Regression Analysis with R

Design and develop statistical nodes to identify unique relationships within data at scale

Giuseppe Ciaburro

BIRMINGHAM - MUMBAI

Regression Analysis with R

Commissioning Editor: Sunith Shetty
Acquisition Editor: Tushar Gupta
Content Development Editor: Cheryl Dsa
Technical Editor: Suwarna Patil
Copy Editor: Safis Editing
Project Coordinator: Nidhi Joshi
Proofreader: Safis Editing
Indexer: Aishwarya Gangawane
Graphics: Tania Dutta
Production Coordinator: Arvindkumar Gupta

First published: January 2018

Production reference: 1290118

Published by Packt Publishing Ltd.
Livery Place
35 Livery Street
Birmingham
B3 2PB, UK.

ISBN 978-1-78862-730-6

www.packtpub.com

`mapt.io`

Mapt is an online digital library that gives you full access to over 5,000 books and videos, as well as industry leading tools to help you plan your personal development and advance your career. For more information, please visit our website.

Why subscribe?

- Spend less time learning and more time coding with practical eBooks and Videos from over 4,000 industry professionals

- Improve your learning with Skill Plans built especially for you

- Get a free eBook or video every month

- Mapt is fully searchable

- Copy and paste, print, and bookmark content

PacktPub.com

Did you know that Packt offers eBook versions of every book published, with PDF and ePub files available? You can upgrade to the eBook version at `www.PacktPub.com` and as a print book customer, you are entitled to a discount on the eBook copy. Get in touch with us at `service@packtpub.com` for more details.

At `www.PacktPub.com`, you can also read a collection of free technical articles, sign up for a range of free newsletters, and receive exclusive discounts and offers on Packt books and eBooks.

Contributors

About the author

Giuseppe Ciaburro holds a PhD in environmental technical physics and two master's degrees. His research was focused on machine learning applications in the study of the urban sound environments. He works at Built Environment Control Laboratory - Università degli Studi della Campania Luigi Vanvitelli (Italy). He has over 15 years of work experience in programming (Python, R, and MATLAB), first in the field of combustion and then in acoustics and noise control. He has several publications to his credit.

About the reviewer

Pierre Paquay holds a master's degree in mathematics from Université de Liège, Belgium, and a certificate in statistical analysis with R programming from the university of Washington. He currently teaches probability, statistics, and data analysis to future mathematics teachers at HEL (Haute École de la Ville de Liège), Belgium. He is also a lifelong learner and is passionate about new discoveries in the field of machine learning.

Packt is searching for authors like you

If you're interested in becoming an author for Packt, please visit `authors.packtpub.com` and apply today. We have worked with thousands of developers and tech professionals, just like you, to help them share their insight with the global tech community. You can make a general application, apply for a specific hot topic that we are recruiting an author for, or submit your own idea.

Table of Contents

Preface   1

Chapter 1: Getting Started with Regression   7

  Going back to the origin of regression   8
  Regression in the real world   12
  Understanding regression concepts   14
  Regression versus correlation   18
  Discovering different types of regression   21
  The R environment   24
  Installing R   27
    Using precompiled binary distribution   29
      Installing on Windows   30
      Installing on macOS   30
      Installing on Linux   30
    Installation from source code   31
  RStudio   31
  R packages for regression   34
    The R stats package   34
    The car package   35
    The MASS package   37
    The caret package   38
    The glmnet package   39
    The sgd package   40
    The BLR package   41
    The Lars package   41
  Summary   42

Chapter 2: Basic Concepts – Simple Linear Regression   43

  Association between variables – covariance and correlation   44
  Searching linear relationships   51
  Least squares regression   55
  Creating a linear regression model   64
    Statistical significance test   69
    Exploring model results   69
    Diagnostic plots   72
  Modeling a perfect linear association   78

Summary 82

Chapter 3: More Than Just One Predictor – MLR 83

Multiple linear regression concepts 84
Building a multiple linear regression model 90
Multiple linear regression with categorical predictor 96
    Categorical variables 96
    Building a model 97
Gradient Descent and linear regression 103
    Gradient Descent 105
    Stochastic Gradient Descent 107
    The sgd package 107
    Linear regression with SGD 108
Polynomial regression 112
Summary 119

Chapter 4: When the Response Falls into Two Categories – Logistic Regression 121

Understanding logistic regression 122
    The logit model 124
Generalized Linear Model 127
    Simple logistic regression 127
Multiple logistic regression 135
    Customer satisfaction analysis with the multiple logistic regression 136
    Multiple logistic regression with categorical data 143
Multinomial logistic regression 156
Summary 162

Chapter 5: Data Preparation Using R Tools 163

Data wrangling 164
    A first look at data 164
    Change datatype 167
    Removing empty cells 169
    Replace incorrect value 170
    Missing values 170
    Treatment of NaN values 173
Finding outliers in data 174
Scale of features 181
    Min–max normalization 182
    z score standardization 185

Discretization in R   187
  Data discretization by binning   188
  Data discretization by histogram analysis   191
Dimensionality reduction   195
  Principal Component Analysis   195
Summary   206

Chapter 6: Avoiding Overfitting Problems - Achieving Generalization   209
  Understanding overfitting   210
    Overfitting detection – cross-validation   213
  Feature selection   228
    Stepwise regression   229
    Regression subset selection   237
  Regularization   245
    Ridge regression   245
    Lasso regression   254
    ElasticNet regression   261
  Summary   264

Chapter 7: Going Further with Regression Models   265
  Robust linear regression   266
  Bayesian linear regression   274
    Basic concepts of probability   275
    Bayes' theorem   281
    Bayesian model using BAS package   283
  Count data model   291
    Poisson distributions   292
    Poisson regression model   294
    Modeling the number of warp breaks per loom   296
  Summary   302

Chapter 8: Beyond Linearity – When Curving Is Much Better   303
  Nonlinear least squares   304
  Multivariate Adaptive Regression Splines   310
  Generalized Additive Model   322
  Regression trees   329
  Support Vector Regression   338
  Summary   342

Chapter 9: Regression Analysis in Practice   345
  Random forest regression with the Boston dataset   346

Exploratory analysis   347
Multiple linear model fitting   357
Random forest regression model   361
Classifying breast cancer using logistic regression   366
Exploratory analysis   368
Model fitting   373
Regression with neural networks   383
Exploratory analysis   385
Neural network model   389
Summary   401
Other Books You May Enjoy   403
Index   407

Preface

Regression analysis is a statistical process that enables predictions of relationships between variables. The predictions are based on the effect of one variable on another. Regression techniques for modeling and analyzing are employed on large sets of data in order to reveal hidden relationships among the variables.

This book will give you a rundown of regression analysis and will explain the process from scratch. The first few chapters explain what the different types of learning are—supervised and unsupervised—and how they differ from each other. We then move on to cover supervised learning in detail, covering the various aspects of regression analysis. The chapters are arranged in such a way that they give a feel of all the steps covered in a data science process: loading the training dataset, handling missing values, EDA on the dataset, transformations and feature engineering, model building, assessing the model fitting and performance, and finally making predictions on unseen datasets. Each chapter starts with explaining the theoretical concepts, and once the reader gets comfortable with the theory, we move to the practical examples to support their understanding. The practical examples are illustrated using R code, including different packages in R such as R stats and caret. Each chapter is a mix of theory and practical examples.

By the end of this book, you will know all the concepts and pain points related to regression analysis, and you will be able to implement what you have learnt in your projects.

Who this book is for

This book is intended for budding data scientists and data analysts who want to implement regression analysis techniques using R. If you are interested in statistics, data science, and machine learning and want to get an easy introduction to these topics, then this book is what you need! A basic understanding of statistics and math will help you to get the most out of the book. Some programming experience with R will also be helpful.

What this book covers

Chapter 1, *Getting Started with Regression*, teaches by example why regression is useful for data science and how to quickly set up R for data science. We provide an overview of the packages used throughout the book.

Chapter 2, *Basic Concepts – Simple Linear Regression*, introduces regression with the simplest algorithm: simple linear regression. The chapter first describes a regression problem and where to fit a regressor, and then gives some intuitions underneath the math formulation.

Chapter 3, *More Than Just One Predictor – MLR*, shows how simple linear regression will be extended to extract predictive information from more than a feature. The stochastic gradient descent technique, explained in the previous chapter, will be scaled to cope with a vector of features.

Chapter 4, *When the Response Falls into Two Categories – Logistic Regression*, shows you how to approach classification and how to build a classifier that predicts class probability.

Chapter 5, *Data Preparation Using R Tools*, teaches you to properly parse a dataset, clean it, and create an output matrix optimally built for regression.

Chapter 6, *Avoiding Overfitting Problems – Achieving Generalization*, helps you avoid overfitting and create models with low bias and variance. Many techniques will be presented here to do so: stepwise selection and regularization (ridge, lasso, and elasticnet).

Chapter 7, *Going Further with Regression Models*, addresses the scaling problem, introducing a new set of techniques. We will learn how to scale linear models to a big dataset and how to deal with incremental data.

Chapter 8, *Beyond Linearity – When Curving Is Much Better*, applies advanced techniques to solve regression problems that cannot be solved with linear models.

Chapter 9, *Regression Analysis in Practice*, presents a series of applications where regression models can be successfully applied, allowing the reader to grasp possible applications for her/his own problems.

To get the most out of this book

This book is focused on regression analysis in an R environment. We have used R version 3.4.2 to build various applications and the open source and enterprise-ready professional software for R, RStudio version 1.0.153. We've focused on how to utilize various R libraries in the best possible way to build real-world applications. These libraries (called `packages`) are available for free at the following URL: https://cran.r-project.org/web/packages/index.html. In that spirit, we have tried to keep all of the code as friendly and readable as possible. We feel that this will enable our readers to easily understand the code and readily use it in different scenarios.

Download the example code files

You can download the example code files for this book from your account at www.packtpub.com. If you purchased this book elsewhere, you can visit www.packtpub.com/support and register to have the files emailed directly to you.

You can download the code files by following these steps:

1. Log in or register at www.packtpub.com.
2. Select the **SUPPORT** tab.
3. Click on **Code Downloads & Errata**.
4. Enter the name of the book in the **Search** box and follow the onscreen instructions.

Once the file is downloaded, please make sure that you unzip or extract the folder using the latest version of:

- WinRAR/7-Zip for Windows
- Zipeg/iZip/UnRarX for Mac
- 7-Zip/PeaZip for Linux

The code bundle for the book is also hosted on GitHub at https://github.com/ PacktPublishing/Regression-Analysis-with-R. We also have other code bundles from our rich catalog of books and videos available at https://github.com/PacktPublishing/. Check them out!

Download the color images

We also provide a PDF file that has color images of the screenshots/diagrams used in this book. You can download it here: https://www.packtpub.com/sites/default/files/ downloads/RegressionAnalysiswithR_ColorImages.pdf.

Conventions used

There are a number of text conventions used throughout this book.

CodeInText: Indicates code words in text, database table names, folder names, filenames, file extensions, pathnames, dummy URLs, user input, and Twitter handles. Here is an example: " In the following figure, the R version 3.4.1 interface is shown."

Any command-line input or output is written as follows:

```
$ mkdir css
$ cd css
```

Bold: Indicates a new term, an important word, or words that you see onscreen. For example, words in menus or dialog boxes appear in the text like this. Here is an example: "The purposes of regression as a statistical tool are of two types **synthesize** and **generalize**, as shown in the following figure."

 Warnings or important notes appear like this.

 Tips and tricks appear like this.

Get in touch

Feedback from our readers is always welcome.

General feedback: Email `feedback@packtpub.com` and mention the book title in the subject of your message. If you have questions about any aspect of this book, please email us at `questions@packtpub.com`.

Errata: Although we have taken every care to ensure the accuracy of our content, mistakes do happen. If you have found a mistake in this book, we would be grateful if you would report this to us. Please visit `www.packtpub.com/submit-errata`, selecting your book, clicking on the Errata Submission Form link, and entering the details.

Piracy: If you come across any illegal copies of our works in any form on the Internet, we would be grateful if you would provide us with the location address or website name. Please contact us at `copyright@packtpub.com` with a link to the material.

If you are interested in becoming an author: If there is a topic that you have expertise in and you are interested in either writing or contributing to a book, please visit `authors.packtpub.com`.

Reviews

Please leave a review. Once you have read and used this book, why not leave a review on the site that you purchased it from? Potential readers can then see and use your unbiased opinion to make purchase decisions, we at Packt can understand what you think about our products, and our authors can see your feedback on their book. Thank you!

For more information about Packt, please visit `packtpub.com`.

1
Getting Started with Regression

Regression analysis is the starting point in data science. This is because regression models represent the most well-understood models in numerical simulation. Once we experience the workings of regression models, we will be able to understand all other machine learning algorithms. Regression models are easily interpretable as they are based on solid mathematical bases (such as matrix algebra for example). We will see in the following sections that linear regression allows us to derive a mathematical formula representative of the corresponding model. Perhaps this is why such techniques are extremely easy to understand.

Regression analysis is a statistical process done to study the relationship between a set of independent variables (**explanatory variables**) and the dependent variable (**response variable**). Through this technique, it will be possible to understand how the value of the response variable changes when the explanatory variable is varied.

Consider some data that is collected about a group of students, on: number of study hours per day, attendance at school, and scores on the final exam obtained. Through regression techniques, we can quantify the average increase in the final exam score when we add one more hour of study. Lower attendance in school (decreasing the student's experience) lowers the scores in the final exam.

A regression analysis can have two objectives:

- **Explanatory analysis**: To understand and weigh the effects of the independent variable on the dependent variable according to a particular theoretical model
- **Predictive analysis**: To locate a linear combination of the independent variable to predict the value assumed by the dependent variable optimally

In this chapter, we will be introduced to the basic concepts of regression analysis, and then we'll take a tour of the different types of statistical processes. In addition to this, we will also introduce the R language and cover the basics of the R programming environment. Finally we will explore the essential tools that R provides for understanding the amazing world of regression.

We will cover the following topics:

- The origin of regression
- Types of algorithms
- How to quickly set up R for data science
- R packages used throughout the book

At the end of this chapter, we will provide you with a working environment that is able to run all the examples contained in the following chapters. You will also get a clear idea about why regression analysis is not just an underrated technique taken from statistics, but a powerful and effective data science algorithm.

Going back to the origin of regression

The word regression sounds like *go back* in some ways. If you've been trying to quit smoking but then yield to the desire to have a cigarette again, you are experiencing an episode of regression. The term **regression** has appeared in early writings since the late 1300s, and is derived from the Latin term **regressus**, which means a return. It is used in different fields with different meanings, but in any case, it is always referred to as the **action of regressing**.

In philosophy, regression is used to indicate the inverse logical procedure with respect to that of the normal apodictic (**apodixis**), in which we proceed from the general to the particular. Whereas in reality, in regression we go back *from the particular to the general*, from the effect to the cause, from the conditioned to the condition. In this way, we can draw completely general conclusions from a particular case. This is the first form of generalization that, as we will see later, represents a crucial part of a statistical analysis.

For example, there is marine regression, which is a geological process that occurs as a result of areas of submerged seafloor being exposed more than the sea level. And there is the opposite event, marine transgression; it occurs when flooding from the sea submerges land that was previously exposed.

The following image shows the results of marine regression on the Aral lake. This lake lies between Kazakhstan and Uzbekistan and has been steadily shrinking since the 1960s, after the rivers that fed it were diverted by Soviet irrigation projects. By 1997, it had declined to ten percent of its original size:

However, in statistics, regression is related to the study of the relationship between the explanatory variables and the response variable. Don't worry! This is the topic we will discuss in this book.

In statistics, the term regression has an ancient origin and a very special meaning. The man who coined this term was a certain Francis Galton, geneticist, who in 1889 published an article in which he demonstrated how *every characteristic of an individual is inherited by their offspring, but on an average to a lesser degree*. For example, children with tall parents are also tall, but on an average their height will be comparatively less than that of their parents. This phenomenon, also graphically described, is called **regression**. Since then, this term has lived on to define statistical techniques that analyze relationships between two or more variables.

The following table shows a short summary of the data used by Galton for his study:

Family	Father	Mother	Gender	Height	Kids
1	78.5	67	M	73.2	4
1	78.5	67	F	69.2	4
1	78.5	67	F	69	4
1	78.5	67	F	69	4
2	75.5	66.5	M	73.5	4
2	75.5	66.5	M	72.5	4
2	75.5	66.5	F	65.5	4
2	75.5	66.5	F	65.5	4
3	75	64	M	71	2
3	75	64	F	68	2
4	75	64	M	70.5	5
4	75	64	M	68.5	5
4	75	64	F	67	5
4	75	64	F	64.5	5
4	75	64	F	63	5
5	75	58.5	M	72	6
5	75	58.5	M	69	6
5	75	58.5	M	68	6
5	75	58.5	F	66.5	6
5	75	58.5	F	62.5	6
5	75	58.5	F	62.5	6

Galton depicted in a chart the average height of the parents and that of the children, noting what he called regression in the data.

The following figure shows this data and a regression line that confirms his thesis:

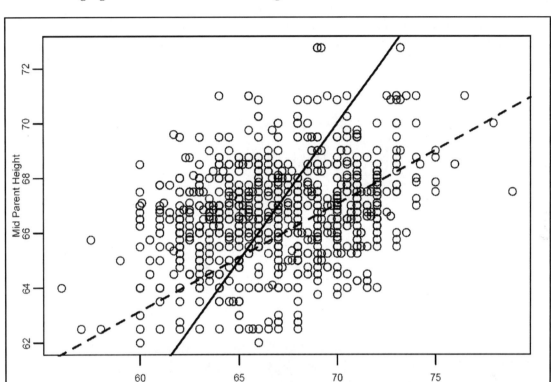

The figure shows a scatter plot of data with two lines. The darker straight line represents the equality line, that is, the average height of the parents is equal to that of the children. The straighter dotted line, on the other hand, represents the linear regression line (defined by Galton) showing a regression in the height of the children relative to that of the parents. In fact, that line has a slope less than that of the continuous line.

Indeed, the children with tall parents are also tall, but on an average they are not as tall as their parents (the regression line is less than the equality line to the right of the figure). On the contrary, children with short parents are also short, but on an average, they are taller than their parents (the regression line is greater than the equality line to the left of the figure). Galton noted that, in both cases, the height of the children approached the average of the group. In Galton's words, this corresponded to the concept of **regression towards mediocrity**, hence the name of the statistical analysis technique.

The **Galton universal regression law** was confirmed by Karl Pearson (Galton's pupil), who collected more than a thousand heights of members of family groups. He found that the average height of the children from a group of short parents was greater than the average height of their fathers' group, and that the average height of the children from a group of tall fathers was lower than the average height of their parents' group. That is, the heights of the tall and short children were regressing toward the average height of all people. This is exactly what we have learned from the observation of the previous graph.

Regression in the real world

In general, statistics—and more specifically, regression—is a math discipline. Its purpose is to obtain information from data about knowledge, decisions, control, and the forecasting of events and phenomena. Unfortunately, statistical culture, and in particular statistical reasoning, are scarce and uncommon. This is due to the institutions that have included the study of this discipline in their programs and study plans inadequately. Often, inadequate learning methods are adopted since this is a rather complex and not very popular topic (as is the case with mathematics in general).

The difficulties faced by students are often due to outdated teaching methods that are not in tune with our modern needs. In this book, we will learn how to deal with such topics with a modern approach, based on practical examples. In this way, all the topics will seem simple and within our reach.

Yet regression, given its cross-disciplinary characteristics, has numerous and varied areas of application, from psychology to agrarianism, and from economics to medicine and business management, just to name a few.

The purpose of regression as a statistical tool are of two types, **synthesize** and **generalize**, as shown in the following figure:

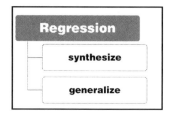

synthesize means predisposing collected data into a form (tables, graphs, or numerical summaries), which allows you to better understand the phenomena on which the detection was performed. The synthesis is met by the need to simplify, which in turn results from the limited ability of the human mind to handle articulated, complex, or multidimensional information. In this way, we can use techniques that allow for a global study of a large number of quantitative and qualitative information to highlight features, ties, differences, or associations between detected variables.

The second purpose (**generalize**) is to extend the result of an analysis performed on data of a limited group of statistical units (sample) to the entire population group (population).

The contribution of regression is not limited to the data analysis phase. It's true that added value is expressed in the formulation of research hypotheses, argumentation of theses, adoption of appropriate solutions and methodologies, choices of methods of detection, formulation of the sample, and the procedure of extending the results to the reference universes.

Keeping these phases under control means producing reliable and economically useful results, and mastering descriptive statistics and data analysis as well as inferential ones. In this regard, we recall that the descriptive statistics are concerned with describing the experimental data with few significant numbers or graphs. Therefore, they photographs a given situation and summarizes its salient characteristics. The inferential statistics use statistical data, also appropriately summarized by the descriptive statistics, to make probabilistic forecasts on future or otherwise uncertain situations.

People, families, businesses, public administrations, mayors, ministers, and researchers constantly make decisions. For most of them, the outcome is uncertain, in the sense that it is not known exactly what will result, although the expectation is that they will achieve the (positive) effects they are hoping for. Decisions would be better and the effects expected closer to those desired if they were made on the basis of relevant data in a decision-making context. Here are some applications of regression in the real world:

- A student who graduates this year must choose the faculty and university degree course on which he/she will enroll. Perhaps he/she has already gained a vocation for his future profession, or studies have confirmed his/her predisposition for a particular discipline. Maybe a well-established family tradition advises him/her to follow the parent's profession. In these cases, the uncertainty of choice will be greatly reduced. However, if the student does not have genuine vocations or is not geared particularly to specific choices, he or she may want to know something about the professional outcomes of the graduates. In this regard, some statistical study on graduate data from previous years may help him/her make the decision.

- A distribution company, such as a supermarket chain, wants to open a new sales outlet in a big city and must choose the best location. It will use and analyze numerous statistical data on the density of the population in different neighborhoods, the presence of young families, the presence of children under the age of six (if it is interested in selling to this category of consumers), and the presence of schools, offices, other supermarkets, and retail outlets.
- Another company wants to invest its profits. It must make a portfolio choice. It has to decide whether to invest in government bonds, national shares, foreign securities, funds, or real estate. To make this choice, it will first conduct an analysis of the returns and risks of different investment alternatives based on statistical data.
- National governments are often called upon to make choices and decisions. To do this, they have statistical production equipment. They have population data and forecasts about population evolution over the coming years, which will calibrate their interventions. A strong decline in birth rates will, for example, recommend school consolidation policies; the emergence of children from the non-community component will signal the need for reviewing multi-ethnic programs and, more generally, school integration policies. On the other hand, statistical data on the presence of national products in foreign markets will suggest the need to export support actions or interventions to promote innovation and business competitiveness.

In the examples we have seen so far, the usefulness of statistical techniques, and particularly of regression in the most diverse working situations, is clear. It is therefore clear how much more information and data companies are required to have to ensure the rationality of decisions and economic behaviors by those who direct them.

Understanding regression concepts

Regression is an inductive learning task that has been widely studied and is widely used in practical applications. Unlike classification processes, where you are trying to predict discrete class labels, regression models predict numeric values.

From a set of data, we can find a model that describes it by the use of the regression algorithms. For example, we can identify a correspondence between input variables and output variables of a given system. One way to do this is to postulate the existence of some kind of mechanism for the parametric generation of data; this, however, does not contain the exact values of the parameters. This process typically makes reference to statistical techniques.

The extraction of general laws from a set of observed data is called **induction**, as opposed to **deduction** in which we start from general laws and try to predict the value of a set of variables. Induction is the fundamental mechanism underlying the scientific method in which we want to derive general laws (typically described in mathematical terms) starting from the observation of phenomena. In the following figure, we can see Peirce's triangle, which represents a scheme of relationships between reasoning patterns:

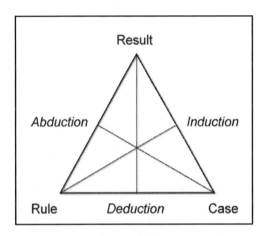

The observation of the phenomena includes the measurement of a set of variables, and therefore the acquisition of data that describes the observed phenomena. Then, the resulting model can be used to make predictions on additional data. The overall process in which, starting from a set of observations, we aim to make predictions on new situations, is called **inference**.

Therefore, inductive learning starts with observations arising from the surrounding environment that, hopefully, are also valid for not-yet-observed cases.

We have already anticipated the stages of the inference process; now let's analyze them in detail through the workflow setting. When developing an application that uses regression algorithms, we will follow a procedure characterized by the following steps:

1. **Collect the data**: Everything starts with the data—no doubt about it—but one might wonder where so much data comes from. In practice, data is collected through lengthy procedures that may, for example, be derived from measurement campaigns or face-to-face interviews. In all cases, data is collected in a database so that it can then be analyzed to obtain knowledge.

If we do not have specific requirements, and to save time and effort, we can use publicly available data. In this regard, a large collection of data is available at the **UCI Machine Learning Repository**, at the following link: http://archive.ics.uci.edu/ml.

The following figure shows the regression process workflow:

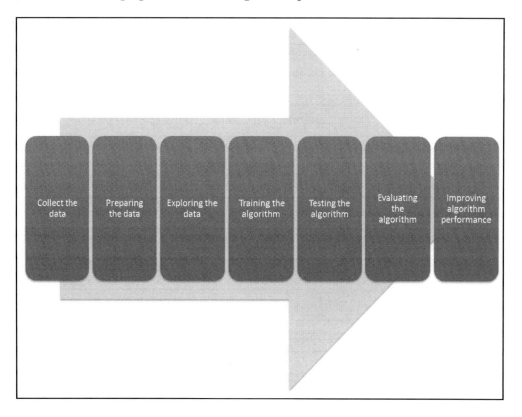

2. **Preparing the data**: We have collected the data; now we have to prepare it for the next step. Once you have this data, you must make sure it is in a format usable by the algorithm you want to use. To do this, you may need to do some formatting. Recall that some algorithms need data in an integer format, whereas some require it in the form of strings, and finally others need it to be in a special format. We will get to this later, but the specific formatting is usually simple compared to data collection.

3. **Exploring the data**: At this point, we can look at the data to verify that it is actually working and we do not have a bunch of empty values. In this step, through the use of plots, we can recognize any patterns or check whether there are some data points that are vastly different from the rest of the set. Plotting data in one, two, or three dimensions can also help.

4. **Training the algorithm**: At this stage, it starts to get serious. The regression algorithm begins to work with the definition of the model and the next training step. The model starts to extract knowledge from the large amounts of data that we have available.

5. **Testing the algorithm**: In this step, we use the information learned in the previous step to see whether the model actually works. The evaluation of an algorithm is for seeing how well the model approximates the real system. In the case of regression techniques, we have some known values that we can use to evaluate the algorithm. So, if we are not satisfied, we can return to the previous steps, change some things, and retry the test.

6. **Evaluating the algorithm**: We have reached the point where we can apply what has been done so far. We can assess the approximation ability of the model by applying it to real data. The model, preventively trained and tested, is then valued in this phase.

7. **Improving algorithm performance**: Finally, we can focus on finishing the work. We have verified that the model works, we have evaluated the performance, and now we are ready to analyze it completely to identify possible room for improvement.

The generalization ability of the regression model is crucial for all other machine learning algorithms as well. Regression algorithms must not only detect the relationships between the target function and attribute values in the training set, but also generalize them so that they may be used to predict new data.

It should be emphasized that the learning process must be able to capture the underlying regimes from the training set and not the specific details. Once the learning process is completed through training, the effectiveness of the model is tested further on a dataset named `testset`.

Regression versus correlation

At the beginning of the chapter, we said that regression analysis is a statistical process for studying the relationship between variables. When considering two or more variables, one can examine the type and intensity of the relationships that exist between them. In the case where two quantitative variables are simultaneously detected for each individual, it is possible to check whether they vary simultaneously and what mathematical relationship exists between them.

The study of such relationships can be conducted through two types of analysis: regression analysis and correlation analysis. Let's understand the differences between these two types of analysis.

Regression analysis develops a statistical model that can be used to predict the values of a variable, called **dependent,** or more rarely predict and identify the effect based on the values of the other variable, called **independent** or **explanatory**, identified as the cause.

With correlation analysis, we can measure the intensity of the association between two quantitative variables that are usually not directly linked to the cause-effect and easily mediated by at least one third variable, but that vary jointly. In the following figure, the meanings of two analyses are shown:

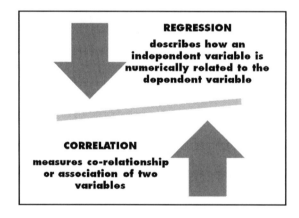

In many cases, there are variables that tend to covariate, but what more can be said about this? If there is a direct dependency relation between two variables—such as whether a variable (dependent) can be determined as a function of a second variable (independent)—then a regression analysis can be used to understand the degree of the relation. For example, blood pressure depends on the subject's age. The existing data used in regression and mathematical equations is defined. Using these equations, the value of one variable can be predicted for the value of one or more variables. This equation can therefore also be used to extract knowledge from the existing data and to predict the outcomes of observations that have not been seen or tested before.

Conversely, if there is no direct dependency relation between variables—such as none of the two variables causing direct variations in the other—the covariate tendency is measured in correlation. For example, there is no direct relationship between the length and weight of an organism, in the sense that the weight of an organism can increase independently of its length. Correlation measures the association between two variables and it quantifies the strength of the relationship. To do this, it evaluates only the existing data.

To better understand the differences, we will analyze in detail the two examples just suggested. For the first example, we list the blood pressure of subjects of different ages, as shown in the following table:

Age	Blood pressure
18	117
22	120
27	122
32	123
37	124
42	125
47	127
52	131
55	133
62	134
68	135

A suitable graphical representation called a scatter plot can be used to depict the relationships between quantitative variables detected on the same units. In the following chapters, we will see in practice how to plot a scatter plot, so let's just make sense of the meaning.

We display this data on a scatter plot, as shown in the following figure:

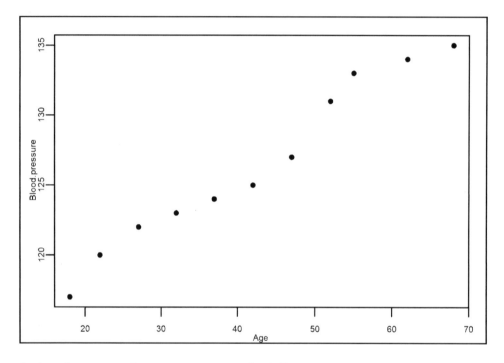

By analyzing the scatter plot, we can answer the following:

- Is there a relationship that can be described by a straight line?
- Is there a relationship that is not linear?
- If the scatter plot of the variables looks similar to a cloud, it indicates that no relationship exists between both variables and one would stop at this point

The scatter plot shows a strong, positive, and linear association between **Age** and **Blood pressure**. In fact, as age increases, blood pressure increases.

Let's now look at what happens in the other example. As we have anticipated, there is no direct relationship between the length and weight of an organism, in the sense that the weight of an organism can increase independently of its length.

We can see an example of an organism's population here:

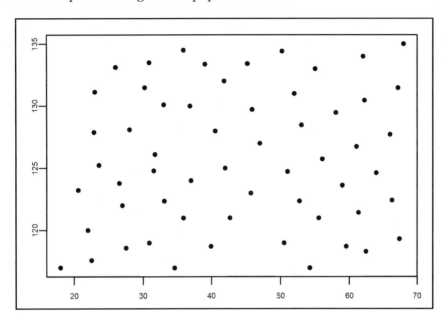

Weight is not related to length; this means that there is no correlation between the two variables, and we conclude that length is responsible for none of the changes in weight.

Correlation provides a numerical measure of the relationship between two continuous variables. The resulting correlation coefficient does not depend on the units of the variables and can therefore be used to compare any two variables regardless of their units.

Discovering different types of regression

As mentioned before, regression analysis is a statistical process for studying the relationship between a set of independent variables (explanatory variables) and the dependent variable (response variable). Through this technique, it will be possible to understand how the value of the response variable changes when the explanatory variable is varied.

The power of regression techniques is due to the quality of their algorithms, which have been improved and updated over the years. These are divided into several main types, depending on the nature of the dependent and independent variables used or the shape of the regression line.

The reason for such a wide range of regression techniques is the variety of cases to be analyzed. Each case is based on data with specific characteristics, and each analysis is characterized by specific objectives. These specifications require the use of different types of regression techniques to obtain the best results.

How do we distinguish between different types of regression techniques? Previously, we said that a first distinction can be made based on the form of the regression line. Based on this feature, the regression analysis is divided into linear regression and nonlinear regression, as shown in the following figure (linear regression to the left and nonlinear quadratic regression to the right):

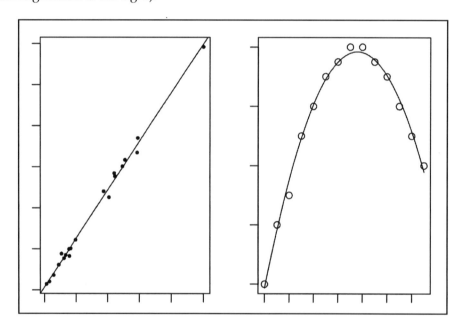

It's clear that the shape of the regression line is dependent on the distribution of data. There are cases where a straight line is the regression line that best approximates the data, while in other cases, you need to fall into a curve to get the best approximation. That said, it is easy to understand that a visual analysis of the distribution of data we are going to analyze is a good practice to be done in advance. By summarizing the shape of distribution, we can distinguish the type of regression between the following:

- Linear regression
- Nonlinear regression

Let us now analyze the nature of the variables involved. In this regard, a question arises spontaneously: can the number of explanatory variables affect the choice of regression technique? The answer to this question is surely positive. For example, in the case of linear regression, if there is only one input variable, then we will do simple linear regression. If, instead, the input variables are two or more, we will need to perform multiple linear regression.

By summarizing, a simple linear regression shows the relationship between a dependent variable Y and an independent variable X. A multiple regression model shows the relationship between a dependent variable Y and multiple independent variables X. In the following figure, the types of regression imposed from the **Number of the explanatory variables** are shown:

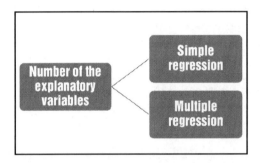

What if we have multiple response variables rather than explanatory variables? In that case, we move from **univariate** models to **multivariate** models. As suggested by the name itself, multivariate regression is a technique with the help of which a single regression model can be estimated with more than one response variable. When there is more than one explanatory variable in a multivariate regression model, the model is a **multivariate multiple regression**.

Finally, let's see what happens when we analyze the type of variables. Usually, regression analysis is used when you want to predict a continuous response variable from a number of explanatory variables, also continuous. But this is not a limitation of regression, in the sense that such analysis is also applicable when categorical variables are at stake.

In the case of a dichotomous explanatory variable (which takes a value of zero or one), the solution is immediate. There are already two numbers (zero and one) associated to this variable, so the regression is immediately applicable. Categorical explanatory variables with more than two values can also be used in regression analyses; however, before they can be used, they need to be converted into variables that have only two levels (such as zero and one). This is called **dummy coding** or **indicator variables**.

Logistic regression should be used if the response variable is dichotomous.

The R environment

After introducing the main topic of the book, it is time to discover the programming environment we will use for our regression analysis. As specified by the title of the book, we will perform our examples in the R environment.

R is an interpreted programming language that allows the use of common facilities for controlling the flow of information, and modular programming using a large number of functions. Most of the available features are written in R. It is also possible for the user to interface with procedures written in C, C ++, or FORTRAN.

R is a GNU project that draws its inspiration from the S language; in fact R is similar to S and can be considered as a different implementation of S. R was developed by John Chambers and his colleagues at Bell Laboratories. There are some significant differences between R and S, but a large amount of the code written for S runs unaltered under R too. R is available as free software under the terms of the **Free Software Foundation's (FSF)** GNU **General Public License (GPL)** in source code form.

Let's specify the definition we just introduced to present R. In fact, R represents a programming environment originally developed for statistical computation and for producing quality graphs. It consists of a language and runtime environment with a graphical interface, a debugger, and access to some system features. It provides the ability to run programs stored in script files. In the following figure, the `R version 3.4.1` interface is shown:

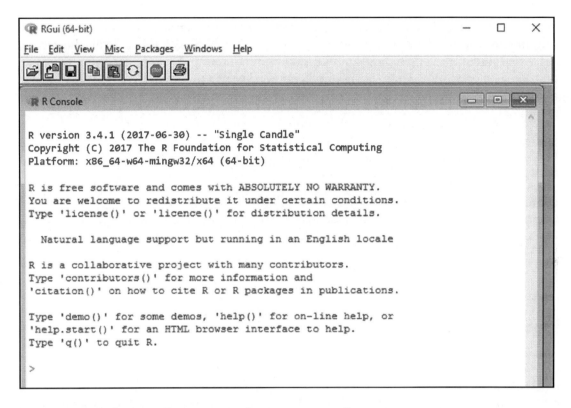

R is an integrated computing system whose resources allow you to:

- Specify a set of commands and require these to run
- View results in text format
- View the charts in an auxiliary window
- Access external archives, even the web-based ones, to capture documents, data, and charts
- Permanently store results and/or graphics

What makes R so useful and explains its quick appreciation from users? The reason lies in the fact that statisticians, engineers, and scientists who have used the software over time have developed a huge collection of scripts grouped in packages. Packages written in R are able to add advanced algorithms, textured color graphics, and data mining techniques to better analyze the information contained in a database.

Its popularity among developers has resulted in its rapid rise among the most widely used programming languages, so over the last 1 year, the TIOBE index has been well ahead by seven positions. The TIOBE programming community index is a way to measure how popular a programming language is, and is updated once a month.

 The TIOBE programming community index is available at the following link: `https://www.tiobe.com/tiobe-index/`.

These ratings are derived on the basis of the number of skilled engineers worldwide, courses, and third-party vendors, and are calculated using popular search engines such as Google, Bing, Yahoo!, Wikipedia, Amazon, YouTube, and Baidu. In the following figure, the first fifteen positions of the TIOBE index for January, 2018 are shown:

Jan 2018	Jan 2017	Change	Programming Language	Ratings	Change
1	1		Java	14.215%	-3.06%
2	2		C	11.037%	+1.69%
3	3		C++	5.603%	-0.70%
4	5	^	Python	4.678%	+1.21%
5	4	v	C#	3.754%	-0.29%
6	7	^	JavaScript	3.465%	+0.62%
7	6	v	Visual Basic .NET	3.261%	+0.30%
8	16	^	R	2.549%	+0.76%
9	10	^	PHP	2.532%	-0.03%
10	8	v	Perl	2.419%	-0.33%
11	12	^	Ruby	2.406%	-0.14%
12	14	^	Swift	2.377%	+0.45%
13	11	v	Delphi/Object Pascal	2.377%	-0.18%
14	15	^	Visual Basic	2.314%	+0.40%
15	9	v	Assembly language	2.056%	-0.65%

R is an open source program, and its popularity reflects a change in the type of software used within the company. We remind you that open source software is free from any constraints not only on its use, but more importantly, on its development. Large IT companies such as IBM, Hewlett-Packard, and Dell are able to earn billions of dollars a year by selling servers running the Linux open source operating system, which is Microsoft Windows' competitor.

The widespread use of open source software is now a consolidated reality. Most websites are managed through an open source web application called Apache, and companies are increasingly relying on the MySQL open source database to store information. Finally, many people see the end results of this technology using the open source Firefox web browser.

R is in many respects similar to other programming languages, such as C, Java, and Perl. Because of its features, it is extremely simple and fast to do a wide range of computing tasks, as it provides quick access through various commands. For statisticians, however, R is particularly useful because it contains a number of integrated mechanisms (built-in functions) to organize data, to perform calculations on information, and to create graphic representations of databases.

Indeed, R is highly extensible and provides a wide variety of statistical (linear and nonlinear modeling, classical statistical tests, time-series analysis, classification, clustering, and so on) and graphical techniques. There is also a wide range of features that provide a flexible graphical environment for creating various types of data presentations. Additional forms of (add-on) packages are available for a variety of specific purposes. These are topics that we will look at in the following sections.

Installing R

After that detailed description of the programming environment R, it is time to install it on our machine. To do this, we will have to get the installation package first.

The packages we will need to install are available on the official website of the language, **Comprehensive R Archive Network (CRAN)**, at the following URL: https://www.r-project.org/.

CRAN is a network of **File Transfer Protocol** (**FTP**) and web servers located around the world that stores identical source and documentation versions of R. CRAN is directly accessible from R's site, and on this site you can also find information about R, some technical manuals, the R magazine, and details about R-developed packages that are stored in CRAN repositories.

Of course, before you download the software versions, we will have to inform you of the type of machine you need and the operating system that must be installed on it. Remember, however, that R is practically available for all operating systems in circulation. In the following screenshot, the CRAN web page is shown:

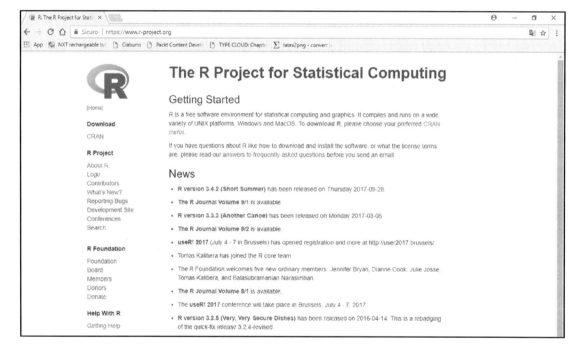

In the drafting period of this book, the current version of the environment R is 3.4.1, which represents the stable one, and that is why, in the examples that will accompany us in the subsequent sections, we will refer to that version.

The following list shows the OSs supported:

- Windows
- macOS
- Unix

In computer science, installation is the procedure whereby the software is copied and configured on the machine. Generally, the software is distributed as a compressed file package, which includes an interface that facilitates and automates the installation (installer).

The installation creates folders on the disk, where all the files used for the program configuration are contained, and the links to make it easier to execute and write the necessary configuration parameters. In the following screenshot, we can see CRAN with all the tools needed for proper software installation:

There are essentially two ways to install R:

- Using existing distributions in the form of binaries
- Using source code

Using precompiled binary distribution

Binary distribution is the simplest choice; it works on most machines and will be the one we will use to make the job as simple as possible. This is a compiled version of R which can be downloaded and installed directly on our system.

Installing on Windows

For the Windows operating system, this version looks like a single EXE file (downloadable from the CRAN site), which can be easily installed with a double-click on it and by following the few steps of the installation. These are the automated installation procedures, the so-called installers, through which the installation phase of the software is reduced by the user to the need to have clicked on the buttons a number of times. Once the process is completed, you can start using R via the icon that will appear on the desktop or through the link available in the list of programs that can be used in our system.

Installing on macOS

Similarly, for macOS, R is available with a unique installation file with a PKG extension; it can be downloaded and installed on our system. The following screenshot shows the directory containing binaries for a base distribution and packages to run on macOS X (release 10.6 and later) extracted from the CRAN website:

Installing on Linux

For a Linux system, there are several versions of the installation file. In the download section, you must select the appropriate version of R, according to the Linux distribution installed on your machine. Installation packages are available in two main formats, .rpm file for Fedora, SUSE, and Mandriva, and .deb extensions for Ubuntu, Debian, and Linux Mint.

Installation from source code

R's installation from source code is available for all supported platforms, though it is not as easy to perform compared to the binary distribution we've just seen. It is especially hard on Windows, since the installation tools are not part of the system.

 Detailed information on installation procedures from source code for Windows, and necessary tools, are available on the CRAN website, at `https://cran.r-project.org/doc/manuals/r-release/R-admin.html`.

On Unix-like systems, the process, on the other hand, is much simpler; the installation must be done following the usual procedure, which uses the following commands:

```
./configure
make
make install
```

These commands, assuming that compilers and support libraries are available, lead to the proper installation of the R environment on our system.

RStudio

To program with R, we can use any text editor and a simple command-line interface. Both of these tools are already present on any operating system, so if you don't want to install anything more, you will be able to ignore this step.

Some find it more convenient to use an **Integrated Development Environment (IDE)**; in this case, as there are several available, both free and paid, you'll be spoilt for choice. Having to make a choice, I prefer the RStudio environment.

RStudio is a set of integrated tools designed to help you be more productive with R. It includes a console, syntax-highlighting editor that supports direct code execution, and a variety of robust tools for plotting, viewing history, debugging, and managing your workspace.

 RStudio is available at the following URL: `https://www.rstudio.com/`.

In the following screenshot you will see the main page of the RStudio website:

This is a popular IDE available in the open source, free, and commercial versions, which works on most operating systems. RStudio is probably the only development environment developed specifically for R. It is available for all major platforms (Windows, Linux, and macOS X) and can run on a local machine such as our computer or even on the web using RStudio Server. With RStudio Server, you can provide a browser-based interface (the so-called IDE) to an R version running on a remote Linux server. It integrates several features that are really useful, especially if you use R for more complex projects or if you want to have more than one developer on a project.

The environment is made up of four different areas:

- **Scripting area**: In this area we can open, create, and write our scripts
- **Console area**: This zone is the actual R console where commands are executed
- **Workspace History area**: In this area you can find a list of all the objects created in the workspace where we are working
- **Visualization area**: In this area we can easily load packages and open R help files, but more importantly, we can view charts

The following screenshot shows the RStudio environment:

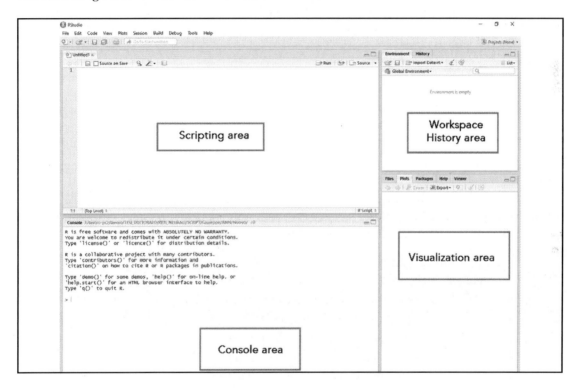

With the use of RStudio, our work will be considerably simplified, displaying all the resources needed in one window.

R packages for regression

Previously, we have mentioned the R packages, which allow us to access a series of features to solve a specific problem. In this section, we will present some packages that contain valuable resources for regression analysis. These packages will be analyzed in detail in the following chapters, where we will provide practical applications.

The R stats package

R stats is a package that contains many useful functions for statistical calculations and random number generation. In the following table you will see some of the information on this package:

Package	stats
Date	October 3, 2017
Version	3.5.0
Title	The R stats package
Author	R core team and contributors worldwide

There are so many functions in the package; we will only mention the ones that are closest to regression analysis. These are the most useful functions used in regression analysis:

- lm: This function is used to fit linear models. It can be used to carry out regression, single stratum analysis of variance, and analysis of co-variance.
- summary.lm: This function returns a summary for linear model fits.
- coef: With the help of this function, coefficients from objects returned by modeling functions can be extracted. Coefficients is an alias for it.
- fitted: Fitted values are extracted by this function from objects returned by modeling functions fitted. Values are an alias for it.
- formula: This function provides a way of extracting formulae which have been included in other objects.
- predict: This function predicts values based on linear model objects.
- residuals: This function extracts model residuals from objects returned by modeling functions.

- `confint`: This function computes confidence intervals for one or more parameters in a fitted model. Base has a method for objects inheriting from the `lm` class.
- `deviance`: This function returns the deviance of a fitted model object.
- `influence.measures`: This suite of functions can be used to compute some of the regression (leave-one-out deletion) diagnostics for linear and **generalized linear models (GLM)**.
- `lm.influence`: This function provides the basic quantities used when forming a wide variety of diagnostics for checking the quality of regression fits.
- `ls.diag`: This function computes basic statistics, including standard errors, t-values, and p-values for the regression coefficients.
- `glm`: This function is used to fit GLMs, specified by giving a symbolic description of the linear predictor and a description of the error distribution.
- `loess`: This function fits a polynomial surface determined by one or more numerical predictors, using local fitting.
- `loess.control`: This function sets control parameters for `loess` fits.
- `predict.loess`: This function extracts predictions from a `loess` fit, optionally with standard errors.
- `scatter.smooth`: This function plots and adds a smooth curve computed by `loess` to a scatter plot.

What we have analyzed are just some of the many functions contained in the stats package. As we can see, with the resources offered by this package we can build a linear regression model, as well as GLMs (such as multiple linear regression, polynomial regression, and logistic regression). We will also be able to make model diagnosis in order to verify the plausibility of the classic hypotheses underlying the regression model, but we can also address local regression models with a non-parametric approach that suits multiple regressions in the local neighborhood.

The car package

This package includes many functions for: ANOVA analysis, matrix and vector transformations, printing readable tables of coefficients from several regression models, creating residual plots, tests for the autocorrelation of error terms, and many other general interest statistical and graphing functions.

In the following table you will see some of the information on this package:

Package	`car`
Date	June 25, 2017
Version	2.1-5
Title	Companion to Applied Regression
Author	John Fox, Sanford Weisberg, and many others

The following are the most useful functions used in regression analysis contained in this package:

- `Anova`: This function returns ANOVA tables for linear and GLMs
- `linear.hypothesis`: This function is used for testing a linear hypothesis and methods for linear models, GLMs, multivariate linear models, and linear and generalized linear mixed-effects models
- `cookd`: This function returns Cook's distances for linear and GLMs
- `outlier.test`: This function reports the Bonferroni p-values for studentized residuals in linear and GLMs, based on a t-test for linear models and a normal-distribution test for GLMs
- `durbin.watson`: This function computes residual autocorrelations and generalized Durbin-Watson statistics and their bootstrapped p-values
- `levene.test`: This function computes Levene's test for the homogeneity of variance across groups
- `ncv.test`: This function computes a score test of the hypothesis of constant error variance against the alternative that the error variance changes with the level of the response (fitted values), or with a linear combination of predictors

What we have listed are just some of the many functions contained in the `stats` package. In this package, there are also many functions that allow us to draw explanatory graphs from information extracted from regression models as well as a series of functions that allow us to make variables transformations.

The MASS package

This package includes many useful functions and data examples, including functions for estimating linear models through **generalized least squares (GLS)**, fitting negative binomial linear models, the robust fitting of linear models, and Kruskal's non-metric multidimensional scaling.

In the following table you will see some of the information on this package:

Package	MASS
Date	October 2, 2017
Version	7.3-47
Title	Support Functions and Datasets for Venables and Ripley's MASS
Author	Brian Ripley, Bill Venables, and many others

The following are the most useful functions used in regression analysis contained in this package:

- `lm.gls`: This function fits linear models by GLS
- `lm.ridge`: This function fist a linear model by Ridge regression
- `glm.nb`: This function contains a modification of the system function
- `glm()`: It includes an estimation of the additional parameter, theta, to give a negative binomial GLM
- `polr`: A logistic or probit regression model to an ordered factor response is fitted by this function
- `lqs`: This function fits a regression to the good points in the dataset, thereby achieving a regression estimator with a high breakdown point
- `rlm`: This function fits a linear model by robust regression using an M-estimator
- `glmmPQL`: This function fits a GLMM model with multivariate normal random effects, using **penalized quasi-likelihood (PQL)**
- `boxcox`: This function computes and optionally plots profile log-likelihoods for the parameter of the **Box-Cox power transformation** for linear models

As we have seen, this package contains many useful features in regression analysis; in addition there are numerous datasets that we can use for our examples that we will encounter in the following chapters.

The caret package

This package contains many functions to streamline the model training process for complex regression and classification problems. The package utilizes a number of R packages.

In the following table you will see listed some of the information on this package:

Package	`caret`
Date	September 7, 2017
Version	6.0-77
Title	Classification and Regression Training
Author	Max Kuhn and many others

The most useful functions used in regression analysis in this package are as follows:

- `train`: Predictive models over different tuning parameters are fitted by this function. It fits each model, sets up a grid of tuning parameters for a number of classification and regression routines, and calculates a resampling-based performance measure.
- `trainControl`: This function permits the estimation of parameter coefficients with the help of resampling methods like cross-validation.
- `varImp`: This function calculates variable importance for the objects produced by train and method-specific methods.
- `defaultSummary`: This function calculates performance across resamples. Given two numeric vectors of data, the mean squared error and R-squared error are calculated. For two factors, the overall agreement rate and Kappa are determined.
- `knnreg`: This function performs **K-Nearest Neighbor** (**KNN**) regression that can return the average value for the neighbors.
- `plotObsVsPred`: This function plots observed versus predicted results in regression and classification models.
- `predict.knnreg`: This function extracts predictions from the KNN regression model.

The `caret` package contains hundreds of machine learning algorithms (also for regression), and renders useful and convenient methods for data visualization, data resampling, model tuning, and model comparison, among other features.

The glmnet package

This package contains many extremely efficient procedures in order to fit the entire Lasso or ElasticNet regularization path for linear regression, logistic and multinomial regression models, Poisson regression, and the Cox model. Multiple response Gaussian and grouped multinomial regression are the two recent additions.

In the following table you will see listed some of the information on this package:

Package	`glmnet`
Date	September 21, 2017
Version	2.0-13
Title	Lasso and Elastic-Net Regularized Generalized Linear Models
Author	Jerome Friedman, Trevor Hastie, Noah Simon, Junyang Qian, and Rob Tibshirani

The following are the most useful functions used in regression analysis contained in this package:

- `glmnet`: A GLM is fit by this function via penalized maximum likelihood. The regularization path is computed for the Lasso or ElasticNet penalty at a grid of values for the regularization parameter lambda. This function can also deal with all shapes of data, including very large sparse data matrices. Finally, it fits linear, logistic and multinomial, Poisson, and Cox regression models.
- `glmnet.control`: This function views and/or changes the factory default parameters in `glmnet`.
- `predict.glmnet`: This function predicts fitted values, logits, coefficients, and more from a fitted `glmnet` object.
- `print.glmnet`: This function prints a summary of the `glmnet` path at each step along the path.
- `plot.glmnet`: This function produces a coefficient profile plot of the coefficient paths for a fitted `glmnet` object.
- `deviance.glmnet`: This function computes the deviance sequence from the `glmnet` object.

As we have mentioned, this package fits Lasso and ElasticNet model paths for regression, logistic, and multinomial regression using coordinate descent. The algorithm is extremely fast, and exploits sparsity in the input matrix where it exists. A variety of predictions can be made from the fitted models.

The sgd package

This package contains a fast and flexible set of tools for large scale estimation. It features many stochastic gradient methods, built-in models, visualization tools, automated hyperparameter tuning, model checking, interval estimation, and convergence diagnostics.

In the following table you will see listed some of the information on this package:

Package	sgd
Date	January 5, 2016
Version	1.1
Title	Stochastic Gradient Descent for Scalable Estimation
Author	Dustin Tran, Panos Toulis, Tian Lian, Ye Kuang, and Edoardo Airoldi

The following are the most useful functions used in regression analysis contained in this package:

- sgd: This function runs **Stochastic Gradient Descent (SGD)** in order to optimize the induced loss function given a model and data
- print.sgd: This function prints objects of the sgd class
- predict.sgd: This function forms predictions using the estimated model parameters from SGD
- plot.sgd: This function plots objects of the sgd class

The BLR package

This package performs a special case of linear regression named Bayesian linear regression. In Bayesian linear regression, the statistical analysis is undertaken within the context of a Bayesian inference.

In the following table you will see listed some of the information on this package:

Package	BLR
Date	December 3, 2014
Version	1.4
Title	Bayesian Linear Regression
Author	Gustavo de los Campos, Paulino Perez Rodriguez

The following are the most useful functions used in regression analysis contained in this package:

- BLR: This function was designed to fit parametric regression models using different types of shrinkage methods.
- sets: This is a vector (*599x1*) that assigns observations to ten disjointed sets; the assignment was generated at random. This is used later to conduct a 10-fold CV.

The Lars package

This package contains efficient procedures for fitting an entire Lasso sequence with the cost of a single least squares fit. Least angle regression and infinitesimal forward stagewise regression are related to the Lasso.

In the following table you will see listed some of the information on this package:

Package	Lars
Date	April 23, 2013
Version	1.2
Title	Least Angle Regression, Lasso and Forward Stagewise
Author	Trevor Hastie and Brad Efron

The following are the most useful functions used in regression analysis contained in this package:

- `lars`: This function fits least angle regression and Lasso and infinitesimal forward stagewise regression models.
- `summary.lars`: This function produces an ANOVA-type summary for a `lars` object.
- `plot.lars`: This function produce a plot of a `lars` fit. The default is a complete coefficient path.
- `predict.lars`: This function make predictions or extracts coefficients from a fitted `lars` model.

Summary

In this chapter, we were introduced to the basic concepts of regression analysis, and then we discovered different types of statistical processes. Starting from the origin of the term regression, we explored the meaning of this type of analysis. We have therefore gone through analyzing the real cases in which it is possible to extract knowledge from the data at our disposal.

Then, we analyzed how to build regression models step by step. Each step of the workflow was analyzed to understand the meaning and the operations to be performed. Particular emphasis was devoted to the generalization ability of the regression model, which is crucial for all other machine learning algorithms.

We explored the fundamentals of regression analysis and correlation analysis, which allows us to study the relationships between variables. We understood the differences between these two types of analysis.

In addition, an introduction, background information, and basic knowledge of the R environment were covered. Finally, we explored a number of essential packages that R provides for understanding the amazing world of regression.

In the next chapter, we will approach regression with the simplest algorithm: simple linear regression. First, we will describe a regression problem in terms of where to fit a regressor and then we will provide some intuitions underneath the math formulation. Then, the reader will learn how to tune the model for high performance and deeply understand every parameter of it. Finally, some tricks will be described to lower the complexity and scale the approach.

Basic Concepts – Simple Linear Regression

In Chapter 1, *Getting Started with Regression*, we understood the concept of regression through the basic principles that govern its algorithms. Moreover, we were been able to discover the different types of regression that make it a real family of algorithms that can solve the most varied types of problems. In this book, we will learn more about all of them, but for now, let us begin with the basic concepts from the simpler algorithm, as indicated by its name: simple linear regression.

As we will see, simple linear regression is easy to understand but represents the basis of regression techniques; once these concepts are understood, it will be easier for us to address the other types of regression. To begin with, let's take an example of applying linear regression taken from the real world.

Consider some data that has been collected about a group of bikers: number of years of use, number of kilometers traveled in 1 year, and number of falls. Through these techniques, we can find that, on average, when the number of kilometers traveled increases, the number of falls also increases. By increasing the number of years of motorcycle usage and so increasing the experience, the number of falls tends to decrease.

The chapter first describes a regression problem, where we fit a regressor, and then gives some intuitions beneath the math formulation. Then, we will learn how to tune the model for higher performances, and understand deeply every parameter of it. Finally, some tricks will be described for lowering the complexity and scaling the approach.

We will cover the following topics:

- Properly defining a simple regression problem
- Applying simple linear regression
- How to get an **Ordinary Least Squares** (**OLS**) estimation
- Giving a sense to the numbers (coefficients) in the model
- Learning methods for measuring the intercept and slope of a straight line
- Evaluating the model's performance

At the end of the chapter, we will be able to perform a simple linear regression. You will know how to apply linear regression methods to your own data and know how the regression algorithm works. You will understand the basic concepts that regression methods use to fit equations to data using the R environment, and learn to format the dataset for regression, fit a linear regressor, and evaluate its performance. We'll also cover topics such as simple linear regression, OLS estimation, and correlations.

Association between variables – covariance and correlation

In the previous chapter, we introduced correlation concepts, and it is now necessary to deepen these concepts. This will help us understand how to use this information in advance and find possible relationships between variables. Let's start with a real example: a company at the launch of a new printer model wants to analyze sales at a number of stores to determine the best price. The following table shows the sales of the product in the last month and the sale price for these stores:

Store	SoldItems	Price	Store	SoldItems	Price
Store1	100	60	Store11	145	42
Store2	150	43	Store12	125	47
Store3	130	48	Store13	135	44
Store4	140	45	Store14	105	54
Store5	110	55	Store15	155	39
Store6	160	40	Store16	110	52
Store7	115	53	Store17	130	46

Store8	135	47	Store18	115	51
Store9	120	52	Store19	150	41
Store10	155	42	Store20	159	41

So far, we have only introduced the basic concepts without elaborating on them practically. It is now time to process the data in the R environment. The first thing to do is load the data into R. To do this, we will use the following code:

```
setwd ("c://R")
Printers=read.csv ("SellingPrinters.csv", header=TRUE, sep=";")
head(Printers)
```

First, `setwd(c://R)` is used to set the working directory to R contained in the root folder. Then we used the `read.csv()` function, which reads a file in table format and creates a data frame from it, with cases corresponding to lines and variables to fields in the file. Finally, we used the `head()` function, which returns the first or last parts of a vector, matrix, table, data frame, or function. The results are shown in the following:

```
> head(Printers)
        X  N.sold.items Price
1 Store1          100     60
2 Store2          150     43
3 Store3          130     48
4 Store4          140     45
5 Store5          110     55
6 Store6          160     40
```

In table form, we can already extract information from the data, but the best way to provide a first look at the data is to plot a chart. Relationships between quantitative variables detected on the same units can be highlighted through a suitable graphical representation, such as a scatter plot.

Here we will consider a Cartesian reference, wherein the values of one variable are plotted on the horizontal axis and the values of the other variable are plotted on the vertical axis. The values of both the variables are represented by a specific pair of numerical coordinates for each point as detected at a specified observation.

The variables that interest us are store sales and pricing. To see how to recall the variables we are interested in, we can use the `str()` function, which shows a compact display of the internal structure of an R object:

```
str(Printers)
```

The results are shown in the following:

```
> str(Printers)
'data.frame':  20 obs. of  3 variables:
 $ X           : Factor w/ 20 levels "Store1","Store10",
               ..: 1 12 14 15 16 17 18 19 20 2 ...
 $ N.sold.items: int  100 150 130 140 110 160 115 135 120 155 ...
 $ Price       : int  60 43 48 45 55 40 53 47 52 42 ...
```

As we can see, the variables contained in the table are identified by their names. There is an easy way to refer to variables by their names in a data frame; namely, by separating the data frame's name from the name of the variable with a dollar sign ($). We can now plot the chart using the `plot` function:

```
plot(Printers$N.sold.items,Printers$Price,cex = 1.3,lwd = 10)
```

The following figure shows a scatter plot of sold item numbers versus the printer's price:

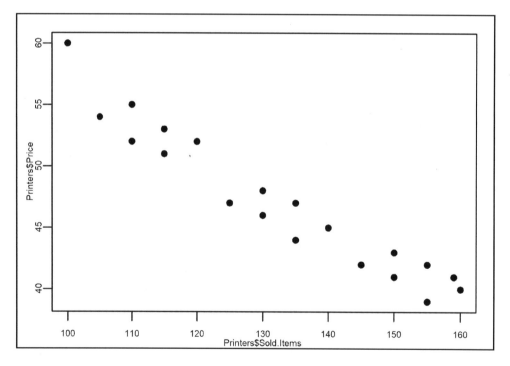

From analysis of the figure, it is possible to note that the points of the scatter plot are arranged according to an elongated cloud. So, we can say that when a variable increases (such as number of sold items), the other variable tends to decrease (such as price).

Without knowing the phenomenon, this data does not tell us whether there is a cause-effect relationship between the two variables. The causes that determine the pattern shown in the figure may be multiple. For example:

- The lowest price increases sales (relationship price - sales)
- Higher sales will lower the price (relationship sales - price)

The one shown in the previous figure is just one of the different relationships that can be observed in a scatter diagram. If this straight line goes from the origin out to high *x-y* values, then it is said that the variables have a concordant association. If the line moves from a high value on the *y* axis to a high value on the *x* axis, the variables have a discordant association. The following figure shows several types of associations between data:

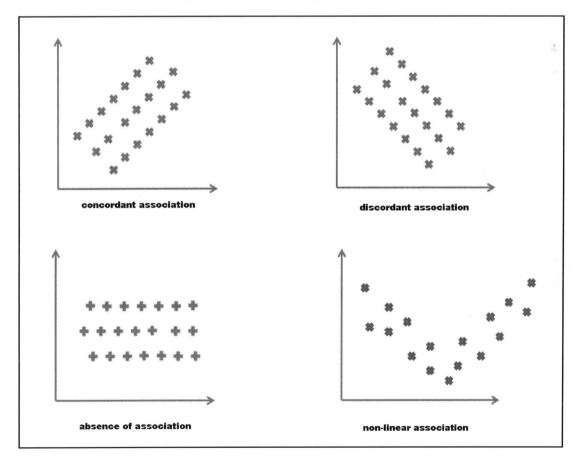

The more we place such points around a straight line, the greater is the correlation between the two variables. At this point, it is permissible to ask the following question: is there a statistical index that expresses the degree of association between two variables? To answer that question, remember what we have said about the association between variables: when changing a variable, the other tends to vary. All this makes us realize that measuring the association between two variables requires a measure of the association variability of the variables.

The most known variability index is variance; it measures how far a set of numbers are spread out from their mean. It represents the mean of the squares of deviations of individual values from their arithmetic mean. The *Variance* is calculated using the following formula:

$$Variance = \frac{1}{N-1} \sum_{i=1}^{n} (x_i - x)^2 = \frac{1}{N-1} \sum_{i=1}^{n} (x_i - x)(x_i - x)$$

Remember that variance is the expectation of the squared deviation of a random variable from its mean. It represents a measure of the spread of data as a whole and is smaller when values are near the mean. In contrast, variance is higher when values are distant from the mean.

To measure the association between variable *x* and variable *y* we can use covariance. Covariance provides an unnormalized measure of their tendency to move together, and is estimated by summing the product deviations from the mean for each variable in each period. Covariance is calculated using the following formula:

$$cov(x, y) = cov(y, x) = \frac{1}{N-1} \sum_{i=1}^{n} (x_i - x)(y_i - y)$$

The covariance sign indicates the type of relationship between the two variables. A positive sign indicates that they move in the same direction while a negative indicates that they move in opposite directions. Also, the tighter the relationship between the variables, the greater the covariance.

Let us calculate the covariant in the example we introduced earlier. Afterward, we will call the covariant among the following variables: `Sold.Items`, `Price`:

```
cov(Printers$Sold.Items,Printers$Price)
```

The result is shown in the following:

```
> cov(Printers$Sold.Items,Printers$Price)
[1] -107.8105
```

The negative sign is indicative of a negative covariance; the value seems to indicate a strong covariance. But are we sure?

> Given two variables x and y, we can say that the covariance is positive if, on average, x and y undergo concordant oscillations (when x exceeds the mean value, y also exceeds the mean value), negative if they suffer discordant oscillations (when x exceeds the mean value, y does not exceed it, and vice versa), it is equal to 0 if they undergo independent oscillations (when x exceeds the mean value, y at times overcomes it but sometimes does not).

In fact, the covariance between two variables cannot tell us whether the bond is tight or not because the value of covariance depends on the size order of the variables (and also on their unit of measurement).

So, it is difficult to understand the intensity of the relationship based exclusively on covariance, as it is not a standardized measure. A standardized measurement of the relationship between two variables is instead represented by the correlation coefficient, which can be calculated starting from covariance using the following formula:

$$corr(x, y) = \frac{cov(x, y)}{sd(x) * sd(y)}$$

Here:

- *cov(x,y)* is the covariance
- *sd(x)* is the standard deviation of *x*
- *sd(y)* is the standard deviation of *y*

The correlation coefficients range between *-1* and *1*, where:

- Values that are derived closer to *1* are an indication of a positive linear relationship between the data columns
- Values closer to *-1* are an indication of one column of data with a negative linear relationship to another column of data (anti-correlation)
- Values that are close to or equal to *0* indicate that a linear relationship between the data columns does not exist

Let us then calculate the correlation coefficient for our example. To do this, we can use the `cor` function as follows:

```
cor(Printers$Sold.Items,Printers$Price)
```

The result is shown in the following:

```
> cor(Printers$Sold.Items,Printers$Price)
[1] -0.9625725
```

This time, we no longer doubt the strong negative correlation, as confirmed by the negative sign and the next value to one. In the formula we analyzed previously, we established the relationship between covariance and the correlation coefficient. Let us verify the correctness by calculating the coefficient of correlation from covariance:

```
CovX_Y=cov(Printers$Sold.Items,Printers$Price)

SdSoldItems=sd(Printers$Sold.Items)

SdPrice=sd(Printers$Price)

CorrCoef=CovX_Y/(SdSoldItems*SdPrice)
```

In this way, we first calculated the covariance, and then the standard deviations of the two variables. Finally, we calculated the correlation coefficient. The result is shown in the following:

```
> CovX_Y=cov(Printers$Sold.Items,Printers$Price)
> CovX_Y
[1] -107.8105
> SdSoldItems=sd(Printers$Sold.Items)
> SdSoldItems
[1] 19.15202
> SdPrice=sd(Printers$Price)
> SdPrice
[1] 5.848077
> CorrCoef=CovX_Y/(SdSoldItems*SdPrice)
> CorrCoef
[1] -0.9625725
```

The result obtained is exactly the same as the application of the `cor` function.

Searching linear relationships

In the previous section, we learned that the coefficient of correlation between two quantitative variables X and Y provides information on the existence of a linear relation between the two variables. This index, however, does not allow determining whether it is X that affects Y, if it is Y that affects X, or whether both X and Y are consequences of a phenomenon that affects both of them. Only more knowledge of the problem under study can allow some hypothesis of the dependence of one variable on another.

If a correlation between two variables is not found, it does not necessarily imply that they are independent, because they might have a nonlinear relationship.

Calculating correlation and covariance is a useful way to investigate whether there exists a linear relationship between variables, without the need to assume or fit a specific model to our data. It may so happen that two variables have a small or no linear correlation, meaning a strong nonlinear relationship. As it may also happen that the two variables have a strong correlation, it will be necessary to find a model that approximates this trend. This suggests that a great way to identify variables that possess a simple relationship is to calculate linear correlation before fitting a model.

We have also shown that a great way to examine the existence of correlations between pairs of variables is to visualize the observations in a Cartesian plane by a scatter plot. We also said that the stronger the link between the two variables, the greater the tendency of the points to fall in a certain direction.

Remember, covariance quantifies the strength of a linear relationship between two variables and correlation provides a measure of the degree of a linear relationship through a dimensionless quantity.

To describe the form of the link between the variables, we can choose to describe the observation behavior by means of a mathematical function that, upon interpolating the data, can represent its tendency and keep its main information. The linear regression method consists of precisely identifying a line that is capable of representing point distribution in a two-dimensional plane. As is easy to imagine, if the points corresponding to the observations are near the line, then the chosen model will be able to effectively describe the link between the variables.

In theory, there are an infinite number of lines that may approximate the observations. In practice, there is only one mathematical model that optimizes the representation of the data. In the case of a linear mathematical relationship, the observations of the variable y can be obtained by a linear function of the observations of the variable x. For each observation we will have the following:

$$y = \alpha * x + \beta$$

In this formula, x is the explanatory variable and y is the response variable. The parameters α and β, which represent respectively the slope of the line and the intercept with the y axis, must be estimated based on the observations collected for the two variables included in the model.

Of particular interest is the slope α, that is, the variation of the mean response for every single increment of the explanatory variable. What about a change in this coefficient? If the slope is positive, the regression line increases from left to right; if the slope is negative, the line decreases from left to right. When the slope is zero, the explanatory variable has no effect on the value of the response. But it is not just the sign of α that establishes the weight of the relationship between the variables; more generally, its value is also important. In the case of a positive slope, the mean response is higher when the explanatory variable is higher; in the case of a negative slope, the mean response is lower when the explanatory variable is higher.

Before looking for the type of relationship between pairs of quantities, it is recommended to conduct a correlation analysis to determine whether there is a linear relationship between these quantities.

The R environment has several functions for performing simple linear regression. In the following sections, we will use some of them, with specific examples. Let's start by using the `lm()` function, which is used to fit linear models, to the example that we have analyzed so far. This function can actually be utilized for carrying out regression, single stratum analysis of variance, and analysis of covariance. Now let's create a linear regression model for the two variables `Sold.Items, Price`:

```
LinMod = lm(Printers$Sold.Items ~ Printers$Price,data=Printers)
```

The model is specified using a formula wherein a ~ separates the response variable present on the left-hand side from the explanatory variables on the right-hand side. Many different functional forms for the relationship can be specified with the help of this formula. The data argument is used to specify the source of the data in which the variables in the formula are contained. The result model is shown in the following:

```
Call:
lm(formula = Printers$Price ~ Printers$Sold.Items, data = Printers)
Coefficients:
        (Intercept)  Printers$Sold.Items
            85.9565              -0.2939
```

More information can be obtained using the summary() function, which produces summaries of the results of various model fitting functions:

```
> summary(LinMod)
Call:
lm(formula = Printers$Price ~ Printers$Sold.Items, data = Printers)
Residuals:
    Min     1Q Median     3Q    Max
 -2.277 -1.353  0.223  1.177  3.436
Coefficients:
                     Estimate Std. Error t value Pr(>|t|)

(Intercept)          85.95647    2.60429   33.01  < 2e-16 ***
Printers$Sold.Items  -0.29392    0.01951  -15.07 1.19e-11 ***
---
Signif. codes:  0 '***' 0.001 '**' 0.01 '*' 0.05 '.' 0.1 ' ' 1
Residual standard error: 1.628 on 18 degrees of freedom
Multiple R-squared:  0.9265,    Adjusted R-squared:  0.9225
F-statistic: 227.1 on 1 and 18 DF,  p-value: 1.195e-11
```

In this case, the amount of information returned may be difficult to understand. Do not worry, we will look at it in detail in the following examples. Let's just focus on adding the regression line to the scatter plot, already shown as previously:

```
abline(LinMod)
```

The following figure shows a scatter plot of sold item numbers versus the printer's price and the regression line:

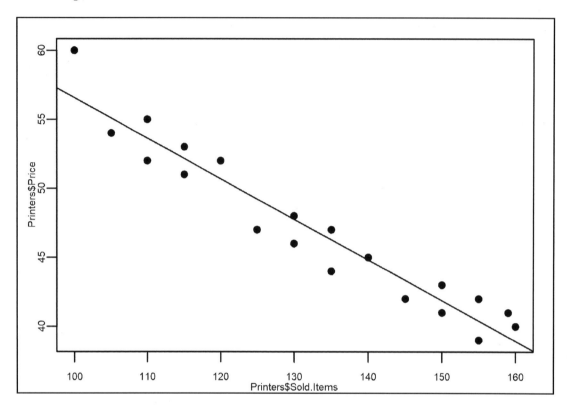

From analysis of the figure it is clear that the regression line approximates the data with excellent results. But we reserve further considerations in the subsequent sections, in which we will have a way of deepening these concepts.

Least squares regression

In the previous section, we saw an example of simple linear regression, built the model, and now have a brief description of it. Next, we will explain the results in detail. We will get started by introducing the key concepts, with another simple linear regression example; we will just use data in the form of a spreadsheet containing the number of vehicles registered in Italy and the population of the different regions. Using this data we will try to determine the line that best estimates the relationship between the population and number of registered vehicles. We can do this in various different ways; we will begin with the simplest. Previously, we said that a linear relationship is represented by the following formula:

$$y = \alpha * x + \beta$$

If we have a set of observations in the form (x_1, y_1), (x_2, y_2), ... (x_n, y_n), for each of these pairs we can write an equation of the type just seen. In this way, we get a system of linear equations. Represent this equation in matrix form as follows:

$$\begin{bmatrix} y_1 \\ y_2 \\ \dots \\ y_n \end{bmatrix} = \begin{bmatrix} x_1 & 1 \\ x_2 & 1 \\ \dots & \dots \\ x_n & 1 \end{bmatrix} \times \begin{bmatrix} \alpha \\ \beta \end{bmatrix}$$

Naming the terms contained in this formula as follows:

$$Y = \begin{bmatrix} y_1 \\ y_2 \\ \dots \\ y_n \end{bmatrix} ; X = \begin{bmatrix} x_1 & 1 \\ x_2 & 1 \\ \dots & \dots \\ x_n & 1 \end{bmatrix} ; A = \begin{bmatrix} \alpha \\ \beta \end{bmatrix}$$

This can be re-expressed using a condensed formulation:

$$Y = X \times A$$

This represents a system of linear equations, and R provides different methods to locate the solution. One of these provides for the use of the `mldivide()` function that performs a symbolic matrix left division. To determine the intercept and the slope, just use the following formula:

$$A = X \backslash Y$$

Let's do it; from the file `VehiclesItaly.xlsx`, import data in a table format. Find the linear regression relation between the vehicle registrations in a state and the population of a state using the `mldivide` function. This function performs a least squares regression. To import `.xlsx` data, we must install a `readxl` library in R.

 Remember, to install a library that is not present in the initial distribution of R, you must use the `install.packages()` function. This function should be used only once and not every time you run the code.

In our case, for example, to install the `readxl` package, we should write the following:

```
install.packages("readxl")
```

This function downloads and installs packages from CRAN-like repositories or from local files. As mentioned, it should be emphasized that this function should be used only once and not every time you run the code. Instead, load the library through the following command, which must be repeated every time you run the code:

```
library(readxl)
```

At this point we can load the contents of the `.xlsx` file into the R environment:

```
setwd ("c://R")
VehicleData <- read_excel("VehiclesItaly.xlsx")
head(VehicleData)
```

First, `setwd(c://R)` is used to set the working directory to R contained in the root folder. Then we used the `read.excel()` function that reads a file in table format and creates a data frame from it, with cases corresponding to lines and variables to fields in the file. Finally, we used the `head()` function that returns the first or last parts of a vector, matrix, table, data frame, or function. The results are shown in the following:

```
> head(VehicleData)
# A tibble: 6 x 3
                   Region Registrations Population
                    <chr>         <dbl>      <dbl>
1          Valle d'Aosta        145263     127329
2                 Molise        204477     312027
3              Basilicata        361034     573694
4                 Umbria        616716     891181
5     Trentino Alto Adige        885665    1059114
6 Friuli Venezia Giulia        773600    1221218
```

As anticipated, the `Registrations` variable contains the number of vehicles registered in Italy and the `Population` variable contains the population of the different regions.

Then, we use the `summary()` function to produce result summaries of the results of the dataset. The function invokes particular methods that depend on the class of the first argument:

```
summary(VehicleData)
```

The results are shown as follows:

```
> summary(VehicleData)
Region              Registrations      Population
Length:20           Min.   : 145263    Min.   :  127329
Class :character    1st Qu.: 814375    1st Qu.: 1180692
Mode  :character    Median :1117087    Median : 1814330
                    Mean   :1866601    Mean   : 3033278
                    3rd Qu.:2886213    3rd Qu.: 4564890
                    Max.   :5923476    Max.   :10008349
```

In this case, a set of data statistics have been obtained. To calculate the slope of the regression line, we will use the `mldivide()` function contained in the `pracma` package. So, we must install the package and then load the library:

```
install.packages("pracma")
library(pracma)
```

Now, assuming vehicle registrations as the response variable (y) and the population of a state as the explanatory variable (x), we can calculate the slope of the regression line simply by typing the following:

```
Y<-VehicleData$Registrations
X<-VehicleData$Population
Alpha<-mldivide(x,y)
```

The result is shown as follows:

```
> alpha
          [,1]
[1,] 0.6061072
```

The linear relationship between the variables is expressed by the following equation:

$$y = 0.6061 \times x$$

In this case, the intercept is equal to zero. Now, let's show the results obtained. To do this, we will first draw a scatter plot with the data in the dataset, and then add the regression line:

```
plot(x,y)
abline(a=0,b=alpha)
```

The following figure shows the scatter plot of distribution with the regression line:

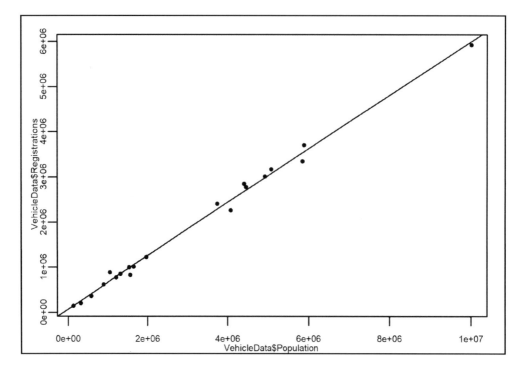

As you might expect, there's a positive association between a state's population and the vehicle registrations, and the regression line fits the data very well.

As just mentioned, the `mldivide()` function performs a least squares regression. But how does least squares regression work? In the least squares method, the coefficients are estimated by determining numerical values that minimize the sum of the squared deviations between the observed responses and the fitted responses.

Given n points (x_1, y_1), (x_2, y_2), ... (x_n, y_n), in the observed population, a least squares regression line is defined as follows:

$$y = \alpha * x + \beta$$

This is the equation line for which the following quantity is minimal:

$$E = \sum_{i=1}^{n} (\alpha x_i + \beta - y_i)^2$$

This quantity represents the sum of the squares of the distances of each experimental datum (x_i, y_i) from the corresponding point on the straight line $(x_i, \alpha x_i + \beta)$, as shown in the following figure:

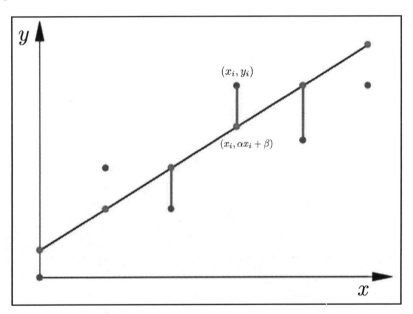

To understand this concept it is easier to draw the distances between these points, formally called residuals, for a couple of data. Once the coefficients are obtained, calculating the residuals is really simple. The observed minus the estimated values, that is:

$$r_i = y_i - (\alpha x_i + \beta)$$

In R, this becomes:

```
VehicleRegFit<- c(alpha)*x
Residual=y-VehicleRegFit
```

Now, we plot the residuals to understand how they are going to distribute:

```
plot(Residual)
abline(a=0,b=0)
```

In the following figure, we can see the scatter plot of **Residual** with a *y=0* line:

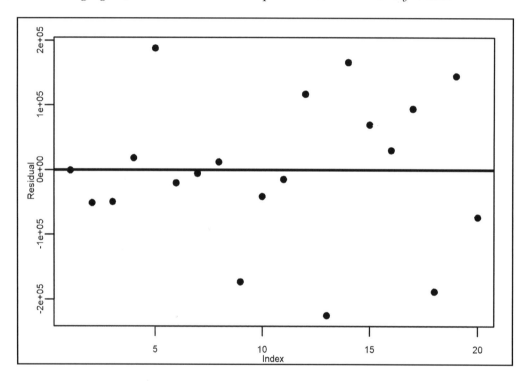

A residual is a measure of how well a regression line fits an individual data point. Therefore, the model is said to fit the data well if the residuals appear to behave randomly. However, the model is clearly said to fit the data poorly if the residuals happen to display a systematic pattern.

The previous figure shows that residuals appear randomly scattered around zero, with a good approximation. To confirm this, we can trace the stem-and-leaf plot of the residuals:

```
stem(Residual)
```

The results are shown as follows:

```
> stem(Residual)
  The decimal point is 5 digit(s) to the right of the |
  -2 | 10
  -1 | 42
  -0 |
   0 | 112333567889
   1 | 348
   2 | 4
```

A stem-and-leaf is a table type used to display data. The stem, on the left, displays the first digit or digits. The leaf, on the right, displays the last digit. In our case, this plot allows us to understand how residuals are distributed. In fact, it is clear that most residuals have the first digit of zero (remember that these values are in exponential format, so they must be multiplied by 10^{+05}). Then, we find four positive (three with the first digit of one and one with the first digit of two) and four negative values.

We have previously seen that the model fits the data very well. But how can we measure this feature? Calculating the coefficient of determination (R-squared) is one method: It is a way to determine a better fit. R-squared measures how well a model can predict the data, and falls between zero and one. The higher the value of the coefficient of determination, the better the model is at predicting the data.

R-squared is defined as the proportion of the variance in the dependent variable that is predictable from the independent variable. To calculate this coefficient, it is necessary to evaluate two quantities:

- The sum of squares of residuals, also called the **residual sum of squares (RSS)**:

$$SS_{res} = \sum_{i=1}^{n}(y_i - \alpha x_i + \beta)^2$$

- The total sum of squares that is proportional to the variance of the data:

$$SS_{tot} = \sum_{i=1}^{n}(y_i - y_{mean})^2$$

The most general definition of the coefficient of determination is:

$$R^2 = 1 - \frac{SS_{res}}{SS_{tot}} = 1 - \frac{\sum_{i=1}^{n}(y_i - \alpha x_i + \beta)^2}{\sum_{i=1}^{n}(y_i - y_{mean})^2}$$

The better the linear regression fits the data in comparison to the simple average, the closer the value of R-squared is to one. Let's see how to calculate it in R:

```
Rsq1 = 1 - sum((y - VehicleRegFit)^2)/sum((y - mean(y))^2)
```

The result is shown as follows:

```
> Rsq1
[1] 0.9934617
```

This result is very close to 1, meaning that the regression line fits the data very well. Are we satisfied with the result or are we trying to improve it? Let's improve the fit by including a y intercept in our model. To do this, insert a column of one into x and use the `mldivide()` function:

```
X1<-cbind(x,1)
alpha_beta = mldivide(x1,y)
```

To calculate the intercept with the y axis, we added a column of 1 to the starting vector. Then, we again applied the `mldivide()` function. The result is shown as follows:

```
> alpha_beta
            [,1]
[1,] 6.061072e-01
[2,] 1.202018e-07
```

Now we calculate the fitted values:

```
VehicleRegFit2 = X1%*%alpha_beta
```

To calculate the product between a vector and a matrix, we used the `%*%` operator. Now, let's plot a graph to compare the two regression lines we have obtained:

```
plot(x,y,cex = 1.3,lwd = 10)
abline(a=0,b=alpha,lwd=5,col="red")
abline(a=alpha_beta[2,],b=alpha_beta[1,],lwd=5,lty=3)
```

To appreciate the differences between the two regression lines, we traced the first in red and the second with a dashed line. As we can see in the following figure, the two overlapping lines mean that the differences are minimal:

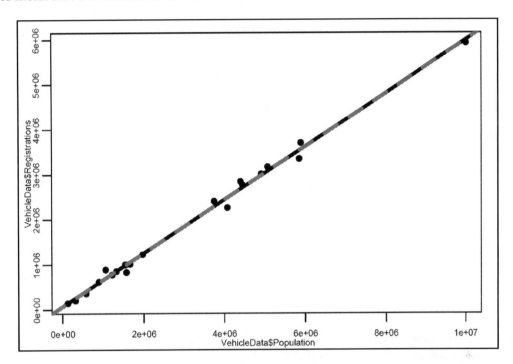

To evaluate any improvement in the regression line, we calculate the coefficient of determination (R-squared) again to compare the performance of the two models:

```
Rsq2 = 1 - sum((y - VehicleRegFit2)^2)/sum((y - mean(y))^2)
```

The result is shown as follows:

```
> Rsq2
[1] 0.9934617
```

From the comparison of the two values (Rsq1 and Rsq2), there is no improvement.

Finally, it is useful to remember that the proportionate amount of variation in the response variable y explained by the independent variable x is suggested by the coefficient of determination (R-squared) in the linear regression model. The larger the R-squared is, the more variability is explained by the linear regression model.

Creating a linear regression model

In the previous section, we adopted an algebraic approach to calculating the regression line. More generally, to create a linear regression model, we use the `lm()` function. This function creates a `LinearModel` object. The object of class `lm` has a series of properties that can be immediately viewed by simply clicking on it. These types of objects can be used for residual analysis and regression diagnosis.

 `LinearModel` is an object comprised of data, model description, diagnostic information, and fitted coefficients for a linear regression.

Models for the `lm()` function are specified symbolically. In fact, the first argument of the function is an object of class `formula`. A typical `formula` object has the following form:

```
response ~ terms
```

`response` represents the (numeric) response vector and `terms` is a series of terms specifying a linear predictor for response. Let us take a look at a terms specification of the following form:

```
A + B
```

This indicates all the terms in `A` together with all the terms in `B`, with duplicates removed. Let's look at another form of specification:

```
A:B
```

This indicates the set of terms obtained by taking the interactions of all terms in `A` with all terms in `B`. Let's see another:

```
A*B
```

This specification indicates the cross of `A` and `B`. This is the same as `A + B + A:B`.

For example, look at the following formula:

```
'Y ~ A + B + C'
```

This represents a three-variable linear model with intercept. To access the documentation of the `lm()` function, simply type `?lm` at the R prompt.

To understand how `lm()` function works, we start from the new dataset containing the number of licensed drivers in the United States from 1960 to 2011. This dataset contains the following fields:

- Year from 1960 to 2011 (named `Year`)
- Number of licensed drivers in the United States in millions (named `LicensedDrivers`)

The data are contained in the `.xlsx` file named `LicensedDrivers.xlsx`.

This file was extracted from the one compiled by the Earth Policy Institute from licensed drivers, vehicle registrations, and resident population - chart, table DV-1C in U.S. **Department of Transportation (DOT)**, **Federal Highway Administration (FHWA)**, Highway Statistics 2011, at `www.fhwa.dot.gov/policyinformation/statistics/011/index.cfm`

Let's start by importing the data into a table:

```
library(readxl)
setwd ("c://R")
LicDrivers <- read_excel("LicensedDrivers.xlsx")
```

To display the internal structure of the `LicDrivers` object, simply type the following:

```
str(LicDrivers)
```

You will obtain the following results:

```
> str(LicDrivers)
Classes 'tbl_df', 'tbl' and 'data.frame':    52 obs. of   2 variables:
 $ Year           : num  1960 1961 1962 1963 1964 ...
 $ LicensedDrivers: num  87 89 91 94 95 99 101 103 105 108 ...
```

Fit a linear regression model for `LicensedDrivers` (number of licensed drivers in the United States in millions), using `Year` (year from 1960 to 2011) as the explanatory variable (predictor):

```
LModel = lm(LicensedDrivers~Year,data = LicDrivers)
```

The results are shown as follows:

```
> LModel
Call:
lm(formula = LicensedDrivers ~ Year, data = LicDrivers)
Coefficients:
(Intercept)          Year
  -4844.307          2.517
```

This means that the linear model for this example is estimated as follows:

$$LicensedDrivers = -4844.307 + 2.517 * Year$$

This equation can be used to make predictions about data not in the source dataset. But, before analyzing the information in the model, we simply draw a plot showing the data and the regression line:

```
plot(LicDrivers$Year,LicDrivers$LicensedDrivers,cex = 1.3,lwd = 10)
abline(LModel,lwd=5)
```

The following figure shows the scatter plot of distribution with regression line:

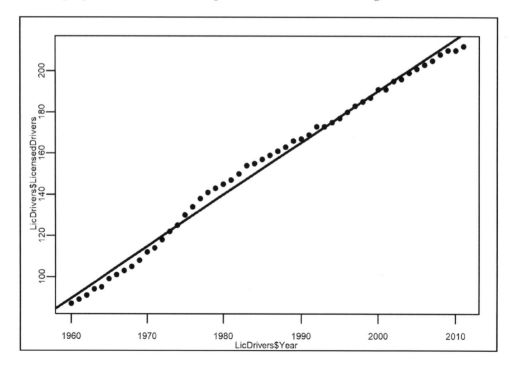

As we have seen before, there's a positive association between a year and the number of licensed drivers, and the regression line fits the data very well. Now, however, is the time to clarify the meaning of the values contained in the model. To look at them, let's see a brief summary using the `summary()` function:

```
summary(LModel)
```

The results are shown as follows:

```
> summary(LModel)
Call:
lm(formula = LicensedDrivers ~ Year, data = LicDrivers)
Residuals:
    Min     1Q  Median     3Q     Max
-5.9601 -2.8996 -0.3038  3.0582  6.5240
Coefficients:
              Estimate Std. Error t value Pr(>|t|)

(Intercept) -4.844e+03  6.445e+01  -75.17   <2e-16 ***
Year         2.517e+00  3.246e-02   77.56   <2e-16 ***
---
Signif. codes:  0 '***' 0.001 '**' 0.01 '*' 0.05 '.' 0.1 ' ' 1
Residual standard error: 3.513 on 50 degrees of freedom
Multiple R-squared:  0.9918,    Adjusted R-squared:  0.9916
F-statistic:  6015 on 1 and 50 DF,  p-value: < 2.2e-16
```

The results show the linear regression model as a formula and following a series of residuals statistics. Now, go to the estimated coefficients, where there is one row for each of the terms included in the model, and the following columns:

- `Estimate`: The estimated coefficient value for each corresponding term in the model. There are two rows: the first is the intercept and the second is the slope.
- `Std.Error`: The standard error of the estimate. The average amount that the coefficient approximates varies from the actual average value of our response variable and is measured by the coefficient standard error. Ideally a lower number relative to its coefficients (as in our case).

- `t value`: The t-statistic for each coefficient, for testing the null hypothesis that the corresponding coefficient is zero against the alternative that it is different from zero, given the other predictors in the model. This is a measure of how many standard deviations our coefficient estimate is far away from zero. This value is required to be far away from zero since this would indicate that the null hypothesis could be rejected—that is, it can be declared that there exists a relationship between speed and distance exists. In our case, the t-statistic values are relatively far away from zero and are large with respect to the standard error, which could suggest that a relationship exists. In general, t-values are also used to compute p-values.

- `Pr(>|t|)`: The `p-value` for the `F-statistic` of the hypotheses tests if the corresponding coefficient is equal to zero or not. In our example, the `p-value` of the `F-statistic` for `Year` is lower than `0.05`, so this term is significant at the five percent significance level, given the other terms in the model.

T-test is a parametric test with the purpose of verifying whether the average value of a distribution differs significantly from a certain reference value.

In addition, we see the following information about the model we have created:

- `Residual standard error`: A measure of the quality of a linear regression fit.

- `Multiple R-squared`: The proportion of total sum of squares explained by the model. It represents the coefficient of determination. In our example, the R-squared value suggests that the model explains approximately *99* percent of the variability in the `LicensedDrivers` response variable.

- `Adjusted R-squared`: This is a modified version of R-squared that has been adjusted for the number of predictors in the model.

- `F-statistic`: The test statistic for the F-test on the regression model. It tests for a significant linear regression relationship between the response variable and the predictor variables.

- `p-value`: The `p-value` for the F-test on the model. In our example, the model is significant with a `p-value` of `2.2e-16`.

Let's look at the result of the last typed R command. Two values are highlighted on the others: R-squared and `p-value`. For the first, a very high value was calculated, equal to `0.992`; it means that there is a strong variation in the response variable, explained by the predictor. On the contrary, the `p-value` is very small, but to understand what this value means, we need to go deeper into the subject.

Statistical significance test

When performing a statistical significance test, the so-called **null hypothesis** is initially assumed. According to it, there is no difference between the groups regarding the parameter being considered. The groups are equal and the observed difference is attributed to the case.

Obviously, the null hypothesis can be true or false. Now we have to decide: do we accept or reject the null hypothesis? To decide, we need to analyze our data with a significance test. If the test recommends rejecting the null hypothesis, then the observed difference is declared statistically significant. If, instead, the test advises us to accept the null hypothesis, then the difference is statistically not significant.

As always, the results of a statistical test do not have absolute value and mathematical certainty, only probability. Therefore, a decision to reject the null hypothesis is probably right, but it may be wrong. Measuring this risk of falling in error is called the significance level of the test.

 This level (called p-value) represents a quantitative estimate of the probability that the observed differences are due to the case.

P is a probability and therefore can only assume values between zero and one. A p-value approaching zero signifies a low probability that the observed difference can be attributed to the case. The significance level of a test can be chosen by the researcher as desired. However, we usually choose a significance level of *0.05* (five percent) or *0.01* (one percent). In our case, we calculated a p-value equal to 2.02e-16, far lower the significance level, indicating that the observed difference is statistically significant.

Exploring model results

We previously said that the lm() function creates a LinearModel object, comprising used data, model description, diagnostic information, and fitted coefficients for a linear regression. Now, we will use some of these properties to extract further knowledge from the model.

The values in the `lm` object depend on the type of model we have built. In this regard, it should be noted that the `lm()` function can be used to carry out regression, single stratum analysis of variance, and analysis of covariance. To see exactly what a linear model fit produces, try the `names` function:

```
names(LModel)
```

For `LModel`, the result are shown as follows:

```
> names(LModel)
 [1] "coefficients"  "residuals"     "effects"       "rank"
"fitted.values" "assign"
 [7] "qr"            "df.residual"   "xlevels"       "call"
"terms"         "model"
```

A brief description of these components is provided in the following list:

- `coefficients`: A named vector of coefficients
- `residuals`: The residuals, that is, response minus fitted values
- `effects`: Returns (orthogonal) effects from a fitted model, usually a linear model
- `rank`: The numeric rank of the fitted linear model
- `fitted.values`: The fitted mean values
- `assing`: An integer vector with an entry for each column in the matrix, giving the term in the formula that gave rise to the column
- `qr`: Computes the QR decomposition of a matrix
- `df.residual`: The residual degrees of freedom
- `xlevels`: A record of the levels of the factors used in fitting
- `call`: Represents the call used to build the model
- `terms`: The `terms` object used
- `model`: The `model` frame used

Let's analyze in detail the most important available values. To call these values, just use the name of the model, followed by the value name and separated by the dollar operator ($). The first values are coefficients of the model. Theoretically speaking, in simple linear regression, coefficients are two unknown constants that represent the intercept and slope terms in the linear model:

```
> LModel$coefficients
 (Intercept)          Year
 -4844.307052     2.517288
```

The first term represents the `Intercept` and the second term is the slope. To access the coefficients we can also use the `coef()` function (`coef(LModel)`). Let us then analyze residuals: As mentioned previously, residuals are essentially the difference between the actual observed response values and the response values that the model predicted:

```
> LModel$residuals
         1          2          3          4          5
-2.5783745 -3.0956629 -3.6129514 -3.1302399 -4.6475284
         6          7          8          9         10
-3.1648169 -3.6821054 -4.1993938 -4.7166823 -4.2339708
        11         12         13         14         15
-2.7512593 -3.2685478 -1.7858363 -0.3031247  0.1795868
        16         17         18         19         20
 2.6622983  4.1450098  5.6277213  6.1104329  5.5931444
        21         22         23         24         25
 5.0758559  4.5585674  5.0412789  6.5239904  5.0067020
        26         27         28         29         30
 4.4894135  3.9721250  3.4548365  2.9375480  3.4202595
        31         32         33         34         35
 1.9029711  1.3856826  2.8683941  0.3511056 -0.1661829
        36         37         38         39         40
-0.6834714 -0.2007598  0.2819517 -0.2353368 -0.7526253
        41         42         43         44         45
 0.7300862 -1.7872023 -0.3044907 -1.8217792 -1.3390677
        46         47         48         49         50
-1.8563562 -2.3736447 -2.8909332 -2.4082216 -2.9255101
        51         52
-5.4427986 -5.9600871
```

The data thus proposed lends itself to a difficult interpretation. It's better to draw a stem-and-leaf plot of `residuals`:

```
> stem (LModel$residuals)
  The decimal point is at the |
  -6 | 0
  -4 | 47622
  -2 | 763211998644
  -0 | 988838733222
   0 | 234749
   2 | 79945
   4 | 015600166
   6 | 15
```

Analyzing the stem-and-leaf plot, we can see that the distribution of residuals appears to be strongly symmetrical. That means that the model predicts the response very well. Afterward, we will try to confirm this through a plot of residuals against fitted values. To access the residuals, we can also use the `residuals` function (`residuals(LModel)`). To extract the fitted value from the model, simply type the following:

```
LModel$fitted.values
```

To access the fitted value we can also use the `fitted` function as follows:

```
fitted(LModel)
```

The `fitted` function is a generic function that extracts fitted values from objects returned by modeling functions. The `fitted.values` command is an alias for it. All object classes that are returned by model fitting functions should provide a `fitted` method. We will use these values in the next section when we view results in specific plots.

To evaluate the performance of the model, we have previously resorted to the values restituted by the `summary()` function. I mean the R-squared that represents the coefficient of determination. Let's see then how to extract it from the model:

```
> summary(LModel)$r.squared
[1] 0.9917559
```

The R-squared value suggests that the model explains approximately 99 percent of the variability in the `LicensedDrivers` response variable. This is a very good result.

Diagnostic plots

The best way to appreciate the results of a simulation is to display them in special charts. In fact, we have already used this technique in this section: I am referring to the chart in which we have drawn the scatter plot of distribution with regression line. Now we will see other plots that will allow us to check the model hypotheses.

Previously, we have already verified whether the model worked well for our data. We did it by analyzing the results of the regression model, such as slope and intercept coefficients, p-value, or R-squared value ,that tell us how a model represents the starting data. That way, however, we did not finish our checks. For example, residuals might show how a model does not represent the data. Residuals remain a result variable after adapting a model (predictors) to data and may reveal unexplained patterns in data from the mounted model. By using this information, we can not only verify whether the linear regression assumptions are met, but also improve our model in an exploratory way.

We have already looked at the residuals, but our analysis was superficial; it is necessary to deepen the subject. We will do it through integrated diagnostic diagrams for the linear regression analysis in R. It is enough to use the `plot` function with the linear regression model as the argument. Six plots are currently available:

- A plot of residuals against fitted values
- A normal q-q plot
- A scale-location plot of sqrt(| residuals |) against fitted values
- A plot of Cook's distances versus row labels
- A plot of residuals against leverages
- A plot of Cook's distances against *leverage/(1-leverage)*

By default, the first three and five are provided, and we will analyze them one by one. To select a single plot, use the `which` argument followed by the number (*1-6*). Alternatively, we can plot the results using the following command:

```
plot(LModel)
```

This will give us the following set of four plots: residuals versus fitted values, a Q-Q plot of standardized residuals, a scale-location plot, and a plot of residuals versus leverage that adds bands corresponding to Cook's distances of *0.5* and *1*. These are the selected plots by default. We will be prompted by R to click on the graph window or press *Enter* before display each plot, but we can do better. Use the `par()` function for your graphics window to be set to show four plots at once, in a layout with 2 rows and 2 columns:

```
par(mfrow=c(2,2))
plot(LModel)
```

To return to a single graph per window, use `par(mfrow=c(1,1))`. Let's start with the plot that shows residuals against fitted values. This plot shows if residuals have nonlinear patterns. There could exist a nonlinear relationship between predictor and outcome variables and the pattern could show up in this plot if the nonlinear relationship is not captured by the model. A good indication that our model fits very well is if there are equally spread residuals around a horizontal line without distinct patterns.

The residuals should be distributed randomly around the horizontal line representing a residual error of zero, such that there should be no clear trend in the distribution of the points. Let's look at residual plots from our model:

```
plot(LModel,which=1)
```

The following figure shows the **Residuals** versus **Fitted values**:

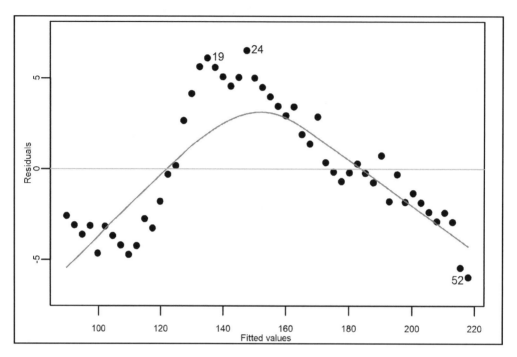

The dotted line at **Residuals** is equal to zero indicates our fit line. Any point on the fit line obviously has zero residuals. Previous points have positive residuals and the following points have negative residuals. In particular, some observations are highlighted by indicating the number. These observations are the most problematic. In this case, observations number **19**, **24**, and **52** are highlighted.

Remember a residual is a measure of how well a regression line fits an individual data point. Therefore, if the residuals appeared to behave randomly, it indicates that the model fits the data well. However, if the residuals appear to show a systematic pattern, we can clearly say that the model fits the data poorly.

In our case, we can see that our residuals have a curved pattern (red line). The fitted line doesn't describe how the response behaves when the input changes, since the relationship is nonlinear. This could mean that we may get a better result if we try a model with a quadratic term included. This is an unexpected result, as the R-squared value was very close to one. All this confirms that there is still much to be observed. We will explore this point further in the following chapters, by actually trying this to see if it helps.

Let's look at the second diagnostic plot: normal q-q plot. This plot shows if residuals are normally distributed. It's good if residuals are lined well on the straight dashed line:

```
plot(LModel,which=2)
```

The following figure shows the **Standardized residuals** against **Theoretical Quantiles**:

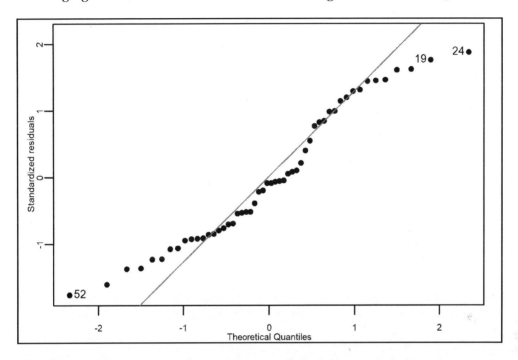

We are looking for if the errors are approximately normally distributed, which is what the q-q plot allows you to see. Analyzing the figure, it can be noted that the residuals do not follow a straight line well. Once again, there are areas where the residuals are located over the dashed lines and areas in which they are located as follows.

Let's look at the third diagnostic plot: scale-location plot, also called a spread-location plot. This plot shows if residuals are spread equally along the ranges of predictors. This is how you can check the assumption of equal variance (homoscedasticity). Indeed, we can also check this assumption with the first diagnostic plot. It's good if you see a horizontal line with equally (randomly) spread points:

```
plot(LModel,which=3)
```

The following figure shows the **Standardized residuals** against **Fitted values**:

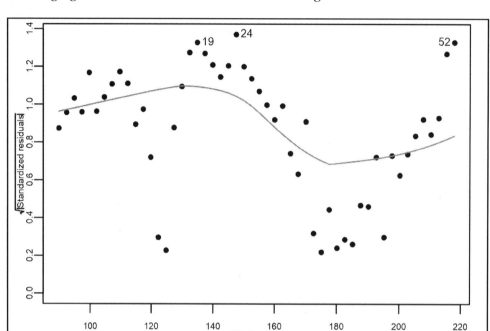

The scale-location plot suggests the spread of points across the predicted values range. Homoscedasticity is one of the assumptions for regression, such that variance should be reasonably equal across the predictor range. It is ideal to have a horizontal red line that would indicate the residuals have uniform variance across the range.

Even in this case, there must be no obvious trend in this plot. Analyzing the figure, it can be noted that the residuals are not equally distributed. Because the residuals focus on some areas at the expense of others, the red smooth line is not horizontal and shows a steep angle.

The last diagnostic plot that we have to analyze is a plot of residuals against leverages. This plot helps us to determine any influential cases, if present. All outliers are not necessarily influential in linear regression analysis. Data might not necessarily be influential in determining a regression line even though the data has extreme values. This means that whether we decide to include or exclude these data from the analysis the results wouldn't be much different.

Before drawing the plot, we must know what influence and leverage are. The amount of change in the predicted scores if an observation is excluded determines the influence of the observation. Cook's distance is a pretty good measure of the influence of an observation. The leverage of an observation is based on how much the observation's value on the predictor variable differs from the mean of the predictor variable. The more the leverage of an observation, the greater potential that point has in terms of influence.

These time patterns are not relevant unlike the other plots. We watch out for outlying values at the upper-right or lower-right corner. Those are the spots where cases can be influential against a regression line. If we find cases outside of a dashed line, these lines are referred to as Cook's distance. The cases are influential to the regression results, when cases are outside of Cook's distance. If those cases are excluded the regression results will be altered.

Let's draw this plot:

```
plot(LModel,which=5)
```

The following figure shows the **Standardized residuals** against **Leverage**:

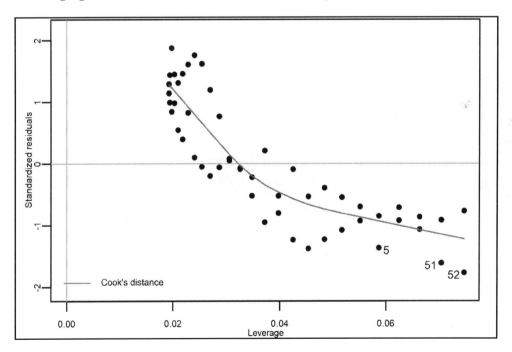

In this plot, **Cook's distance** is represented by the dotted red lines and the ones outside the dotted line at the top-right or bottom-right corner are the ones that are of interest to us. We say that the observation has high leverage or that the potential for influencing our model is higher if any point falls in that region and if we exclude that point. As we can notice there are points in the bottom right corner. We will take a look at this in the following sections.

Modeling a perfect linear association

So far, we have explored several real cases for which we have searched linear associations, and therefore we have built models of simple linear regression. Next, we tried to analyze the results to confirm the goodness of fit in the simulation of the real system. At this point, it is reasonable to wonder what results of a model perfectly fit a linear system. In this way we will know how to distinguish between a model with a good approximation to what is wrong. In this last case, clearly indicating a nonlinear relationship remains the best solution.

Previously, we said that a simple linear relationship is represented by the following formula:

$$y = \alpha * x + \beta$$

Here, α and β, represent, respectively, the slope and the intercept with the y axis of the regression line. That being said, we build a dummy system by deciding a priori an intercept and a slope:

```
x<-seq(from = 1, to = 100, by = 0.1)
y<-2.7*x+6
```

In this way, we first created an integer vector (x) containing numbers from 1 to 100 with a step of 0.1. So, we calculated the value of y according to the following formula:

$$y = 2.7 * x + 6$$

The relationship we have built up is a perfect linear association; it is clear that we cannot use it to build the model. We would not have any benefit and the algorithm would not be able to tell us anything. Now, we can add an error to the system, distributing it randomly on all data:

```
len<-length(y)

er<-runif(len, min=-1, max=1)
```

We first determined the length of vector y, so we created a vector of the same length consisting of random numbers within the range (-1, 1). Such a vector will represent our error that we will add to vector y:

```
y<-y+er
dataxy<-table(rep(x, y))
```

With that code, we added an error to vector y, so we inserted the two x and y vectors to a table. At this point, we have the dummy data needed to build our linear regression model:

```
LModel = lm(y~x,data = dataxy)
```

To look at them, let's see a brief summary using the summary function:

```
summary(LModel)
```

The result are shown as follows:

```
> summary(LModel)
Call:
lm(formula = y ~ x, data = dataxy)
Residuals:
     Min        1Q    Median        3Q       Max
-0.96387  -0.50036   0.00546   0.45533   1.04603
Coefficients:
              Estimate Std. Error t value Pr(>|t|)
(Intercept) 5.9304973  0.0360546    164.5   <2e-16 ***
x           2.7004560  0.0006212   4347.1   <2e-16 ***
---
Signif. codes:   0 '***' 0.001 '**' 0.01 '*' 0.05 '.' 0.1 ' ' 1
Residual standard error: 0.5594 on 989 degrees of freedom
Multiple R-squared:  0.9999,     Adjusted R-squared:  0.9999
F-statistic: 1.89e+07 on 1 and 989 DF,  p-value: < 2.2e-16
```

As was obvious, the results are excellent: R-squared = 0.999, and p-value: < 2.2e-16. Of course, the intercept and the slope of the regression line are very close to those we set off at the start. Therein is the error we intentionally introduced to create the model.

Now, simply draw a plot showing the data and the regression line:

```
plot(x,y,cex = 1.3,lwd = 10)
abline(LModel,lwd=5)
```

The following figure shows the scatter plot of distribution with regression line:

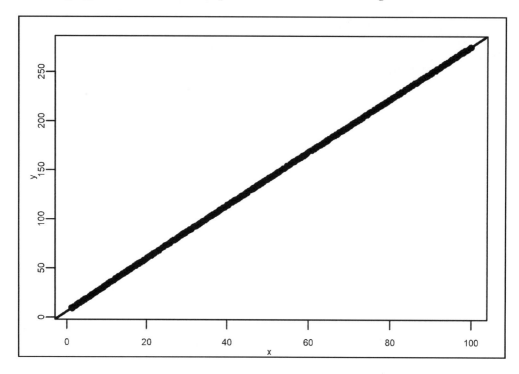

Analyzing the plot, we can confirm the perfect fitting of the regression line to the data. But such results do not have to make us think it's over. We have seen in the example analyzed in the previous section; to confirm the goodness of fit, it is necessary to perform a residuals analysis.

We will do this through integrated diagnostic diagrams for the linear regression analysis in R. As already done in the previous section, we will use the `plot` function with the linear regression model as the argument. We plot the charts provided by default; furthermore, we will use the `par` function to set the graphics window to show four plots at once, in a layout with 2 rows and 2 columns:

```
par(mfrow=c(2,2))
plot(LModel)
```

The following figure shows four plots: a plot of **Residuals** against **Fitted values**, a normal q-q plot, a scale-location plot, and a plot of **Standardized residuals** against **Leverage**:

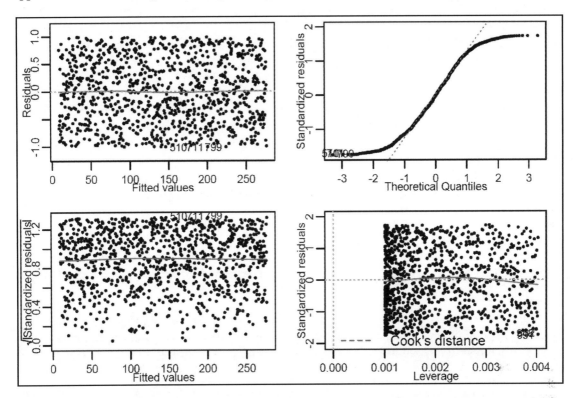

In the previous section, at the residuals analysis we repeatedly underlined the need for the residuals to be distributed equally, as a condition necessary for the success of the model. Now we can see that the residuals are equally distributed. In addition, except in the case of normal q-q plot, in the other three plots, the red line is almost horizontal. In the case of the normal q-q plot, the data fitted well to the dashed line. All this did not happen in the example analyzed earlier, indicating that the model was nonlinear.

Summary

In this chapter, we introduced regression with the simplest algorithm: simple linear regression. We first described a regression problem and where to fit a regressor, and then provided some intuitions underneath the math formulation. Then, we learned how to tune the model for higher performance, and came to deeply understand every parameter of it. In addition, some tricks were described to lower the complexity and scaling of the approach.

To start, we explored the coefficient of correlation between two quantitative variables X and Y, which provides information on the existence of a linear relation between the two variables. We understood that this coefficient does not allow us to determine whether it is X that affects Y, of whether it is Y that affects X, or whether both X and Y are consequences of a phenomenon that affects both of them. Only more knowledge of the problem under study can allow some hypothesis of the dependence of a variable on another.

Then, we analyzed a real-life example by adopting an algebraic approach to calculating the linear regression model. We saw that a method for finding the better fit is calculating the coefficient of determination (R-squared). An R-squared measure shows how well a model can predict the data, and falls between zero and one. The higher the value of the coefficient of determination, the better the model is at predicting the data.

We learned to use the `lm()` function to build a linear regression model, so we analyzed in detail all the results offered by the model to evaluate its performance. Subsequently, we saw how to run a residuals analysis to confirm the goodness of the fitting on the model.

Finally, we fitted a dummy model to understand what results to expect from a linear regression model.

In the next chapter, simple linear regression will be extended to extract predictive information from more than one feature. The **Stochastic Gradient Descent (SGD)** technique will be scaled to cope with a vector of features. Finally, polynomial regression will be introduced for when linear regression is not good enough.

3
More Than Just One Predictor – MLR

In Chapter 2, *Basic Concepts – Simple Linear Regression*, we understood the concept of simple linear regression that covers the relationship between only one independent variable (explanatory variable) and the dependent variable (response variable). It's not very often that we find a variable that depends solely on another. Usually, we find that the response variable depends on at least two predictors.

Let's take a look at an example. Getting to the workplace can often be a path full of variables. Scheduling your departure to arrive on time can be a difficult task. That is why you need to take different variables into account: the distance from your home, the type of route to follow (street type), traffic along the route, the number of stops (if you need to drop your children to school), weather conditions, and so on. Have you ever thought about it? Every morning, we have to plan all these things in order to get to work on time.

In this chapter, simple linear regression will be extended to extract predictive information from more than one feature. We will learn how to tune the multiple linear regression model for higher performance and deeply understand every parameter of it. We will explore the **Stochastic Gradient Descent (SGD)** technique for optimization of the algorithms used on regression to find a good set of model parameters for a given training dataset. Finally, polynomial regression will be introduced where linear regression is not good enough.

We will cover the following topics:

- Multiple linear regression
- Model results explained
- Evaluating the model's performance
- Linear regression using SGD
- Polynomial regression

At the end of the chapter, you will be able to perform multiple linear regression. You will have learned how to apply multiple linear regression methods to your own data and how the regression algorithm works. You will understand the basic concepts that multiple regression methods use to fit equations to data using the R environment. You will also learn how to use the SGD technique to improve the model's performance.

Multiple linear regression concepts

So far, we have resolved simple linear regression problems; they study the relation between a dependent variable, y, and an independent variable, x, based on the regression equation:

$$y = \alpha * x + \beta$$

In this equation, the explanatory variable is represented by x and the response variable is represented by y. To solve this problem, the least squares method was used. In this method, we can find the best fit by minimizing the sum of squares of the vertical distances from each data point on the line. As mentioned before, we don't find that a variable depends solely on another very often. Usually, we find that the response variable depends on at least two predictors. In practice, we will have to create models with a response variable that depends on more than one predictor. These models are named multiple linear regression, a straightforward generalization of single predictor models. According to multiple linear regression models, the dependent variable is related to two or more independent variables. The general model for n variables is of the form:

$$y = \beta_0 + \beta_1 * x_1 + \beta_2 * x_2 + \ldots + \beta_n * x_n$$

Here, $x_1, x_2,.. x_n$ are the n predictors and y is the only response variable. The coefficients β_i measure the change in the y value associated with a change in x_i, keeping all the other variables constant. The simple linear regression model is used to find a straight line that best fits the data. On the other hand, multiple linear regression models, for example, with two independent variables, are used to find a plane that best fits the data; more generally, it is a multidimensional plane. The goal is to find the surface that best fits our predictors in terms of minimizing the overall squared distance between itself and the response variable. In order to estimate β, similarly to what we did in the simple linear regression case, we want to minimize the following term over all possible values of intercepts and slopes:

$$\sum_i [y_i - (\beta_0 + \beta_1 * x_1 + \beta_2 * x_2 + \ldots + \beta_n * x_n)]^2$$

Just as we did in the case of simple linear regression, we can represent the previous equation in matrix form as:

$$
\begin{bmatrix} y_1 \\ y_2 \\ \ldots \\ y_n \end{bmatrix}
=
\begin{bmatrix}
1 & x_1,1 & x_1,2 & \ldots & x_1,n \\
1 & x_2,1 & x_2,2 & \ldots & x_2,n \\
\ldots & & & & \\
1 & x_n,1 & x_n,2 & \ldots & x_n,n
\end{bmatrix}
\times
\begin{bmatrix} \beta_0 \\ \beta_1 \\ \beta_2 \\ \ldots \\ \beta_n \end{bmatrix}
$$

Naming the terms contained in this formula as follows:

$$
Y = \begin{bmatrix} y_1 \\ y_2 \\ \ldots \\ y_n \end{bmatrix}
; X =
\begin{bmatrix}
1 & x_1,1 & x_1,2 & \ldots & x_1,n \\
1 & x_2,1 & x_2,2 & \ldots & x_2,n \\
\ldots & & & & \\
1 & x_n,1 & x_n,2 & \ldots & x_n,n
\end{bmatrix}
; \beta = \begin{bmatrix} \beta_0 \\ \beta_1 \\ \beta_2 \\ \ldots \\ \beta_n \end{bmatrix}
$$

This can be re-expressed using a condensed formulation:

$$Y = X * \beta$$

Finally, to determine the intercept and slope through the least squares method, we have to solve the previous equation with respect to β as follows (we must estimate the coefficients with the normal equation):

$$\beta = (X^T * X)^{-1} * X^T * Y$$

In the previous equation, there are three mathematical operations involving matrices: transpose, inverse, and matrix multiplication. Let's see them in detail.

The matrix transpose, X^T, for any $m{\times}n$ matrix X, is the $n{\times}m$ matrix obtained by writing its columns as rows and its rows as columns. Let's see an example:

```
X = matrix( c(1,2,3,4,5,6), nrow=3,ncol=2)
> X
     [,1] [,2]
[1,]   1    4
[2,]   2    5
[3,]   3    6
> t(X)
     [,1] [,2] [,3]
[1,]   1    2    3
[2,]   4    5    6
```

As we can see, with the transpose operation, we exchanged the rows with the columns.

In matrix multiplication, the elements of the product are computed in a row-by-column mode. For example, in the $A*B$ multiplication, the value at position $(AB)_{i,j}$ is computed by element-wise multiplication of the entries in row i of A by the entries in column j of B, and then by summing the results. To perform matrix multiplication, we can use the matrix product operator, written with percent symbols as %*%. By using the same matrix X used in the previous code, we can obtain:

```
> t(X)%*%X
     [,1] [,2]
[1,]   14   32
[2,]   32   77
```

Finally, to do a matrix inversion, we can use the solve() R function as follows (recall that inversion of a matrix is only allowed for square matrices):

```
> solve(t(X)%*%X)
            [,1]        [,2]
[1,]  1.4259259 -0.5925926
[2,] -0.5925926  0.2592593
```

Now we know how to do the required three steps to solve the following equation:

$$\beta = (X^T * X)^{-1} * X^T * Y$$

We can then calculate the intercept and slope of the regression line.

To practice these methods, we can draw on the many examples in the software distribution. In this case, we will load in the R environment the .csv file named CementData.csv, which contains observations of heat of reaction of various cement mixtures.

 Source: Woods, H., Steinour, H.H., and Starke, H.R. (1932). *Effect of composition of Portland cement on heat evolved during hardening. Industrial Engineering and Chemistry, 24, 1207–1214.*

This file contains five columns. The first four columns (ingredients variables) contain the percentage of the following mixture elements:

- **Column1**: 3CaO.Al2O3 (tricalcium aluminate)
- **Column2**: 3CaO.SiO2 (tricalcium silicate)
- **Column3**: 4CaO.Al2O3.Fe2O3 (tetracalcium aluminoferrite)
- **Column4**: 2CaO.SiO2 (beta-dicalcium silicate)

The fifth column (the heat variable) contains the heat of reaction of the cement mixtures. From such data, to get the regression coefficients, we have several solutions that can be adopted. We will soon see some of these so that we can explore many solutions available in R to solve the same problem.

Let's start with importing data into the R environment:

```
setwd ("c://R")
CementData=read.csv("CementData.csv", header=TRUE,sep=",")
str(CementData)
```

We analyze the content of the CementData variable using the str() function:

```
> str(CementData)
'data.frame':  13 obs. of  5 variables:
 $ Ingredient_1: int  7 1 11 11 7 11 3 1 2 21 ...
 $ Ingredient_2: int  26 29 56 31 52 55 71 31 54 47 ...
 $ Ingredient_3: int  6 15 8 8 6 9 17 22 18 4 ...
 $ Ingredient_4: int  60 52 20 47 33 22 6 44 22 26 ...
 $ Heat         : num  78.5 74.3 104.3 87.6 95.9 ...
```

To determine the intercept and the coefficients, we will add a column containing 1 at the matrix containing the ingredients:

```
x <- as.matrix(cbind(rep(1,13), CementData[,1:4]))
y <- CementData[,5]
```

Now we can calculate the intercept and slope of the regression line:

```
Beta<-solve(t(x)%*%x)%*%t(x)%*%y
```

The results are shown here:

```
> Beta
                    [,1]
rep(1, 13)    62.4053693
Ingredient_1   1.5511026
Ingredient_2   0.5101676
Ingredient_3   0.1019094
Ingredient_4  -0.1440610
```

But what is this data? The first term represents the intercept and the others represent the coefficient of each predictor. With such values, our model is represented by the following equation:

$$y = 62.4053693 + 1.5511026 * x_1 + 0.5101676 * x_2 + 0.1019094 * x_3 - 0.1440610 * x_4$$

Now we can calculate the residuals; once the coefficients are obtained, calculating the residuals is really simple. It is observed minus fitted values:

$$r_i = y_i - (\beta_0 + \beta_1 * x_1 + \beta_2 * x_2 + \ldots + \beta_n * x_n)$$

In R, this becomes:

```
HeatRegFit<- x%*%Beta[,1]
Residual=y-HeatRegFit
```

Now, we plot the residuals to understand how they are going to distribute:

```
plot(Residual,cex = 1.3,lwd = 10)
abline(a=0,b=0,lwd=5)
```

The following figure shows the scatter plot of a residual with the *y=0* line:

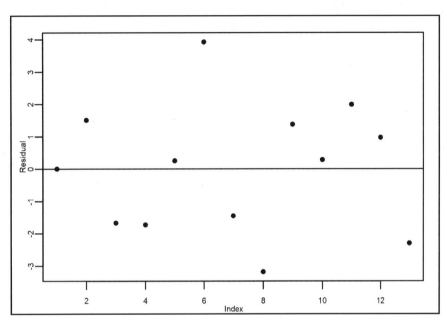

A residual is a measure of how well a regression line fits an individual data point. Therefore, if the residuals appear to behave randomly, it is an indication of the model fitting the data well. However, if they show a systematic pattern, we can safely deduce that the model fits the data poorly.

The previous figure shows that residuals appear randomly scattered around zero, with a good approximation. To measure the accuracy of the fit, we now calculate the coefficient of determination (R-squared). R-squared measures how well a model can predict the data, and falls between zero and one. The higher the value of the coefficient of determination, the better the model is at predicting the data.

In Chapter 2, *Basic Concepts – Simple Linear Regression*, we learned to calculate R-squared, so we can simply apply the formula:

```
Rsq = 1 - sum((y - HeatRegFit)^2)/sum((y - mean(y))^2)
```

The result is shown as follows:

```
> Rsq
[1] 0.9823756
```

This result is very close to 1, meaning the regression line fits the data very well.

Building a multiple linear regression model

In Chapter 2, *Basic Concepts – Simple Linear Regression,* we learned to use the lm() function to create a simple linear regression model. We can also use it to solve this kind of problem.

To practice this method, we can draw on the many datasets available on the internet. In this case, we will load a .csv file named EscapingHydrocarbons.csv into the R environment; it contains the quantity of hydrocarbons escaping, depending on different variables.

 Source: *Linear Regression Datasets* offered by the Department of Scientific Computing, Florida State University (http://people.sc.fsu.edu/~jburkardt/datasets/regression/regression.html).

When petrol is pumped into tanks, hydrocarbons escape. To evaluate the effectiveness of pollution controls, experiments were performed. The quantity of hydrocarbons escaping was measured as a function of the tank temperature, the temperature of the petrol pumped in, the initial pressure in the tank, and the pressure of the petrol pumped in.

There are 32 rows of data. The data includes:

- TankTemperature
- PetrolTemperature
- InitialTankPressure
- PetrolPressure
- AmountEscapingHydrocarbons

Let's start with importing data into the R environment:

```
setwd ("c://R")
PetrolData=read.csv ("EscapingHydrocarbons.csv", header=TRUE,sep=";")
str(PetrolData)
```

We analyze the content of the PetrolData variable using the str() function:

```
> str(PetrolData)
'data.frame':  32 obs. of  5 variables:
 $ TankTemperature     : int  33 31 33 37 36 35 59 60 59 60 ...
 $ PetrolTemperature   : int  53 36 51 51 54 35 56 60 60 60 ...
 $ InitialTankPressure : num  3.32 3.1 3.18 3.39 3.2 3.03 4.78 4.72 4.6
                               4.53 ...
 $ PetrolPressure      : num  3.42 3.26 3.18 3.08 3.41 3.03 4.57 4.72 4.41
```

```
                         4.53 ...
$ AmountEscapingHydrocarbons: int   29 24 26 22 27 21 33 34 32 34 ...
```

To create a multiple linear regression model, use the `lm()` function. This function creates a `LinearModel` object. The object of class `lm` has a series of properties that can be immediately viewed by simply clicking on it in the RStudio environment.

Models for `lm` are specified symbolically. In fact, the first argument of the function is an object of class `formula`. So the first thing to do is build the formula. To do so, we retrieve the names of the variables using `names` function :

```
> names(PetrolData)
[1] "TankTemperature"           "PetrolTemperature"
"InitialTankPressure"
[4] "PetrolPressure"            "AmountEscapingHydrocarbons"
```

Now, we can discover that the names of the variables are long, and so writing the function would take too long. Let's see whether we can automate the procedure:

```
n<-names(PetrolData)
form1 = as.formula(paste("AmountEscapingHydrocarbons ~", paste(n[!n %in%
"AmountEscapingHydrocarbons"], collapse = " + ")))
```

In this piece of code, we first recover all the variable names using the `names` function. This function gets or sets the name of an object. Next, we build the formula that we will use to build the regression model.

Fit a multiple linear regression model for the amount of escaping hydrocarbons using the rest of the variables as explanatory variables (predictors):

```
MLModel = lm(form1,data =PetrolData)
```

The results are shown as follows:

```
> MLModel
Call:
lm(formula = form1, data = PetrolData)
Coefficients:
          (Intercept)       TankTemperature       PetrolTemperature
              1.01502              -0.02861                 0.21582
  InitialTankPressure        PetrolPressure
             -4.32005               8.97489
```

This means that the multiple linear model for this example is estimated as follows:

```
AmountEscapingHydrocarbons =  1.01502
                            - 0.02861 * TankTemperature
                            + 0.21582 * PetrolTemperature
                            - 4.32005 * InitialTankPressure
                            + 8.97489 * PetrolPressure
```

Now, it's time to clarify the meaning of the values contained in the model. To look at them, let's see a brief summary using the summary() function:

summary(MLModel)

The results are shown as follows:

```
> summary(MLModel)
Call:
lm(formula = form1, data = PetrolData)
Residuals:
    Min     1Q Median     3Q    Max
 -5.586 -1.221 -0.118  1.320  5.106
Coefficients:
                    Estimate Std. Error t value Pr(>|t|)
(Intercept)          1.01502    1.86131   0.545  0.59001
TankTemperature     -0.02861    0.09060  -0.316  0.75461
PetrolTemperature    0.21582    0.06772   3.187  0.00362 **
InitialTankPressure -4.32005    2.85097  -1.515  0.14132
PetrolPressure       8.97489    2.77263   3.237  0.00319 **
---
Signif. codes:  0 '***' 0.001 '**' 0.01 '*' 0.05 '.' 0.1 ' ' 1
Residual standard error: 2.73 on 27 degrees of freedom
Multiple R-squared:  0.9261,    Adjusted R-squared:  0.9151
F-statistic: 84.54 on 4 and 27 DF,  p-value: 7.249e-15
```

From the results obtained, the model seems to work. In fact, we have obtained a value of Multiple R-squared equal to 0.9261, very close to one. In other words, 92.6 percent of the variations in hydrocarbons escaping with respect to the average can be explained by the four regression variables. This shows that the initial model is appropriate for determining the amount of hydrocarbons escaping.

Based on the output, TankTemperature has the highest p-value (0.75461). The high p-value indicates that it may not be a good explanatory variable. To improve the model's performance, we need to remove the TankTemperature variable from the model. Variable selection procedures to improve the performance of regression models will be dealt with in later chapters.

To further test the model's capacity in predicting the amount of escaping hydrocarbons as a function of other variables, we can display the predicted values against the current ones. To do this, we first perform the prediction on all the observations contained in the starting dataset. We can use the predict() function. This is a generic function for predictions from the results of various model fitting functions:

```
Pred <- predict(MLModel)
```

Now, we can trace the Actual values against the Predicted ones:

```
plot(PetrolData[,5],Pred,
     xlab="Actual",ylab="Predicted")
abline(a=0,b=1)
```

In the previous commands, we first plot the Actual values against the Predicted ones, and then we add a line with zero intercept and *slope=1*, as shown in the following figure:

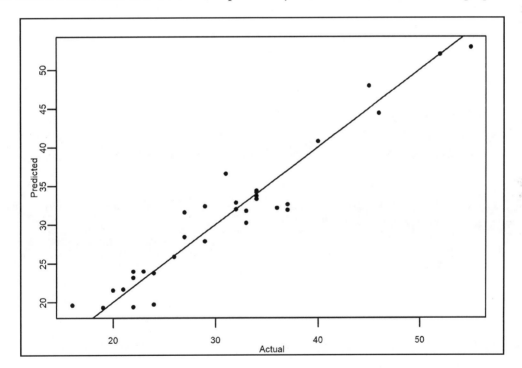

A **Predicted** versus **Actual** plot shows the effect of the model. For a good fit, the points should be close to the fitted line (the line with the *x=y* equation). Points that are horizontally distant from the line have the most leverage, and they effectively try to pull the fitted line toward themselves. Points that are vertically distant from the line represent possible outliers. Both types of points can adversely affect the fit.

An important way of checking whether or not a multiple linear regression has achieved its goal (that is, to explain as much variation as possible in a dependent variable while respecting the underlying assumption) is to check the residuals of a regression. In other words, have a detailed look at what is left over after explaining the variation in the dependent variable using independent variables meaning, the unexplained variation.

Ideally, all residuals should be small and unstructured; this would mean that the regression analysis has been successful in explaining the essential part of the variation of the dependent variable. If, however, residuals exhibit a structure or present any special aspect that does not seem random, they challenge the results obtained so far.

To perform a residuals analysis, we can rely on a number of tools in R. Some of these are the diagnostic diagrams that are obtained using the `plot` function on the `lm` class object.

We plot the charts provided by default:

- A plot of residuals against fitted values
- A normal Q-Q plot
- A scale-location plot of *sqrt(| residuals |)* against fitted values
- A plot of residuals against leverages

Furthermore, we will use the `par()` function to set the graphics window to show four plots at once, in a layout with 2 rows and 2 columns:

```
par(mfrow=c(2,2))
plot(MLModel)
```

In the following figure, there are four plots—**Residuals vs Fitted** values, **Normal Q-Q**, **Scale-Location**, and **Residuals vs Leverage**:

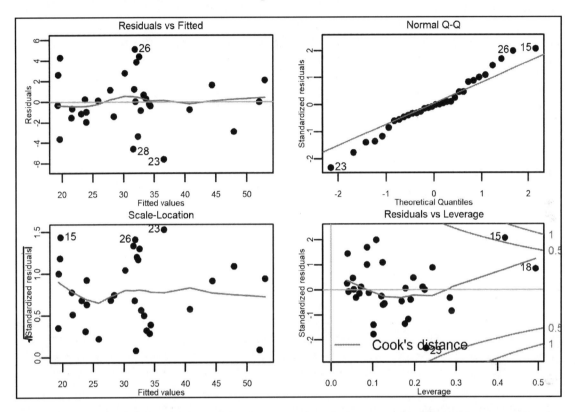

In the previous chapter, in the residuals analysis, we repeatedly underlined the need for the residuals to be distributed equally as a condition necessary for the success of the model. Now we can see that the residuals are equally distributed. In addition, except in the case of the **Normal Q-Q** plot, the red line is almost horizontal. In the **Normal Q-Q** plot, the data does not fit to the straight line very well. All this tells us is that the model we have built is able to predict the system with good approximation, but at the same time, the model assumptions are not strictly verified, so the model may be wrong.

Multiple linear regression with categorical predictor

After dealing with several examples of linear regression, we can certainly claim to have understood the mechanisms underlying this statistical technique. So far, we've used only continuous variables, such as predictors. What happens when the predictors are categorical variables? Don't worry, because the underlying principles of regression techniques remain the same.

Categorical variables

Categorical variables are variables that are not numerical. They do not derive from measurement operations (and do not have units of measurement), but from classification and comparison operations; for instance, they describe data that fits into specific categories. Categorical variables can be further grouped as nominal, dichotomous, or ordinal:

- **Nominal variables** are variables that have two or more categories but do not have an intrinsic order. For example, the blood group variable, limited to the *ABO* system, can assume the values *A*, *B*, *AB*, and *O*. If we try to sort the values that this variable can assume (for example, from smallest to largest), we immediately realize that there is no solution. These variables cannot be used for mathematical operations, but they can be used as a grouping of subjects in a sample. There are no intermediaries and there is no order or hierarchy between them.

- **Dichotomous variables** are a special case of nominal variables that have only two categories or levels, for example, gender. This leads us to classify people as male or female. This is an example of a dichotomous variable, as well as a nominal variable.

- **Ordinal variables** are variables that have two or more categories, just like nominal variables, but they can be ordered or ranked. For example, the presence of blood in urine may take the following values: absent, traces, +, ++, or +++. In this example, the order in which values are assigned to the variable has been listed to follow a precise logic, proceeding regularly from the absence of blood to the most massive presence. The position occupied in the ordinal scale not only allows us to determine whether there is a difference between two values, but also defines the sign of that difference. In the case of ordinal variables, it is not possible to define how much a variable value is greater/less than another variable value.

Building a model

Let's now look at a practical case: in a company, we have been collecting employee wages based on years of experience. We now want to create a model that allows us to see an employee's salary progression over time. Three types of employees were considered: `Management`, `TechnicalStaff`, and `GeneralStaff`. Let's start by importing data into the R environment; we have a worksheet named `employees.xlsx`:

```
library(readxl)
setwd ("c://R")
EmployeesSalary <- read_excel("employees.xlsx")
summary(EmployeesSalary)
```

First, we loaded the library through the `library` command.

Remember that to install a library that is not present in the initial distribution of R, you must use the `install.package` function. This is the main function used to install packages. It takes a vector of names and a destination library, downloads the packages from the repositories, and installs them.

We then used the `setwd()` function to set the working directory to R, contained in the root folder. We used the `read.excel()` function, which reads a file in table format and creates a data frame from it, with cases corresponding to lines and variables to fields in the file. Finally, we used the `summary()` function to return a brief description of the dataset. The results are shown here:

```
> summary(EmployeesSalary)
 YearsExperience      Salary        LevelOfEmployee
 Min.   : 1.00   Min.   :20.00   Length:120
 1st Qu.:10.75   1st Qu.:27.71   Class :character
 Median :20.50   Median :41.00   Mode  :character
 Mean   :20.50   Mean   :43.83
 3rd Qu.:30.25   3rd Qu.:58.12
 Max.   :40.00   Max.   :82.00
```

Now we have a table with three variables: `YearsExperience`, `Salary`, and `LevelOfEmployee`. Their content is easily deducible. While the first two are `double`, the third contains `character` vectors. In fact, it is easy to understand that this is a categorical variable, as it contains the three types of employees already listed before. But R does not know this, and we have to tell it. In practice, we will have to transform that variable, making it categorical (`factor`):

```
EmployeesSalary$LevelOfEmployee <-
            as.factor(EmployeesSalary$LevelOfEmployee)
```

Let's repeat the `summary` command to see what has changed:

```
> summary(EmployeesSalary)
 YearsExperience     Salary            LevelOfEmployee
 Min.   : 1.00    Min.   :20.00    GeneralStaff   :40
 1st Qu.:10.75    1st Qu.:27.71    Management     :40
 Median :20.50    Median :41.00    TechnicalStaff:40
 Mean   :20.50    Mean   :43.83
 3rd Qu.:30.25    3rd Qu.:58.12
 Max.   :40.00    Max.   :82.00
```

In the column related to the `LevelOfEmployee` variable, there are now three factors, with the number of occurrences. We have, in fact, transformed a `character` vector into a `factor` vector.

Conceptually, factors are variables in R that take on a limited number of different values; such variables are often referred to as categorical variables. One of the most important uses of factors is in statistical modeling. Since categorical variables enter into statistical models differently than continuous variables, storing data as factors ensures that the modeling functions will treat such data correctly.

The time has come to look at the data. In this regard, we draw a simple scatter plot of the employee's salary versus years of experience, by distinguishing according to the types of employees. To distinguish the types of employees, we can use a `plot()` function option. I refer to the `pch` option to specify symbols to use when plotting points:

```
pch.list <- as.numeric(EmployeesSalary$LevelOfEmployee)
plot(EmployeesSalary$YearsExperience, EmployeesSalary$Salary,
            pch=c(pch.list))
```

In the previous code, we first retrieved the list of employee levels in numeric format, and so we traced the chart by assigning a different mark to each level.

The results clearly show the wage differences that the three categories have recorded. However, in all three cases, the linear trend is equally evident, as is shown in the following figure. It shows the salaries of employees (`Salary`) versus years of experience (`YearsExperience`), grouped by level (`LevelOfEmployee`):

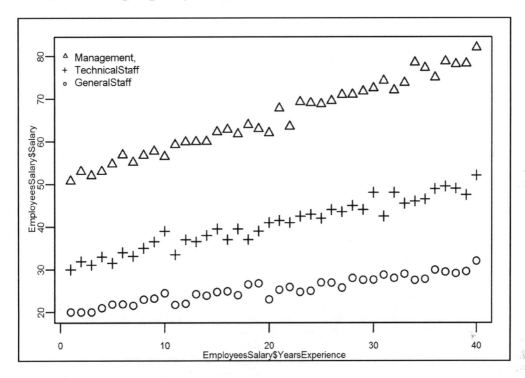

The plot suggests a linear trend, but highlights a clear separation between the three types of categorical data. So, we can fit a regression model with `Salary` as the dependent variable and `YearsExperience` and `LevelOfEmployee` as the independent variables. Considering that `LevelOfEmployee` is a categorical variable with three levels (`Management`, `TechnicalStaff`, and `GeneralStaff`), it appears in the model as two indicator variables. Based on the deductions derived from plot analysis, we can create the model using the `lm` function

Remember, R includes categorical predictors as dummy indicator variables. An indicator variable has values zero and one. A categorical variable with n categories can be represented by n–1 indicator variables.

To take into account the differences between the types of employees, we can include `YearsExperience*LevelOfEmployee` interaction terms. In this case, the model becomes more complex; in fact, to the predictors considered up to now, others are added, represented by the product of the original predictors:

```
LMcat <- lm('Salary~YearsExperience*LevelOfEmployee',data=EmployeesSalary)
```

The results are shown in the following code:

```
> LMcat
Call:
lm(formula = "Salary~YearsExperience*LevelOfEmployee",
                        data = EmployeesSalary)
Coefficients:
(Intercept)                                     20.1986
YearsExperience                                  0.2506
LevelOfEmployeeManagement                       30.2473
LevelOfEmployeeTechnicalStaff                   10.3687
YearsExperience:LevelOfEmployeeManagement        0.4876
YearsExperience:LevelOfEmployeeTechnicalStaff 0.2375
```

Based on the results, the model equation is as follows:

```
Salary =
   20.1986
+ 0.2506   * YearsExperience
+ 30.2473 * LevelOfEmployee(Management)
+ 10.3687 * LevelOfEmployee(TechnicalStaff)
+ 0.4876   * YearsExperience * LevelOfEmployee(Management)
+ 0.2375   * YearsExperience * LevelOfEmployee(TechnicalStaff)
```

In this equation, the term `LevelOfEmployee(GeneralStaff)` does not appear, due to the fact that the first level is the reference group by default. On the contrary, there are the first-order terms for `YearsExperience` and `LevelOfEmployee`, and all interactions.

It is easy to understand that only one equation for the whole system does not allow us to get an adequate estimate of wages. We need to distinguish three models, one for each category of employees, thus obtaining the following three equations:

```
LevelOfEmployee(GeneralStaff):
Salary = 20.2 + 0.25 * YearsExperience
LevelOfEmployee(TechnicalStaff):
Salary = (20.2 + 10.4) + (0.25 + 0.24) * YearsExperience
LevelOfEmployee(Management)
Salary = (20.2 + 30.2) + (0.25 + 0.49) * YearsExperience
```

To better understand what we have done so far, we add these lines to the scatter plot already proposed. To add the three regression lines to the scatter plot, we must perform some calculations. First, we extract the coefficients from the model:

```
LMcat.coef <- coef(LMcat)
```

The results are shown in the following figure:

```
> LMcat.coef
                                (Intercept)                              YearsExperience
                                 20.1985769                                    0.2506060
                 LevelofEmployeeManagement                 LevelofEmployeeTechnicalStaff
                                 30.2472692                                   10.3687308
 YearsExperience:LevelofEmployeeManagement  YearsExperience:LevelofEmployeeTechnicalStaff
                                  0.4875600                                    0.2374522
```

At this point, we just have to calculate the intercept and slope for each of the three regression equations already seen before:

```
> LMcat.GeneralStaff
    (Intercept) YearsExperience
      20.198577        0.250606
> LMcat.TechnicalStaff <-
      c(LMcat.coef[1]+LMcat.coef[4],LMcat.coef[2]+LMcat.coef[6])
> LMcat.TechnicalStaff
    (Intercept) YearsExperience
      30.5673077       0.4880582
> LMcat.Management <-
      c(LMcat.coef[1]+LMcat.coef[3],LMcat.coef[2]+LMcat.coef[5])
> LMcat.Management
    (Intercept) YearsExperience
      50.445846        0.738166
```

Here, we have simply added the values of the coefficients according to what was previously reported in the three equations. As can be seen, these coefficients coincide (apart from the approximation in the description of the equations used for space reasons). To add regression lines, we will use the form required by the optional `coef` argument `abline`, which lets us superimpose these straight lines on a rough data plot:

```
abline(coef=LMcat.GeneralStaff,lwd=2)
abline(coef=LMcat.TechnicalStaff,lwd=2)
abline(coef=LMcat.Management,lwd=2)
```

Now it is clear that the three straight lines, representing the three equations, are distinguished by both intercepts and slopes, as shown in this figure (scatter plot with three straight lines that fit three data groups):

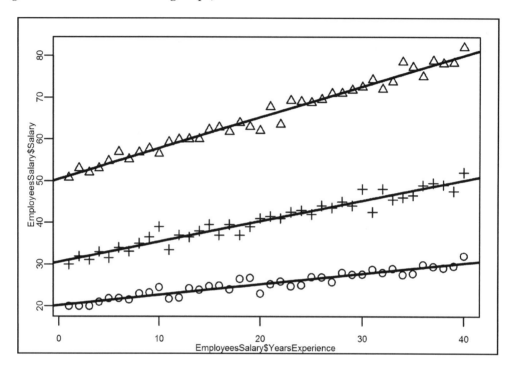

From the analysis of the figure, it can be seen that the three regression lines obtained from the model fit well with the distribution of the data. This means the model is characterized by good performance. To confirm this, we will show the model results with the summary function:

```
summary(LMcat)
```

The results are shown in the following figure:

```
> summary(LMcat)

Call:
lm(formula = "Salary~YearsExperience*LevelOfEmployee", data = EmployeesSalary)

Residuals:
    Min      1Q  Median      3Q     Max
-3.2092 -0.8512  0.0314  0.7345  3.5521

Coefficients:
                                          Estimate Std. Error t value Pr(>|t|)
(Intercept)                               20.19858    0.40884  49.404   <2e-16 ***
YearsExperience                            0.25061    0.01738  14.421   <2e-16 ***
LevelOfEmployeeManagement                 30.24727    0.57819  52.314   <2e-16 ***
LevelOfEmployeeTechnicalStaff             10.36873    0.57819  17.933   <2e-16 ***
YearsExperience:LevelOfEmployeeManagement  0.48756    0.02458  19.839   <2e-16 ***
YearsExperience:LevelOfEmployeeTechnicalStaff 0.23745 0.02458   9.662   <2e-16 ***
---
Signif. codes:  0 '***' 0.001 '**' 0.01 '*' 0.05 '.' 0.1 ' ' 1

Residual standard error: 1.269 on 114 degrees of freedom
Multiple R-squared:  0.9951,    Adjusted R-squared:  0.9949
F-statistic:  4664 on 5 and 114 DF,  p-value: < 2.2e-16
```

From the results obtained, the model seems to work. In fact, we have obtained a value of `Multiple R-squared` equal to `0.9951`, very close to one. In other words, *99.5* percent of the variations in salary from the average can be explained by the years of experience, level of employee, and their interaction terms. This shows that the initial model is appropriate for determining how much an employee's salary varies over the years, differentiating them by job type.

By analyzing the results obtained for p-value, we can state that the null hypothesis is rejected. For every contribution, the p-value value is extremely low (`p-value <2.2e-16`).

Gradient Descent and linear regression

The **Gradient Descent (GD)** is an iterative approach for minimizing the given function, or, in other words, a way to find a local minimum of a function. The algorithm starts with an initial estimate of the solution that we can give in several ways: one approach is to randomly sample values for the parameters. We evaluate the slope of the function at that point, determine the solution in the negative direction of the gradient, and repeat this process. The algorithm will eventually converge where the gradient is zero, corresponding to a local minimum.

The steepest descent step size is replaced by a similar size from the previous step. The gradient is basically defined as the slope of the curve, as shown in the following figure:

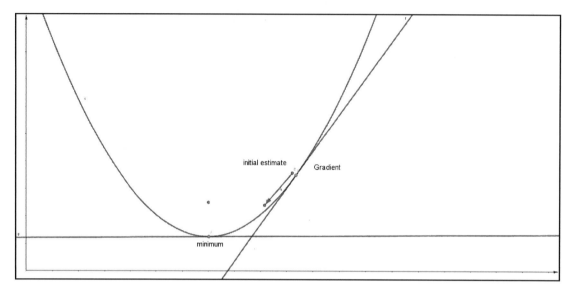

In Chapter 2, *Basic Concepts – Simple Linear Regression*, we saw that the goal of OLS regression is to find the line that best fits the predictor in terms of minimizing the overall squared distance between itself and the response. In order to estimate α and β, we want to minimize the following term:

$$\sum_{i=1}^{n}(y_i - \alpha x_i + \beta)^2$$

Now, we can implement a linear regression model for performing OLS regression using one of the following approaches:

- Solving the model parameters analytically (solving a normal equation)
- Using an optimization algorithm (GD, SGD, and so on)

When adopting the first approach (solving a normal equation), we must resolve the following equation:

$$\beta = (X^T * X)^{-1} * X^T * Y$$

As we explained earlier, this means dealing with three mathematical operations involving matrices: transpose, inverse, and matrix multiplication. In the case of smaller datasets, if a costly computing matrix inverse is not a concern, this method is preferred. For very large datasets, or datasets where the inverse of $X^T * X$ may not exist, the other approaches are to be preferred.

Gradient Descent

To perform OLS regression using the GD algorithm, we have to minimize the cost function that measures how good a given regression line is.

This cost function will take in an (α , β) pair and return an error value based on how well the line fits our data. To compute this error for a given line, we'll iterate through each (x,y) point in our dataset and sum the square distances between each point's y value and the candidate line's y value (computed at $\alpha x + \beta$).

The cost function looks like the following:

$$CostFunction = \frac{1}{N} * \sum_{i=1}^{n} (y_i - (\alpha x_i + \beta))^2$$

If we plot the loss function (z axis) with respect to the coefficients of linear regression (α and β), the 3D plot looks like this:

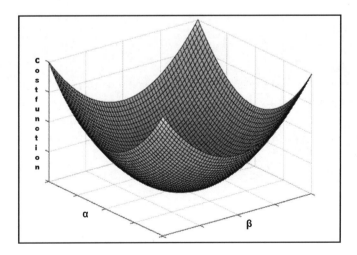

Now we just need to identify the minimum value of the cost function by adjusting the coefficients (α and β). GD reaches the bottom of the curve by iterative calculation of both α and β.

To run GD on this cost function (this is particularly convenient, as it is a convex function), we first need to compute its gradient. The gradient will act like a compass and always point us downhill. To compute it, we will need to differentiate our cost function. Since our function is defined by two parameters (α and β), we will need to compute a partial derivative for each. These derivatives work out to be:

$$\frac{\partial}{\partial \alpha} = \frac{2}{N} * \sum_{i=1}^{n} -x_i * (y_i - (\alpha x_i + \beta))$$

$$\frac{\partial}{\partial \beta} = \frac{2}{N} * \sum_{i=1}^{n} -(y_i - (\alpha x_i + \beta))$$

We now have all the tools needed to run GD. We can initialize our search to start at any pair of α and β values and let the GD algorithm march downhill on our cost function towards the best line. Each iteration will update α and β to a line that yields a slightly lower error than the previous iteration.

For example, to update the slope of the regression line, the algorithm uses the following equation:

$$\alpha_{n=1} = \alpha_n - \eta * \frac{\partial}{\partial \alpha_n}$$

Here, η is the step size (learning rate); this parameter determines how quickly or slowly we will move towards the optimal values. It decides how large a step we take downhill during each iteration. If we take too large a step, we may step over the minimum. However, if we take small steps, it will require too much iteration to arrive at the minimum. The new position of $\alpha(\alpha_{n+1})$ is decided by the previous position of $\alpha(\alpha_n)$ moving along the slope provided by the partial derivative.

A similar procedure is followed in the search for the intercept of the regression line. In this case, the equation takes the following form:

$$\beta_{n+1} = \beta_n - \eta * \frac{\partial}{\partial \beta_n}$$

The iterative process proceeds until convergence is reached.

Stochastic Gradient Descent

As we have seen, in the GD algorithm, we calculate the gradient of the cost function on the complete set of data at our disposal; this is why it is also called **batch GD**. If the dataset is very large, GD usage can be quite expensive, as we only take a single step for one pass over the whole dataset. So the bigger the dataset, the slower our algorithm is at refreshing the weights, and the longer it will take to converge to the minimum global cost.

The SGD algorithm is a simplification of the GD algorithm. Instead of calculating the gradient exactly, for each iteration, the gradient of one of the randomly selected observations is used.

The term **stochastic** derives from the fact that the gradient based on a single training sample is a stochastic approximation of the whole cost gradient. Due to its stochastic nature, the path towards the global cost minimum is not direct, as in GD, but may zigzag if we visualize the cost surface in a 2D space. However, it has been shown that SGD almost surely converges to the global cost minimum if the cost function is convex (or pseudo-convex).

In other words, in a full batch GD, the gradient is computed for the full dataset, whereas SGD takes a single sample and performs gradient calculations. It can also take mini-batches and perform the calculations. One advantage of SGD is faster computation of gradients.

To perform regression analysis with the SGD algorithm in R, we can use the sgd package.

The sgd package

This package contains a fast and flexible set of tools for large-scale estimation. It features many stochastic gradient methods, built-in models, visualization tools, automated hyperparameter tuning, model checking, interval estimation, and convergence diagnostics.

The following table gives some information about this package:

Package	sgd
Date	January 05, 2016
Version	1.1
Title	Stochastic Gradient Descent for Scalable Estimation
Authors	Dustin Tran, Panos Toulis, Tian Lian, Ye Kuang, and Edoardo Airoldi

Here are the most useful functions used in regression analysis contained in this package:

- sgd: This function runs SGD in order to optimize the induced loss function given a model and data
- print: This function prints objects of class sgd
- predict: This function forms predictions using the estimated model parameters from SGD
- plot: This function plots objects of class sgd

Linear regression with SGD

To perform a linear regression analysis with the SGD algorithm, we use the example available in the sgd package:

```
library(sgd)
N <- 10000
d <- 10
set.seed(42)
X <- matrix(rnorm(N*d), ncol=d)
theta <- rep(5, d+1)
eps <- rnorm(N)
y <- cbind(1, X) %*% theta + eps
dat <- data.frame(y=y, x=X)
sgd.theta <- sgd(y ~ ., data=dat, model="lm")
sprintf("Mean squared error: %0.3f", mean((theta -
            as.numeric(sgd.theta$coefficients))^2))
plot(sgd.theta, theta, type="mse-param")
```

Now, let's go through the code to understand how to apply the sgd package to solve a linear regression problem.

To start, we must install the `sgd` package in the R environment.

Remember that to install a library that is not present in the initial distribution of R, you must use the `install.packages()` function. This function should be used only once and not every time you run the code.

It is important to note that we can use the visualization area of RStudio to install a package. We need to choose the **Packages** tab and click on the **Install** button. This will open the **Install Packages** window, where we can type the name of the package and then click the **Install** button, as shown in the following figure:

This procedure downloads and installs packages from CRAN-like repositories or from local files. As mentioned before, it is emphasized that this procedure should be used only once and not every time you run the code. Instead, load the library through the following command, and this must be repeated every time you run the code:

```
library(sgd)
```

At this point, we can build the dataset; first, we set the dimension:

```
N <- 10000
d <- 10
```

Here, N is the number of observations, while d is the number of explanatory variables. Let's analyze the next line of code:

```
set.seed(42)
```

This command sets the seed of R's random number generator, which is useful for creating simulations or random objects that can be reproduced. Now we can generate the data; we will start from the predictors:

```
X <- matrix(rnorm(N*d), ncol=d)
```

To generate *10,000* observations of the explanatory variables, we used the rnorm() and matrix() functions. The rnorm function generates multivariate normal random variates in the space defined by the argument (N*d). The matrix function creates a matrix from the given set of values, rnorm(N*d). We also have the number of columns equal to the number of explanatory variables (d). Now we can switch to the response variable:

```
theta <- rep(5, d+1)
eps <- rnorm(N)
y <- cbind(1, X) %*% theta + eps
```

With these lines of code, we generate the response variable from the explanatory variables by multiplying them for the theta variable (estimator) and adding a random error (the eps variable). At this point, we create the data frame:

```
dat <- data.frame(y=y, x=X)
```

The data.frame() function creates data frames, tightly coupled collections of variables which share many of the properties of matrices and of lists, used as the fundamental data structure by most of R's modeling software. Now we can create the model:

```
sgd.theta <- sgd(y ~ ., data=dat, model="lm")
```

The sgd() function runs SGD in order to optimize the induced loss function, given a model and data. The first argument is an object of class formula, a symbolic description of the model to be fitted. The . notation in a formula is commonly taken to mean *all other variables in data that do not already appear in the formula*. The second argument of the sgd function is the data frame containing the variables in the model. The last argument is the character specifying the model to be used. Items available are: lm, glm, cox, gmm, and m. Our choice is the linear model.

Let's look at the model we just created:

```
str(sgd.theta)
```

The results are shown in the following figure:

```
> str(sgd.theta)
List of 7
 $ model       : chr "lm"
 $ coefficients: num [1:11, 1] 5.02 5.05 4.95 5.01 4.93 ...
 $ converged   : logi TRUE
 $ estimates   : num [1:11, 1:70] 0.595 0.816 0.692 -0.354 0.405 ...
 $ pos         : num [1:70] 1 1 1 1 2 2 2 2 2 3 ...
 $ times       : num [1:70] 0.001 0.001 0.001 0.001 0.001 0.001 0.001 0.001 0.001 0.001 ...
 $ model.out   :List of 2
  ..$ transfer: chr "identity"
  ..$ family  :List of 11
  .. ..$ family     : chr "gaussian"
  .. ..$ link       : chr "identity"
  .. ..$ linkfun    :function (mu)
  .. ..$ linkinv    :function (eta)
  .. ..$ variance   :function (mu)
  .. ..$ dev.resids :function (y, mu, wt)
  .. ..$ aic        :function (y, n, mu, wt, dev)
  .. ..$ mu.eta     :function (eta)
  .. ..$ initialize: expression({ n <- rep.int(1, nobs)  if (is.null(etastart) && is.null(start) && is.null(mustart) && ((fam
nk| ....truncated....
  .. ..$ validmu    :function (mu)
  .. ..$ valideta   :function (eta)
  .. ..- attr(*, "class")= chr "family"
 - attr(*, "class")= chr "sgd"
```

We can now calculate the **Mean Square Error (MSE)**. The MSE of an estimator θ', of a parameter θ, is the function of θ, defined by the following equation:

$$MSE = \frac{1}{n} \sum_{i=1}^{N} (\theta' - \theta)^2$$

Here, θ' is an estimator and θ is an estimated parameter. All this, in R, becomes:

```
sprintf("Mean squared error: %0.3f", mean((theta -
            as.numeric(sgd.theta$coefficients))^2))
```

The results are shown here:

```
> sprintf("Mean squared error: %0.3f", mean((theta -
as.numeric(sgd.theta$coefficients))^2))
[1] "Mean squared error: 0.006"
```

Finally, we plot the **Mean Squared Error** against the **log-Iteration**:

```
plot(sgd.theta, theta, type="mse-param")
```

This command plots objects of class `sgd`. In the arguments, the model, the estimator, and the type of plot are present. We have chosen MSE in the predictions.

The results are shown in the following figure:

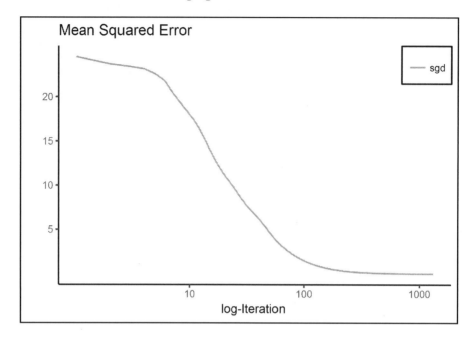

From the analysis of the figure, it can be noticed that the algorithm converges quickly.

Polynomial regression

Polynomial models can be used in situations where the relationship between response and explanatory variables is curvilinear. Sometimes, a nonlinear relationship in a small range of explanatory variables can also be modeled by polynomials.

A polynomial quadratic (squared) or cubic (cubed) term turns a linear regression model into a polynomial curve. However, since it is the explanatory variable that is squared or cubed and not the Beta coefficient, it still qualifies as a linear model. This makes it a nice, straightforward way to model curves, without having to model complicated nonlinear models.

In polynomial regression, some predictors appear in degrees equal to or greater than two. The model continues to be linear in its parameters. For example, a second-degree parabolic regression model looks like this:

$$y = \beta_0 + \beta_1 * x + \beta_2 * x^2$$

This model can easily be estimated by introducing a second-degree term in the regression model. The difference is that in polynomial regression, the equation produces a curved line, not a straight line. Polynomial regression will usually be used when the relationship between the variables looks curved. A simple curve can sometimes be straightened out by transforming one or both of the variables. A more complicated curve, however, is best handled with polynomial regression.

More generally, a polynomial regression equation assumes the following form:

$$y = \beta_0 + \beta_1 * x + \beta_2 * x^2 + \beta_3 * x^3 + ... + \beta_n * x^n$$

In the next example, we will only deal with the case of a second-degree parabolic regression in R, and then we will compare the model obtained with the third-degree. Now we'll show how to model data with a polynomial. Let's start with a simple example. We have measured the temperature (in degrees Celsius) in a few hours of the day. We want to know the temperature trend, even in those times of the day when we did not notice it. Those moments are, however, understood between the initial moment and the final moment in which our measurements took place:

```
Time=c(6,7,8,9,10,11,12,13,14,15,16,17,18,19)
Temp=c(4,6,7,9,10,11,11.5,12,12,11.5,11,10,9,8)
```

Let's see how these values are distributed in a scatter plot:

```
plot(Time,Temp,cex.axis=0.6)
```

In the following figure, **Temp** versus **Time** is shown:

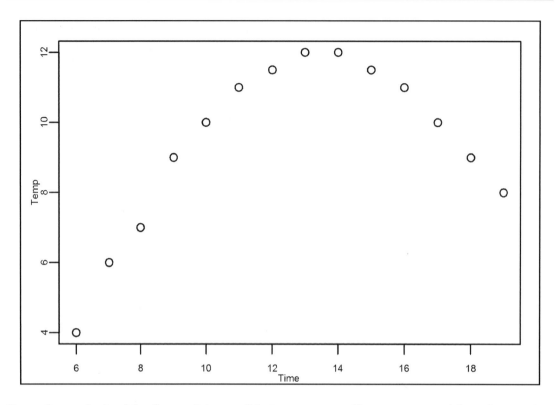

From the analysis of the figure, it is possible to note a curvilinear pattern of data that can be modeled through a second-degree polynomial as the following equation:

$$Temp = \beta_0 + \beta_1 * Time + \beta_2 * Time^2$$

The unknown coefficients, β_0, β_1, and β_2, are computed by minimizing the sum of squares of deviations of the data from the model (least squares fit).

At this point, we can begin by searching for a polynomial model that appropriately approximates our data. First of all, we specify that what we want is a polynomial as a function of time (that is, a raw polynomial, which is different from an orthogonal polynomial). This is an important clarification, because the commands and results will change in the two cases in R. So we look for a function of the following type:

$$y = \beta_0 + \beta_1 * x + \beta_2 * x^2 + \beta_3 * x^3 + ... + \beta_n * x^n$$

Here, *x=time*.

At what degree of polynomial must we stop? It depends on the degree of precision we are looking for. The higher the degree of the polynomial, the greater the precision of the model, but the more difficult it is to calculate. In addition, it is necessary to verify the significance of the coefficients that are found, but let's get to it right away.

In R, to fit a polynomial regression model, we have two methods identical to each other. Suppose we look for the values of the beta coefficients for a polynomial of the second degree and then of the third degree:

```
Polyfit2 <- lm(Temp ~ Time + I(Time^2))
Polyfit3 <- lm(Temp ~ Time + I(Time^2) + I(Time^3))
```

Alternatively, we can build second-order and third-order polynomials more quickly through the following code:

```
Polyfit2b <- lm(Temp ~ poly(Time, 2, raw=TRUE))
Polyfit3b <- lm(Temp ~ poly(Time, 3, raw=TRUE))
```

The `poly()` function is especially useful when you want to obtain a high degree, because it avoids explicitly writing the formula. If we specify `raw = TRUE`, the two methods seen just now provide the same output. If we do not specify `raw = TRUE`, the `poly()` function will provide the values of the beta parameters of an orthogonal polynomial, which is different from the general formula written previously, although the templates are both effective.

Otherwise, with `raw = FALSE`, `poly()` computes an orthogonal polynomial. It internally sets up the model matrix with the raw coding x, x^2, x^3, ... first, and then scales the columns so that each column is orthogonal to the previous ones. This does not change the fitted values, but has an advantage: you can see whether a certain order in the polynomial significantly improves the regression over the lower orders.

At this point, we have the polynomial regression models of the second and third order. We analyze the results obtained:

```
summary(Polyfit2)
```

The results are shown as follows:

```
> summary(Polyfit2)
Call:
lm(formula = Temp ~ Time + I(Time^2))
Residuals:
     Min       1Q    Median        3Q       Max
-0.52005  -0.06387   0.03970   0.15543   0.21250
Coefficients:
              Estimate Std. Error t value Pr(>|t|)
```

```
(Intercept) -13.710165    0.601247   -22.80 1.30e-10 ***
Time          3.760920    0.102822    36.58 7.69e-13 ***
I(Time^2)    -0.138393    0.004071   -33.99 1.71e-12 ***
---
Signif. codes:  0 '***' 0.001 '**' 0.01 '*' 0.05 '.' 0.1 ' ' 1
Residual standard error: 0.2197 on 11 degrees of freedom
Multiple R-squared:  0.9931,    Adjusted R-squared:  0.9918
F-statistic: 791.3 on 2 and 11 DF,  p-value: 1.301e-12
```

The `summary` output (`Polyfit2b`) is absolutely identical. We have obtained the β_0 = -13.710165, β_1 = 3.760920, and β_2 = -0.138393 values, and all three are significant (*p-value<0,05*). Therefore, the equation of the second-degree polynomial of our model is:

$$Temp = -13.710165 + 3.760920 * Time - 0.138393 * Time^2$$

From the results obtained, the model seems to work. In fact, we have obtained a value of `Multiple R-squared` equal to `0.9931`, very close to one. In other words, *99.3* percent of the variation of temperature from the average can be explained by the time.

Now we can draw a plot of what we got. In R, there is no function to plot polynomials. We must first draw the starting data in a scatter plot, and then plot the curve obtained through the prediction based on the model we got.

Let's start by getting predictions using the `predict` function:

```
PredData = data.frame(Time = seq(min(Time), max(Time), length.out = 100))
PredData$Temp = predict(Polyfit2, newdata = PredData)
```

In the first line, we need to insert a column containing the `Time` variable into a data frame. There are `100` equidistant elements between the minimum and the maximum of the starting values. In the second line, we use the `predict()` function for predictions from the results of the model fitting function.

Now we can plot the graph:

```
plot(Time,Temp)
with(PredData, lines(x = Time, y = Temp))
```

The first line draws a scatter plot of **Time** against **Temp**; the second code line adds a line of predicted values. The results are shown in the following figure:

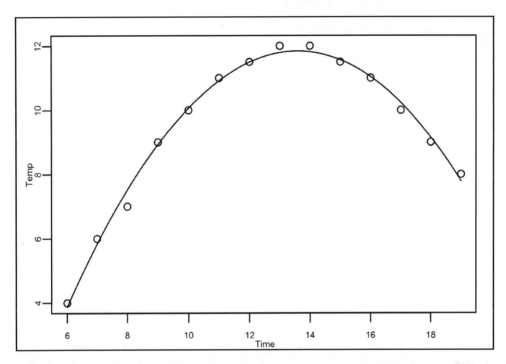

From an analysis of the figure, it can be seen that the regression line obtained from the model fits well to the distribution of the data. This means the model is characterized by good performance.

Now let's see what happens with the third-order polynomial regression model:

```
summary(Polyfit3)
```

The results are shown as follows:

```
> summary(Polyfit3)
Call:
lm(formula = Temp ~ Time + I(Time^2) + I(Time^3))
Residuals:
     Min       1Q   Median       3Q      Max
-0.51293 -0.06900  0.04628  0.15067  0.22794
Coefficients:
            Estimate Std. Error t value Pr(>|t|)
(Intercept) -13.42402    2.05505  -6.532 6.62e-05 ***
```

```
Time              3.68179     0.55157     6.675 5.53e-05 ***
I(Time^2)        -0.13164     0.04633    -2.841   0.0175 *
I(Time^3)        -0.00018     0.00123    -0.146   0.8866
---
Signif. codes:  0 '***' 0.001 '**' 0.01 '*' 0.05 '.' 0.1 ' ' 1
Residual standard error: 0.2302 on 10 degrees of freedom
Multiple R-squared:  0.9931,    Adjusted R-squared:  0.991
F-statistic: 480.6 on 3 and 10 DF,  p-value: 4.183e-11
```

In this case, we get the following equation:

$$Temp = -13.42402 + 3.68179 * Time\ -0.13164 * Time^2 - 0.00018 * Time^3$$

From the results obtained, the model seems to work. In fact, we have obtained a value of `Multiple R-squared` equal to 0.9931 (the same as in the previous model), very close to one. If we analyze the results of the t-test, we notice that the third degree term has a *p-value>* *0.05*, so it is not statistically significant. All of this means that the second-degree polynomial regression model provides better results.

In regression analysis, it's important to keep the order of the model as low as possible. In the first analysis, we keep the model at the first order. If this is not satisfactory, then a second-order polynomial is tried. The use of polynomials of higher orders can lead to incorrect evaluations.

To confirm what we say, we will also show the regression curve. We will use the same procedure as for the second-order polynomial regression model. Let's first create the data frame with the `Time` variable; then we will obtain the prediction of the data with the polynomial regression model of the third order:

```
PredData2 = data.frame(Time = seq(min(Time), max(Time), length.out = 100))
PredData2$Temp = predict(Polyfit3, newdata = PredData)
```

Now we can plot the graph:

```
plot(Time,Temp)
with(PredData2, lines(x = Time, y = Temp))
```

The first line draws a scatter plot of **Time** against **Temp**; the second line adds a line of predicted values. The results are shown here:

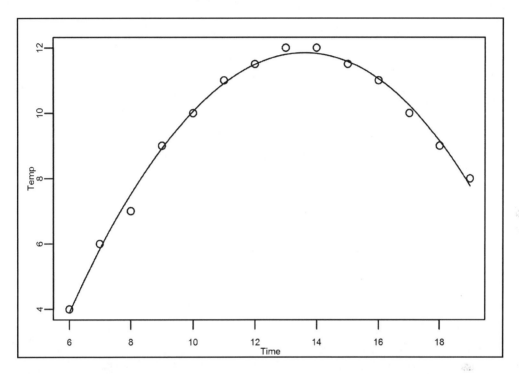

The differences between the two models are such that it is not possible to evaluate them graphically. In fact, they appear to be substantially equivalent at first sight. But by analyzing the results of the t-test, we have been able to verify that the performance of the second-order model is better.

Summary

In this chapter, we learned the basic concepts of multiple linear regression, where linear regression is extended to extract predictive information from more than one feature. We saw how to tune the multiple linear regression model for higher performance and deeply understood every parameter of it. We understood the information contained in linear regression models that we can build with the lm function. Furthermore, we have learned to carry out a proper residuals analysis to understand, in depth, whether the model we built has been effective in predicting our system. We dealt with the case of a linear regression model with categorical variables.

We then explored the SGD technique for optimization of algorithms used on regression to find a good set of model parameters given a training dataset. After analyzing the GD algorithms in detail, we solved a multiple linear regression problem with the use of the `sgd` package.

Finally, polynomial regression was introduced where linear regression is not good enough. With polynomial regression, we approached a model in which some predictors appear in degrees equal to or greater than two, to fit data with a curved line. Polynomial regression is usually used when the relationship between variables looks curved.

In the next chapter, we will approach logistic regression, a special type of regression. First we will describe a regression problem to fit a regressor, and then we will give some intuitions underneath the math formulation. Then, the reader will learn how to tune the model for higher performance and deeply understand every parameter of it. Finally, some practical examples will be solved to discover how to apply such techniques to real-life cases.

4

When the Response Falls into Two Categories – Logistic Regression

In previous chapters, we studied linear regression models in detail. In particular, we found that in all the models described, the response variable takes quantitative values. Often in everyday life, response variables are qualitative instead. For example, we want to determine whether a device is on or off, depending on the noise detected in the environment. Or we want to know whether to issue a credit based on financial information and other personal information. Or we want to diagnose a patient's disease first to select the immediate treatment pending final results.

In each of these cases, we want to explain the probability of having an attribute, or an event occurring, in relation to the number of possible variations of multiple explanatory variables. In other words, we are trying to classify a phenomenon. The term **classification** can cover any context in which certain decisions or forecasts are made on the basis of the information currently available. So, a classification procedure is a formal method for repeatedly making judgments in new situations.

In this chapter, we will learn to perform classifications through logistic regression techniques. We will learn how to define a classification problem and how to apply logistic regression to resolve this type of problem. We will understand how to use the **Generalized Linear Models (GLMs)** to perform logistic regression. We will also learn how to use useful tools to evaluate performances, and deeply understand every parameter of it. We will explore the **Stochastic Gradient Descent (SGD)** technique to optimize the algorithms used on logistic regression to find a good set of model parameters, given a training dataset.

We will cover the following topics:

- Properly defining a classification problem
- Applying logistic regression
- GLMs
- Model results explained
- Evaluating the model's performance

At the end of the chapter, you will be able to perform a logistic regression and be able to apply logistic regression methods to your own data. You will see how the logistic regression algorithm works, understand the basic concepts that logistic regression methods use to fit equations to data using the R environment. Finally, we will learn how to improve the model's performance. We'll also cover the GLMs to perform logistic regression where linear regression is not good enough.

Understanding logistic regression

In linear regression, the dependent variable y (response variable) is continuous and its estimated value can be thought of as a conditional mean estimation for each value of x. In this case, it is assumed that the variable y is distributed according to normal distribution. When the dependent variable is dichotomous, and can be coded as having two values, zero or one (such as *on = one, off = zero*), the theoretical distribution of reference should not be normal but binomial distribution.

In fact, as we have seen in `Chapter 2`, *Basic Concepts – Simple Linear Regression*, the linear model is based on the following regression equation:

$$y = \alpha * x + \beta$$

Here, the values of the dependent variable can go from -∞ to +∞. All this does not agree with the expected values for a dichotomous variable, which as we have said, assumes only two values *(0;1)*.

Let's try to understand this concept better by analyzing a simple example. Let's suppose we've put the data of a certain observation on a scatter plot. Since the answer is dichotomous, in the graph we observe the data placed on two horizontal lines, corresponding to the two possible values that the answer can assume (*0,1*). If we trace the trend line determined by the linear model, we can notice that when predictor increases, the values expected for the response become greater than one, as well as for certain values of the predictor, the response becomes less than zero, as shown in the following figure:

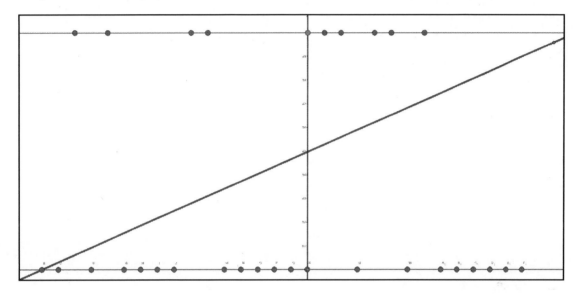

This prediction is inadequate for the dependent variable that, as mentioned, can only assume only one of two values, zero or one. In fact, if the dependent variable is dichotomous, and if it is influenced by the variable *x*, then it should be noted that for very high values of *x* (or very low, if the relation is negative), the value in *y* should be very close to one and should not exceed that limit. The same should occur near zero. In practice, the curve representing the relationship between *x* and *y* should be logistic and nonlinear, as shown in the following figure:

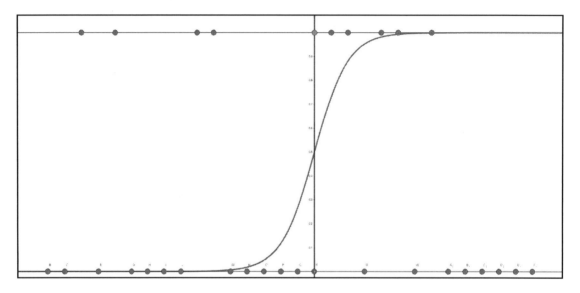

In these cases, therefore, it would be more appropriate to fit a nonlinear regression model.

The logit model

As anticipated, the linear function is not suitable to represent the relationship between the independent variable and the dependent variable, in cases where the response takes dichotomous values. Now, we try to model the probabilities that the response belongs to the reference class. If we use the standard linear model to represent these probabilities, then our system is described by the following equation:

$$P(x) = \alpha * x + \beta$$

In this case, we have predictions that both classification options may exceed the expected values (-∞ to +∞), as we could see from the figure shown in the previous section. Then, to solve this problem we can apply an exponential function at the right end of the equation of the linear regression model. By working on this transformation we get:

$$P(x) = e^{\alpha * x + \beta}$$

Even though this transformation allows us to narrow the values of the equation within the range of *0* to +∞, it does not completely solve the problem. Since we have once again overcome the two classification options only for the upper limit of the expected values, we can apply the logistic transformation that allows us to control the values and narrow them to the probability range (*0; 1*):

$$P(x) = \frac{e^{\alpha * x + \beta}}{1 + e^{\alpha * x + \beta}}$$

As with linear regression, in the analysis of logistic regression, the interpretation of the relationship between independent variables and dependent variables is done by evaluating the parameters of the model. In the estimation of the logistic regression parameters, the maximum likelihood algorithm that estimates the model parameters is used, to maximize the log-likelihood function indicating how likely the expected *Y* value is to obtain the values of independent variables. In the method of maximum likelihood, the optimal solution is achieved starting from test values for parameters (arbitrary values) which are subsequently modified to see if the function can be improved. The process is repeated (iteration) until the ability to improve the function is infinitesimal (converges).

In logistic regression, the dependent variable characterizes membership of a group. The values that are assigned to the levels are arbitrarily attributed. What matters is therefore not the expected value (or predicted), as in linear regression, but the probability that a given subject belongs to the reference group. Despite this, it is important to emphasize that the choice of values to assign affects the results of the analysis. One way to solve the dilemma of assigning values to levels, is to replace the probability with odds.

Odds is a way of expressing a probability through a ratio. It is calculated by making the ratio between the frequencies observed in one level with the frequencies observed in the other. The value of the odds expresses the relationship between two categories. Odds are defined as the ratio of the probability of success and the probability of failure. Previously, we calculated the probability by applying the following equation:

$$P(x) = \frac{e^{\alpha * x + \beta}}{1 + e^{\alpha * x + \beta}}$$

Calculate the odds using this equation. With the ratio between the probabilities of obtaining the two values we get the following equation:

$$\frac{P(x)}{1 - P(x)} = e^{\alpha * x + \beta}$$

Here, $P(x)/(1-P(x))$ represent the odds. This quantity can take on any value between 0 and ∞. If we define this quantity by the ratio of the probability of success and the probability of failure, then values of the odds close to zero indicate very low probabilities of success. Values of the odds close to ∞ indicate very high probabilities of success.

As stated previously, the odds, even though it allows narrowing the values of the equation within the range of 0 to +∞, does not completely solve the problem. Let's take the logarithm of the previous equation:

$$\log\left(\frac{P(x)}{1 - P(x)}\right) = \alpha * x + \beta$$

Here, this quantity is called **log-odds** or **logit**, and it's linear in x. It is important to point out that probability, odds, and logit are three different ways of expressing exactly the same thing. Transformation into logit only serves to ensure mathematical correctness of the analysis.

Generalized Linear Model

In the previous chapters, we have worked with regression models where the response variable is quantitative and normally distributed. Now, we turn our attention to models where the response variable is discrete and the error terms do not follow a normal distribution. Such models are called GLMs.

GLMs are extensions of traditional regression models that allow the mean to depend on the explanatory variables through a `link` function, and the response variable to be any member of a set of distributions called the **exponential family** (such as Binomial, Gaussian, Poisson, and others).

In R, to fit GLMs we can use the `glm()` function. The model is specified by giving a symbolic description of the linear predictor and a description of the error distribution. Its usage is similar to that of the function `lm()` which we previously used for multiple linear regression. The main difference is that we need to include an additional argument family to describe the error distribution and `link` function to be used in the model.

Simple logistic regression

Recent studies argue that people who are extremely stressed due to work and many other reasons, may be exposed to the risk of type two diabetes. According to the researchers, the results of the study show that chronic stress, resulting from work activities, whose key aspects are emotional exhaustion, physical and mental fatigue, could be a risk factor for the onset of type two diabetes in apparently healthy subjects.

It has been hypothesized that stress has a significant role in the development of type two diabetes, so emotional stress can pose a health risk. Previous studies have already stressed its association with the risk of cardiovascular disease, sleep disorders, fertility alterations, and musculoskeletal pain. The results obtained suggest that potential adverse health effects may be greater than you think and also include the risk of diabetes.

In this example, we will see how to make a logistic regression model if it has categorical or qualitative variables arranged in double-entry contingency tables. In this model, the dependent variable Y is a Bernoulli variable, which can assume values zero or one.

We will look at a simple logistic regression model (one regressor only). Both the dependent variable and the independent variable are dichotomous, so they can only assume zero or one.

The following table shows the results of a type two diabetes study. It is to be considered how much the presence of a stress factor can influence the onset of this disease:

Stress	DiabNo	DiabYes	Total
No	326	8	334
Yes	160	64	224
Total	486	72	558

To start, we import the values in the table in R. We need to create a double-entry table; let's proceed as follows:

```
diabetes <- matrix(c(326,160,8,64), nrow=2)
colnames(diabetes) <- c("DiabNO", "DiabYes")
rownames(diabetes) <- c("StressNO", "StressYes")
TableDiabetes <- as.table(diabetes)
```

Let's look at the table by invoking the `TableDiabetes` variable:

```
> TableDiabetes
          DiabNO DiabYes
StressNO     326       8
StressYes    160      64
```

We now organize the data to carry out logistic regression. We need to create a data frame:

```
DfBiabetes <- as.data.frame(TableDiabetes)
```

We see the result:

```
> DfBiabetes
       Var1     Var2 Freq
1  StressNO   DiabNO  326
2 StressYes   DiabNO  160
3  StressNO  DiabYes    8
4 StressYes  DiabYes   64
```

At this point, we can use the `glm()` function to build the logistic regression model:

```
LogModel <- glm(Var2 ~ Var1, weights = Freq, data = DfBiabetes, family =
              binomial(logit))
```

We now comment on the code used to build the regression model. Logistic regression is called by imposing the family: `family = binomial (logit)`. The `Var2 ~ Var1` code means that we want to create a model that explains the `Var2` variable (presence or absence of diabetes) depending on the `Var1` variable (presence or absence of stress events). In practice, `Var1` is the independent variable X, and `Var2` is the dependent variable Y. The `weights` argument is used to give the number of trials when the response is the proportion of successes, in our case data contained in the `Freq` column of the `DfBiabetes` data frame (so we write `weights = Freq`). Then we read `data = DfBiabetes` to specify the location where the values are contained.

The `family` objects provide a convenient way to specify the details of the models used by the `glm()` function. The following `family` type objects are available:

- binomial (link = "logit")
- gaussian (link = "identity")
- Gamma (link = "inverse")
- inverse.gaussian (link = "1/mu^2")
- poisson (link = "log")
- quasi (link = "identity", variance = "constant")
- quasibinomial (link = "logit")
- quasipoisson (link = "log")

To produce result summaries of the results of the model fitting function, we use the `summary()` function:

```
summary (LogModel)
```

The results are shown in the following:

```
> summary (LogModel)
Call:
glm(formula = Var2 ~ Var1, family = binomial(logit), data = DfBiabetes,
    weights = Freq)
Deviance Residuals:
       1         2         3         4
 -3.976   -10.377     7.727    12.663
Coefficients:
              Estimate Std. Error z value Pr(>|z|)

(Intercept)    -3.7075     0.3579 -10.360  < 2e-16 ***
Var1StressYes   2.7912     0.3872   7.208 5.67e-13 ***
---
```

```
Signif. codes:  0 '***' 0.001 '**' 0.01 '*' 0.05 '.' 0.1 ' ' 1
(Dispersion parameter for binomial family taken to be 1)
    Null deviance: 429.15  on 3  degrees of freedom
Residual deviance: 343.54  on 2  degrees of freedom
AIC: 347.54
Number of Fisher Scoring iterations: 6
```

Let's find out what was being returned to us: the first thing we see is the call, what model we ran, what options we specified, and so on.

Next, we see the deviance residuals, which are a measure of model fit. This part of the output shows the distribution of the deviance residuals for individual cases used in the model.

The next part of the summary results shows the coefficients, their standard errors, the z-statistic, and the associated p-values. This is the essential part of the model as it defines the equation. Based on the results, our model is represented by the following equation:

$$P(x) = \frac{e^{(+2.7912*x-3.7075)}}{1 + e^{(+2.7912*x-3.7075)}}$$

We can also see that both coefficients are significant (*p-value <0.05*). The logistic regression coefficients give the change in the log odds of the outcome for a single unit increase in the predictor variable. So, for every single unit change in `Var1`, the log odds of diabetes onset (versus non-diabetes onset) increases by *2.7912*.

Below the table of coefficients are fit indices, including the null and deviance residuals and the **Akaike Information Criterion** (**AIC**). Null deviance indicates the response predicted by a model with nothing but an intercept. The lower the value, the better the model. Residual deviance indicates the response predicted by a model on adding independent variables. The lower the value, the better the model. Deviance is a measure of the goodness of the fit of a GLM. Or rather, it's a measure of badness of fit–higher numbers indicate worse fit.

The analogous metric of adjusted R-squared in logistic regression is AIC. AIC is the measure of fit which penalizes the model for the number of model coefficients. Therefore, we always prefer models with minimum AIC value.

Finally, the number of Fisher scoring iterations is returned. Fisher's scoring algorithm is a derivative of Newton's method for solving maximum likelihood problems, numerically. For our model we see that Fisher's scoring algorithm needed six iterations to perform the fit. This doesn't really tell you a lot that you need to know, other than the fact that the model did indeed converge, and had no trouble doing it.

Previously, we wrote the equation of our system (let's call it precisely):

$$P(x) = \frac{e^{(+2.7912*x-3.7075)}}{1 + e^{(+2.7912*x-3.7075)}}$$

Here, the independent x variable can assume zero or one. If it assumes zero (so in the absence of stressful events) then the probability of having diabetes is provided by the following equation:

$$P(x = 0) = \frac{e^{(-3.7075)}}{1 + e^{(-3.7075)}}$$

We evaluate this equation in R:

```
Px0=(exp(-3.7075))/(1+exp(-3.7075))
```

The result is shown in the following:

```
> Px0
[1] 0.02395106
```

So, the probability of having diabetes is equal to 2.4 percent. If there are stress events ($x = 1$), the probability of having diabetes is provided by the following equation:

$$P(x = 1) = \frac{e^{(2.7912-3.7075)}}{1 + e^{(2.7912-3.7075)}}$$

We evaluate this equation in R:

```
Px1=(exp(-3.7075+2.7912))/(1+exp(-3.7075+2.7912))
```

The result is shown in the following:

```
> Px1
[1] 0.2857124
```

So, the probability of having diabetes is equal to *28.6* percent. Now, can you notice a noticeable increase? We now calculate *odds*, as we have indicated in the previous section, the *odds* formula is:

$$odds(x = 0) = \frac{P(x = 0)}{1 - P(x = 0)} = e^{\beta} = e^{-3.7075}$$

Calculate *odds* for *x = 0* in R:

```
Oddsx0=exp(-3.7075)
```

The result is shown in the following:

```
> Oddsx0
[1] 0.02453879
```

Calculate the odds for *x = 1*:

```
Oddsx1=exp(2.7912-3.7075)
```

The result is shown in the following:

```
> Oddsx1
[1] 0.3999963
```

We can finally calculate the odd ratio *OR* using the following formula:

$$OR = \frac{odds(x = 1)}{odds(x = 0)}$$

All this in R becomes:

```
OR = exp(2.7912-3.7075)/exp(-3.7075)
```

The result is shown in the following:

```
> OR
[1] 16.30057
```

A person who has experienced a stressful event has a tendency to develop type two diabetes 16.30057 times greater than the person who has not undergone stressful events.

So far, to calculate this data, we first defined the quantities by indicating the respective equations, so we made the relative calculations in R. The choice of this approach was intended to understand these concepts in detail. In fact, to calculate these values, we can take advantage of the data contained in the model that we have built. Let's see how.

To extract the model coefficients we can write:

```
Beta = LogModel$coefficient[1]
Alpha = LogModel$coefficient[2]
```

The results are shown in the following:

```
> Beta
(Intercept)
  -3.707456
> Alpha
Var1StressYes
     2.791165
```

Calculate the probabilities associated with the two conditions imposed by the regressor:

```
P0 <- exp(LogModel$coefficient[1]) / (1 + exp(LogModel$coefficient[1]))
P1 <- exp(LogModel$coefficient[1] + LogModel$coefficient[2]) / (1 +
exp(LogModel$coefficient[1]+LogModel$coefficient[2]))
```

Obtaining the following results:

```
> P0
(Intercept)
  0.0239521
> P1
(Intercept)
  0.2857143
```

We can then calculate odds:

```
odds0 <- P0 / (1 - P0)
odds1 <- P1 / (1 - P1)
```

The results are shown in the following:

```
> odds0
(Intercept)
 0.02453988
> odds1
(Intercept)
        0.4
```

We can finally calculate the odd ratio:

```
OR1 <- odds1 / odds0
```

Obtaining the following result:

```
> OR1
(Intercept)
      16.3
```

By comparing the results obtained following the two approaches, it is possible to verify that we have achieved the same results.

Finally, we can analyze the most well-known formula for calculating the odds-ratio that allows us to compute this value from the double-entry table presented at the beginning of this example. To recall this data in the formula, we use letters as shown in the following figure:

Stress	Diabetes No	Diabetes Yes	Total
No	326 **a**	8 **b**	334
Yes	160 **c**	64 **d**	224
Total	486	72	558

Using the data available in that table we can write:

$$OR = \frac{a/c}{b/d} = \frac{a*d}{b*c}$$

All this in R becomes:

```
OR2 <- (TableDiabetes[1,1]*TableDiabetes[2,2]) /
         (TableDiabetes[1,2]*TableDiabetes[2,1])
```

The result is shown in the following:

```
> OR2
[1] 16.3
```

Once again, we got the same result.

Multiple logistic regression

In the previous section, we introduced the simple logistic regression model, where the dichotomous response depends on only one explanatory variable. As in the case of linear regression, which we analyzed in Chapter 2, *Basic Concepts – Simple Linear Regression*, and Chapter 3, *More Than Just One Predictor – MLR*, the popularity of a modeling technique lies in its ability to model many variables, which can be on different measurement scales. Now, we will generalize the logistic model to the case of more than one independent variable.

Central arguments in dealing with multiple logistic models will be the estimate of the coefficients in the model and the tests for their significance. This will follow the same lines as the univariate model already seen in the previous section. In multiple regression, the coefficients are called **partial** because they express the specific relationship that an independent variable has with the dependent variable net of the other independent variables considered in the model.

Similarly to what is done for the univariate case, we can derive the equation of the multivariate logistic regression model starting with the probabilities that the response takes the value *1*:

$$P(x) = \beta_0 + \beta_1 * x_1 + \beta_2 * x_2 + \ldots + \beta_n * x_n$$

By applying the logistic transformation at the right end of the equation of the linear regression model, we get:

$$P(x) = \frac{e^{(\beta_0 + \beta_1 * x_1 + \beta_2 * x_2 + \ldots + \beta_n * x_n)}}{1 + e^{(\beta_0 + \beta_1 * x_1 + \beta_2 * x_2 + \ldots + \beta_n * x_n)}}$$

By making the ratio between the probabilities of obtaining the two values, we get the following equation:

$$\frac{P(x)}{1 - P(x)} = e^{(\beta_0 + \beta_1 * x_1 + \beta_2 * x_2 + \ldots + \beta_n * x_n)}$$

Finally, let's take the logarithm of the previous equation:

$$\log\left(\frac{P(x)}{1 - P(x)}\right) = \beta_0 + \beta_1 * x_1 + \beta_2 * x_2 + \ldots + \beta_n * x_n$$

Again, in this case, the *log* odds are linear in *x*. In the following section, an example of a multiple logistic regression analysis is proposed to understand how to perform it in the R environment.

Customer satisfaction analysis with the multiple logistic regression

To begin with, let us consider the data collected at a restaurant through customer interviews. The customers were asked to give a score to the following aspects: Service, Ambience, and Food. They were also asked whether they would leave the tip on the basis of these scores. In this case, the number of inputs is three and the output is a categorical value (Tip=1 and No-tip=0).

The input file to be used is shown in the following screenshot:

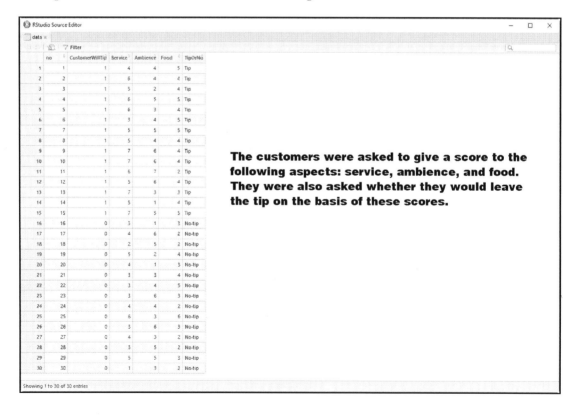

The customers were asked to give a score to the following aspects: service, ambience, and food. They were also asked whether they would leave the tip on the basis of these scores.

All the variables are shown in the following list:

- `CustomerWillTip`
- `Service`
- `Ambience`
- `Food`

This is a classification problem with three inputs and one dichotomy output. We will try to solve this classification problem with logistic regression. Let's start by uploading the content data into a `.csv` file named `RestaurantTips.csv` in the R environment:

```
setwd("C:/R")
data=read.csv('RestaurantTips.csv',sep=",",header=TRUE)
View(data)
```

This first command sets the working directory where we will have inserted the dataset for the next reading. The second command use the `read.csv()` function that reads a file in table format and creates a data frame from it, with cases corresponding to rows and variables to columns in the file. The last command invokes a spreadsheet-style data viewer on a matrix-like R object. Now let's look at the variables in the dataset:

```
names(data)
```

As anticipated, there are three predictors (`Service`, `Ambience`, and `Food`) and one response (`CustomerWillTip`). Before proceeding with the fitting of the model, let's see if you can extract useful information through a first exploratory investigation. First, we trace a plot of the variables we just found:

```
plot(data[,2:5])
```

This command draws a scatter plot matrix. But what is the scatter plot matrix? For a set of variables $A_1, A_2, .. , A_k$, the scatter plot matrix shows all the scatter plots of the variables in a matrix format. So, if there are n variables, the scatter plot matrix will have n rows and n columns and the ith row and j^{th} column of this matrix is a plot of A_i versus A_j.

The scatter plot matrix for the four variables, **CustomerWillTip**, **Service**, **Ambience**, and **Food**, is shown in the following figure:

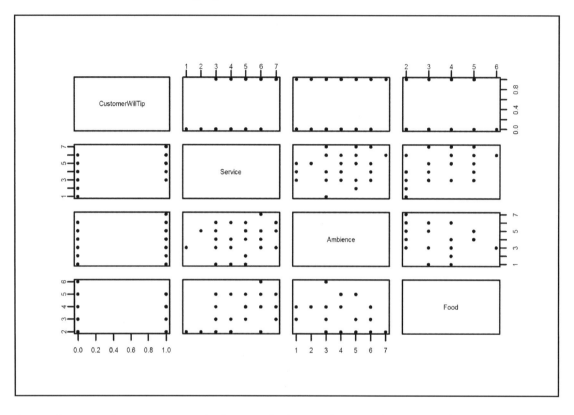

As can be seen, there are no particular trends. Let us then conduct a correlation analysis using the cor() function:

```
cor(data[,2:5])
```

The results are shown in the following:

```
> cor(data[,2:5])
                CustomerWillTip    Service    Ambience        Food
CustomerWillTip       1.0000000  0.6607721   0.1634356   0.4665695
Service               0.6607721  1.0000000   0.1550232   0.4065033
Ambience              0.1634356  0.1550232   1.0000000  -0.1108067
Food                  0.4665695  0.4065033  -0.1108067   1.0000000
```

From the analysis of the results, it seems that the possibility of leaving tips is more correlated with the Service. Then comes the Food and ultimately Ambience. It is important to remember these results as we will look for a confirmation in the simulation model.

Now, we build the object of formula type which we will include in the glm() function:

```
formula1=CustomerWillTip ~ Service + Food + Ambience
```

Then we can build the model:

```
LGModel<-glm(formula1 , data = data, family = binomial(logit))
```

To produce result summaries of logistic regression model fitting, we use the summary() function as follows:

```
summary(LGModel)
```

The results are shown in the following:

```
> summary(LGModel)
Call:
glm(formula = formula1, family = binomial(logit), data = data)
Deviance Residuals:
      Min         1Q     Median         3Q        Max
 -2.73481   -0.48223    0.04048    0.52687    1.51540
Coefficients:
              Estimate Std. Error z value Pr(>|z|)
(Intercept) -10.4691      3.9993  -2.618  0.00885 **
Service       1.2810      0.4935   2.596  0.00943 **
Food          0.9351      0.5810   1.609  0.10752
Ambience      0.2960      0.3389   0.873  0.38256
---
Signif. codes:   0 '***' 0.001 '**' 0.01 '*' 0.05 '.' 0.1 ' ' 1
(Dispersion parameter for binomial family taken to be 1)
    Null deviance: 41.589  on 29  degrees of freedom
Residual deviance: 21.882  on 26  degrees of freedom
AIC: 29.882
Number of Fisher Scoring iterations: 6
```

From the analysis of model coefficients, it can be noticed that only Intercept and the Service variable are statistically significant. Recall that correlation analysis had also shown similar results. In fact, even in that case the most correlated variable with the response was Service. Let's try then to see what happens if we remove from the model, terms that are not statistically significant (Ambience and Food):

```
LGModel1<-glm(CustomerWillTip ~ Service, data = data, family =
binomial(logit))
summary(LGModel1)
```

The results of the new model are shown in the following:

```
> summary(LGModel1)
Call:
glm(formula = CustomerWillTip ~ Service, family = binomial(logit), data =
data)
Deviance Residuals:
    Min       1Q    Median       3Q       Max
-2.03716  -0.46420   0.07336   0.51801   2.13608
Coefficients:
            Estimate Std. Error z value Pr(>|z|)
(Intercept)  -6.2882     2.2405  -2.807  0.00501 **
Service       1.3715     0.4756   2.884  0.00393 **
---
Signif. codes:  0 '***' 0.001 '**' 0.01 '*' 0.05 '.' 0.1 ' ' 1
(Dispersion parameter for binomial family taken to be 1)
    Null deviance: 41.589  on 29   degrees of freedom
Residual deviance: 25.301  on 28   degrees of freedom
AIC: 29.301
Number of Fisher Scoring iterations: 5
```

In this case, both terms are statistically significant. At this point we can use the model to make predictions. To do this, we will use the predict() function. The function predict() is a generic function for predictions from the results of various model fitting functions. This function invokes particular methods which depend on the class of the first argument:

```
LGModel1Pred <- round(predict(LGModel1, data, type="response"))
```

In this line of code, we applied the predict() function to the previously built logistic regression model (LGModel1), passing the entire set of data at our disposal. The results were then rounded off using the round() function.

To analyze the performance of the model in the classification, we can calculate the confusion matrix. In a confusion matrix, our classification results are compared to real data. The strength of a confusion matrix is that it identifies the nature of the classification errors, as well as their quantities. In this matrix, the diagonal cells show the number of cases that were correctly classified, all the other cells show the misclassified cases.

To calculate the confusion matrix, we can use the `confusionMatrix()` function contained in the `caret` package. The `caret` package contains functions to streamline the model training process for complex regression and classification problems. This package utilizes a number of R packages but tries not to load them all at package startup. A description of the `caret` package is contained at the end of the Chapter 1, *Getting Started with Regression*.

First, we will install the package:

```
install.package(caret)
```

 Remember, to install a library that is not present in the initial distribution of R, you must use the `install.package` function. This is the main function to install packages. It takes a vector of names and a destination library, downloads the packages from the repositories and installs them.

Then, we will load the library through the `library` command:

```
library(caret)
```

Now, we can apply the `confusionMatrix()` function:

```
LGModel1 <- confusionMatrix(LGModel1Pred, data[,"CustomerWillTip"])
LGModel1
```

The `confusionMatrix()` function calculates a cross-tabulation of observed and predicted classes with associated statistics. The results are shown in the following:

```
> LGModel1CM
Confusion Matrix and Statistics
          Reference
Prediction  0  1
         0 12  2
         1  3 13

                  Accuracy : 0.8333
                    95% CI : (0.6528, 0.9436)
       No Information Rate : 0.5
       P-Value [Acc > NIR] : 0.0001625
                     Kappa : 0.6667
    Mcnemar's Test P-Value : 1.0000000
               Sensitivity : 0.8000
```

```
            Specificity : 0.8667
          Pos Pred Value : 0.8571
          Neg Pred Value : 0.8125
             Prevalence : 0.5000
         Detection Rate : 0.4000
   Detection Prevalence : 0.4667
      Balanced Accuracy : 0.8333
         'Positive' Class : 0
```

From the analysis of the confusion matrix, we can see that the logistic regression model has been able to properly classify *25* cases out of *30* available. Classification errors were therefore only *5*. As it is possible to verify, the model has a high accuracy (0.8333), but also the sensitivity and the specificity are greater than *80* percent (0.8000, and 0.8667). Then we understand how these values are calculated.

All evaluation metrics present in the results can be derived from the same confusion matrix, let's see how. Suppose we have the values of the classification plotted in an *nxn* matrix (*2x2* in case of binary classification) as follows:

	Predicted value	Predicted value
Actual values	TRUE	FALSE
TRUE	TP	FN
FALSE	FP	TN

Now, let's look at some evaluation metrics in detail.

True Positive Rate (TPR) or **sensitivity** or **recall** or **hit rate** is a measure of how many true positives were identified out of all the positives identified:

$$TPR = \frac{TP}{P} = \frac{TP}{TP + FN}$$

Ideally, the model is better if we have this closer to one.

True Negative Rate (TNR) or **specificity** is the ratio of true negatives and total number of negatives we have predicted:

$$TNR = \frac{TN}{N} = \frac{TN}{TN + FP}$$

If this ratio is closer to zero, the model is more accurate.

Accuracy is the measure of how good our model is. It is expected to be closer to one, if our model is performing well. Accuracy is the ratio of correct predictions and all the total predictions:

$$ACC = \frac{TP + TN}{P + N} = \frac{TP + TN}{TP + TN + FP + FN}$$

Precision and recall are again ratios between the *TP* with (*TP+FP*) and *TP* with (*TP+FN*) respectively. These ratios determine how relevant our predictions are compared to the actual.

Precision is defined as how many selected items are relevant. That is, how many of the predicted ones are actually correctly predicted. The equation is:

$$Precision = \frac{TP}{TP + FP}$$

If *Precision* is closer to one, we are more accurate in our predictions.

Recall, on the other hand, tells us how many relevant items we selected. Mathematically, it is:

$$Recall = \frac{TP}{TP + FN}$$

Multiple logistic regression with categorical data

To improve our practice with the multiple logistic regression, we look at another example. This time, we will use the UCBAdmissions dataset that contains aggregate data on applicants to graduate school at Berkeley for the six largest departments in 1973, classified by admission and sex. As such, this is a multiple logistic regression modeling problem. Input attributes include things like sex, departments, and admission attributes. A brief database description is given in the following list:

- **Name**: UCBAdmissions
- **Package**: datasets
- **Number of instances**: 4526
- **Number of attributes**: 3 categorical attributes

Each of the attributes is detailed in the following table:

No	Name	Levels
1	Admit	Admitted, Rejected
2	Gender	Male, Female
3	Dept	A, B, C, D, E, F

This dataset is contained in the R `datasets` package: there are around *90* datasets available in this package. Most of them are small and easy to feed into functions in R.
To see a list of the available dataset, type the following statement in the R prompt:

```
> library(help="datasets")
```

The following screenshot shows part of the documentation that is displayed:

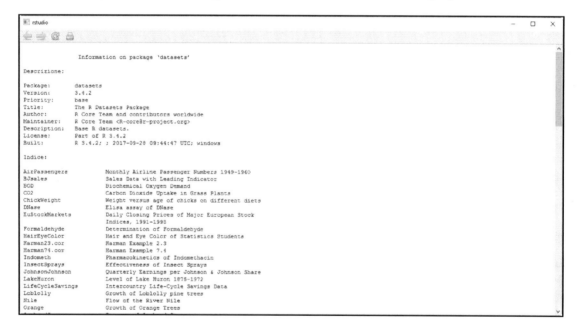

As can be seen after a series of package's information, all available datasets with a brief description are proposed.

Let's start by loading the `UCBAdmissions` dataset through the following command which, as we anticipated, is contained in the `datasets` library and saves it in a given frame:

```
data = UCBAdmissions
```

Use the `str()` function to view a compact display of the structure of an arbitrary R object. In our case, using `str(data)`, we will obtain the following results:

```
> str(data)
 table [1:2, 1:2, 1:6] 512 313 89 19 353 207 17 8 120 205 ...
 - attr(*, "dimnames")=List of 3
  ..$ Admit : chr [1:2] "Admitted" "Rejected"
  ..$ Gender: chr [1:2] "Male" "Female"
  ..$ Dept  : chr [1:6] "A" "B" "C" "D" ...
```

The dataset is stored in table format with three variables: `Admit`, `Gender`, and `Dept`. Of these three variables, two are dichotomy (only two values) while the third one has six levels. To extract more information, use the `summary()` function:

```
summary(data)
```

The results are shown in the following:

```
> summary(data)
Number of cases in table: 4526
Number of factors: 3
Test for independence of all factors:
    Chisq = 2000.3, df = 16, p-value = 0
```

As we anticipated, the table contains `4526` cases with three variables. In particular, all three already have the `factor` attribute. To begin with, we can extract the total admissions by `Gender`:

```
TotalAdmit=apply(data, c(1, 2), sum)
> TotalAdmit
          Gender
Admit      Male Female
  Admitted 1198    557
  Rejected 1493   1278
```

Thus, for the six departments overall, 1198 males were Admitted, 1493 males were Rejected, 557 females were Admitted, and 1278 females were Rejected. Now, we calculate the admission rates by gender:

```
>MaleAdmit = 1198/(1198+1493)
[1] 0.4451877
> FemaleAdmit= 557/(557+1278)
[1] 0.3035422
```

Of the male applicants, the *44.5* percent were admitted whereas for the female applicants, only *30.4* percent were admitted. Let's display a barplot of these values:

```
barplot(TotalAdmit,legend = rownames(TotalAdmit))
```

The following figure shows the total **Admitted** and **Rejected** by gender:

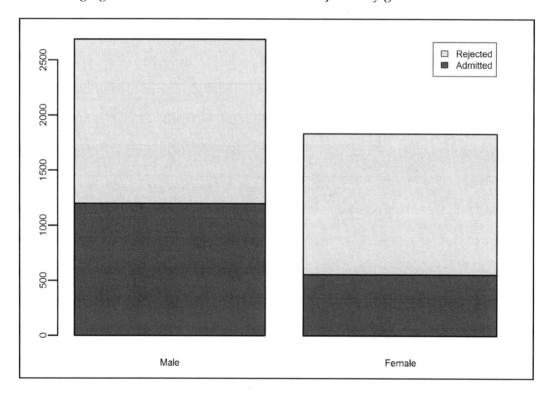

It is legitimate to ask: Is there gender bias in the graduate admissions? It is reasonable to ask: was there a gender discrimination in the Berkeley graduate admissions in 1973? We can calculate the odds ratio.

In the previous section, saw that from a table of this type it is easy to calculate the odds ratio. Let's recall the formula:

$$OR = \frac{a/c}{b/d} = \frac{a*d}{b*c}$$

Here the *a, b, c, d* terms are defined as follows:

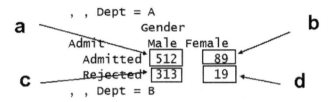

According to what we saw, we can write:

```
ODTotal=TotalAdmit[1,1]*TotalAdmit[2,2]/(TotalAdmit[1,2]*TotalAdmit[2,1])
> ODTotal
[1] 1.84108
```

The odds ratio of 1.84108 illustrates that the odds for men being admitted is higher. A first statistic on data can be obtained by simply invoking the data object:

```
> data
, , Dept = A
          Gender
Admit      Male Female
  Admitted  512     89
  Rejected  313     19
, , Dept = B
          Gender
Admit      Male Female
  Admitted  353     17
  Rejected  207      8
, , Dept = C
          Gender
Admit      Male Female
  Admitted  120    202
  Rejected  205    391
, , Dept = D
          Gender
Admit      Male Female
  Admitted  138    131
  Rejected  279    244
```

```
, , Dept = E
           Gender
Admit        Male Female
   Admitted    53     94
   Rejected   138    299
, , Dept = F
           Gender
Admit        Male Female
   Admitted    22     24
   Rejected   351    317
```

In this way, the number of Admitted and Rejected per Gender is returned for each department. As we can see for each department, we have a table with admissions (Admitted, Rejected) by Gender.

Now, we can calculate the odds ratio for each department. To avoid writing the same formula for the six values for the different departments, we write a function that we can later use whenever necessary:

```
odds.ratio=function(x,addtocounts=0){
  x=x+addtocounts
  (x[1,1]*x[2,2])/(x[1,2]*x[2,1])
}
```

Now, we can calculate the odds ratio for each department using this function:

```
OD<-round(apply(data,3,odds.ratio),2)
```

In this line of code, we used the apply() function to apply the odds.ratio function to the third attribute of the data table (Dept). Next, we used the round() function to round off the results obtained at the second decimal place. The results are shown in the following:

```
> OD<-round(apply(data,3,odds.ratio),2)
   A    B    C    D    E    F
0.35 0.80 1.13 0.92 1.22 0.83
```

Beware, as these values are relative to the male gender, they are greater than those of females for departments C and E and are lower than those of females for departments A, B, D and F. But we had previously seen that other values were derived from the total calculation (ODTotal=1.84108). So, the Simpson's paradox is confirmed, in which a trend appears in different groups of data but disappears or reverses when these groups are combined.

 Simpson's paradox indicates a situation in which a relationship between two phenomena appears to be modified, or even inverted, by the data in possession because of other phenomena not taken into consideration in the analysis (hidden variables).

How to explain these conflicting results? Calculate the Admitted/Rejected rates for the different departments:

```
AdmitRates<-round(prop.table(margin.table(UCBAdmissions,c(1,3)),2),2)
```

The results are shown in the following:

```
> AdmitRates
         Dept
Admit        A    B    C    D    E    F
  Admitted 0.64 0.63 0.35 0.34 0.25 0.06
  Rejected 0.36 0.37 0.65 0.66 0.75 0.94
```

From the analysis of the results obtained, the trend reversal that we previously found is now clear. In fact, most males move towards departments A and B where acceptance has a higher rate, while most women are heading towards departments C, D, E and F where acceptance has a lower rate.

We can confirm this by analyzing the percentages of Admitted and Rejected by gender for each department:

```
par(mfrow=c(2,3))
for (i in 1:6)
  barplot(data[,,i],legend.text=FALSE,main=paste("Dept",LETTERS[i],sep="
"))
```

The following figure shows the `Admitted` and `Rejected` by gender for each department (in dark gray the `Admitted` while in light gray the `Rejected`):

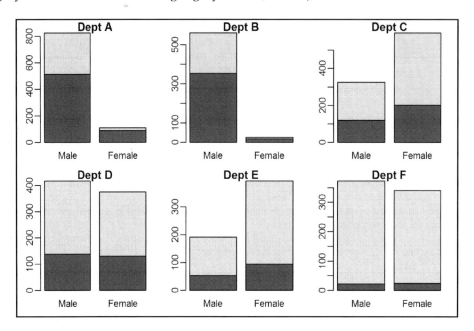

From the analysis of the figure, it is clear that in the first two departments (**A** and **B**) the percentages of admitted ones are higher than the other departments, in fact the dark gray area is higher (`Admitted`). On the other hand, in the departments **C**, **D**, **E**, and **F**, the light gray (`Rejected`) prevails.

Finally, we calculate the acceptance and rejection rates for each gender and for each department:

```
DeptResults <- prop.table(data,c(2,3))
```

The results are shown in the following:

```
> DeptResults
, , Dept = A
                Gender
Admit           Male       Female
  Admitted 0.62060606 0.82407407
  Rejected 0.37939394 0.17592593
, , Dept = B
                Gender
Admit           Male       Female
```

```
Admitted 0.63035714 0.68000000
Rejected 0.36964286 0.32000000
, , Dept = C
                      Gender
Admit             Male      Female
  Admitted 0.36923077 0.34064081
  Rejected 0.63076923 0.65935919
, , Dept = D
                      Gender
Admit             Male      Female
  Admitted 0.33093525 0.34933333
  Rejected 0.66906475 0.65066667
, , Dept = E
                      Gender
Admit             Male      Female
  Admitted 0.27748691 0.23918575
  Rejected 0.72251309 0.76081425
, , Dept = F
                      Gender
Admit             Male      Female
  Admitted 0.05898123 0.07038123
  Rejected 0.94101877 0.92961877
```

To get an immediate comparison, let's just see the percentage of admissions for each gender and each department:

```
DeptResults[1,,]
```

The results are shown in the following:

```
> DeptResults[1,,]
        Dept

Gender           A          B          C          D
  Male    0.62060606 0.63035714 0.36923077 0.33093525
  Female  0.82407407 0.68000000 0.34064081 0.34933333
                 E          F
  Male    0.27748691 0.05898123
  Female  0.23918575 0.07038123
```

Thus, females are admitted at a higher rate in the Dept of A, B, D, F and at a lower rate in Dept of C and E. The preference for males is quite slight in the C and E, whereas the preference for females is quite large in A and F. In B and D, females are admitted at a slightly higher rate than males. Finally, we can conclude, in the overall data, males are admitted at a higher rate. Broken by department, males are admitted at much lower rates in the Dept of A and F and a slightly lower rate in the Dept of B and D. Males are admitted at a slightly higher rate in the Dept of C and E.

After exploring the data, we are ready to build the logistic regression model. The first thing to do is to set up the response in a format compatible with the glm() function that we will use to fit the model.

For the binomial families, the response can be specified in one of three ways:

- As a factor
- As a numerical vector with values between zero and one, interpreted as the proportion of successful cases (with the total number of cases given by the weights)
- As a two-column integer matrix: the first column gives the number of successes and the second the number of failures

We choose to adopt the third format. To do this, we will report Admitted and Rejected in the first two columns, while in the third we will place Gender and finally in the fourth the department:

```
FirstTwoColumn<-
matrix(data,ncol=2,byrow=TRUE,dimnames=list(NULL,c("Admitted","Rejected")))
Gender<-rep(c("Male","Female"),6)
Dept<-rep(c("A","B","C","D","E","F"),each=2)
```

At this point, we just have to put the four columns into a data frame:

```
data1 <- data.frame(FirstTwoColumn,Gender,Dept)
```

Now, we can use the glm() function to build the model, let us consider the simplest logit model that provides the sum of the two predictors (Gender and Dept):

```
MLogit1=glm(cbind(Admitted,Rejected)~Gender+Dept,
            family=binomial(link=logit),data=data1)
```

To analyze the results, we use the summary function:

```
summary(MLogit1)
```

The results are shown in the following screenshot:

```
> summary(MLogit1)

Call:
glm(formula = cbind(Admitted, Rejected) ~ Gender + Dept, family = binomial(link = logit),
    data = data1)

Deviance Residuals:
      1        2        3        4        5        6        7        8        9       10       11       12
-1.2487   3.7189  -0.0560   0.2706   1.2533  -0.9243   0.0826  -0.0858   1.2205  -0.8509  -0.2076   0.2052

Coefficients:
            Estimate Std. Error z value Pr(>|z|)
(Intercept)  0.68192    0.09911   6.880 5.97e-12 ***
GenderMale  -0.09987    0.08085  -1.235    0.217
DeptB       -0.04340    0.10984  -0.395    0.693
DeptC       -1.26260    0.10663 -11.841  < 2e-16 ***
DeptD       -1.29461    0.10582 -12.234  < 2e-16 ***
DeptE       -1.73931    0.12611 -13.792  < 2e-16 ***
DeptF       -3.30648    0.16998 -19.452  < 2e-16 ***
---
Signif. codes:  0 '***' 0.001 '**' 0.01 '*' 0.05 '.' 0.1 ' ' 1

(Dispersion parameter for binomial family taken to be 1)

    Null deviance: 877.056  on 11  degrees of freedom
Residual deviance:  20.204  on  5  degrees of freedom
AIC: 103.14

Number of Fisher Scoring iterations: 4
```

Let's find out what was being returned to us: the first thing we see is the call, the model we ran, what options we specified, and so on.

Next, we see the deviance residuals, which are a measure of model fit. This part of the output shows the distribution of the deviance residuals for individual cases used in the model.

The next part of the summary results shows the coefficients, their standard errors, the z-statistic, and the associated p-values. This is the essential part of the model as it defines the equation. In the coefficients list, the term Dept A does not appear, due to the fact that the first level is the reference group, by default.

From the analysis of results, you can notice that this simple model does not work well. Demonstration is the value of `Residual deviance` which is equal to `20.204 on 5 degrees of freedom`. All this should not be surprising, in fact, if we go to analyze the `Deviance Residuals`, we note that the second value is `3.7189`, which differs considerably from the others. This value corresponds to `Admitted/Rejected` counts for female candidatures at department `A`, which is thus in contrast to the other recorded values. Department `A` seems a clear outlier. Let's get it out of the model and see what's happening:

```
MLogit2=glm(cbind(Admitted,Rejected)~Gender+Dept,
      family=binomial(link=logit),data=data1,subset = (Dept != "A"))
summary(MLogit2)
```

The results are shown in the following screenshot:

```
> summary(MLogit2)

Call:
glm(formula = cbind(Admitted, Rejected) ~ Gender + Dept, family = binomial(link = logit),
    data = data1, subset = (Dept != "A"))

Deviance Residuals:
      3        4        5        6        7        8        9       10       11       12
-0.1191   0.5680   0.5239  -0.3914  -0.5164   0.5440   0.6868  -0.4892  -0.5024   0.5158

Coefficients:
            Estimate Std. Error z value Pr(>|z|)
(Intercept)  0.51349    0.11936   4.302 1.69e-05 ***
GenderMale   0.03069    0.08676   0.354    0.724
DeptC       -1.14008    0.12188  -9.354  < 2e-16 ***
DeptD       -1.19456    0.11984  -9.968  < 2e-16 ***
DeptE       -1.61308    0.13928 -11.581  < 2e-16 ***
DeptF       -3.20527    0.17880 -17.927  < 2e-16 ***
---
Signif. codes:  0 '***' 0.001 '**' 0.01 '*' 0.05 '.' 0.1 ' ' 1

(Dispersion parameter for binomial family taken to be 1)

    Null deviance: 539.4581  on 9  degrees of freedom
Residual deviance:   2.5564  on 4  degrees of freedom
AIC: 71.791

Number of Fisher Scoring iterations: 3
```

Performance improvements are apparent: `Residual deviance` now equals `2.5564 on 4 degrees of freedom` and `Deviance Residuals` do not seem to be outliers. Another way to compare the two models is to consider the `AIC`. This is an estimator of the relative quality of statistical models for a given set of data. Given a collection of models for the data, `AIC` estimates the quality of each model, relative to each of the other models. Thus, `AIC` provides a means for model selection. The rule is to prefer the models with the lowest `AIC`.

In this case, we have a clear improvement of AIC which ranges from 103.14 to 71.791. But even in this case we cannot be satisfied with it. From the analysis of the results provided by the model we notice that the term that takes into account the gender is not statistically significant in both models (0.217 and 0.724). This prompts us to remove it from the model:

```
MLogit3=glm(cbind(Admitted,Rejected)~Dept,family=binomial(link=logit),
          data=data1,subset = (Dept != "A"))
summary(MLogit3)
```

The results are shown in the following screenshot:

```
> summary(MLogit3)

Call:
glm(formula = cbind(Admitted, Rejected) ~ Dept, family = binomial(link = logit),
    data = data1, subset = (Dept != "A"))

Deviance Residuals:
      3        4        5        6        7        8        9       10       11       12
-0.1041   0.4978   0.6950  -0.5177  -0.3764   0.3952   0.8119  -0.5754  -0.4341   0.4418

Coefficients:
            Estimate Std. Error z value Pr(>|z|)
(Intercept)  0.54286    0.08575    6.33 2.44e-10 ***
DeptC       -1.15855    0.11017  -10.52  < 2e-16 ***
DeptD       -1.20774    0.11394  -10.60  < 2e-16 ***
DeptE       -1.63237    0.12824  -12.73  < 2e-16 ***
DeptF       -3.21851    0.17490  -18.40  < 2e-16 ***
---
Signif. codes:  0 '***' 0.001 '**' 0.01 '*' 0.05 '.' 0.1 ' ' 1

(Dispersion parameter for binomial family taken to be 1)

    Null deviance: 539.4581  on 9  degrees of freedom
Residual deviance:   2.6815  on 5  degrees of freedom
AIC: 69.916

Number of Fisher Scoring iterations: 3
```

Note that the deviance for the reduced model is 2.6815 on 5 degrees of freedom, indicating a good fit. Moreover, all the terms in the model are now statistically significant.

Multinomial logistic regression

A generalization of logistic regression techniques makes it possible to deal with the case where the dependent variable is categorical on more than two levels. This is a case of multinomial or polynomial logistic regression.

A first distinction to operate is between nominal and ordinal logistic regression. We refer to nominal logistic regression when there is no natural order among the categories of the dependent variable, as can be the choice between four pizza types or between some singers. When, on the other hand, you can classify the dependent variable levels in an orderly scale, you are talking about ordinal logistic regression.

To perform multinomial logistic regression analysis, we can use the `mlogit` package. `mlogit` is a package for R which enables the estimation of the multinomial logit models with individual and/or alternative specific variables. The main extensions of the basic multinomial model (heteroscedastic, nested and random parameter models) are implemented.

The following table lists some of the information on this package:

Package	`mlogit`
Date	December 20, 2013
Version	0.2-4
Title	Multinomial logit model
Author	Yves Croissant

The following lists the most useful functions used in the multinomial logistic regression analysis, contained in this package:

- `mlogit`: This function runs estimation by maximum likelihood of the multinomial logit model, with alternative-specific and/or individual specific variables
- `mlogit.data`: This function shapes `data.frame` in a suitable form for the use of the `mlogit` function
- `mlogit.optim`: This function performs efficiently the optimization of the likelihood functions for multinomial logit models parameters from SGD
- `plot.mlogit`: This function contains methods for `rpar` and `mlogit` objects which provide a plot of the distribution of one or all of the estimated random parameters

To perform a multinomial logistic regression example, we can use the datasets included into the package. These datasets deal with some individuals, which make one or a sequential choice of one alternative among a set of several alternatives. The determinants of these choices are variables that can be alternative specific or purely individual specific. Such data has therefore a specific structure that can be characterized by three indexes:

- The alternative
- The choice situation
- The individual

The last index being only relevant if we have repeated observations for the same individual. For this example, we will use the dataset named `Heating` that contains the heating system choice in several California houses. This dataset is contained in the `mlogit` package.

A data frame with 900 rows and 16 variables:

- `idcase`: ID
- `depvar`: Heating system, one of **gas central (gc)**, **gas room (gr)**, **electric central (ec)**, **electric room (er)**, **heat pump (hp)**
- `ic.z`: Installation cost for heating system z (defined for the five heating systems)
- `oc.z`: Annual operating cost for heating system z (defined for the five heating systems)
- `pb.z`: Ratio `oc.z/ic.z`
- `income`: Annual income of the household
- `agehed`: Age of the household head
- `rooms`: Numbers of rooms in the house

The observations consist of single-family houses in California that were newly built and had central air-conditioning. The goal is to model the choice among heating systems. To recapitulate, we have the following choices:

- gc
- gr
- ec
- er
- hp

To start, we must install the `mlogit` package in the R environment.

Remember, to install a library that is not present in the initial distribution of R, you must use the `install.packages()` function. This function should be used only once and not every time you run the code.

Instead, load the library through the following command and repeat every time you run the code:

```
library(mlogit)
```

At this point, we can load the dataset:

```
data("Heating")
```

As we have already said, the dataset is contained in the `mlogit` package, so to load it we can use the `data()` function. To display a compact summary of the dataset simply type:

```
str(Heating)
```

The results are shown in the following:

```
> str(Heating)
'data.frame':   900 obs. of  16 variables:
 $ idcase: num  1 2 3 4 5 6 7 8 9 10 ...
 $ depvar: Factor w/ 5 levels "gc","gr","ec",..: 1 1 1 4 4 1 1 1 1 1 ...
 $ ic.gc : num  866 728 599 835 756 ...
 $ ic.gr : num  963 759 783 793 846 ...
 $ ic.ec : num  860 797 720 761 859 ...
 $ ic.er : num  996 895 900 831 986 ...
 $ ic.hp : num  1136 969 1048 1049 883 ...
 $ oc.gc : num  200 169 166 181 175 ...
 $ oc.gr : num  152 169 138 147 139 ...
 $ oc.ec : num  553 520 439 483 404 ...
 $ oc.er : num  506 486 405 425 390 ...
 $ oc.hp : num  238 199 171 223 178 ...
 $ income: num  7 5 4 2 2 6 4 6 5 7 ...
 $ agehed: num  25 60 65 50 25 65 35 20 60 20 ...
 $ rooms : num  6 5 2 4 6 7 2 7 6 2 ...
 $ region: Factor w/ 4 levels "valley","scostl",..: 4 2 4 2 1 2 2 1 2 2 ...
```

As anticipated, there are `16` variables in the dataset among which we can see that `14` are numeric and `2` factor. The `depvar` variable is the response and the others will be our predictors.

The `mlogit` function requires its own special type of data frame, and there are two data formats:

- `wide`: In this case, there is one row for each choice situation
- `long`: In this case, there is one row for each alternative and, therefore, as many rows as there are alternatives for each choice situation

To convert ordinary data frames to a type required by `mlogit`, we can use the `mlogit.data()` function:

```
DataHeating <- mlogit.data(Heating, shape="wide", choice="depvar",
                    varying=c(3:12))
```

In the `mlogit.data()` function, the mandatory arguments are:

- `choice`: The variable indicating the choice made. It can be either a logical vector, a numerical vector with zero where the alternative is not chosen, a factor with level `yes` when the alternative is chosen.
- `shape`: The shape of `data.frame`. Whether long if each row is an alternative or wide if each row is an observation.
- `varying`: The indexes of the variables that are alternative specific.

Let's take a look at the first 10 lines of the new object we just created:

```
head(DataHeating, 10)
```

The results are shown in the following screenshot:

```
> head(DataHeating, 10)
     idcase depvar income agehed rooms region alt      ic     oc chid
1.ec      1  FALSE      7     25     6 ncostl  ec  859.90 553.34    1
1.er      1  FALSE      7     25     6 ncostl  er  995.76 505.60    1
1.gc      1   TRUE      7     25     6 ncostl  gc  866.00 199.69    1
1.gr      1  FALSE      7     25     6 ncostl  gr  962.64 151.72    1
1.hp      1  FALSE      7     25     6 ncostl  hp 1135.50 237.88    1
2.ec      2  FALSE      5     60     5 scostl  ec  796.82 520.24    2
2.er      2  FALSE      5     60     5 scostl  er  894.69 486.49    2
2.gc      2   TRUE      5     60     5 scostl  gc  727.93 168.66    2
2.gr      2  FALSE      5     60     5 scostl  gr  758.89 168.66    2
2.hp      2  FALSE      5     60     5 scostl  hp  968.90 199.19    2
```

An `mlogit.data` object is returned, which is `data.frame` in long format, which means one line for each alternative. It has an index attribute, which is `data.frame` that contains the index of the choice made (`chid`), and the index of the alternative (`alt`). The `depvar` variable is a Boolean which indicates the choice made and the individual specific variable (income) is repeated five times. So ultimately, every record of the starting dataset is transformed into five records into the arrival dataset. To confirm this, we can note that starting from a data frame containing 900 observations now there are 4500 observations.

At this point, we can build the model. As always, we must specify the formula to be included in the model before proceeding. Previously, we have often used a formula; a basic formula has the name of the dependent variable on the left, and the specification of the independent variables is on the right, with the two parts separated by a tilde (~).

Generally, the right-hand side of the formula consists of a series of names of variables, separated by + signs. An intercept is automatically included. By specifying *-1* or *+0* on the right-hand side we can omit this term. Finally, we can save a formula into a variable and then supply the name of the variable whenever a formula is called for.

In the `mlogit` package, there are some useful extensions to the formula concept, specially adapted to discrete choice models. A specific model formula for `logit` models is `mFormula` that provides a relevant class to deal with this specificity, and suitable methods to extract the elements of the model.

In `mlogit`, two kinds of variables are used: alternative specific and individual specific variables. An `mFormula` is a formula for which the right-hand side may contain three parts:

- The first one contains the alternative specific variables with a generic coefficient, that is, a unique coefficient for all the alternatives
- The second one contains the individual specific variables for which one coefficient is estimated for all the alternatives except one of them
- The third one contains the alternative specific variables with alternative specific coefficients

The different parts are separated by a | sign. If a standard formula is written, it is assumed that there are only alternative specific variables with generic coefficients.

In this respect, we build the formula:

```
form1 <- mFormula(depvar~ic+oc|0)
```

This formula specifies the `depvar` variable as a response, while `ic` and `oc` are explanatory variables. We remember that `ic` represents the installation cost for the heating system (defined for the five heating systems), while `oc` is the annual operating cost for the heating system. Previously, we said that by default, an intercept is added to the model. We removed it by using *+0* in the second part. Now, we can use the `mlogit()` function to estimate the multinomial logistic model by maximum likelihood:

```
MlogitModel <- mlogit(form1, DataHeating)
```

To produce result summaries of the model fitting function, we use the `summary()` function:

```
summary(MlogitModel)
```

The results are shown in the following:

```
> summary(MlogitModel)
Call:
mlogit(formula = form1, data = DataHeating, method = "nr", print.level = 0)
Frequencies of alternatives:
      ec       er       gc       gr       hp
0.071111 0.093333 0.636667 0.143333 0.055556
nr method
4 iterations, 0h:0m:0s
g'(-H)^-1g = 1.56E-07
gradient close to zero
Coefficients :
      Estimate  Std. Error t-value  Pr(>|t|)
ic -0.00623187  0.00035277 -17.665 < 2.2e-16 ***
oc -0.00458008  0.00032216 -14.217 < 2.2e-16 ***
---
Signif. codes:  0 '***' 0.001 '**' 0.01 '*' 0.05 '.' 0.1 ' ' 1
Log-Likelihood: -1095.2
```

The `summary()` function returns the following results: a brief indication of the model, the estimated coefficients, their estimated standard errors, the t-statistics, the probability, under the null hypothesis that the true value of the coefficient is zero, of observing a t-value greater than the computed one; then a graphical indication (stars) of the significance level of the coefficient is displayed.

Finally, the `Log-Likelihood` of the fitted `model` is returned. `mlogit` maximizes the `Log-Likelihood` function to find optimal values of the estimated coefficients. We can use `Log-Likelihood` to compare two models that use the same data to estimate the coefficients. Because the values are negative, the closer to zero the value is, the better the model fits the data.

Now, we can see both coefficients are highly significant and have the predicted negative sign, meaning that as the cost of a system increases (and the costs of the other systems remain the same) the probability of that system being chosen reduces.

Summary

In this chapter, we introduced classifications through logistic regression techniques. We have first described a logistic model and then we have provided some intuitions underneath the math formulation. We learned how to define a classification problem and how to apply logistic regression to solve this type of problem. We introduced the simple logistic regression model, where the dichotomous response depends on only one explanatory variable.

Then, we generalized the logistic model to the case of more than one independent variable in the multiple logistic regression. Central arguments in dealing with multiple logistic models have been the estimate of the coefficients in the model and the tests for their significance. This has followed the same lines as the univariate model. In multiple regression, the coefficients are called partial because they express the specific relationship that an independent variable has with the dependent variable net of the other independent variables considered in the model.

We learnt how to use the GLMs to perform multiple logistic regression. GLMs are extensions of traditional regression models that allow the mean to depend on the explanatory variables through a `link` function, and the response variable to be any member of a set of distributions called the exponential family. We have explored useful tools to evaluate performances, and we now have a deep understanding of every parameter. Furthermore, we have explored multiple logistic regression with categorical data.

Finally, we have discovered multinomial logistic regression, a generalization of logistic regression techniques makes it possible to deal with the case where the dependent variable is categorical on more than two levels.

In the next chapter, we will learn about the different datatypes in regression analysis and how to clean the data and identify missing data. In addition, we will understand how to work with outliers and derived variables, learn the most used descriptive statistical techniques, and understand some data analysis techniques. We will understand how to properly parse a dataset, clean it and create an output matrix optimally built for regression.

5
Data Preparation Using R Tools

Real world datasets are very varied: variables can be textual, numerical, or categorical and observations can be missing, false, or wrong (outliers). To perform a proper data analysis, we will understand how to correctly parse a dataset, clean it, and create an output matrix optimally built for regression. To extract knowledge, it is essential that the reader is able to create an observation matrix, using different techniques of data analysis and cleaning.

In the previous chapters, we analyzed how to perform a single and multiple regression analysis while how to carry out a multiple and multinomial logistic regression. But in all cases analyzed, to get the correct indication from the models, the data must be processed in advance to eliminate any anomalies.

In this chapter, we will explore the data preparation techniques to obtain a high-performing regression analysis. To do this, we have to get the data into a form that the algorithm can use to build a predictive analytical model. We start from discovering different ways to transform data, and the degree of cleaning the data. We will analyze the techniques available for the preparation of the most suitable data for analysis and modeling, which includes imputation of missing data, detecting and eliminating outliers, and adding derived variables. Then we will learn how to normalize the data, in which data units are eliminated, allowing you to easily compare data from different locations.

We will cover the following topics:

- Different ways to transform data
- Learn how to organize the data
- Dealing with missing data
- Detecting outliers

- Data normalization
- Discretization, standardization of features
- Dimensionality reduction

At the end of the chapter, we will be able to perform a data preparation so that their information content is best exposed to the regression tools. We learn how to apply transforming methods to own data and how these technique works. We discover how to clean the data, identify missing data, and how to work with outliers and with missing entries. We learn how to use normalization techniques to compare data from different locations. We'll also cover the dimensionality reduction, discretization, and standardization of features topics.

Data wrangling

Once data collection has been completed and imported into the R environment, it is finally time to start the analysis process. This is what a novice might think; conversely, we must first proceed to the preparation of data (**data wrangling**). This is a laborious process that can take a long time, in some cases about *80* percent of the entire data analysis process. However, it is a fundamental prerequisite for the rest of the data analysis workflow, so it is essential to acquire the best practices in such techniques.

Before submitting our data to any regression algorithm, we must be able to evaluate the quality and accuracy of our observations. If we cannot access the data stored in R correctly, or if we do not know how to switch from raw data to something that can be analyzed, we cannot go ahead.

A first look at data

Before passing our data to regression algorithms, we need to give a first look at what we've imported into the R environment to see if there are any issues. Often, raw data is messy and poorly formatted. In other cases, it may not have the appropriate details for our study.

 Correcting the data in progress can be destructive because it can be overwritten without the ability to restore the original data.

To get started, it's good practice to keep your original data. To do this, every change will be performed on a copy of the dataset. Putting order in the data is the first step and it will make data cleaning more easily, but let's ask a question. When can we say that our data is tidy? According to Hadley Wickham, a dataset is tidy if it satisfies the following conditions:

- Observations are in rows
- Variables are in columns
- Data is contained in a single dataset

But what else can we find in raw data? There are various things that can go wrong in collecting data. Here are some of the most commonly found problems:

- A table contains more types of observed phenomena
- A single observed phenomenon is stored in several tables
- Column headers do not contain variable names
- A column contains multiple variables
- Variables are stored in both rows and columns

Let's move on to a practical example, we will use a file designed ad hoc that contains the data for a small sample of observation; it lists the results of a test. We'll grab `CleaningData.xls`, a spreadsheet that contains some of the issues we just listed. To import this file into R, we need to set the R working directory to the folder where we saved the file, in my case `C://R`. To do this, we will use the `setwd()` function that set the R working directory to a `dir` specified by the user:

```
setwd ("c://R")
```

Then we will use the `read.csv()` function that reads a file in CSV format and creates a data frame from it, with cases corresponding to lines and variables to fields in the file:

```
SampleData=read.csv("CleaningData.csv", header=TRUE,sep=";")
```

Finally, we will use the `head()` function that returns the first or last parts of a vector, matrix, table, data frame or function:

```
head(SampleData)
```

The results are shown in the following:

```
> head(SampleData)
    name gender age right wrong
1   Emma      F  24    80    20
2   Liam      M -19     .    47
3 Olivia          32    75    25
4   Noah      M  15    60    40
5    Ava      F  18    45    55
6  Mason      M  21    54    46
```

As you can see, there are five columns corresponding to as many variables as:

- `name`: Name
- `gender`: Sex
- `age`: Age
- `right`: Percentage of right answers
- `wrong`: Percentage of wrong answers

Now that we have the data in a data frame in the R workspace, first we print a summary of the main features with `summary` command:

```
summary(SampleData)
> summary(SampleData)
      name     gender      age            right          wrong
 Ava      :1   :1    Min.   :-19.0   NaN      :2   Min.   : 2.00
 Elijah   :1   F:5   1st Qu.: 19.5   -19      :1   1st Qu.:24.00
 Emma     :1   M:6   Median : 24.0   .        :1   Median :43.00
 Isabella:1          Mean   : 27.0   13       :1   Mean   :46.08
 Liam     :1         3rd Qu.: 29.0   45       :1   3rd Qu.:62.50
 Lucas    :1         Max.   :100.0   5        :1   Max.   :95.00
 (Other)  :6         NA's   :1       (Other) :5
```

Already, we can see that the `age` variable has one missing value. Missing values of any type of variable are indicated by the `NA` code, which means not available. The **Not a Number (NaN)** code, on the other hand, indicates invalid numeric values, such as a numeric value divided by zero. If a variable contains missing values, R cannot apply some functions to it. For this reason, it is necessary to process the missing values in advance. Let's look at the data frame to see what it contains:

```
SampleData
> SampleData
    name gender age right wrong
1   Emma      F  24    80    20
```

2	Liam	M	-19	.	47
3	Olivia		32	75	25
4	Noah	M	15	60	40
5	Ava	F	18	45	55
6	Mason	M	21	54	46
7	Isabella	F	28	-19	85
8	Lucas	M	30	13	87
9	Sophia	F	26	NaN	30
10	Elijah	M	100	98	2
11	Mia	F	22	5	95
12	Oliver	M	NA	NaN	21

A quick look, and we notice that there are some problems:

- Empty cells
- Cell containing the string NA
- Cells containing the string NaN
- Cell containing a period (.)
- Cells containing a negative number (-19)

In this case, we were fast because the file is small—only twelve records—but in the case of large files, we would not have been as quick.

Change datatype

In the previous section we noticed some anomalies in the dataset. But before proceeding with any removal, additional control over the type attributed by R to the variables should be carried out. To do this, we will use the str() function that returns a compact display of the internal structure of an R object:

```
str(SampleData)
```

The results are shown in the following:

```
> str(SampleData)
'data.frame':   12 obs. of  5 variables:
 $ name  : Factor w/ 12 levels "Ava","Elijah",..: 3 5 11 9 1 7 4 6 12 2 ...
 $ gender: Factor w/ 3 levels "","F","M": 2 3 1 3 2 3 2 3 2 3 ...
 $ age   : int  24 -19 32 15 18 21 28 30 26 100 ...
 $ right : Factor w/ 11 levels "-19",".","13",..: 9 2 8 7 4 6 1 3 11 10 ...
 $ wrong : int  20 47 25 40 55 46 85 87 30 2 ...
```

For the most part, the type attributed by R to the variables is correct. The exception is represented by the `right` variable that appears as a `Factor` while we would expect an `int` value. The anomalies in the data also confused R.

So let's see how to correct that mistake. We will simply have to do a type conversion. In particular, we will have to transform the `right` variable from the `Factor` type to the `int` type. R has several features that allow datatype conversion. A list of the most used conversion features is shown in the following:

- `as.numeric()`
- `as.character()`
- `as.vector()`
- `as.matrix()`
- `as.data.frame`

In our case, we will use the first one to allow us to convert the `right` column from `Factor` to numeric. Unfortunately, if the argument of the `as.numeric()` function is `Factor`, this function will return the underlying numeric (integer) representation, which is often meaningless as it may not correspond to the factor levels. To transform a factor `f` to approximately its original numeric values, `as.numeric(levels(f))[f]` is recommended:

```
SampleData$right<-
as.integer(as.numeric(levels(SampleData$right))[SampleData$right])
> SampleData$right<-
as.integer(as.numeric(levels(SampleData$right))[SampleData$right])
Warning message:
NAs introduced by coercion
```

A warning massage is returned which warns us that `NAs introduced by coercion`. Let's see what happened:

```
> SampleData
        name gender age right wrong
1       Emma      F   24    80    20
2       Liam      M  -19    NA    47
3     Olivia          32    75    25
4       Noah      M   15    60    40
5        Ava      F   18    45    55
6      Mason      M   21    54    46
7   Isabella      F   28   -19    85
8      Lucas      M   30    13    87
9     Sophia      F   26   NaN    30
10    Elijah      M  100    98     2
11       Mia      F   22     5    95
```

| 12 | Oliver | M | NA | NaN | 21 |

By comparing the new version of the dataset with the original, we can see that in the `right` column where the term . (period in the second row) was first present, the term NA now appears.

Removing empty cells

From the data analysis, we detect an empty cell at the third row and second column. It is necessary to eliminate this anomaly before you can analyze the data frame. To do this, we can enter a NA value in the empty cell.

To set all of the empty cells to a NA value we can act as follows:

```
SampleData[SampleData==""]<-NA
```

To confirm the operation, we'll see the summary using `summary` function again:

```
summary(SampleData)
```

The results are shown in the following figure:

```
> summary(SampleData)
      name        gender       age              right            wrong
 Ava     :1            :0   Min.   :-19.0   Min.   :-19.00   Min.   : 2.00
 Elijah  :1    F    :5   1st Qu.: 19.5   1st Qu.: 13.00   1st Qu.:24.00
 Emma    :1    M    :6   Median : 24.0   Median : 54.00   Median :43.00
 Isabella:1    NA's:1   Mean   : 27.0   Mean   : 45.67   Mean   :46.08
 Liam    :1            3rd Qu.: 29.0   3rd Qu.: 75.00   3rd Qu.:62.50
 Lucas   :1            Max.   :100.0   Max.   : 98.00   Max.   :95.00
 (Other) :6            NA's   :1   NA's   :3
```

Now, in the `age` column there is an NA value. The same result could be done when reading the dataset, when we use the `read.csv` function. Let's see how:

```
SampleData=read.csv ("CleaningData.csv",
        header=TRUE,na.strings=c("",  "NA"),sep=";")
```

Here, we used the `na.strings` argument of the `read.csv()` function that is a character vector of strings which are to be interpreted as NA values. Blank fields are also considered to be missing values in logical, integer, numeric and complex fields. Note that the test happens after white space is stripped from the input, so `na.strings` values may need their own white space stripped in advance.

Replace incorrect value

The next step will allow us to replace the incorrect value indicators. If we give a look at the data again, we can see that in the `right` column the value -19 is displayed, which is obviously an incorrect value since for that variable, permissible values are between 0 and 100 (this is a percentage):

```
> SampleData$right
 [1]   80   NA   75   60   45   54  -19   13 NaN   98    5 NaN
```

We can replace that value with the missing value indicator that is said to be NA. To do this we will write:

```
SampleData$right[SampleData$right == -19 ] <- NA
```

Let's try to see this variable again:

```
> SampleData$right
 [1]   80   NA   75   60   45   54   NA   13 NaN   98    5 NaN
```

The incorrect value is no longer present, in its place there is a further NA value.

Missing values

A missing value occurs when an unknown value is stored for the variable in an observation. Missing data is a common occurrence and can have a significant effect on the operations that can be done on the data. In R, missing values are represented by the NA symbol. This symbol is a special value whose properties are different from other values. NA is one of the very few reserved words in R: we cannot give anything this name.

To detect missing values, we can use the `is.na()` function that indicates which elements are missing. This function returns a logical vector the same length as its argument, with TRUE for missing values and FALSE for non-missings. We apply this function to the data frame so far used:

```
is.na(SampleData)
```

The results are shown in the following figure:

```
> is.na(SampleData)
         name gender   age right wrong
 [1,] FALSE   FALSE FALSE FALSE FALSE
 [2,] FALSE   FALSE FALSE  TRUE FALSE
 [3,] FALSE    TRUE FALSE FALSE FALSE
 [4,] FALSE   FALSE FALSE FALSE FALSE
 [5,] FALSE   FALSE FALSE FALSE FALSE
 [6,] FALSE   FALSE FALSE FALSE FALSE
 [7,] FALSE   FALSE FALSE  TRUE FALSE
 [8,] FALSE   FALSE FALSE FALSE FALSE
 [9,] FALSE   FALSE FALSE  TRUE FALSE
[10,] FALSE   FALSE FALSE FALSE FALSE
[11,] FALSE   FALSE FALSE FALSE FALSE
[12,] FALSE   FALSE  TRUE  TRUE FALSE
```

In the previous figure, six TRUE values are present. From the comparison with the original dataset, it can be seen that the six TRUE values correspond to the cells that contain the NA and NaN values. To locate the missing value index, we can use the which() function. Let's see how to use this feature to the newly seen case:

```
which(is.na(SampleData))
```

The results are as follows:

```
> which(is.na(SampleData))
[1] 15 36 38 43 45 48
```

Six values are returned: there are the indexes of the NA values in the data frame. These are six integers that indicate the progressive position of the six values when the matrix is read, according to the columns. To obtain the array indices we can add the arr.ind argument as follows:

```
which(is.na(SampleData), arr.ind=TRUE)
```

The results are as follows:

```
> which(is.na(SampleData), arr.ind=TRUE)
      row col
[1,]    3   2
[2,]   12   3
[3,]    2   4
[4,]    7   4
[5,]    9   4
[6,]   12   4
```

Now, row and column indexes are specified for both values. To find all the rows indexes in a data frame with at least one NA, we can use the following command:

```
unique(unlist(lapply(SampleData, function(x) which(is.na(x)))))
```

In this command, three functions are used: `lapply`, `unlist`, and `unique`. The first function, (`lapply()`) applies the function declared as an argument to each column and returns a list whose i^{th} element is a vector containing the indices of the elements which have missing values in column i. The `unlist()` function turns that list into a vector. Finally, the `unique()` function returns a data frame like the one passed as an argument but with duplicate rows removed. The results are as follows:

```
> unique (unlist (lapply (SampleData, function(x) which(is.na(x)))))
[1]  3 12  2  7  9 12
```

The 3, 12, 2, 7, 9, and 12 rows contain missing values.

Once we have detected, what do we do with missing values? Of course, the procedure we have followed so far aims to remove missing values. So let's find out the techniques at our disposal to do so. To begin, we can analyze the `na.omit()` function. This function returns the object with incomplete cases removed. The following is an example of this function at work:

```
SampleDataMinor<-na.omit(SampleData)
summary(SampleDataMinor)
```

The results are as follows:

```
> summary(SampleDataMinor)
      name     gender        age               right            wrong
 Ava    :1    :0     Min.   : 15.00    Min.   : 5.00    Min.   : 2.00
 Elijah :1    F:3    1st Qu.: 19.50    1st Qu.:29.00    1st Qu.:30.00
 Emma   :1    M:4    Median : 22.00    Median :54.00    Median :46.00
 Lucas  :1           Mean   : 32.86    Mean   :50.71    Mean   :49.29
 Mason  :1           3rd Qu.: 27.00    3rd Qu.:70.00    3rd Qu.:71.00
 Mia    :1           Max.   :100.00    Max.   :98.00    Max.   :95.00
 (Other):1
```

As we can see, there is no missing data in the data frame. The `na.omit()` function drops out any rows with missing values anywhere in them and forgets them forever. What do I mean by that? To understand this, we consider a variation of this function: `na.exclude`. The function `na.exclude` differs from `na.omit` only in the class of the `na.action` attribute of the result, which is `exclude`. When `na.exclude` is used, the residuals and predictions are padded to the correct length by inserting NA for cases omitted by `na.exclude`.

In the previous chapters, we have seen several modeling functions. These functions provide the `na.action` attribute we just mentioned. This is actually a function that specifies what to do when you encounter an NA. When the modeling function meets NA, it recalls the function for the treatment of missing values contained in `na.action`. These functions replace the original dataset from a new dataset where NA have been changed. By default, `na.action` provides the `na.omit` function, which, as mentioned, removes all lines with missing values. When `na.exclude` is provided, then it excludes all lines with missing values but keeps track of where they were. An additional alternative is `na.action = na.fail`, which instead just stops when it encounters missing values.

Treatment of NaN values

Previously we saw that the `is.na()` function is able to detect both NA and NaN values. In the previous procedure, we removed both. If we analyze the original version of the data frame we can still see some NaN values:

```
> SampleData
      name gender  age right wrong
1     Emma      F   24    80    20
2     Liam      M  -19    NA    47
3    Olivia          32    75    25
4     Noah      M   15    60    40
5      Ava      F   18    45    55
6    Mason      M   21    54    46
7 Isabella      F   28   -19    85
8    Lucas      M   30    13    87
9   Sophia      F   26   NaN    30
10   Elijah     M  100    98     2
11      Mia      F   22     5    95
12   Oliver      M   NA   NaN    21
```

The presence of the `NaN` value is evident. What does this symbol represent? `NaN` is a symbol indicating that the result of a numeric operation was executed on invalid operands and therefore did not produce any result. Examples are the division by zero or the square root of a negative number. `NaN` values are associated only with numeric observations.

So, `NaN` is the unintended result of attempting a calculation that's impossible to perform with the specified values. To detect `NaN` values, we can use the `is.nan()` function that tests if a numeric value is `NaN`. This function returns a logical vector the same length as its argument, with `TRUE` for `NaN` values and `FALSE` for non-NaN. We apply this function to the data frame so far used:

```
> is.nan(SampleData$right)</strong>
 [1] FALSE FALSE FALSE FALSE FALSE FALSE FALSE FALSE  TRUE FALSE FALSE  TRUE
```

Two values of `TRUE` are returned. As we have seen in the previous section, to remove lines containing `NaN` values we can use the `na.omit()` function.

Finding outliers in data

Outliers are the values that, compared to others, are particularly extreme (a value clearly distant from the other available observations.). Outliers are a problem because they tend to distort data analysis results, in particular in descriptive statistics and correlations. These should be identified in the data cleaning phase, but can also be dealt in the next step of data analysis. Outliers can be univariate when they have an extreme value for a single variable, or multivariate when they have an unusual combination of values on a number of variables.

Outliers are the extreme values of a distribution that are characterized by being extremely high or extremely low compared to the rest of the distribution, and thus representing isolated cases with respect to the rest of the distribution.

There are different methods to detect the outliers, we will use the Tukey's method which uses the **interquartile range (IQR)** range approach. This method is not dependent on distribution of data, and ignores the mean and standard deviation, which are influenced by the outliers.

As said before, to determine the outlier values refer to the IQR given by the difference between the third and the first quartile, that is, the amplitude of the range within which it falls the *50* percent of the observations that occupy the central positions in the ordered series of data. Its outlier, a value with positive deviation from the third quartile greater than *1.5* times the IQR or, symmetrically, a value with a negative deviation from the first quartile (in absolute value) greater than *1.5* times the IOR.

To identify a possible outlier, the `boxplot()` function can be used. Generally, the `boxplot()` function is used to plot a boxplot. A boxplot, also referred to as a whiskers chart, is a graphical representation used to describe the distribution of a sample by simple dispersion and position indexes. A boxplot can be represented, either horizontally or vertically, by means of a rectangular partition divided by two segments. The rectangle (box) is delimited by the first quartile (25th percentile) and the third quartile (75th percentile), and divided by the median (50th percentile), as shown in the following figure:

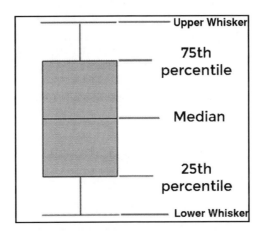

Segments outside the box (whiskers) represent the lower and the upper whiskers. By default, the whiskers will extend up to 1.5 times the interquartile range from the top (bottom) of the box to the furthest datum within that distance. In this way, the four equally populated ranges delineated by quartiles are graphically represented. To plot a boxplot in R, we can use the `boxplot()` function that produce box-and-whisker plot(s) of the given (grouped) values:

```
boxplot(SampleDataMinor)
```

As already mentioned, the `SampleDataMinor` data frame contains five variables as follows:

- `name`: Name
- `gender`: Sex
- `age`: Age
- `right`: Percentage of right answers
- `wrong`: Percentage of wrong answers

The first two are factors and only the last three are numerics. In the following figure, five boxplots are shown, one for each variable contained in the dataset (`SampleDataMinor`):

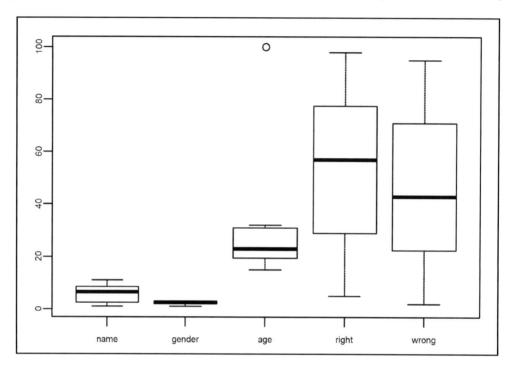

From a first look at the chart, it's clear that something weird was detected for the `age` variable. In fact, in this case, besides the typical whiskers diagrams, there is a circle which indicates a possible outlier. Let's look at this aspect by accessing the statistics made available by the `boxplot` function:

```
boxplot.stats(SampleDataMinor$age)
```

The `boxplot.stats()` function returns a matrix: each column contains the extreme of the lower whisker, the lower hinge, the median, the upper hinge and the extreme of the upper whisker for one plot. If all the inputs have the same class attribute, so will this component. The results are as follows:

```
> boxplot.stats(SampleDataMinor$age)
$stats
[1] 15.0 19.5 22.0 27.0 30.0
$n
[1] 7
$conf
```

```
[1] 17.52112 26.47888
$out
[1] 100
```

The out column contains the values of any data points which lie beyond the extremes of the whiskers, in our case there is only one element (100). This is our outlier.

In some cases, you may be tempted to remove outliers that are influential or have an excessive impact on the synthesis measures you want to consider (such as the mean, or the linear correlation coefficient). However, this way of proceeding is not always cautious, unless the reasons for an abnormal observation have been identified and it can be assumed that it can be excluded from the analysis, as it is inconsistent with the reference collective. In other cases, it is not sensible to remove abnormal observations.

After all, a question arises spontaneously: why is outliers detection important? Because, it can drastically change the fit estimates and predictions.

Treating or altering the outliers in a dataset is not a standard operating procedure. However, it is essential to understand their impact on your predictive models. It is left to the best judgment of the researcher to decide whether treating outliers is necessary and how to go about it. Let me illustrate this using the SellingPrinters.csv dataset which we have used before.

To understand the implications of outliers better, I am going to compare the fit of a simple linear regression model on SellingPrinters dataset, with and without outliers. In order to distinguish the effect clearly, I manually introduce extreme values to the original dataset. Then, I built the model on both the datasets.

In Chapter 2, *Basic Concepts – Simple Linear Regression*, we solved a real case: a company at the launch of a new printer model wants to analyze sales at a number of stores to determine the best price. In the dataset named SellingPrinters.csv, are stored the sales of the product in the last month and the sale price for these stores.

To begin, load the dataset into R, to do this we will use the following code:

```
setwd ("c://R")
Printers1=read.csv ("SellingPrinters.csv", header=TRUE, sep=";")
```

First, `setwd(c://R)` is used to set the working directory to R contained in the root folder. Then we used the `read.csv()` function that reads a file in table format and creates a data frame from it, with cases corresponding to rows and variables to columns in the file. To remember what it contains, let's look at the internal structure of the imported data frame:

```
str(Printers1)
> str(Printers1)
'data.frame':  20 obs. of  3 variables:
 $ X         : Factor w/ 20 levels "Store1","Store10",..: 1 12 14 15 16 17
18 19 20 2 ...
 $ Sold.Items: int  100 150 130 140 110 160 115 135 120 155 ...
 $ Price     : int  60 43 48 45 55 40 53 47 52 42 ...
```

Three variables are stored:

- `X`: Store
- `Sold.Items`: Number of printers sold
- `Price`: Price of the printers

At this point, we will display some data statistics using the `summary()` function. We will then need to compare the two data frames:

```
summary(Printers1)
> summary(Printers1)
       X            Sold.Items          Price
 Store1 : 1    Min.   :100.0    Min.    :39.0
 Store10: 1    1st Qu.:115.0    1st Qu.:42.0
 Store11: 1    Median :132.5    Median :46.5
 Store12: 1    Mean   :132.2    Mean    :47.1
 Store13: 1    3rd Qu.:150.0    3rd Qu.:52.0
 Store14: 1    Max.   :160.0    Max.    :60.0
 (Other):14
```

Let's now create a linear regression model for the two variables: `Sold.Items`, `Price`:

```
LinMod1 <- lm( Printers1$Price ~ Printers1$Sold.Items,data=Printers1)
```

The result model is shown in the following:

```
> LinMod1
Call:
lm(formula = Printers1$Price ~ Printers1$Sold.Items, data = Printers1)
Coefficients:
          (Intercept)    Printers1$Sold.Items
             85.9565                  -0.2939
```

Now we just introduce two outliers:

```
PrintersOutlier<-
data.frame(X=c("Store21","Store22"),Sold.Items=c(210,50),Price=c(47,50))
```

So, we introduced two new stores (Store21 and Store22). These are two special stores. The first, Store21, recorded a large number of sales at an average price. The particular success is due to a contest associated with the sale of printers. The second, Store22, has recorded a low number of sales, again offering an average price. The particular failure is due to the bad character of the seller who mistreats the customers. Add these data to the original ones:

```
Printers2 <- rbind(Printers1,PrintersOutlier)
```

Let's now create a linear regression model for the second dataset:

```
LinMod2 <- lm( Printers2$Price ~ Printers2$Sold.Items,data=Printers2)
```

The resulting model is shown in the following:

```
> LinMod2
Call:
lm(formula = Printers2$Price ~ Printers2$Sold.Items, data = Printers2)
Coefficients:
          (Intercept)    Printers2$Sold.Items
               62.538                  -0.116
```

Only two outliers have changed the model. But to better understand the differences, we can see on a chart, the original data and the regression line:

```
par(mfrow=c(1, 2))
plot(Printers1$Sold.Items,Printers1$Price,xlim=c(48, 212), ylim=c(37, 62))
abline(LinMod1,lwd = 10)
plot(Printers2$Sold.Items,Printers2$Price,xlim=c(48, 212), ylim=c(37, 62))
abline(LinMod2,lwd = 10)
```

The plots of the two models are shown in the following figure (without outliers to the left, and with outliers to the right):

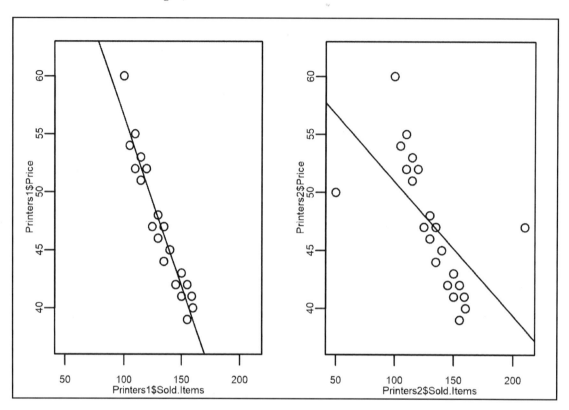

As can be seen, even just two outliers have created a lot of damage. It is clear that the regression line changes considerably: by comparing the two figures the slope is clearly different. But the most important thing is that in the figure to the right (with outliers), now the regression line is unable to fit the data. All this proves that the treatment of outliers is of crucial importance in order to obtain a regression model that fits the data very well. The performance of regression analysis methods, in practice, also depends on the quality of the data.

Scale of features

Data scaling is a preprocessing technique usually employed before feature selection and classification. Many artificial intelligence-based systems use features that are generated by many different feature extraction algorithms, with different kinds of sources. These features may have different dynamic ranges. Popular distance measures, for example the Euclidean distance, implicitly assign more weighting to features with large ranges than those with small ranges. Feature scaling is thus required to approximately equalize ranges of the features and make them have approximately the same effect in the computation of similarity.

In addition, in several data mining applications with huge numbers of features with large dynamic ranges, feature scaling may improve the performance of the fitting model. However, the appropriate choice of these techniques is an important issue, since applying scaling on the input could change the structure of data and thereby affect the outcome of multivariate analysis used in data mining.

So far we have worked on the data to correct any errors or omissions. We can say that at this point all variables contained in the dataset are complete with consistent data. What about different variables characterized by different ranges and units? There can be variables in a data frame where values for one feature could range between *1–10* and values for other feature could range from *1–1000*.

In data frames like these, owing to mere greater numeric range, the impact on response variables by the feature having greater numeric range could be more than the one having less numeric range, and this could, in turn, impact prediction accuracy. Our goal is to improve predictive accuracy and not allow a particular feature to impact the prediction due to a large numeric value range. Thus, we may need to scale values under different features such that they fall under a common range. Through this statistical procedure, it is possible to compare identical variables belonging to different distributions, but also different variables, or variables expressed in different units. Two methods are usually well known for rescaling data: normalization, and standardization.

 Remember, it is good practice to rescale the data before training a regression algorithm. With rescaling, data units are eliminated, allowing you to easily compare data from different locations.

Min–max normalization

Min-max normalization, (usually called **feature scaling**) performs a linear transformation on the original data. This technique gets all the scaled data in the range *[0,1]*. The formula to achieve this is the following:

$$x_{scaled} = \frac{x - x_{min}}{x_{max} - x_{min}}$$

Min-max normalization preserves the relationships among the original data values. The cost of having this bounded range is that we will end up with smaller standard deviations, which can suppress the effect of outliers.

To normalize the data, we use the `scale()` function, which is a generic function whose default method centers and/or scales the columns of a numeric matrix. The function syntax is as follows:

```
scale(x, center, scale)
```

Here:

- x: This is a numeric matrix
- center: This is either a logical value or a numeric vector of length equal to the number of columns of x
- scale: This is either a logical value or a numeric vector of length equal to the number of columns of x

The value of `center` determines how column centering is performed. If `center` is a numeric vector with a length equal to the number of columns of x, then each column of x has the corresponding value from center subtracted from it.

The value of `scale` determines how column scaling is performed (after centering). If `scale` is a numeric vector with length equal to the number of columns of x, then each column of x is divided by the corresponding value from `scale`.

That being said, to run the min-max normalization using the `scale()` function, just set the arguments as follows:

- center = xmin
- scale = xmax - xmin

To better understand how to perform a min-max normalization by `scale()` function, just analyze an example. We will use a dataset contained in the R `datasets` package. I refer to the dataset called `airquality`. These are the daily readings of the following air quality values for May 1, 1973 (a Tuesday) to September 30, 1973:

- `Ozone`: Mean ozone in parts per billion from *1300* to *1500* hours at Roosevelt Island
- `Solar.R`: Solar radiation in Langleys in the frequency band *4000–7700* Angstroms from *0800* to *1200* hours at Central Park
- `Wind`: Average wind speed in miles per hour at *0700* and *1000* hours at LaGuardia Airport
- `Temp`: Maximum daily temperature in degrees Fahrenheit at La Guardia Airport

The data was obtained from the New York State Department of Conservation (ozone data) and the **National Weather Service (NWS)** (meteorological data).

A data frame consists of *154* observations on *6* variables.

Name	Type	Units
Ozone	numeric	ppb
Solar.R	numeric	lang
Wind	numeric	mph
Temp	numeric	degrees F
Month	numeric	1--12
Day	numeric	1--31

As can be seen, the six variables are characterized by different units of measurement.

To begin loading the data we use:

```
Airquality<-as.data.frame(airquality)
```

To display the range of values of the six variables, we use the `summary` function that returns a series of statistical calculations on the data:

```
summary(Airquality)
```

The results are shown in the following figure:

```
> summary(Airquality)
     Ozone            Solar.R           Wind            Temp           Month            Day
 Min.   :  1.00   Min.   :  7.0   Min.   : 1.700   Min.   :56.00   Min.   :5.000   Min.   : 1.0
 1st Qu.: 18.00   1st Qu.:115.8   1st Qu.: 7.400   1st Qu.:72.00   1st Qu.:6.000   1st Qu.: 8.0
 Median : 31.50   Median :205.0   Median : 9.700   Median :79.00   Median :7.000   Median :16.0
 Mean   : 42.13   Mean   :185.9   Mean   : 9.958   Mean   :77.88   Mean   :6.993   Mean   :15.8
 3rd Qu.: 63.25   3rd Qu.:258.8   3rd Qu.:11.500   3rd Qu.:85.00   3rd Qu.:8.000   3rd Qu.:23.0
 Max.   :168.00   Max.   :334.0   Max.   :20.700   Max.   :97.00   Max.   :9.000   Max.   :31.0
 NA's   :37       NA's   :7
```

There are `na`, before we proceed we have to remove them:

```
Airquality<-na.omit(Airquality)
```

As you can see, the variables ranges are very varied. We want to eliminate this feature through min-max normalization. As stated earlier, in order to apply this procedure we have to calculate the minimum and maximum for each variable. To do this, we use the `apply()` function. This function returns a vector or an array or a list of values obtained by applying a function to margins of an array or matrix. Let's understand the meaning of the arguments used:

```
max_data <- apply(Airquality, 2, max)
min_data <- apply(Airquality, 2, min)
```

The first argument of the `apply()` function specifies the dataset to apply the function, in our case, the dataset named `Airquality`. The second argument must contain a vector giving the subscripts which the function will be applied over. In our case, one indicates rows and two indicates columns. The third argument must contain the function to be applied; in our case, the `max()` and `min()` function. As said before, to normalize the data, we use the `scale` function:

```
data_scaled1 <- scale(Airquality,center = min_data,
                  scale = max_data - min_data)
```

Here, `center` and `scale` arguments were set as described previously when we analyzed the formula. To analyze the results, let's apply the `summary()` function again but this time on the scaled data (`data_scaled1`):

```
summary(data_scaled1)
```

The results are shown in the following figure:

```
> summary(data_scaled)
      Ozone             Solar.R            Wind             Temp             Month             Day
 Min.   :0.0000    Min.    :0.0000   Min.   :0.0000   Min.   :0.0000   Min.    :0.0000   Min.    :0.0000
 1st Qu.:0.1018    1st Qu.:0.3257    1st Qu.:0.2772   1st Qu.:0.3500   1st Qu.:0.2500    1st Qu.:0.2667
 Median :0.1796    Median :0.6116    Median :0.4022   Median :0.5500   Median :0.5000    Median :0.5000
 Mean   :0.2461    Mean    :0.5437   Mean   :0.4152   Mean   :0.5198   Mean    :0.5541   Mean    :0.4982
 3rd Qu.:0.3653    3rd Qu.:0.7599    3rd Qu.:0.5000   3rd Qu.:0.6875   3rd Qu.:1.0000    3rd Qu.:0.7167
 Max.   :1.0000    Max.    :1.0000   Max.   :1.0000   Max.   :1.0000   Max.    :1.0000   Max.    :1.0000
```

It is apparent that now the data is all between zero and one, this happens for each column of the data frame, then for each variable. The scale differences due to the different units of measurement have therefore been removed.

z score standardization

This technique consists of subtracting the mean of the column to each value in a column, and then dividing the result for the standard deviation of the column. The formula to achieve this is the following:

$$x_{scaled} = \frac{x - mean}{sd}$$

The result of standardization is that the features will be rescaled so that they'll have the properties of a standard normal distribution as follows:

- $\mu=0$
- $\sigma=1$

where μ is the mean and σ is the standard deviation from the mean.

In summary, the z score (also called the **standard score**) represents the number of standard deviations with which the value of an observation point or data is greater than the mean value of what is observed or measured. Values more than the mean have positive z scores, while values less than the mean have negative z scores. The z score is a quantity without dimension, obtained by subtracting the population mean from a single rough score and then dividing the difference for the standard deviation of the population.

Once again, to standardize the data, we will use the `scale()` function. This time the two topics (`center` and `scale`) will be set as follows:

- `center = mean`
- `scale = standard deviation`

To perform a z score standardization by `scale()` function, just analyze an example. We will use the same dataset used for min-max normalization. I refer to datasets called `airquality`, which contains the daily readings of the following air quality values for May 1, 1973 (a Tuesday) to September 30, 1973. As always, we start loading the dataset:

```
Airquality<-as.data.frame(airquality)
```

To display the range of values of the six variables, we use the `summary()` function that returns a series of statistical calculations on the data:

```
summary(Airquality)
```

The results are shown in the following figure:

```
> summary(Airquality)
     Ozone           Solar.R           Wind            Temp           Month            Day
 Min.   :  1.00   Min.   :  7.0   Min.   : 1.700   Min.   :56.00   Min.   :5.000   Min.   : 1.0
 1st Qu.: 18.00   1st Qu.:115.8   1st Qu.: 7.400   1st Qu.:72.00   1st Qu.:6.000   1st Qu.: 8.0
 Median : 31.50   Median :205.0   Median : 9.700   Median :79.00   Median :7.000   Median :16.0
 Mean   : 42.13   Mean   :185.9   Mean   : 9.958   Mean   :77.88   Mean   :6.993   Mean   :15.8
 3rd Qu.: 63.25   3rd Qu.:258.8   3rd Qu.:11.500   3rd Qu.:85.00   3rd Qu.:8.000   3rd Qu.:23.0
 Max.   :168.00   Max.   :334.0   Max.   :20.700   Max.   :97.00   Max.   :9.000   Max.   :31.0
 NA's   :37       NA's   :7
```

There are `na`, before we proceed we have to remove them:

```
Airquality<-na.omit(Airquality)
```

Standardizing the features so that they are centered around zero with a standard deviation of one is not only important if we are comparing measurements that have different units, but it is also a general requirement for many machine learning algorithms. Now, we need to compute the mean and standard deviation. To notice that the scale() function do this standardizing by default (without having to mention center and scale parameters). Another time we can use the `apply()` function as follows:

```
mean_data <- apply(Airquality, 2, mean)
sd_data <- apply(Airquality, 2, sd)
```

Just use the `scale()` function:

```
data_scaled2 <- scale(Airquality,center = mean_data,
                      scale = sd_data)
```

To display the results, we will use the `summary()` function:

```
summary(data_scaled2)
```

The results are shown in the following figure:

```
> summary(data_scaled2)
     Ozone              Solar.R             Wind               Temp              Month               Day
 Min.   :-1.2351    Min.    :-1.9506    Min.   :-2.14735    Min.   :-2.1818    Min.    :-1.5041    Min.    :-1.716505
 1st Qu.:-0.7242    1st Qu.:-0.7822    1st Qu.:-0.71384    1st Qu.:-0.7128    1st Qu.:-0.8254    1st Qu.:-0.797725
 Median :-0.3335    Median : 0.2435    Median :-0.06736    Median : 0.1267    Median :-0.1467    Median : 0.006208
 Mean   : 0.0000    Mean    : 0.0000    Mean   : 0.00000    Mean   : 0.0000    Mean    : 0.0000    Mean    : 0.000000
 3rd Qu.: 0.5981    3rd Qu.: 0.7756    3rd Qu.: 0.43859    3rd Qu.: 0.7038    3rd Qu.: 1.2106    3rd Qu.: 0.752717
 Max.   : 3.7835    Max.    : 1.6368    Max.   : 3.02452    Max.   : 2.0155    Max.    : 1.2106    Max.    : 1.728921
```

According to the assumptions, all variables have `mean = 0`. Let's verify that they also have `sd = 1`:

```
SDdata_scaled2<-apply(data_scaled2,2,sd)
```

The results are as follows:

```
> SDdata_scaled2
  Ozone Solar.R    Wind    Temp   Month     Day
      1       1       1       1       1       1
```

So, we have verified that all six variables have a standard deviation of 1.

Discretization in R

Discretization techniques can be used to convert continuous attributes to nominal attributes. In this way, the number of values for a given continuous attribute is reduced by dividing the attribute into a range of values. Actual data values are replaced with interval value labels.

Machine-learning algorithms are typically recursive; to process large amounts of data a great deal of time is spent to sort the data at every step. It is clear that the smaller the number of distinct values to be ordered, the faster these methods should be. That is why these techniques are particularly beneficial.

In discretization, the raw values of a numeric attribute are replaced by labels or conceptual labels. For example, the continuous value of the measured temperature in one day can be divided into three bins (*0-10, 11-20, 21-30*) or can be divided into the three conceptual labels (low, medium, high).

There are several discretization techniques including the following:

- **Data discretization by binning**: This is a technique based on a specified number of bins
- **Data discretization by histogram analysis**: In this technique, a histogram partitions the values of an attribute into disjoint ranges called buckets or bins

Data discretization by binning

Binning is based on a specified number of bins. These methods are used as discretization methods for data reduction and concept hierarchy generation. For example, attribute values can be discretized by distributing the values into bin and replacing each bin by the mean bin value or bin median value. These techniques can be applied recursively to the resulting partitions to generate concept hierarchies. Binning is sensitive to the user-specified number of bins, as well as the presence of outliers.

To perform data discretization by binning we will use the `discretize()` function contained in the `arule` package. This function implements several basic unsupervized methods to convert continuous variables into a categorical variables (factor) suitable for association rule mining. The general form of the function is as follows:

```
discretize(x, method="interval", categories = 3, labels = NULL,
                           ordered=FALSE, onlycuts=FALSE, ...)
```

The arguments with a brief explanation are listed in the following table:

Argument	Brief description
x	A numeric vector (continuous variable).
method	Discretization method. Available are: `interval` (equal interval width), `frequency` (equal frequency), `cluster` (k-means clustering) and `fixed` (categories specifies interval boundaries).
categories	Number of categories or a vector with boundaries (all values outside the boundaries will be set to NA).

labels	Names for categories (character vector).
ordered	Return a factor with ordered levels (logical).
onlycuts	Return only computed interval boundaries (logical).
...	For method cluster further arguments are passed on to k-means.

To better understand how to perform a data discretization by binning by discretize() function, just analyze an example. We will use a dataset contained in the R datasets package. I refer to a dataset called Nile. This dataset contains measurements of the annual flow of the river Nile at Aswan (formerly Assuan), 1871–1970, in *10^8 m^3*, with apparent changepoint near 1898. This is a time series of length 100.

To begin loading the data we use:

```
Nile<-as.data.frame(Nile)
```

To display the range of values of the only one variable we use the summary() function that returns a series of statistical calculations on the data:

```
summary(Nile)
```

The results are shown in the following:

```
> summary(Nile)
       x

 Min.    : 456.0
 1st Qu.: 798.5
 Median : 893.5
 Mean    : 919.4
 3rd Qu.:1032.5
 Max.    :1370.0
```

As we can see, the Nile flow in 100 years has undergone considerable fluctuations. We see everything in a chart:

```
plot(Nile)
```

The plots of the flow of the river Nile at Aswan from 1871 to 1970 are shown in the following figure:

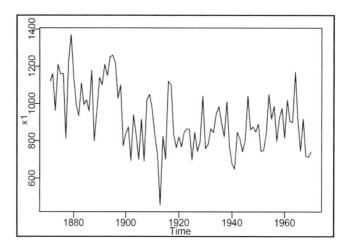

We have confirmed the fluctuation of water flow in the Nile over time. We can now proceed to discretization. First, we must install the `arule` package.

 Remember, to install a library that is not present in the initial distribution of R, you must use the `install.package` function. This is the main function to install packages. It takes a vector of names and a destination library, downloads the packages from the repositories and installs them.

Then, we will load the library through the `library` command:

```
library(arule)
```

We decide to transform the only continuous variable contained in the data frame into a categorical three bin variable (`Low`, `Med`, `High`):

```
NileDiscr<-discretize(Nile$x, method="interval", categories = 3,
               labels = c("Low","Med","High"),
               ordered=FALSE, onlycuts=FALSE)
```

Let's see the results:

```
summary(NileDiscr)
> summary(NileDiscr)
 Low  Med High
  18   61   21
```

Only three values are returned with the occurrences frequency for each of them. The interval boundaries are shown in the following:

```
456.0000  760.6667 1065.3333 1370.0000
```

These values will serve as an example to compare the two techniques.

Data discretization by histogram analysis

A histogram is a graphical representation of a numerical distribution, showing the shape of a distribution. It consists of adjacent rectangles (bins), whose bases are aligned on an axis oriented and equipped with a unit of measure (the axis assumes the unit of measure of the character and can be safely understood as the *x* axis). The adjacency of the rectangles reflects the continuity of the character. Each rectangle has a base length equal to the width of the corresponding class; the height is calculated as a frequency density, so it is equal to the ratio between the frequencies (absolute) associated with the class and the amplitude of the class.

Thus, in a histogram, the values are partitioned according to an attribute. You can use different partitioning rules to define histograms. For example, the histogram with the same width, subdivides the values into equal size partitions or ranges, and an even frequency histogram divides the values so that each partition contains the same number of data. The histogram analysis algorithm can be applied recursively to each partition to automatically generate a hierarchy of multilevel concepts, with the procedure ending once a certain number of conceptual levels have been reached.

To perform data discretization by histogram analysis, we will use the hist() function that computes a histogram of the given data values. The function provides a number of arguments, so to view the documentation type the following command:

```
?hist
```

R's default with equi-spaced breaks (also the default) is to plot the counts in the cells defined by breaks. Thus, the height of a rectangle is proportional to the number of points falling into the cell, as is the area provided the breaks are equally spaced. The default with non-equi-spaced breaks is to give a plot of area one, in which the area of the rectangles is the fraction of the data points falling in the cells.

Now, we use the same dataset used for data discretization by the binning example. That is the `Nile` dataset contained in the `datasets` package.

To begin loading the data:

```
Nile<-as.data.frame(Nile)
```

To display the range of values of the only one variable, we use the `summary()` function that returns a series of statistical calculations on the data:

```
summary(Nile)
```

The results are shown in the following:

```
> summary(Nile)
       x
 Min.   : 456.0
 1st Qu.: 798.5
 Median : 893.5
 Mean   : 919.4
 3rd Qu.:1032.5
 Max.   :1370.0
```

We use the `hist()` function as follows:

```
HistNile<-hist(Nile$x, breaks =3)
```

The histogram of the flow of the river Nile at Aswan from 1871 to 1970 is shown in the following figure:

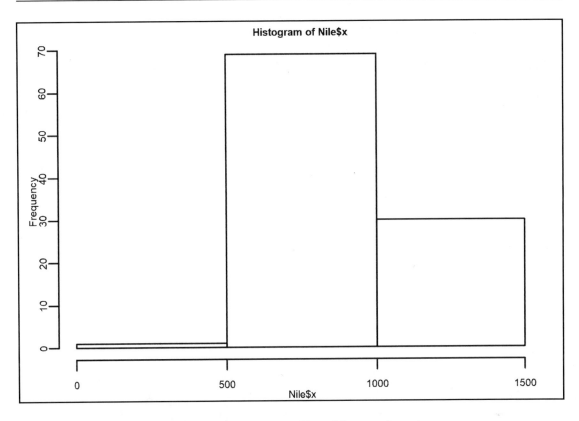

But an object of class `histogram` also returns a list with components:

`breaks`	The *n+1* cell boundaries (=*breaks* if that was a vector). These are the nominal breaks, not with the boundary fuzz.
`counts`	*n* integers; for each cell, the number of *x[]* inside.
`density`	Values $f^\wedge(x[i])$, as estimated density values. If *all(diff(breaks)) == 1)*, they are the relative frequencies *counts/n* and in general satisfy *sum[i; $f^\wedge(x[i])$ (b[i+1]-b[i])] = 1*, where *b[i] =* breaks[i].
`mids`	The *n* cell midpoints.
`xname`	A character string with the actual *x* argument name.
`equidist`	Logical, indicating if the distances between breaks are all the same.

In the following are shown values returned for our analysis:

```
> HistNile
$breaks
[1]     0   500 1000 1500
$counts
[1]    1 69 30
$density
[1] 0.00002 0.00138 0.00060
$mids
[1]    250   750 1250
$xname
[1] "Nile$x"
$equidist
[1] TRUE
attr(,"class")
[1] "histogram"
```

Comparing the results obtained with those obtained with binning, it is possible to notice a difference in the counts. It is easy to see that this is due to a different time division subdivision. Let's try, for example, setting the same intervals for bin:

```
HistNile2<-hist(Nile$x, breaks =c(456,760.67,1065.33,1370))
HistNile2
```

The results are shown in the following:

```
> HistNile2
$breaks
[1]    456.00   760.67 1065.33 1370.00
$counts
[1] 18 61 21
$density
[1] 0.0005908032 0.0020022320 0.0006892704
$mids
[1]    608.335   913.000 1217.665
$xname
[1] "Nile$x"
$equidist
[1] FALSE
attr(,"class")
[1] "histogram"
```

Now the results coincide.

Dimensionality reduction

Dimensionality reduction is the process of converting a set of data with many variables into data with lesser dimensions while ensuring similar information. The aim is to reduce the number of dimensions in a dataset through either feature selection or feature extraction without significant loss of details. Feature selection approaches try to find a subset of the original variables. Feature extraction reduces the dimensionality of the data by transforming it into new features.

Principal Component Analysis

Principal Component Analysis (PCA) generates a new set of variables, among them uncorrelated, called **principal components**; each main component is a linear combination of the original variables. All principal components are orthogonal to each other, so there is no redundant information. The principal components as a whole, constitute an orthogonal basis for the data space. The goal of PCA is to explain the maximum amount of variance with the fewest number of principal components. It is a form of multidimensional scaling. It is a linear transformation of the variables into a lower dimensional space that retains the maximum amount of information about the variables. A principal component is therefore a combination of the original variables after a linear transformation.

In R, PCA is performed by using the `prcomp()` function; it performs a PCA on the given data matrix and returns the results as an object of class `prcomp`. The general syntax of the `prcomp()` function is as follows:

```
prcomp(x, retx = TRUE, center = TRUE, scale. = FALSE,
                tol = NULL, rank. = NULL, ...)
```

The arguments with a brief explanation are listed in the following table:

Argument	Brief description
formula	A formula with no response variable, referring only to numeric variables.
data	An optional data frame containing the variables in the formula. By default, the variables are taken from environment(formula).
subset	An optional vector used to select rows (observations) of the data matrix x.
na.action	A function which indicates what should happen when the data contain NA. The default is set by the na.action setting of options, and is na.fail if that is unset. The factory-fresh default is na.omit.

...	Arguments passed to or from other methods. If x is a formula one might specify `scale` or `tol`.
x	A numeric or complex matrix (or data frame) which provides the data for the PCA.
retx	A logical value indicating whether the rotated variables should be returned.
center	A logical value indicating whether the variables should be shifted to be zero centered. Alternately, a vector of length equal the number of columns of x can be supplied. The value is passed to `scale`.
scale	A logical value indicating whether the variables should be scaled to have unit variance before the analysis takes place. The default is FALSE for consistency with S, but in general, scaling is advisable. Alternatively, a vector of length equal the number of columns of x can be supplied. The value is passed to scale.
tol	A value indicating the magnitude below which components should be omitted. (Components are omitted if their standard deviations are less than or equal to `tol` times the standard deviation of the first component.) With the default null setting, no components are omitted (unless `rank.` is specified less than `min(dim(x))`.). Other settings for `tol` could be `tol = 0` or `tol = sqrt(.Machine$double.eps)`, which would omit essentially constant components.
rank.	Optionally, a number specifying the maximal rank, that is, a maximal number of principal components to be used. Can be set as alternative or in addition to `tol`, useful notably when the desired rank is considerably smaller than the dimensions of the matrix.
object	Object of class inheriting from `prcomp`.
newdata	An optional data frame or matrix in which to look for variables with which to predict. If omitted, the scores are used. If the original fit used a formula or a data frame or a matrix with column names, `newdata` must contain columns with the same names. Otherwise it must contain the same number of columns, to be used in the same order.

The calculation is done by a singular value decomposition of the (centered and possibly scaled) data matrix, not by using Eigen values and Eigen vectors of the covariance matrix. This is generally a preferred method for numerical accuracy. The print method for these objects prints the results in a nice format and the plot method produces a scree plot.

As always, we begin by getting the data to be analyzed.

 To get the data, we draw on the large collection of data available from the UCI Machine Learning Repository at the following link: `http://archive.ics.uci.edu/ml`.

In this study, we use a `seeds` dataset, which contains measurements of the geometrical properties of kernels belonging to three different varieties of wheat. As reported on the site, the examined group comprises kernels belonging to three different varieties of wheat (Kama, Rosa, and Canadian), with *70* elements each, randomly selected for the experiment.

High-quality visualization of the internal kernel structure was detected using a soft X-ray technique. The images were recorded on *13x18* cm X-ray KODAK plates. Studies were conducted using combine-harvested wheat grain originating from experimental fields, explored at the Institute of Agrophysics of the Polish Academy of Sciences in Lublin.

The `seeds` dataset is multivariate, consisting of *210* instances. Seven geometric parameters of the wheat kernel are used as real-valued attributes organizing an instance. These seven attributes are:

- Area, `A`
- Perimeter, `P`
- Compactness, `C = 4*pi*A/P^2`
- Length of kernel
- Width of kernel
- Asymmetry coefficient
- Length of kernel groove

The seeds dataset contains *210* records of three kinds of wheat seed specification; there are *70* points of each kind. To start, we download the data from the UCI Machine Learning Repository and save it in our current folder. The data are contained into dataset named `Seed.csv`.

To begin, load the dataset into R, to do this, we will use the following code:

```
setwd ("c://R")
Seed<-read.csv ("seeds_dataset.csv", header=TRUE, sep="")
```

First, `setwd(c://R)` is used to set the working directory to R contained in the root folder. Then, we used the `read.csv()` function that reads a file in table format and creates a data frame from it, with cases corresponding to rows and variables to columns in the file. To remember what it contains, let's look the internal structure of the imported data frame:

```
str(SeedData)
> str(SeedData)
'data.frame':  209 obs. of  8 variables:
 $ X15.26: num  14.9 14.3 13.8 16.1 14.4 ...
 $ X14.84: num  14.6 14.1 13.9 15 14.2 ...
 $ X0.871: num  0.881 0.905 0.895 0.903 0.895 ...
 $ X5.763: num  5.55 5.29 5.32 5.66 5.39 ...
 $ X3.312: num  3.33 3.34 3.38 3.56 3.31 ...
 $ X2.221: num  1.02 2.7 2.26 1.35 2.46 ...
 $ X5.22 : num  4.96 4.83 4.8 5.17 4.96 ...
 $ X1    : int  1 1 1 1 1 1 1 1 1 ...
```

We must change the variables names:

```
names(SeedData) = c('Area', 'Perimeter', 'Compactness', 'LengthK',
                    'WidthK','AsymCoef','LengthKG','Seeds')
```

To display the range of values of the only one variable, we use the `summary()` function that returns a series of statistical calculations on the data:

```
summary(SeedData)
```

The results are shown in the following figure:

```
> summary(SeedData)
Area             Perimeter        Compactness      LengthK
Min.   :10.59    Min.   :12.41    Min.   :0.8081   Min.   :4.899
1st Qu.:12.26    1st Qu.:13.45    1st Qu.:0.8567   1st Qu.:5.262
Median :14.34    Median :14.29    Median :0.8735   Median :5.520
Mean   :14.85    Mean   :14.56    Mean   :0.8710   Mean   :5.628
3rd Qu.:17.32    3rd Qu.:15.73    3rd Qu.:0.8879   3rd Qu.:5.980
Max.   :21.18    Max.   :17.25    Max.   :0.9183   Max.   :6.675

WidthK           AsymCoef         LengthKG         Seeds
Min.   :2.630    Min.   :0.7651   Min.   :4.519    Min.   :1.000
1st Qu.:2.941    1st Qu.:2.5870   1st Qu.:5.045    1st Qu.:1.000
Median :3.232    Median :3.6000   Median :5.224    Median :2.000
Mean   :3.258    Mean   :3.7073   Mean   :5.409    Mean   :2.005
3rd Qu.:3.562    3rd Qu.:4.7730   3rd Qu.:5.877    3rd Qu.:3.000
Max.   :4.033    Max.   :8.4560   Max.   :6.550    Max.   :3.000
```

The first seven columns contain the measured variables, while the eighth variable is the type of seed. Let's first try to find out whether the variables are related to each other. We can do this using the `pairs()` function to create a matrix of sub-axes containing scatter plots of the columns of a matrix:

```
pairs(SeedData[1:7],cex.labels = 2, font.labels = 2)
```

The scatter plot matrix of the measured variables is shown in the following figure:

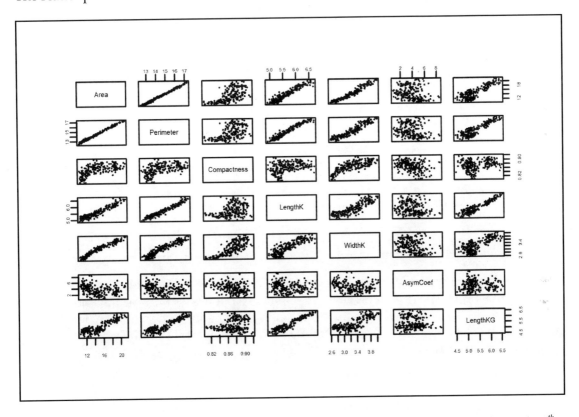

In the last figure, the plots are scatter plots of the columns of a matrix (the subplot in the ith row and j^{th} column of the matrix is a scatter plot of the ith column against the jth column). As we can see in the figure, scatter plot matrices are a great way to roughly determine whether you have a linear correlation between multiple variables. This is particularly helpful in locating specific variables that might have mutual correlations, indicating a possible redundancy of data. In the diagonal are the name of the measured variables. The rest of the plots are scatter plots of the matrix columns. Specifically, each plot is present twice; the plots on the ith row are the same as those in the ith column (mirror image).

From a first analysis of the last figure, you can see several plots showing a linear relationship between the variables. This is the case of the plot showing the relationship between Area and Perimeter, as well as between Perimeter and LengthK, just to name a couple, while no correlation can be found for other pairs of variables. For example, the variable AsymCoef has no correlation with any variable; in fact, the data is distributed throughout the plot area.

This first visual analysis can be confirmed by calculating the linear correlation between the measured variables. We will use the cor() function to return a matrix containing the pairwise linear correlation coefficient (r) between each pair of columns in the matrix given by the user:

```
R<-cor(SeedData[1:7])
```

The results are shown in the following figure:

```
> R
                 Area  Perimeter Compactness    LengthK     WidthK    AsymCoef    LengthKG
Area        1.0000000  0.9943529   0.6083178  0.9500348  0.9707678 -0.22944735  0.86429955
Perimeter   0.9943529  1.0000000   0.5293023  0.9724320  0.9448336 -0.21685286  0.89159222
Compactness 0.6083178  0.5293023   1.0000000  0.3679965  0.7616711 -0.33224447  0.22690481
LengthK     0.9500348  0.9724320   0.3679965  1.0000000  0.8604405 -0.17056196  0.93389992
WidthK      0.9707678  0.9448336   0.7616711  0.8604405  1.0000000 -0.25798121  0.74969146
AsymCoef   -0.2294474 -0.2168529  -0.3322445 -0.1705620 -0.2579812  1.00000000 -0.01292354
LengthKG    0.8642996  0.8915922   0.2269048  0.9338999  0.7496915 -0.01292354  1.00000000
```

The correlation coefficient has to be between –1.0 and 1.0 (*0= no correlation; -1/1=high negative/positive correlation*). What is suggested in the last figure is confirmed by the preceding table. To better understand the concept of correlation, we analyze in detail the first row of plots shown in the last figure; for each of them, we provide the value of the newly calculated correlation coefficient, as shown in the following figure:

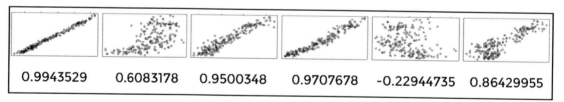

| 0.9943529 | 0.6083178 | 0.9500348 | 0.9707678 | -0.22944735 | 0.86429955 |

From the last figure, we can understand a lot:

- In the first plot to the left, the data points are placed on a straight line, showing a correlation of nearly +1, as confirmed by the correlation coefficient (**0.9943529**).
- In the second plot, the data shows an increasing trend but is less grouped on the straight line, indicating a moderate linear relationship (**0.6083178**).
- In the third plot, the data is again placed on a straight line showing a correlation of nearly +1, but to a lesser extent than the first plot, as confirmed by the correlation coefficient (**0.9500348**).
- A similar thing happens for the fourth plot (**0.9707678**).
- The fifth plot, however, shows a different trend than the ones seen so far. In it, the trend is decreasing (r is negative) and the data is extremely scattered. Indeed, the correlation coefficient is close to zero (**-0.22944735**).
- Finally, the sixth plot shows a strong uphill (positive) linear relationship (**0.86429955**).

You may ask why we must analyze both the graphs and the coefficients. In some cases, the plots tell us what r does not. Indeed, if the scatter plot doesn't indicate there's at least somewhat of a linear relationship, the correlation calculation doesn't mean much. Then, two things can happen:

- If no relationship at all exists, calculating the correlation doesn't make sense, Because correlation only applies to linear relationships
- If a strong relationship exists but it's not linear, the correlation may be misleading, because in some cases a strong curved relationship exists

That's why it's critical to examine the scatter plot. As we can see in the R matrix, the correlation among some variables is as high as *0.85*. This means that there is a good linear correlation between some variables, so there is some data redundancy in the data matrix measured. This means it is possible to reduce dimensionality without losing large amounts of information. PCA constructs new independent variables that are linear combinations of the original variables. It's time to run PCA:

```
PCAObj<-prcomp(SeedData[1:7])
```

The `prcomp()` function returns an object of class `prcomp`, which has some methods available. The `print` method returns the standard deviation of each of the seven PCs, and their rotation (or loadings), which are the coefficients of the linear combinations of the continuous variables. Let's see what the `print` method returns:

```
print(PCAObj)
```

The results are shown in the following figure:

```
> print(PCAObj)
Standard deviations (1, .., p=7):
[1] 3.292885365 1.459447704 0.271984920 0.112900389 0.052524599 0.039707693 0.005458657

Rotation (n x k) = (7 x 7):
                  PC1          PC2         PC3         PC4          PC5          PC6          PC7
Area        -0.884290165  0.100244681  0.26466763 -0.19919292  0.137171430 -0.280701799 -0.025409348
Perimeter   -0.395405729  0.056600920 -0.28288632  0.57948700 -0.573925893  0.301484220  0.065856820
Compactness -0.004311869 -0.002919315  0.05906820 -0.05794088  0.052887064  0.045206902  0.994125738
LengthK     -0.128533090  0.030852285 -0.40049920  0.43386023  0.787784068  0.115270049  0.001464877
WidthK      -0.111065346  0.002260619  0.31934700 -0.23556118  0.142896269  0.896170038 -0.081533559
AsymCoef     0.127102112  0.989502046  0.06414376  0.02452927  0.001566863 -0.003299595  0.001142113
LengthKG    -0.129055836  0.081655029 -0.76153843 -0.61386838 -0.089277603  0.108863647  0.008949347
```

Basically, the number of principal components in rotation is equal to number of variables in the dataset. The rotation matrix columns contain the Eigen vectors. The rows of the rotation matrix contain the coefficients for the first seven variables contained in the data frame, and its columns correspond to seven principal components. Each column of the rotation matrix contains coefficients for one principal component, and the columns are in descending order of component variance. Each column contains coefficients that determine the linear combination of the starting variables that represent the information in the new dimensional space.

A generic principal component is defined as a linear combination of the original variables p weighed for a vector u. The first principal component is the linear combination of p variables with higher variance; the second is the linear combination of p variables with an immediately lower variance, subject to the constraint of being orthogonal to the previous component; and so on. For example, the first principal component is represented by the following equation:

```
PC1 = -0.8843* Area - 0.3954 * Perimeter - 0.0043 * Compactness - 0.1285 *
LengthK - 0.1110 * WidthK + 0.1271 * AsymCoef - 0.1290 * LengthKG
```

There are as many principal components as there are observed variables, and each one is obtained as a linear combination at maximum variance under the non-correlation constraint with all the previous ones. Now we plot the scree plot. A scree plot displays the explained variance associated with a principal component in descending order versus the number of the principal component.

```
plot(PCAObj)
```

We can use scree plots in PCA to visually assess which components explain most of the variability in the data, as shown in the following figure:

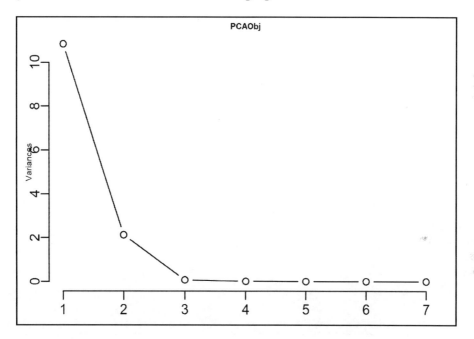

Generally, we extract the components on the steep slope. The components on the shallow slope contribute little to the solution. The last big drop occurs between the second and third components, so we choose the first two components.

To better understand this choice, we can make a scree plot of the percent variability explained by the first two principal component. The percent variability explained is returned in the explained variables from the summary() function:

```
SumPCAObj<-summary(PCAObj)
> SumPCAObj
Importance of components:
                        PC1     PC2     PC3     PC4     PC5
```

```
Standard deviation      3.293 1.459 0.27198 0.11290 0.05252
Proportion of Variance 0.830 0.163 0.00566 0.00098 0.00021
Cumulative Proportion  0.830 0.993 0.99869 0.99967 0.99988
                        PC6       PC7
Standard deviation      0.03971 0.005459
Proportion of Variance 0.00012 0.000000
Cumulative Proportion  1.00000 1.000000
```

Now we plot the proportion of variance:

```
ScreePlot <- barplot(SumPCAObj$importance[2,]*100,
                             ylim = c(0, 100))
lines(x = ScreePlot, y = SumPCAObj$importance[3,]*100)
points(x = ScreePlot, y = SumPCAObj$importance[3,]*100)
```

The bar plot of the proportion of variance by each principal component is shown in the following figure:

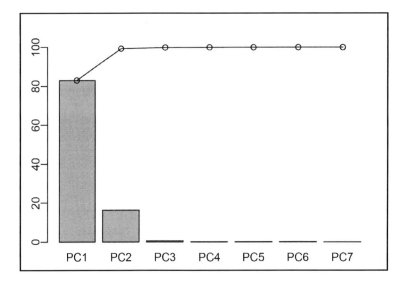

In the previous figure, there are two pieces of information; the bar plot shows the proportion of variance for each principal component, while the upper line shows the cumulative variance explained by the components. An analysis of figure confirms the choice made earlier, since the first two main components offer more than *99* percent of the explained variance.

Finally, we just have to visualize both the principal component coefficients for each variable and the principal component scores for each observation in a single plot. This type of plot is named `biplot`:

```
biplot(PCAObj,scale=0, cex=1.3)
```

Biplots are a type of exploration plot used to simultaneously display graphic information on the samples and variables of a data matrix. Samples are displayed as points, while variables are displayed as vectors. In the following figure, a biplot of the principal component coefficients for each variable and principal component scores for each observation is shown:

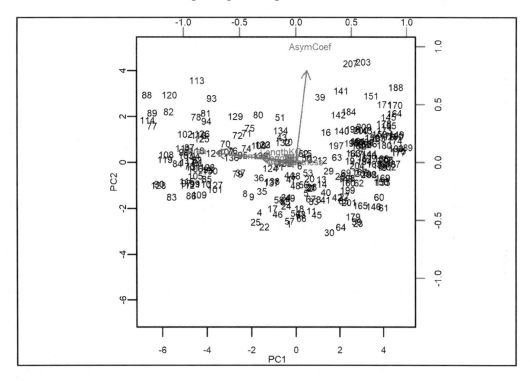

All seven variables are represented in this biplot by a vector, and the direction and length of the vector indicate how each variable contributes to the two principal components in the plot. For example, the first principal component, on the horizontal axis, has negative coefficients for six variables; only the `AsymCoef` variable has a positive coefficient. That is why six vectors are directed into the left half of the plot and only one is directed into the right half. The largest coefficient in the first principal component is the first element, corresponding to the variable `Area`.

The second principal component, on the vertical axis, has positive coefficients for six variables and only one negative coefficient for the Compactness variables (close to zero). Moreover, the length of the vectors makes us understand clearly what the weight of each variable is in the corresponding principal component. It is clear then, that the Area variable assumes a preponderant weight over the others in the first principal component. The same applies to the AsymCoef variable for the second principal component.

Summary

In this chapter, we explored the data preparation techniques to obtain a high-performing regression analysis. These techniques can improve the quality of the data, thereby helping to improve the accuracy and efficiency of the subsequent knowledge extraction process. Analyzing data that has not been carefully screened for such problems can produce misleading results. For this reason, we have to get the data into a form that the algorithm can use to build a predictive analytical model. We started by discovering different ways to transform data, and the degree of cleaning the data. We analyzed the techniques available for the preparation of the most suitable data for analysis and modeling, which includes imputation of missing data, detecting and eliminating outliers, and adding derived variables.

Then we learned how to scale the data, in which data units are eliminated, allowing you to easily compare data from different locations. Data scaling is a preprocessing technique usually employed before feature selection and classification. Two methods are usually well known for rescaling data: normalization, and standardization. Min-max normalization performs a linear transformation on the original data. These techniques get all the scaled data in the range *[0,1]*. A z score standardization consists of subtracting the mean of the column to each value in a column, and then dividing the result for the standard deviation of the column.

So, we discovered the discretization techniques that can be used to convert continuous attributes to nominal attributes. In this way, the number of values for a given continuous attribute is reduced by dividing the attribute into a range of values. Actual data values are replaced with interval value labels. Two methods have been analyzed: discretization by binning and discretization by histogram analysis. Discretization by binning is based on a specified number of bins. These methods are used as discretization methods for data reduction and concept hierarchy generation. The histogram analysis algorithm can be applied recursively to each partition to automatically generate a hierarchy of multilevel concepts, with the procedure ending once a certain number of conceptual levels have been reached.

Finally, dimensionality reduction was explored. Dimensionality reduction is the process of converting a set of data with many variables into data with lesser dimensions while ensuring similar information. We learned PCA that generates a new set of variables, among them uncorrelated, called principal components; each main component is a linear combination of the original variables.

In the next chapter, we will try to achieve generalization for our models. We will explore several techniques, avoiding overfitting, and creating models with low bias and variance. Many techniques will be presented to achieve this: stepwise selection, regularization (Ridge, Lasso, and ElasticNet). These are the techniques that allow you to improve the performance of the models in order to make them particularly reliable. There's no universal solution to overfitting, but experience and good advice will help create better models.

6
Avoiding Overfitting Problems - Achieving Generalization

In the previous chapters, we have emphasized the importance of the training phase for successful modeling. In the training phase, the model is developed by accurately specifying the level of detail that the system will be able to predict. The higher the degree of detail required, the greater the ability to predict from the model. So far, nothing strange has been found. Problems arise when we use that model to make new predictions based on data that the model does not know. The risk we run is that we push the precision in the details so much that we lose the ability to generalize.

Let's consider a practical example: suppose we build a face recognition model. Since each pixel can be compared between one image and the other, it may happen that minor details become overwhelming: hair, background, shirt color, and so on. The number of details on which the model can play is so wide that it is able to identify individual images.

The result is that it recognizes the images used in the learning phase perfectly, but then it is not able to recognize new ones. It is based on insignificant details, and does not do the most important thing: it does not generalize. It does not identify the fundamental distinctive features between one face and the other.

In this chapter, we will try to achieve generalization for our models. We will explore several techniques for avoiding overfitting and creating models with low bias and variance. Many techniques will be presented here to do so, such as stepwise selection and regularization (Ridge, Lasso, and ElasticNet). These are the techniques that allow improving the performance of the models in order to make them particularly reliable. There's no universal solution to overfitting, but experience and good advice will help create better models.

We will cover the following topics:

- What overfitting is, and what bias-variance is
- Cross-validation
- Stepwise regression
- Subset selection
- Regularization, Ridge, Lasso, and ElasticNet regressors
- Stability selection for regression and classification

At the end of the chapter, we will be able to recognize an overfitting problem and simultaneously minimize two sources of error (bias and variance) that prevent regression algorithms from generalizing beyond their training set. We will learn how to apply stepwise regression, in which the choice of predictive variables is carried out by an automatic procedure. We will understand how to add a greater accuracy to the datasets, implementing regression with regularization using Lasso or Ridge. Regularization means modifying the optimization problem to prefer small weights.

Understanding overfitting

General overfitting occurs when a very complex statistical model suits the observed data because it has too many parameters compared to the number of observations. The risk is that an incorrect model can perfectly fit data, just because it is quite complex compared to the amount of data available. Although, it is possible for overfitting to occur when the amount of data is adequate. Consequently, when the model is used to predict new observations, there is a problem, because it is not able to generalize.

The concept of overfitting is also very important in regression analysis. Usually, a learning algorithm is trained using a set of examples (training set), the output of which is already known. It is assumed that the learning algorithm will reach a state in which it will be able to predict outputs for all the other examples it has not yet seen, assuming that the learning model will be able to generalize.

However, especially in cases where there is a small number of training examples, the model can adapt to features that are specific only to the training set, but do not have the remainder of cases; therefore, in the presence of overfitting, the performance (the ability to adapt/predict) on the training data will increase, while performance on data not yet used will be worse.

On the contrary, underfitting occurs when a regression algorithm cannot capture the underlying trend of the data. Underfitting would occur, for example, when fitting a linear model to nonlinear data. Such a model would have poor predictive performance. In the following figure, three models that represent three solutions to the problem are shown. The first, on the left, is clearly underfitted; the one in the center is the correct model; the one on the right presents an overfitting problem:

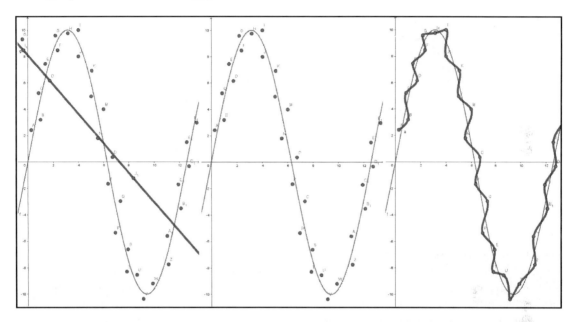

Overfitting exists because the criterion used for model selection is not the same as the criterion used to judge the goodness of fit. For example, a model could be selected by maximizing its performance on some training datasets, yet its goodness of fit may be determined by its ability to perform well on new data; overfitting occurs when a model begins to memorize training data, rather than learning to generalize from a trend.

Usually, we look for a data model that provides, on average, the best predictions possible for the dataset. This goal can conflict with the simple task of modeling a good set of learning data. So, it can happen that if the number of parameters is equal to or higher than the number of observations, the prediction of training data can take place with a simple model. This model simply memorizes the whole training data, but fails drastically when predicting.

In the case of an underfitted model, a bias problem will usually occur; conversely, if the model is overfitted, then it is usually a variance problem. Recall that bias is a measure of how far off the model estimated values are from the true values. It is the error from erroneous assumptions in the learning algorithm. Variance refers to the change in parameter estimates across different datasets. It is the error from sensitivity to small fluctuations in the training set.

Based on the previous example, it becomes crucial to understand whether the predictive model is affected by a polarization problem or a variance problem during the modeling process. To do this, you need to perform bias-variance diagnosis by dividing the dataset into two parts: training and testing. Then we will have to analyze the prediction error on these two parts.

Let's suppose we have a set of data that represents a phenomenon. We can think of such points as generated by a regular function, *h(x)*, with the addition of a noise, *ε*. Our goal is to build a model that approximates the function *h(x)*, given a specific set of *y(x)* data, generated as:

$$y(x) = h(x) + \epsilon$$

We want to approximate the points using a *g(x)* function, with a small number of parameters: a straight line. This model has the advantage of being very simple; there are only two free parameters. However, it does not do a good job of linking the data, and therefore, it does not correctly predict any new data. It is said that the simple model has a high bias. In contrast, a model built using many free parameters does a great job of approximating data points, and therefore, the data point error is close to zero.

It must be noted that this is usually true; however, if the *h(x)* function is linear, a straight line would be the best model to use.

However, it does not have a good predictive value of $h(x)$ for the new x input values. The model has a high variance and does not reflect the structure you expect in any dataset generated by the previous equation. The following figure shows a simple model with high bias (to the left), and a more complex model with high variance (to the right):

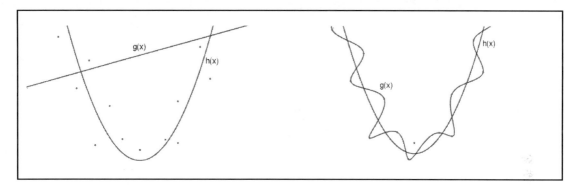

Clearly, what you want is a middle ground: a model that is powerful enough to represent the data structure ($h(x)$), but not so powerful to faithfully follow the pattern, even on noise associated with data samples.

The trend of variance or bias is likely to become a problem if you have a dataset with a few points. In the opposite case, where there is an infinite number of data points (as in a continuous learning line), there is no danger of data overfitting, since the noise associated with any given point plays an insignificant role in the overall shape of the model. However, this is never the case in practice.

Overfitting detection – cross-validation

Cross-validation is a model evaluation technique generally used to evaluate a machine learning algorithm's performance in making predictions on new datasets that it has not been trained on. In fact, it is not advisable to compare the predictive accuracy of a set of models using the same observations as used for model estimation. Therefore, to evaluate the predictive performance of the models, we must use an independent set of data.

In the cross-validation procedure, a dataset partitions a subset of data used to train the algorithm, and the remaining data is used for testing. Subdivision is usually randomly performed to ensure that the two parts have the same distribution. Because cross-validation does not use all of the data to build a model, it is a commonly used method to detect overfitting during training. The following figure, for instance, shows how an **Original dataset** has been divided:

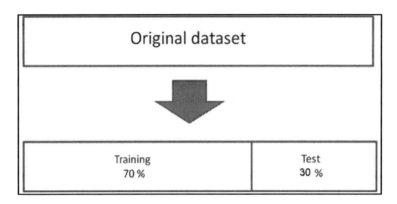

In cross-validation, each round involves randomly partitioning the original dataset into a training set and a testing set. The training set is then used to train a regression algorithm, and the testing set is used to evaluate its performance. So, the model is fit on the training set, and the fitted model is used to predict the responses for the observations in the testing set. This process is repeated several times, and the average cross-validation error is used as a performance indicator. The model showing the lowest error on the test set is identified as the best.

Several cross-validation techniques are available. The following lists the most used:

- **k-fold**: This technique subdivides data into k randomly chosen subsets (named **folds**) of roughly equal sizes. One subset is used to validate the model, while the remaining subsets are used for training. This process is repeated k times, such that each subset is used exactly once for validation.
- **Leave-one-out cross-validation (LOOCV)**: This technique subdivides data using the k-fold approach, where k is equal to the total number of observations in the data. This time, a single observation is used for the testing set, and the remaining observations make up the training set.

In addition, two more resampling methods are available:

- **Data splitting**: This technique subdivides into exactly two subsets of specified ratios for training and validation.
- **Bootstrap resampling**: This techniques creates bootstrap samples by randomly collecting observations from the original dataset with replacements against which to evaluate the model. Typically, a large number of resampling iterations are performed.

To improve our practice with the cross-validation techniques, we look at an example. This time, we will use the Motor Trend Car Road Tests dataset (mtcars) contained in the datasets package. The data was extracted from the 1974 *Motor Trend US* magazine and comprises fuel consumption and ten aspects of automobile design and performance for *32* automobiles (1973–74 models).

The data consists of *32* observations on *11* variables, as follows:

- Mpg: Miles/(US) gallon
- cyl: Number of cylinders
- disp: Displacement (cu.in.)
- hp: Gross horsepower
- drat: Rear axle ratio
- wt: Weight (1000 lbs)
- qsec: *1/4* mile time
- vs: V/S
- am: Transmission (*0 = automatic, 1 = manual*)
- gear: Number of forward gears
- carb: Number of carburetors

Let's start by loading the mtcars dataset through the following command which, as we anticipated, is contained in the dataset's library and saves it in a given frame:

```
data(mtcars)
```

Use the `str()` function to view a compact display of the structure of an arbitrary R object. In our case, using `str(mtcars)`, we will obtain the following results:

```
> str(mtcars)
'data.frame':  32 obs. of  11 variables:
 $ mpg : num  21 21 22.8 21.4 18.7 18.1 14.3 24.4 22.8 19.2 ...
 $ cyl : num  6 6 4 6 8 6 8 4 4 6 ...
 $ disp: num  160 160 108 258 360 ...
 $ hp  : num  110 110 93 110 175 105 245 62 95 123 ...
 $ drat: num  3.9 3.9 3.85 3.08 3.15 2.76 3.21 3.69 3.92 3.92 ...
 $ wt  : num  2.62 2.88 2.32 3.21 3.44 ...
 $ qsec: num  16.5 17 18.6 19.4 17 ...
 $ vs  : num  0 0 1 1 0 1 0 1 1 1 ...
 $ am  : num  1 1 1 0 0 0 0 0 0 0 ...
 $ gear: num  4 4 4 3 3 3 3 4 4 4 ...
 $ carb: num  4 4 1 1 2 1 4 2 2 4 ...
```

The dataset is stored in `data.frame` format, with eleven variables: `mpg`, `cyl`, `disp`, `hp`, `drat`, `wt`, `qsec`, `vs`, `am`, `gear`, and `carb`. All of these variables are numeric. To extract more information, use the `summary()` function:

```
> summary(mtcars)
      mpg             cyl             disp             hp
 Min.   :10.40   Min.   :4.000   Min.   : 71.1   Min.   : 52.0
 1st Qu.:15.43   1st Qu.:4.000   1st Qu.:120.8   1st Qu.: 96.5
 Median :19.20   Median :6.000   Median :196.3   Median :123.0
 Mean   :20.09   Mean   :6.188   Mean   :230.7   Mean   :146.7
 3rd Qu.:22.80   3rd Qu.:8.000   3rd Qu.:326.0   3rd Qu.:180.0
 Max.   :33.90   Max.   :8.000   Max.   :472.0   Max.   :335.0
      drat             wt             qsec             vs
 Min.   :2.760   Min.   :1.513   Min.   :14.50   Min.   :0.0000
 1st Qu.:3.080   1st Qu.:2.581   1st Qu.:16.89   1st Qu.:0.0000
 Median :3.695   Median :3.325   Median :17.71   Median :0.0000
 Mean   :3.597   Mean   :3.217   Mean   :17.85   Mean   :0.4375
 3rd Qu.:3.920   3rd Qu.:3.610   3rd Qu.:18.90   3rd Qu.:1.0000
 Max.   :4.930   Max.   :5.424   Max.   :22.90   Max.   :1.0000
      am             gear             carb
 Min.   :0.0000   Min.   :3.000   Min.   :1.000
 1st Qu.:0.0000   1st Qu.:3.000   1st Qu.:2.000
 Median :0.0000   Median :4.000   Median :2.000
 Mean   :0.4062   Mean   :3.688   Mean   :2.812
 3rd Qu.:1.0000   3rd Qu.:4.000   3rd Qu.:4.000
 Max.   :1.0000   Max.   :5.000   Max.   :8.000
```

As we anticipated, all variables are numeric, and brief statistics for each one are returned. Let's first try to find out whether the variables are related to each other. For this purpose, we will calculate the linear correlation between the measured variables. We will use the `cor()` function to return a matrix containing the pairwise linear correlation coefficient (r) between each pair of columns in the matrix given by the user:

```
R<-cor(mtcars)
```

The results are shown in the following figure:

	mpg	cyl	disp	hp	drat	wt	qsec	vs	am	gear	carb
mpg	1.0000000	-0.8521620	-0.8475514	-0.7761684	0.68117191	-0.8676594	0.41868403	0.6640389	0.59983243	0.4802848	-0.55092507
cyl	-0.8521620	1.0000000	0.9020329	0.8324475	-0.69993811	0.7824958	-0.59124207	-0.8108118	-0.52260705	-0.4926866	0.52698829
disp	-0.8475514	0.9020329	1.0000000	0.7909486	-0.71021393	0.8879799	-0.43369788	-0.7104159	-0.59122704	-0.5555692	0.39497686
hp	-0.7761684	0.8324475	0.7909486	1.0000000	-0.44875912	0.6587479	-0.70822339	-0.7230967	-0.24320426	-0.1257043	0.74981247
drat	0.6811719	-0.6999381	-0.7102139	-0.4487591	1.00000000	-0.7124406	0.09120476	0.4402785	0.71271113	0.6996101	-0.09078980
wt	-0.8676594	0.7824958	0.8879799	0.6587479	-0.71244065	1.0000000	-0.17471588	-0.5549157	-0.69249526	-0.5832870	0.42760594
qsec	0.4186840	-0.5912421	-0.4336979	-0.7082234	0.09120476	-0.1747159	1.00000000	0.7445354	-0.22986086	-0.2126822	-0.65624923
vs	0.6640389	-0.8108118	-0.7104159	-0.7230967	0.44027846	-0.5549157	0.74453544	1.0000000	0.16834512	0.2060233	-0.56960714
am	0.5998324	-0.5226070	-0.5912270	-0.2432043	0.71271113	-0.6924953	-0.22986086	0.1683451	1.00000000	0.7940588	0.05753435
gear	0.4802848	-0.4926866	-0.5555692	-0.1257043	0.69961013	-0.5832870	-0.21268223	0.2060233	0.79405876	1.0000000	0.27407284
carb	-0.5509251	0.5269883	0.3949769	0.7498125	-0.09078980	0.4276059	-0.65624923	-0.5696071	0.05753435	0.2740728	1.00000000

The correlation coefficient has to be between *–1.0* and *1.0* (*0= no correlation; -1/1=high negative/positive correlation*). Analyzing the first column of the screenshot, we notice that the mpg variable is largely correlated with the variables wt, cyl, and disp. We will confirm this in the subsequent analyzes.

Now we have a dataset from which we want to extract knowledge; to do this, we will build a multi-component linear regression model. It is natural that doubts arise about the goodness of the fit of this model.

Having trained and evaluated the model on the same dataset, we will have an algorithm performance on that dataset, but we will have no indication of how the algorithm performs on data that the model has not been trained on.

This will require cross-validation of the data. We will start with data splitting, as previously mentioned: subdividing data into exactly two subsets of a specified ratio for training and validation.

This technique is particularly useful when you have a very large dataset. In this case, the dataset is divided into two partitions: training and test. The training set is used to train the model, while the test set will provide us with a significant performance estimate. This method is very advantageous when using slow methods and needing a quick approximation of performance.

The following example divides the dataset so that *70* percent is used to train a linear regression model and the remaining *30* percent is used to evaluate model performance. To perform data splitting, we can use the `createDataPartition()` function (contained in the `caret` package) that returns a list or matrix of row position integers corresponding to the training data. For bootstrap samples, simple random sampling is used. For other data splitting, the random sampling is done within the levels of `y`, when `y` is a factor, in an attempt to balance the class distributions within the splits. For numeric `y`, the sample is split into groups based on percentiles, and sampling is done within these subgroups. The general form of the function is shown in the following:

```
createDataPartition(y, times = 1, p = 0.5, list = TRUE,
                    groups = min(5, length(y)))
```

The arguments, with brief explanations, are listed in the following table:

Arguments	Explanation
y	A vector of outcomes. For `createTimeSlices`, these should be in chronological order.
times	The number of partitions to create.
p	The percentage of data that goes to training.
list	If (TRUE) the results are returned in a list, or a matrix with the number of rows equal to floor (p * length(y)) and `times` columns (Logical).
groups	For numeric y, the number of breaks in the quantiles.
k	An integer for the number of folds.
returnTrain	A logical. When TRUE, the values returned are the sample positions corresponding to the data used during training. This argument only works in conjunction with list = TRUE.
initialWindow	The initial number of consecutive values in each training set sample.
horizon	The number of consecutive values in the test set sample.
fixedWindow	Logical; if FALSE, all training samples start at one.

skip	Integer; how many (if any) resamples to skip to thin the total amount.
group	A vector of groups whose length matches the number of rows in the overall dataset.

Then, we split the dataset:

```
DataSplit<-createDataPartition(y = mtcars$mpg, p = 0.7, list = FALSE)
```

In the code just suggested, the dataset is split into *70:30*, with the intention of using *70* percent of the data at our disposal to train the model and the remaining *30* percent to test the model. Now, we will create two datasets:

```
TrainData<-mtcars[DataSplit,]
TestData<-mtcars[-DataSplit,]
```

In these two lines, the data of the data frame named mtcars is subdivided into two new data frames, called TrainData and TestData. Now we can build the model: to do this, we will use the train() function. This function can be used to estimate the coefficient values for various modeling functions, like regression, and others. This function sets up a grid of tuning parameters, and can also compute resampling based performance measures. Let's see how it works:

```
LmFit1<-train(mpg~., data = TrainData, method = "lm")
```

A string specifying which regression model to adopt has been used (in our case, lm). Possible values are found using a names (getModelInfo()) command. To look at the model, let's see a brief summary using the summary() function:

```
summary(LmFit1)
```

The results are shown as follows:

```
> summary(LmFit1)
Call:
lm(formula = .outcome ~ ., data = dat)
Residuals:
    Min     1Q Median     3Q    Max
 -2.838 -1.393 -0.152  1.465  3.772
Coefficients:
              Estimate Std. Error t value Pr(>|t|)
(Intercept)  1.0132568 27.0569121   0.037   0.9707
cyl          0.8208032  1.4098159   0.582   0.5704
disp         0.0001679  0.0200953   0.008   0.9935
hp          -0.0038351  0.0236248  -0.162   0.8735
```

```
drat          0.2553228   1.7023173    0.150    0.8831
wt           -4.9016239   2.4596012   -1.993    0.0677 .
qsec          1.4920162   1.2364704    1.207    0.2491
vs            0.9581446   4.1871121    0.229    0.8226
am            3.8512042   3.4207886    1.126    0.2806
gear          0.1381449   2.3683050    0.058    0.9544
carb         -0.0984429   0.9316262   -0.106    0.9175
---
Signif. codes:   0 '***' 0.001 '**' 0.01 '*' 0.05 '.' 0.1 ' ' 1
Residual standard error: 2.494 on 13 degrees of freedom
Multiple R-squared:  0.9133,    Adjusted R-squared:  0.8466
F-statistic: 13.69 on 10 and 13 DF,   p-value: 2.43e-05
```

A linear regression model that uses the least squares approach to determine optimal parameters for the given data has been returned. Now, a test must be performed on the TestData or other new data using parameter estimates obtained from the model building process. The following shows how the testing activity is performed on the TestData sample using the coefficients obtained from the model built on the TrainData sample. This step can be easily implemented with the help of the predict() function. This function is a generic function for predictions from the results of various model fitting functions. The function invokes particular methods, which depend on the class of the first argument:

```
PredictedTest<-predict(LmFit1,TestData)
```

At this point, we have to build data.frame with the values of the current and estimated mpg variable to compare them:

```
ModelTest1<-data.frame(obs = TestData$mpg, pred=PredictedTest)
```

To see model performance metrics on the TestData sample, you can use a defaultSummary() function that, given two numeric vectors of data, calculates the **mean squared error** (**MSE**) and R-squared. For two factors, the overall agreement rate and kappa are determined:

```
defaultSummary(ModelTest1)
```

This example returns the values of the RMSE and metrics:

```
> defaultSummary(ModelTest1)
     RMSE   Rsquared
3.9641704 0.8150085
```

Let's try with another cross-validation method. In this case, we will adopt the k-fold technique that subdivides data into randomly selected subsets (named *folds*) of roughly equal sizes. One subset is used to validate the model, while the remaining subsets are used to train the model. This process is repeated *k* times, such that each subset is used exactly once for validation. The k-fold is a robust method for estimating accuracy, and the size of *k* and to tune the amount of bias in the estimate. *k* values are, in general, set to three, five, seven and ten. To perform the k-fold cross-validation technique, just use the `train()` function as follows:

```
Control1<-trainControl(method = "cv", number = 10)
LmFit2<-train(mpg ~ ., data = mtcars, method = "lm",
              trControl = Control1, metric="Rsquared")
```

The first line is used for setting the method adopted. To do this, the `trainControl()` function is used to control the computational methods of the `train()` function. In the `trainControl` function, the `cv` method is used (that means k-fold cross-validation), and the `number` of folds is set to `10`. Then, the `train()` function is used to build a regression model with the k-fold cross-validation technique. Let's see a brief summary using the `summary` function:

```
summary(LmFit2)
```

The results are shown as follows:

```
> summary(LmFit2)
Call:
lm(formula = .outcome ~ ., data = dat)
Residuals:
    Min      1Q  Median      3Q     Max
-3.4506 -1.6044 -0.1196  1.2193  4.6271
Coefficients:
            Estimate Std. Error t value Pr(>|t|)
(Intercept) 12.30337   18.71788   0.657   0.5181
cyl         -0.11144    1.04502  -0.107   0.9161
disp         0.01334    0.01786   0.747   0.4635
hp          -0.02148    0.02177  -0.987   0.3350
drat         0.78711    1.63537   0.481   0.6353
wt          -3.71530    1.89441  -1.961   0.0633 .
qsec         0.82104    0.73084   1.123   0.2739
vs           0.31776    2.10451   0.151   0.8814
am           2.52023    2.05665   1.225   0.2340
gear         0.65541    1.49326   0.439   0.6652
carb        -0.19942    0.82875  -0.241   0.8122
---
Signif. codes:  0 '***' 0.001 '**' 0.01 '*' 0.05 '.' 0.1 ' ' 1
```

```
Residual standard error: 2.65 on 21 degrees of freedom
Multiple R-squared:  0.869,      Adjusted R-squared:  0.8066
F-statistic: 13.93 on 10 and 21 DF,   p-value: 3.793e-07
```

Also, in this case, a test must be performed on the data. To do this, we use the `predict()` function once again:

```
PredictedTest2<-predict(LmFit2,mtcars)
ModelTest2<-data.frame(obs = mtcars$mpg, pred=PredictedTest2)
defaultSummary(ModelTest2)
```

The results are shown as follows:

```
> defaultSummary(ModelTest2)
    RMSE Rsquared
2.330856 0.868611
```

As we have seen in `Chapter 3`, *More Than Just One Predictor – Multiple Linear Regression*, we need to check whether a multiple linear regression has achieved its goal to explain as much variation as possible in a dependent variable while respecting the underlying assumption. An important way to do this is to check the residuals of a regression. In other words, have a detailed look at what is left over after explaining the variation in the dependent variable using independent variables, meaning the unexplained variation.

Ideally, all residuals should be small and unstructured; this will then mean that the regression analysis has been successful in explaining the essential part of the variation of the dependent variable. If, however, residuals exhibit a structure or present any special aspect that does not seem random, this challenges the results obtained so far.

To perform a residuals analysis, we can use the `residuals()` function, which extracts model residuals from objects returned by modeling functions:

```
ResData<-residuals(LmFit2)
```

To plot actual against predicted values, we must first calculate predicted values:

```
PredictedValues2<-predict(LmFit2)
```

Now we can plot actual values against residual values:

```
plot(mtcars$mpg,ResData)
abline(0,0)
```

In the second line of code, we used the `abline()` function to add an y=0 line. This function adds one or more straight lines through the current plot. Then we plot actual against predicted values:

```
plot(mtcars$mpg,PredictedValues2)
abline(0,1)
```

In the second line of code, we used the `abline()` function to add a *y=x* line. This line is useful for understanding how data is positioned. Specifically, if the actual and predicted data coincide, then the data is positioned on that line. In the following figure, the plot of the actual values against residual values is shown at the top, and the plot of the actual values against predicted values is shown at the bottom:

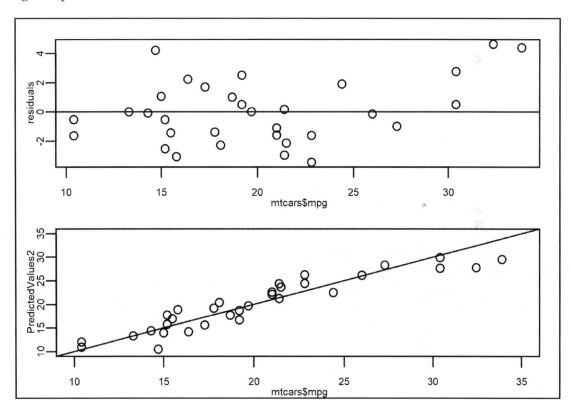

The previous figure (at the top) shows that residuals appear randomly scattered around zero, with a good approximation. The actual against predicted plot shows the effect of the model and compares it against the null model. For a good fit, the points should be close to the fitted line (the line with the *x=y* equation). Points on the left or right of the plot, furthest from the mean, have the most leverage, and effectively try to pull the fitted line toward the point. Points that are vertically distant from the line represent possible outliers. Both types of points can adversely affect the fit. In our case, the points are very close to the line; that means it is a good fit.

Let's deal with another cross-validation method, LOOCV. This technique subdivides data using the k-fold approach, where *k* is equal to the total number of observations in the data. This time, a single observation is used for the testing set, and the remaining observations make up the training set.

The procedure is similar to that seen for the previous case. Again, we will use the `trainControl()` function to control the computable methods of the `train()` function, and then use the `train ()` function to build a regression model:

```
Control2<-trainControl(method="LOOCV")
LmFit3<-train(mpg ~ ., data = mtcars, method = "lm", trControl = Control2)
summary(LmFit3)
```

The results are shown as follows:

```
> summary(LmFit3)
Call:
lm(formula = .outcome ~ ., data = dat)
Residuals:
     Min      1Q  Median      3Q     Max
 -3.4506 -1.6044 -0.1196  1.2193  4.6271
Coefficients:
            Estimate Std. Error t value Pr(>|t|)
(Intercept) 12.30337   18.71788   0.657   0.5181
cyl         -0.11144    1.04502  -0.107   0.9161
disp         0.01334    0.01786   0.747   0.4635
hp          -0.02148    0.02177  -0.987   0.3350
drat         0.78711    1.63537   0.481   0.6353
wt          -3.71530    1.89441  -1.961   0.0633 .
qsec         0.82104    0.73084   1.123   0.2739
vs           0.31776    2.10451   0.151   0.8814
am           2.52023    2.05665   1.225   0.2340
gear         0.65541    1.49326   0.439   0.6652
carb        -0.19942    0.82875  -0.241   0.8122
---
Signif. codes:  0 '***' 0.001 '**' 0.01 '*' 0.05 '.' 0.1 ' ' 1
Residual standard error: 2.65 on 21 degrees of freedom
```

```
Multiple R-squared:  0.869,    Adjusted R-squared:  0.8066
F-statistic: 13.93 on 10 and 21 DF,  p-value: 3.793e-07
```

In the `caret` package, a method for computation of variable importance for regression models is also available. This is the `varImp()` function that computes the variable's importance for objects produced by the `train()` function. So, we calculate the relative importance of variables for the last model:

```
varImp(LmFit3)
```

The results are shown as follows:

```
> varImp(LmFit3)
lm variable importance
        Overall
wt      100.000
am       60.325
qsec     54.826
hp       47.462
disp     34.516
drat     20.202
gear     17.917
carb      7.225
vs        2.392
cyl       0.000
```

To better understand the weight of each variable, we can also plot a graph:

```
plot(varImp(LmFit3))
```

This command produces a Pareto-type plot, where the variables are ranked by their importance, and a needle-plot is used to show the top variables, as follows:

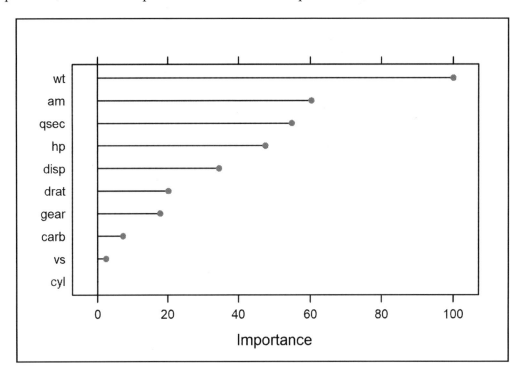

Finally, the bootstrap resampling method is used. This technique creates bootstrap samples by randomly collecting observations from the original dataset with replacements against which to evaluate the model. Typically, a large number of resampling iterations are performed:

```
Control3<-trainControl(method="boot", number=100)
LmFit4<-train(mpg ~ ., data = mtcars, method = "lm", trControl = Control3)
summary(LmFit4)
```

The previous example uses a bootstrap with 100 resamples to prepare a linear regression model. The results are shown as follows:

```
> summary(LmFit4)
Call:
lm(formula = .outcome ~ ., data = dat)
Residuals:
    Min     1Q  Median     3Q     Max
-3.4506 -1.6044 -0.1196  1.2193  4.6271
```

```
Coefficients:
              Estimate Std. Error t value Pr(>|t|)
(Intercept) 12.30337    18.71788   0.657   0.5181
cyl         -0.11144     1.04502  -0.107   0.9161
disp         0.01334     0.01786   0.747   0.4635
hp          -0.02148     0.02177  -0.987   0.3350
drat         0.78711     1.63537   0.481   0.6353
wt          -3.71530     1.89441  -1.961   0.0633 .
qsec         0.82104     0.73084   1.123   0.2739
vs           0.31776     2.10451   0.151   0.8814
am           2.52023     2.05665   1.225   0.2340
gear         0.65541     1.49326   0.439   0.6652
carb        -0.19942     0.82875  -0.241   0.8122
---
Signif. codes:   0 '***' 0.001 '**' 0.01 '*' 0.05 '.' 0.1 ' ' 1
Residual standard error: 2.65 on 21 degrees of freedom
Multiple R-squared:  0.869,      Adjusted R-squared:  0.8066
F-statistic: 13.93 on 10 and 21 DF,   p-value: 3.793e-07
```

Also, in this case, a test must be performed on the data. To do this, we use the `predict()` function another time:

```
PredictedTest4<-predict(LmFit4,mtcars)
ModelTest4<-data.frame(obs = mtcars$mpg, pred=PredictedTest4)
defaultSummary(ModelTest4)
```

The results are shown as follows:

```
> defaultSummary(ModelTest4)
      RMSE   Rsquared
2.1469050 0.8690158
```

Now we have all the tools to compare the different models.

Feature selection

In general, when we work with high-dimensional datasets, it is a good idea to reduce the number of features to only the most useful ones and discard the rest. This can lead to simpler models that generalize better. Feature selection is the process of reducing inputs for processing and analyzing or identifying the most significant features over the others. This selection of features is necessary to create a functional model, so as to achieve a reduction in cardinality, imposing a limit greater than the number of features that must be considered during its creation. In the following figure, a general scheme of a feature selection process is shown:

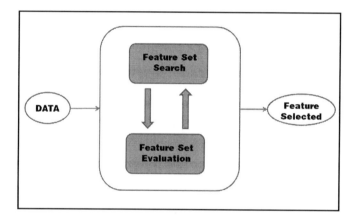

Usually, the data contains redundant information, or more than the necessary information; in other cases, it may contain incorrect information. Feature selection makes the process of creating a model more efficient, for example, decreasing the load on the CPU and the memory needed to train the algorithm. Moreover, selection of features produces a general improvement in reducing the problem of overfitting, that is, a reduction in variance.

Feature selection is based on finding a subset of the original variables, usually iteratively, thus detecting new combinations of variables and comparing prediction errors. The combination of variables that produces minimum error will be labeled as a selected feature and used as input for the machine learning algorithm.

To perform feature selection, we must set the appropriate criteria in advance. Usually, these selection criteria determine the minimization of a specific predictive error measure for models fit for different subsets. Based on these criteria, the selection algorithms seek a subset of predictors that optimally model the measured responses. Such research is subject to constraints, such as the necessary or excluded characteristics and the size of the subset.

Function selection is particularly useful in cases where the modeling goal is to identify an influencing subset. It becomes essential when categorical features are present and numerical transformations are inadequate.

Stepwise regression

At the beginning of Chapter 1, *Getting Started with Regression*, we said that regression analysis can be conducted for dual purposes; one of these is to understand and weigh the effects of the independent variable on the dependent variable. In other words, with this method, we can select predictors that have a greater influence on the response of the model. Stepwise regression is a method of selecting independent variables in order to choose a set of predictors that have the best relationship with the dependent variable. Among variable selection algorithms, we have three methods:

- **Forward method**: It starts with an empty model in which no predictors are selected; in the first step, the variable with the most significant association at the statistical level is added. At each subsequent step, the remaining variable with the largest statistically significant association is added into the model. This process continues until it is no longer a variable with a statistically significant association with the dependent variable.
- **Backward method**: It begins with a model that includes all the variables. Then, we proceed step-by-step to delete the variables, starting from the one with the least significant association.
- **Stepwise method**: It moves back and forth between the two processes by adding and removing variables that gain or lose significance in the various model adjustments (with the addition or reinsertion of a variable).

In the following figure, the criteria adopted from these three methods to select the variables are shown:

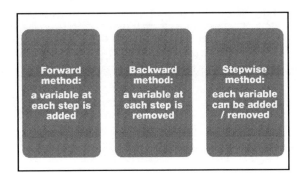

The stepwise method requires more computational resources than the forward or backward selection, while the controlled models are larger. So the probability of choosing the best models in sample data is greater in stepwise regression, though it is not guaranteed. It is worth mentioning that such algorithms fall into the greedy algorithms category.

Stepwise selection methods generally include criteria for terminating the selection process. The more commonly used criteria are listed in the following:

- Coefficient of determination R^2
- Residual mean square RMS
- Adjusted coefficient of determination (Adjusted R^2)
- Mallow's Cp statistic
- AIC, SBC, and BIC

We will adopt the AIC. AIC is the measure of fit which penalizes model for the number of model coefficients. Therefore, we always prefer a model with a minimum AIC value.

To learn how to use a feature selection algorithm, we perform a stepwise regression analysis. Stepwise regression is an automated tool used in the exploratory stages of model building to identify a useful subset of predictors. In R, to create a stepwise regression model, use the `step()` function that performs stepwise model selection by AIC. The general form of the function is as follows:

```
step(object, scope, scale = 0,
     direction = c("both", "backward", "forward"),
     trace = 1, keep = NULL, steps = 1000, k = 2, ...)
```

The arguments, with brief explanations, are listed in the following table:

Agrument	Explanation
object	An object representing a model of an appropriate class (mainly `lm` and `glm`). This is used as the initial model in the stepwise search.
scope	Defines the range of models examined in the stepwise search. This should be either a single formula, or a list containing components upper and lower, both formulas. See the details for how to specify the formulas and how they are used.
scale	Used in the definition of the AIC statistic for selecting the models, currently only for `lm`, `aov`, and `glm` models. The default value, zero, indicates the scale should be estimated: see `extractAIC`.

direction	The mode of stepwise search; can be one of `both`, `backward`, or `forward`, with a default of `both`. If the `scope` argument is missing, the default for direction is `backward`. Values can be abbreviated.
trace	If positive, information is printed during the running of step. Larger values may give more detailed information.
keep	A filter function whose input is a fitted model object and the associated AIC statistic, and whose output is arbitrary. Typically, `keep` will select a subset of the components of the object and return them. The default is to not keep anything.
steps	The maximum number of steps to be considered. The default is `1000` (essentially, as many as required). It is typically used to stop the process early.
k	The multiple of the number of degrees of freedom used for the penalty. Only `k = 2` gives the genuine AIC; `k = log(n)` is sometimes referred to as BIC or SBC.
...	Any additional arguments to `extractAIC`.

We begin, as always, by getting the data to be analyzed.

 To get the data, we draw on the large collection of data available at the UCI Machine Learning Repository, at the following link: `http://archive.ics.uci.edu/ml`

We use the `YachtHydrodynamics` dataset, which is used to predict the hydrodynamic performance of sailing yachts from dimensions and velocity. Predicting the residuary resistance of sailing yachts at the initial design stage is of great value for evaluating the performance of the ship and for estimating the required propulsive power. Essential inputs include the basic hull dimensions and the boat velocity. The inputs are concerned with hull geometry coefficients and the **Froude number**, while the output is the residuary resistance per unit weight of displacement. This dataset contains the following fields:

- Longitudinal position of the center of buoyancy, adimensional
- Prismatic coefficient, adimensional
- Length-displacement ratio, adimensional
- Beam-draught ratio, adimensional
- Length-beam ratio, adimensional

- Froude number, adimensional
- Residuary resistance per unit weight of displacement, adimensional

To start, we use the `read.table()` function that reads a file in table format and creates a data frame from it, with cases corresponding to lines and variables to fields in the file. In the `read.table()` function, the name of the file which the data is to be read from can also be a complete URL:

```
YachtHydrodynamics <-
read.table(url("https://archive.ics.uci.edu/ml/machine-learning-
databases/00243/yacht_hydrodynamics.data"))
```

Here is the URL of the dataset on the UCI Machine Learning Repository. We set the names of the variables in accordance with the previous list:

```
names(YachtHydrodynamics)<- c('LongPos', 'PrismaticCoef',
            'LengDispRatio','BeamDraughtRatio',
            'LengthBeamRatio ','FroudeNumber',
            'ResResistance')
```

So, the data is now available in the R environment, in table form; now we can perform a stepwise regression. In the following figure, the first rows of the `YachtHydrodynamics` table are shown:

	LongPos	PrismaticCoef	LengDispRatio	BeamDraughtRatio	LengthBeamRatio	FroudeNumber	ResResistance
1	-2.3	0.568	4.78	3.99	3.17	0.125	0.11
2	-2.3	0.568	4.78	3.99	3.17	0.150	0.27
3	-2.3	0.568	4.78	3.99	3.17	0.175	0.47
4	-2.3	0.568	4.78	3.99	3.17	0.200	0.78
5	-2.3	0.568	4.78	3.99	3.17	0.225	1.18
6	-2.3	0.568	4.78	3.99	3.17	0.250	1.82
7	-2.3	0.568	4.78	3.99	3.17	0.275	2.61
8	-2.3	0.568	4.78	3.99	3.17	0.300	3.76
9	-2.3	0.568	4.78	3.99	3.17	0.325	4.99
10	-2.3	0.568	4.78	3.99	3.17	0.350	7.16
11	-2.3	0.568	4.78	3.99	3.17	0.375	11.93
12	-2.3	0.568	4.78	3.99	3.17	0.400	20.11
13	-2.3	0.568	4.78	3.99	3.17	0.425	32.75
14	-2.3	0.568	4.78	3.99	3.17	0.450	49.49
15	-2.3	0.569	4.78	3.04	3.64	0.125	0.04
16	-2.3	0.569	4.78	3.04	3.64	0.150	0.17
17	-2.3	0.569	4.78	3.04	3.64	0.175	0.37
18	-2.3	0.569	4.78	3.04	3.64	0.200	0.66
19	-2.3	0.569	4.78	3.04	3.64	0.225	1.06
20	-2.3	0.569	4.78	3.04	3.64	0.250	1.59
21	-2.3	0.569	4.78	3.04	3.64	0.275	2.33
22	-2.3	0.569	4.78	3.04	3.64	0.300	3.29

Showing 1 to 23 of 308 entries

Now we print a summary of the main features:

```
> summary(YachtHydrodynamics)
     LongPos          PrismaticCoef      LengDispRatio     BeamDraughtRatio
 Min.   :-5.000    Min.   :0.5300    Min.   :4.340    Min.   :2.810
 1st Qu.:-2.400    1st Qu.:0.5460    1st Qu.:4.770    1st Qu.:3.750
 Median :-2.300    Median :0.5650    Median :4.780    Median :3.955
 Mean   :-2.382    Mean   :0.5641    Mean   :4.789    Mean   :3.937
 3rd Qu.:-2.300    3rd Qu.:0.5740    3rd Qu.:5.100    3rd Qu.:4.170
 Max.   : 0.000    Max.   :0.6000    Max.   :5.140    Max.   :5.350
 LengthBeamRatio   FroudeNumber       ResResistance
 Min.   :2.730    Min.   :0.1250    Min.   : 0.0100
 1st Qu.:3.150    1st Qu.:0.2000    1st Qu.: 0.7775
 Median :3.150    Median :0.2875    Median : 3.0650
 Mean   :3.207    Mean   :0.2875    Mean   :10.4954
 3rd Qu.:3.510    3rd Qu.:0.3750    3rd Qu.:12.8150
 Max.   :3.640    Max.   :0.4500    Max.   :62.4200
```

Before passing our data to the `step()` function, we need to give a first look to what we've got in the `YachtHydrodynamics` dataset. To do this, we will draw a simple scatter plot for each predictive variable versus the response variable:

```
par(mfrow=c(2,3))
plot(YachtHydrodynamics$LongPos,YachtHydrodynamics$ResResistance,
                    xlab="LongPos",ylab="ResResistance")
plot(YachtHydrodynamics$PrismaticCoef,YachtHydrodynamics$ResResistance,
                    xlab="PrismaticCoef",ylab="ResResistance")
plot(YachtHydrodynamics$LengDispRatio,YachtHydrodynamics$ResResistance,
                    xlab="LengDispRatio",ylab="ResResistance")
plot(YachtHydrodynamics$BeamDraughtRatio,YachtHydrodynamics$ResResistance,
                    xlab="BeamDraughtRatio",ylab="ResResistance")
plot(YachtHydrodynamics$LengthBeamRatio,YachtHydrodynamics$ResResistance,
                    xlab="LengthBeamRatio",ylab="ResResistance")
plot(YachtHydrodynamics$FroudeNumber,YachtHydrodynamics$ResResistance,
                    xlab="FroudeNumber",ylab="ResResistance")
```

A table of scatter plots is shown in the following figure; each plot represents a scatter plot of predictive variables versus response variables:

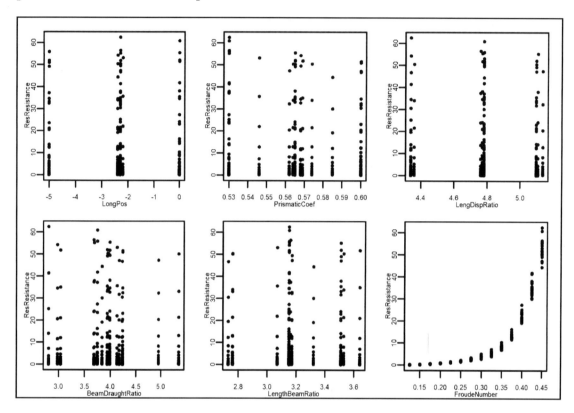

From a quick analysis of the plots, we can see that the sixth predictive variable (FroudeNumber) seems to be particularly correlated with the response variable (the bottom right plot of the previous figure). Let's see if we can find confirmation from the feature selection analysis.

In the regression analysis, the choice of regressors to be included in the model is an essential part of the whole procedure. This is a fairly delicate problem, since only those explanatory variables should be included in the model, the variation of which makes a real contribution to the variation of the response variable. Generally, by increasing the number of regressors in the model, residual deviance tends to decrease. We should also consider that some explanatory variables may be statistically significant, and may therefore be included in the model only due to factors relevant to the case.

Conversely, fundamental explanatory variables may be statistically non-significant, and thus excluded from the model. As a result, it is clear how difficult it is to get to a good model, in general. It is more appropriate to consider a number of equally statistically significant models, among which the researcher can choose the one he thinks most appropriate, also based on considerations related to the interpretation of the phenomenon being analyzed.

This is what we will do in this example: we will build different models, and then choose which one best approximates the data. In the `step()` function, we need to pass an object representing a model of an appropriate class (mainly `lm` and `glm`). This is used as the initial model in the stepwise search. We build a first model:

```
Lm1 <- lm(ResResistance ~ ., data = YachtHydrodynamics)
```

We started from the simplest case, which includes all the terms added to each other. Let's see model statistics:

```
> summary(Lm1)
Call:
lm(formula = ResResistance ~ ., data = YachtHydrodynamics)
Residuals:
    Min      1Q  Median      3Q     Max
-11.770  -7.565  -1.881   6.112  31.572
Coefficients:
                  Estimate Std. Error t value Pr(>|t|)
(Intercept)      -19.2367    27.1133  -0.709    0.479
LongPos            0.1938     0.3381   0.573    0.567
PrismaticCoef     -6.4194    44.1590  -0.145    0.885
LengDispRatio      4.2330    14.1651   0.299    0.765
BeamDraughtRatio  -1.7657     5.5212  -0.320    0.749
LengthBeamRatio   -4.5164    14.2000  -0.318    0.751
FroudeNumber     121.6676     5.0658  24.018   <2e-16 ***
---
Signif. codes:   0 '***' 0.001 '**' 0.01 '*' 0.05 '.' 0.1 ' ' 1
Residual standard error: 8.96 on 301 degrees of freedom
Multiple R-squared:  0.6576,     Adjusted R-squared:  0.6507
F-statistic: 96.33 on 6 and 301 DF,  p-value: < 2.2e-16
```

Here, we may notice that all the predictors are not statistically significant, except one (`FroudeNumber`). Let's see if the stepwise regression confirms this result:

```
Slm1 <- step(Lm1)
```

No arguments are passed, except the model. In this case, the default for direction is `backward`. Recall that the `backward` method begins with a model that includes all the variables. In the `direction` argument, we can indicate whether to use backward (`direction = "backward"`), forward (`direction = "forward"`), or both (`direction = "both"`) procedures. Then, we proceed step-by-step to delete the variables, starting from the one with the least significant association. Let's see the results:

```
> Slm1 <- step(Lm1)
Start:  AIC=1357.64
ResResistance ~ LongPos + PrismaticCoef + LengDispRatio + BeamDraughtRatio
+ LengthBeamRatio + FroudeNumber
                   Df Sum of Sq    RSS    AIC
- PrismaticCoef     1         2  24164 1355.7
- LengDispRatio     1         7  24170 1355.7
- LengthBeamRatio   1         8  24171 1355.7
- BeamDraughtRatio  1         8  24171 1355.7
- LongPos           1        26  24189 1356.0
<none>                           24163 1357.6
- FroudeNumber      1     46306  70468 1685.3
Step:  AIC=1355.66
ResResistance ~ LongPos + LengDispRatio + BeamDraughtRatio +
    LengthBeamRatio + FroudeNumber
                   Df Sum of Sq    RSS    AIC
- LongPos           1        27  24191 1354.0
- LengDispRatio     1        51  24215 1354.3
- LengthBeamRatio   1        54  24218 1354.3
- BeamDraughtRatio  1        64  24228 1354.5
<none>                           24164 1355.7
- FroudeNumber      1     46306  70470 1683.3
Step:  AIC=1354
ResResistance ~ LengDispRatio + BeamDraughtRatio + LengthBeamRatio +
    FroudeNumber
                   Df Sum of Sq    RSS    AIC
- LengDispRatio     1        51  24242 1352.7
- LengthBeamRatio   1        53  24244 1352.7
- BeamDraughtRatio  1        64  24255 1352.8
<none>                           24191 1354.0
- FroudeNumber      1     46306  70497 1681.4
Step:  AIC=1352.65
ResResistance ~ BeamDraughtRatio + LengthBeamRatio + FroudeNumber
                   Df Sum of Sq    RSS    AIC
- LengthBeamRatio   1         3  24245 1350.7
- BeamDraughtRatio  1        14  24255 1350.8
<none>                           24242 1352.7
- FroudeNumber      1     46306  70547 1679.7
Step:  AIC=1350.68
```

```
ResResistance ~ BeamDraughtRatio + FroudeNumber
                    Df Sum of Sq   RSS    AIC
- BeamDraughtRatio  1         11 24255 1348.8
<none>                           24245 1350.7
- FroudeNumber      1      46306 70550 1677.7
Step:  AIC=1348.82
ResResistance ~ FroudeNumber
                Df Sum of Sq   RSS    AIC
<none>                       24255 1348.8
- FroudeNumber   1      46306 70561 1675.7
```

Starting from a linear model that contains linear terms for each predictor, subsequently, step-by-step, terms with no statistical significance are removed. Finally, a model with only one predictor (FroudeNumber) is returned. This model makes the lowest value for AIC. What we had expected from the visual analysis of the data was confirmed by the variable selection procedure.

Regression subset selection

In Chapter 3, *More Than Just One Predictor – Multiple Linear Regression*, we saw that multiple linear regression models are easy to assemble, and they are also easy to interpret. These models are particularly accurate in many cases, especially when the relationship between the response and the predictors is clearly linear. However, it is often the case that not all variables used in a multiple regression model are associated with the response.

Unrelated variables with the response are not only irrelevant, but their presence leads to useless complexity in the model. By removing them, we can get a more easily interpretable model.

Subset selection refers to the task of finding a small subset of available independent variables that are correlated to the response, and therefore, able to predict the dependent variable with good performance.

To perform regression subset selection, including exhaustive search, we can use the leaps package. The leaps() function performs an exhaustive search for the best subsets of the variables in x for predicting y in linear regression, using an efficient branch-and-bound algorithm. It is a compatibility wrapper for regsubsets, which does the same thing better. Since the algorithm returns the best model of each size, the results do not depend on a penalty model for model size: it doesn't make any difference whether you want to use AIC, BIC, CIC, DIC, and so on.

To learn how to use subset selection to feature selection, we will use the Swiss Fertility and Socioeconomic Indicators (1888) dataset (swiss) contained in the datasets package. This is standardized fertility measure and socio-economic indicators for each of the 47 French speaking provinces of Switzerland in about 1888. The swiss dataset consists of a data frame with 47 observations on six variables, as follows:

- Fertility index of marital fertility (Ig), a common standardized fertility measure
- Agriculture percentage of males involved in agriculture as an occupation
- Examination percentage of draftees receiving the highest mark on army examination
- Education percentage of education beyond primary school for draftees
- Catholic percentage of catholics (as opposed to protestant)
- Infant.Mortality live births who lived less than one year

Each of which is in percent, such that, in *[0,100]*. Let's start by loading the swiss dataset through the following command:

```
SwissData <- data.frame(swiss)
```

Use the str() function to view a compact display of the structure of an arbitrary R object. In our case, using str(SwissData), we will obtain the following results:

```
> str(SwissData)
'data.frame':   47 obs. of  6 variables:
 $ Fertility       : num  80.2 83.1 92.5 85.8 76.9 76.1 83.8 92.4
                          82.4 82.9 ...
 $ Agriculture     : num  17 45.1 39.7 36.5 43.5 35.3 70.2 67.8
                          53.3 45.2 ... $ Examination
   : int  15 6 5 12 17 9 16 14 12 16 ...
 $ Education       : int  12 9 5 7 15 7 7 8 7 13 ...
 $ Catholic        : num  9.96 84.84 93.4 33.77 5.16 ...
 $ Infant.Mortality: num  22.2 22.2 20.2 20.3 20.6 26.6 23.6 24.9
                          21 24.4 ...
```

Before we start the variable selection procedure, let's look at what's in the dataset. We can start from the basic statistics returned by the summary() function:

```
> summary(SwissData)
   Fertility        Agriculture       Examination        Education
 Min.   :35.00    Min.   : 1.20    Min.   : 3.00    Min.   : 1.00
 1st Qu.:64.70    1st Qu.:35.90    1st Qu.:12.00    1st Qu.: 6.00
 Median :70.40    Median :54.10    Median :16.00    Median : 8.00
 Mean   :70.14    Mean   :50.66    Mean   :16.49    Mean   :10.98
```

```
3rd Qu.:78.45    3rd Qu.:67.65    3rd Qu.:22.00    3rd Qu.:12.00
Max.    :92.50   Max.    :89.70   Max.    :37.00   Max.    :53.00
   Catholic         Infant.Mortality
Min.    :  2.150  Min.    :10.80
1st Qu.:   5.195  1st Qu.:18.15
Median :  15.140  Median :20.00
Mean   :  41.144  Mean   :19.94
3rd Qu.:  93.125  3rd Qu.:21.70
Max.   : 100.000  Max.    :26.60
```

We now have a first visual analysis by tracing the `boxplot` of the variables contained in the dataset:

```
boxplot(SwissData)
```

The following figure shows boxplots of the given variables:

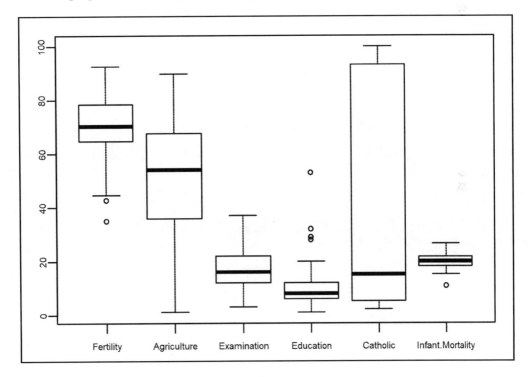

As we can see, the **Catholic** variable covers a wide range of values, while the infant mortality variable is condensed. The **Education** variable also shows possible outliers. Let's analyze the possible relationships between these variables. To do that, we will use the `cor()` function to return a matrix containing the pairwise linear correlation coefficient (r) between each pair of columns in the matrix given by the user:

```
R<-cor(SwissData)
```

The results are shown in the following:

```
> R
                        Fertility Agriculture Examination
Fertility              1.0000000   0.35307918  -0.6458827
Agriculture            0.3530792   1.00000000  -0.6865422
Examination           -0.6458827  -0.68654221   1.0000000
Education             -0.6637889  -0.63952252   0.6984153
Catholic               0.4636847   0.40109505  -0.5727418
Infant.Mortality       0.4165560  -0.06085861  -0.1140216
                        Education    Catholic Infant.Mortality
Fertility              -0.66378886   0.4636847       0.41655603
Agriculture            -0.63952252   0.4010951      -0.06085861
Examination             0.69841530  -0.5727418      -0.11402160
Education               1.00000000  -0.1538589      -0.09932185
Catholic               -0.15385892   1.0000000       0.17549591
Infant.Mortality       -0.09932185   0.1754959       1.00000000
```

To produce a grid of scatter plots, allowing us to visualize the correlation between all pairs of variables in this dataset, we can type the following command:

```
plot(SwissData[,1:6])
```

A matrix of scatter plots is produced. The following figure shows the scatter plot matrix of the variables:

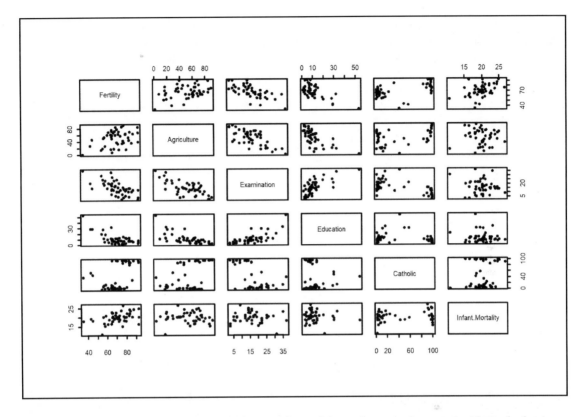

In the previous figure, the plots are scatter plots of the columns of a matrix (the subplot in the ith row and j^{th} column of the matrix is a scatter plot of the ith column against the jth column). As we can see in the figure, scatter plot matrices are a great way to roughly determine whether you have a linear correlation between multiple variables. This is particularly helpful in locating specific variables that might have mutual correlations, indicating a possible redundancy of data. In the diagonal are the names of the measured variables. The rest of the plots are scatter plots of the matrix columns. Specifically, each plot is present twice; the plots on the ith row are the same as those in the ith column (a mirror image).

From the analysis of the matrix of correlation coefficients and from the previous figure, we can note that **Infant.Mortality** is positively correlated with **Fertility** and with being **Catholic**, and negatively with **Examination** and **Education**. Additionally, we see that **Fertility** is positively correlated with being **Catholic** and with **Agriculture** and negatively with **Education** and **Examination**.

Our aim is to build a linear regression model that is able to predict **Infant.Mortality** as much as possible on other variables. Before doing this, however, we want to select only the most correlated variables with the response through the subset selection. To do this, we will use the `leaps` package. First, we must install the `leaps` package.

Remember, to install a library that is not present in the initial distribution of R, you must use the `install.package` function. This is the main function to install packages. It takes a vector of names and a destination library, downloads the packages from the repositories, and installs them.

Then, we will load the library through the `library` command:

```
library(leaps)
```

Now, we will use the `regsubsets()` function that performs model selection by exhaustive search:

```
SubsetSelection <- regsubsets(Infant.Mortality~., SwissData,
                                                  nvmax=5)
```

Let's see what we got:

```
SumSubsetSelection<-summary(SubsetSelection)
```

The results are shown in the following:

```
> SumSubsetSelection
Subset selection object
Call: regsubsets.formula(Infant.Mortality ~ ., SwissData, nvmax = 5)
5 Variables   (and intercept)
              Forced in Forced out
Fertility        FALSE     FALSE
Agriculture      FALSE     FALSE
Examination      FALSE     FALSE
Education        FALSE     FALSE
Catholic         FALSE     FALSE
1 subsets of each size up to 5
Selection Algorithm: exhaustive
         Fertility Agriculture Examination Education Catholic
1  ( 1 )  "*"       " "         " "         " "       " "
2  ( 1 )  "*"       " "         " "         "*"       " "
3  ( 1 )  "*"       "*"         " "         "*"       " "
4  ( 1 )  "*"       "*"         "*"         "*"       " "
5  ( 1 )  "*"       "*"         "*"         "*"       "*"
```

Moreover, the `summary()` function returns a matrix with the best subset of predictors for one to five predictor models. For example, the best model with two variables includes `Fertility` and `Education` as predictors for `Infant.Mortality`. We can also see that all models include `Fertility`, and that all models with at least two variables also include `Education`. The `summary` object also includes metrics, such as adjusted R-squared, CP, or BIC, that we can use to determine the best overall model.

For example, we can check which of the five subsets provides the maximum value of the R^2 adjusted:

```
BestSubsetAdjr2 <- which.max(SumSubsetSelection$adjr2)
```

The result is shown in the following:

```
> BestSubsetAdjr2
[1] 2
```

This result tells us that the best model is that with two variables, that is, `Fertility` and `Education`. Let's see what happens using Mallow's `cp` element:

```
BestSubsetCp<- which.min(SumSubsetSelection$cp)
```

The result is shown in the following:

```
> BestSubsetCp
[1] 2
```

The result is the same; the best subsets include the `Fertility` and `Education` variables. From these results, we will be able to build a rigorous model that will show good results. Now, we see two results in two plots:

```
par(mfrow=c(1,2))
plot(SumSubsetSelection$adjr2, xlab="Variables selected",
                        ylab="Adjusted RSq", type="l")
points(BestSubsetAdjr2, SumSubsetSelection$adjr2[BestSubsetAdjr2],
                        col="black", cex =1, pch =20)
plot(SumSubsetSelection$cp, xlab="Variables selected", ylab="CP",
                        type="l")
points(BestSubsetCp, SumSubsetSelection$cp[BestSubsetCp],
                        col="black", cex =1, pch =20)
```

The following figure shows the value of the `Adjusted RSq` and `cp` for all the subsets selected, with the best value for each one:

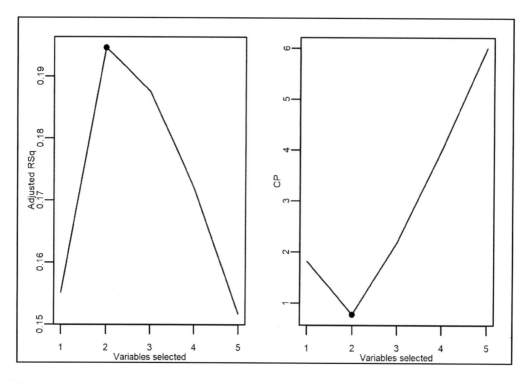

Finally, we extract the coefficients of the best model selected with the **Adjusted RSq** and **CP** metrics:

```
coef(SubsetSelection,2)
```

The results are shown in the following:

```
> coef(SubsetSelection,2)
(Intercept)    Fertility    Education
 8.63757624   0.14615350   0.09594897
```

As anticipated, the best model will be able to predict infant mortality on the basis of only two variables, which are `Fertility` and `Education`, respectively.

Regularization

As an alternative to the selection methods discussed in the previous sections (forward, backward, stepwise), it is possible to adopt methods that use all predictors but bind or adjust the coefficients by bringing them to very small or zero values (shrinkage). These methods are actually defined as automatic feature selection methods, as they improve generalization. They are called regularization methods and involve modifying the performance function, normally selected as the sum of the squares of regression errors on the training set.

When a large number of variables are available, the least square estimates of a linear model often have a low bias but a high variance with respect to models with fewer variables. Under these conditions, as we have seen in previous sections, there is an overfitting problem. To improve precision prediction by allowing greater bias but a small variance, we can use variable selection methods and dimensionality reduction, but these methods may be unattractive for computational burdens in the first case or provide a difficult interpretation in the other case.

Another way to address the problem of overfitting is to modify the estimation method by neglecting the requirement of an unbiased parameter estimator and instead considering the possibility of using a biased estimator, which may have smaller variance. There are several biased estimators, most based on regularization: Ridge, Lasso, and ElasticNet are the most popular methods.

Ridge regression

In Chapter 2, *Basic Concepts – Simple Linear Regression*, we saw that in order to estimate the regression coefficients β in the least squares method, we must minimize the following term **Residual Sum of Squares (RSS)**:

$$RSS = \sum_{i=1}^{n}(y_i - \beta_1 x_i + \beta_0)^2$$

The general linear regression model can be expressed using a condensed formulation:

$$Y = X * \beta$$

Here, $\beta = [\beta_0, \beta_1]$. To determine the intercept and the slope through the least squares method, we have to solve the previous equation with respect to β, as follows (we must estimate the coefficients with the normal equation):

$$\beta = (X^T * X)^{-1} * X^T * Y$$

When the predictors are most correlated and the columns of the matrix X have an approximate linear dependence, the term $(X^T * X)^{-1}$ becomes close to singular. As a result, the least squares estimate becomes highly sensitive to random errors in the observed response Y, producing a large variance. This situation is defined as **multicollinearity**, and means that the information contained in a variable is actually already present in the dataset through the other variables. When multicollinearity occurs, least squares estimates are unbiased, but their variances are large, so they may be far from the true value. By adding a degree of bias to the regression estimates, Ridge regression reduces the standard errors.

Ridge regression is very similar to least squares, except that the Ridge coefficients are estimated by minimizing a slightly different quantity. In particular, the Ridge regression coefficients β are the values that minimize the following quantity:

$$\sum_{i=1}^{n}(y_i - \beta_1 x_i + \beta_0)^2 + \lambda * \beta_1^2 = RSS + \lambda * \beta_1^2$$

Here, $\lambda \geq 0$ is a tuning parameter, to be determined separately. The term $\lambda \beta_1^2$ is a shrinkage penalty that decreases when the β parameters withdraw (shrink) towards the zero. Parameter λ controls the relative impact of the two components: RSS and the penalty term. If $\lambda = 0$, the Ridge regression coincides with the least squares method. If $\lambda \to \infty$, all estimated coefficients tend to zero. The regression Ridge produces different estimates for different values of λ. The optimal choice of λ is crucial and is usually done with cross-validation.

Note that the shrinkage penalty is not applied to β_0, as it would not make sense. Ridge regression addresses the problem by estimating regression coefficients using the following equation:

$$\beta = (X^T * X + \lambda * I)^{-1} * X^T * Y$$

Here, λ is the Ridge parameter and I is the identity matrix. Small positive values of λ improve the conditioning of the problem and reduce the variance of the estimates. While biased, the reduced variance of Ridge estimates often result in a smaller mean square error when compared to least squares estimates. It is worth mentioning that now, the matrix $(X^T*X + \lambda *I)$ is never singular.

In the least squares estimates, the scale change of a variable has no practical effect: if the predictor X_j is multiplied by a constant k, its estimated coefficient is automatically divided by k by the algorithm. In other words, the $\beta_j X_j$ effect remains the same regardless of the X_j measurement scale.

In the regression Ridge, a scale transformation has substantial effects, and therefore, to avoid obtaining different results depending on the predicted scale of measurement, it is advisable to standardize all predictors before estimating the model. To standardize the variables, we must subtract their means and divide by their standard deviations.

To learn how to use a regularization algorithm, we perform a Ridge regression analysis step-by-step. We begin, as always, by getting the data to be analyzed. This time, we will use the **Road Casualties Great Britain (RCGB)** 1969–84 dataset (`Seatbelts`) contained in the `datasets` package. This is a multiple time-series dataset that was commissioned by the department of transport in 1984 to measure differences in deaths before and after front seatbelt legislation was introduced on January 31, 1983. It provides monthly total numerical data on numbers of incidents, including those related to death and injury in **Road Traffic Accidents (RTA)**. The dataset starts in January 1969, and observations run until December 1984.

There are 192 observations of the following eight variables:

- `driversKilled`: Car drivers killed.
- `drivers`: Same as `UKDriverDeaths`.
- `front`: Front-seat passengers killed or seriously injured.
- `rear`: Rear-seat passengers killed or seriously injured.
- `kms`: Distance driven.
- `PetrolPrice`: Petrol price.
- `VanKilled`: Number of van (light goods vehicle) drivers.
- `Law`: Was the law in effect that month? Two values are available (zero/one).

Let's start by loading the `Seatbelts` dataset through the following command, which, as we anticipated, is contained in the `datasets` library, and saves it in a given frame:

```
Seatbelts <- data.frame(Seatbelts)
```

Use the `str()` function to view a compact display of the structure of an arbitrary R object. In our case, using `str(Seatbelts)`, we will obtain the following results:

```
> str(Seatbelts)
'data.frame':   192 obs. of  8 variables:
 $ DriversKilled: num  107 97 102 87 119 106 110 106 107 134 ...
 $ drivers      : num  1687 1508 1507 1385 1632 ...
 $ front        : num  867 825 806 814 991 ...
 $ rear         : num  269 265 319 407 454 427 522 536 405 437 ...
 $ kms          : num  9059 7685 9963 10955 11823 ...
 $ PetrolPrice  : num  0.103 0.102 0.102 0.101 0.101 ...
 $ VanKilled    : num  12 6 12 8 10 13 11 6 10 16 ...
 $ law          : num  0 0 0 0 0 0 0 0 0 0 ...
```

There are 192 observations of 8 variables in a numerical class. To gain a better understanding, the first 10 records can be looked at:

```
> head(Seatbelts,n=10)
   DriversKilled drivers front rear   kms
1            107    1687   867  269  9059
2             97    1508   825  265  7685
3            102    1507   806  319  9963
4             87    1385   814  407 10955
5            119    1632   991  454 11823
6            106    1511   945  427 12391
7            110    1559  1004  522 13460
8            106    1630  1091  536 14055
9            107    1579   958  405 12106
10           134    1653   850  437 11372
   PetrolPrice VanKilled law
1    0.1029718        12   0
2    0.1023630         6   0
3    0.1020625        12   0
4    0.1008733         8   0
5    0.1010197        10   0
6    0.1005812        13   0
7    0.1037740        11   0
8    0.1040764         6   0
9    0.1037740        10   0
10   0.1030264        16   0
```

Then, a summary of each subset is given:

```
> summary(Seatbelts)
DriversKilled        drivers              front
Min.    : 60.0   Min.    :1057   Min.    : 426.0
1st Qu.:104.8    1st Qu.:1462    1st Qu.: 715.5
Median :118.5    Median :1631    Median : 828.5
Mean    :122.8   Mean    :1670   Mean    : 837.2
3rd Qu.:138.0    3rd Qu.:1851    3rd Qu.: 950.8
Max.    :198.0   Max.    :2654   Max.    :1299.0
      rear               kms             PetrolPrice
Min.    :224.0   Min.    : 7685   Min.    :0.08118
1st Qu.:344.8    1st Qu.:12685    1st Qu.:0.09258
Median :401.5    Median :14987    Median :0.10448
Mean    :401.2   Mean    :14994   Mean    :0.10362
3rd Qu.:456.2    3rd Qu.:17203    3rd Qu.:0.11406
Max.    :646.0   Max.    :21626   Max.    :0.13303
   VanKilled             law
Min.    : 2.000   Min.    :0.0000
1st Qu.: 6.000    1st Qu.:0.0000
Median : 8.000    Median :0.0000
Mean    : 9.057   Mean    :0.1198
3rd Qu.:12.000    3rd Qu.:0.0000
Max.    :17.000   Max.    :1.0000
```

As mentioned, seatbelt legislation was introduced on January 31, 1983, so it is convenient to split the dataset into two (before/after the legislation). This subdivision will be executed with the subset() function that returns subsets of vectors, matrices, or data frames which meet conditions. The condition will be law == 0 (before the legislation), and law ==1 (after the legislation):

```
BeforeLaw <-subset(Seatbelts,law ==0)
AfterLaw <- subset(Seatbelts,law!=0)
```

To check for any changes following the entry into force of the law, we can plot the boxplots of the two newly obtained data frames:

```
par(mfrow=c(1,2))
boxplot(BeforeLaw$DriversKilled,ylim=c(50,200),main="Before
Law",ylab="Drivers Killed")
boxplot(AfterLaw$DriversKilled,ylim=c(50,200),main="After
Law",ylab="Drivers Killed")
```

The following figure shows the **Drivers Killed** boxplot **Before Law** (to the left), and the **Drivers Killed** boxplot **After Law** (to the right):

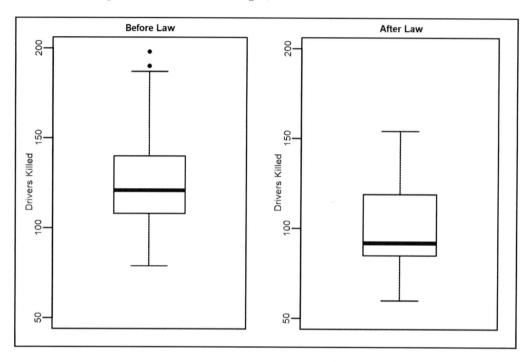

It can be seen that there were less drivers killed after the legislation was passed. After carrying out an exploratory analysis, we return to our goal: we are interested in predicting drivers killed using a multi-linear model. To perform Ridge regression, we will use the `glmnet` package that provides methods to algorithm regularization.

This package provides extremely efficient procedures for fitting the Ridge, Lasso, and ElasticNet regularization paths for linear regression, logistic and multinomial regression models, Poisson regression, and the Cox model. The algorithm is extremely fast and exploits sparsity in the input matrix where it exists. A variety of predictions can be made from the fitted models. The main function in the package is `glmnet()`. This function fits a **generalized linear model (GLM)** via penalized maximum likelihood. The regularization path is computed for the Ridge, Lasso, or ElasticNet penalty at a grid of values for the regularization parameter lambda. Can deal with all shapes of data, including very large sparse data matrices.

First, we must install the `glmnet` package.

Remember, to install a library that is not present in the initial distribution of R, you must use the `install.package` function. This is the main function to install packages. It takes a vector of names and a destination library, downloads the packages from the repositories, and installs them.

Then, we will load the library through the `library` command:

```
library(glmnet)
```

To use the `glmnet()` function, we must first set the input matrix and the response variable:

```
x <- model.matrix(DriversKilled~., BeforeLaw)[,-c(1,8)]
y <- BeforeLaw$DriversKilled
```

In the first line of the code, we used the `model.matrix()` function that creates a model matrix by expanding factors to a set of dummy variables (depending on the contrasts) and expanding interactions similarly. The term `[,-c(1,8)]` is used to remove the intercept and the last columns. Then we set the response variable. Now we can use the `glmnet()` function to build the linear regression model with Ridge regularization. The `glmnet()` function provides an `alpha` argument that determines what method is used. If `alpha=0`, then Ridge regression is used, and if `alpha=1`, then the Lasso is used:

```
RidgeMod <- glmnet(x, y, alpha=0, nlambda=100,
                   lambda.min.ratio=0.0001)
```

In the `glmnet` function are used the following arguments:

- `nlambda=100`: Set the number of lambda values (the default is `100`)
- `lambda.min.ratio=0.0001`: Set the smallest value for lambda, as a fraction of `lambda.max`, the (data derived) entry value (that is, the smallest value for which all coefficients are zero)

Let us now see how the coefficient values change according to the `lambda` value. To do that, we will use the `plot.glmnet()` function that produces a coefficient profile plot of the coefficient paths for a fitted `glmnet` object:

```
plot(RidgeMod,xvar="lambda",label=TRUE)
```

The `xvar` argument sets what is on the *x* axis. The following options are available:

- `norm`: Plots against the L1-norm of the coefficients
- `lambda`: Against the log-lambda sequence
- `dev`: Against the percent deviance explained

The following figure shows a coefficient profile plot of the coefficient paths for a `RidgeMod` model:

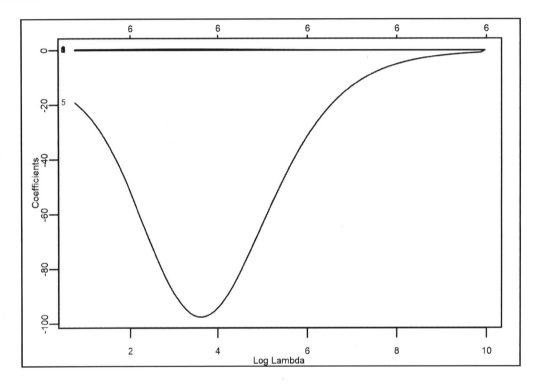

When lambda is very large (the log of lambda is ten), the regularization effect dominates the squared loss function and the coefficients tend to zero. At the beginning of the path, as lambda tends toward zero and the solution tends towards the **Ordinary Least Square (OLS)**, coefficients exhibit big oscillations (they are unregularized). In practice, it is necessary to tune lambda in such a way that a balance is maintained between both.

The Ridge regression draws a whole model path; our goal is to select the best. In this regard, we can use the `cv.glmnet()` function available in the `glmnet` package. This function does k-fold cross-validation for `glmnet`, produces a plot, and returns a value for the best lambda value:

```
CvRidgeMod <- cv.glmnet(x, y, alpha=0, nlambda=100,
                        lambda.min.ratio=0.0001)
```

The function runs `glmnet` *nfolds+1* times; the first to get the lambda sequence, and then the remainder to compute the fit with each of the folds omitted. The error is accumulated, and the average error and standard deviation over the folds is computed. Now we will plot the cross-validation curve produced by `plot.cv.glmnet()`:

```
plot(CvRidgeMod)
```

The `plot.cv.glmnet()` function plots the cross-validation curve, and upper and lower standard deviation curves, as a function of the lambda values used, as follows:

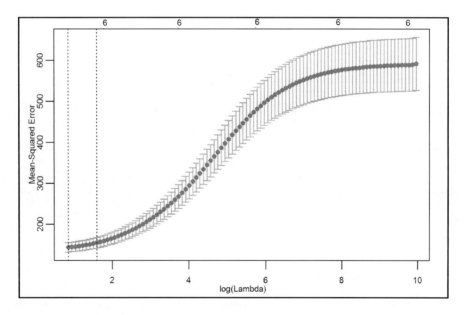

The previous figure includes the cross-validation curve (red dotted line) and upper and lower standard deviation curves along the λ sequence (error bars). In the beginning of the procedure (to the right of the figure), the MSE is very high, and the coefficients are restricted to be too small; and then at some point, it kind of levels off. This seems to indicate that the full model is doing a good job.

There are two vertical lines: one is at the minimum, and the other vertical line is within one standard error of the minimum. The second line is a slightly more restricted model that does almost as well as the minimum, and sometimes, we'll go for that.

These lines then lie at two lambda values:

- `lambda.min` is the value of λ that gives the minimum mean cross-validated error
- `lambda.1se`, gives the most regularized model such that the error is within one standard error of the minimum

At the top of the plot, you actually see how many nonzero variables' coefficients are in the model. There are all six variables in the model (five variables, plus the intercept), and no coefficient is zero. At this point, we extract the best lambda value:

```
best.lambda <- CvRidgeMod$lambda.min
```

The result is shown in the following:

```
> best.lambda
[1] 2.335042
```

Once we have the best lambda, we can use `predict` to obtain `coefficients`:

```
predict(RidgeMod, s=best.lambda, type="coefficients")[1:6, ]
```

The results are shown in the following:

```
> predict(RidgeMod, s=best.lambda, type="coefficients")[1:6, ]
  (Intercept)        drivers         front           rear
-10.884410054    0.065576651    0.019258743   -0.002439347
          kms     PetrolPrice
  0.000538637  -20.498674980
```

This is the best regression model for our data.

Lasso regression

In the previous section, we saw Ridge regression: this is a method for regularization and for avoiding overfitting. In Ridge regression, the regression coefficients are shrunk by introducing a penalty, as follows:

$$\sum_{>i=1}^{n}(y_i - \beta_1 x_i + \beta_0)^2 + \lambda * \beta_1 2 = RSS + \lambda * \beta_1 2$$

Here, the term $\lambda\beta_1^2$ is a shrinkage penalty that decreases when the β parameters withdraw (shrink) towards zero. The Lasso regression is a shrinkage method like Ridge, with subtle but important differences. The Lasso estimate is defined by the following equation:

$$\sum_{i=1}^{n}(y_i - \beta_1 x_i + \beta_0)^2 + \lambda * |\beta_1| = RSS + \lambda * |\beta_1|$$

Here, the term $\lambda|\beta_1|$ is a shrinkage penalty for the Lasso regression. It is clear that Ridge and Lasso regression use two different penalty functions. Ridge uses L2-norm, whereas Lasso goes with L1-norm. In Ridge regression, the penalty is the sum of the squares of the coefficients, and for Lasso, it's the sum of the absolute values of the coefficients. It's a shrinkage towards zero using an absolute value (L1-norm) rather than a sum of squares (L2-norm).

These are two normalization procedures (Loss functions) commonly used in the machine learning algorithm. L1-norm is also known as **least absolute deviations**, or **least absolute errors**. It is basically minimizing the sum of the absolute differences between the target value and the estimated values. L2-norm is also known as **least squares**. It is basically minimizing the sum of the square of the differences between the target value and the estimated values.

The Ridge regression produces a model with all the variables, of which the part with coefficients is closer to zero. Increasing λ forces more coefficients to be close to zero, but almost never exactly equal to zero, unless $\lambda = \infty$. For forecasting this is not a problem, while interpretation can sometimes be problematic. Lasso regression tries to overcome this aspect.

The Lasso regression penalty term, using the absolute value (rather than the square, as in the regression Ridge), forces some coefficients to be exactly equal to zero, if λ is large enough. In practice, Lasso automatically performs a real selection of variables.

To perform Lasso regression, we will use the same dataset used in the previous example (Ridge regression). I'm referring to the Road Casualties in Great Britain 1969–84 dataset (Seatbelts) contained in the datasets package. Let's start by loading the Seatbelts dataset through the following command:

```
Seatbelts <- data.frame(Seatbelts)
```

To have a preview of the dataset, we use the View() function, as follows:

```
View(Seatbelts)
```

The following figure shows a spreadsheet-style data viewer on a matrix-like `Seatbelts` object:

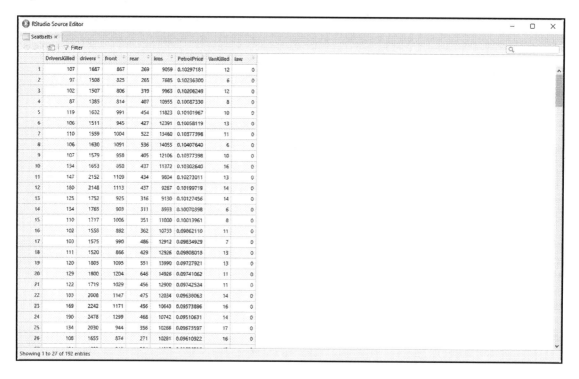

As mentioned, seatbelt legislation was introduced on January 31, 1983, so it is convenient to split the dataset into two (before/after the legislation). This subdivision will be executed with the `subset()` function that returns subsets of vectors, matrices, or data frames which meet conditions. The condition will be `law ==0` (before the legislation), and `law ==1` (after the legislation):

```
BeforeLaw <-subset(Seatbelts,law ==0)
AfterLaw <- subset(Seatbelts,law!=0)
```

We have already done an exploratory analysis of the data in the previous section. So let's go straight to our goal: make a Lasso regression with the data before the law came into force (`BeforeLaw` data frame). To do that, we will once again use the `glmnet()` function contained in the `glmnet` package.

First, we load the library through the following command:

```
library(glmnet)
```

To use the `glmnet()` function, we must first set the input matrix and the response variable:

```
x <- model.matrix(DriversKilled~., BeforeLaw)[,-c(1,8)]
y <- BeforeLaw$DriversKilled
```

In the first line of the code, we used the `model.matrix()` function that creates a model matrix by expanding factors to a set of dummy variables (depending on the contrasts) and expanding interactions similarly. The term `[,-c(1,8)]` is used to remove the intercept and the last columns. Then we set the response variable. Now we can use the `glmnet()` function to build the linear regression model with Ridge regularization. The `glmnet()` function provides an `alpha` argument that determines what method is used. If `alpha=1`, the Lasso method is used:

```
LassoMod <- glmnet(x, y, alpha=1, nlambda=100,
                   lambda.min.ratio=0.0001)
```

In the glmnet function are used the following arguments:

- `nlambda=100`: Sets the number of lambda values (the default is `100`)
- `lambda.min.ratio=0.0001`: Sets the smallest value for lambda, as a fraction of `lambda.max`, the (data derived) entry value (the smallest value for which all coefficients are zero)

Let us now see how the coefficient values change according to the lambda value. To do that, we will use the `plot.glmnet()` function that produces a coefficient profile plot of the coefficient paths for a fitted `glmnet` object:

```
plot(LassoMod,xvar="norm",label=TRUE)
```

The `xvar` argument sets what is on the *x* axis. In this case, we used the `norm` option that plots coefficients against the L1-norm, as follows:

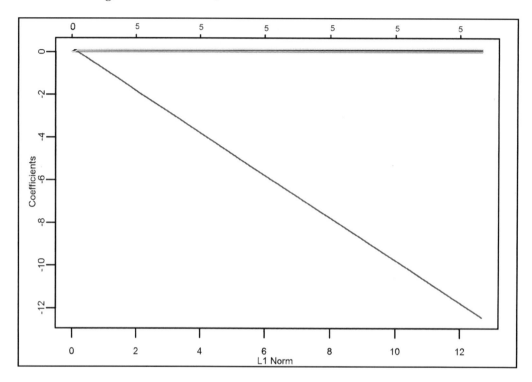

In the previous figure, each curve corresponds to a variable. This plot shows the path of its coefficient against the L1-norm of the whole coefficient vector when λ varying. The previous axis indicates the number of nonzero coefficients at the current λ, which is the effective degrees of freedom for the Lasso. We have also annotated the curves; this can be done by setting `label=TRUE` in the `plot` command.

A summary of the `glmnet` path at each step is displayed by the `print` function:

```
print (LassoMod)
```

The results are shown in the following (for space reasons, we only reported the head and tail of the returned print):

```
> print (LassoMod)
Call:  glmnet (x = x, y = y, alpha = 1, nlambda = 100, lambda.min.ratio =
1e-04)
      Df    %Dev    Lambda
 [1,]  0 0.0000 21.28000
```

```
 [2,]  1 0.1314 19.39000
 [3,]  1 0.2404 17.66000
 [4,]  1 0.3309 16.09000
 [5,]  1 0.4061 14.66000
 [6,]  1 0.4685 13.36000
 [7,]  1 0.5203 12.17000
 [8,]  1 0.5633 11.09000
 [9,]  1 0.5990 10.11000
[10,]  1 0.6287  9.21000
.....................................................
[54,]  5 0.7802  0.15360
[55,]  5 0.7802  0.14000
[56,]  5 0.7802  0.12750
[57,]  5 0.7803  0.11620
[58,]  5 0.7803  0.10590
[59,]  5 0.7803  0.09648
[60,]  5 0.7803  0.08791
[61,]  5 0.7803  0.08010
[62,]  5 0.7803  0.07299
[63,]  5 0.7803  0.06650
[64,]  5 0.7803  0.06059
```

The results show, from left to right, the number of nonzero coefficients (degrees of freedom), the percent (of null) of deviance explained (`%dev`), and the value of λ (lambda). Even if we set `100` lambda values, the program stops early if `%dev` does not change sufficiently from one lambda to the next, typically near the end of the path.

The `glmnet` function returns a sequence of models implied by lambda fitted by coordinate descent; our goal is to select the best. In this regard, we can use the `cv.glmnet()` function available in the `glmnet` package. This function does k-fold cross-validation for `glmnet`, produces a plot, and returns a value for the best lambda value:

```
CvLassoMod <- cv.glmnet(x, y, alpha=1, nlambda=100,
                        lambda.min.ratio=0.0001)
```

The function runs `glmnet` *nfolds+1* times; the first to get the lambda sequence, and then the remainder to compute the fit with each of the folds omitted. The error is accumulated, and the average error and standard deviation over the folds is computed. Now we will plot the cross-validation curve produced by `plot.cv.glmnet()`:

```
plot(CvLassoMod)
```

The `plot.cv.glmnet()` function plots the cross-validation curve, and upper and lower standard deviation curves, as a function of the lambda values used, as follows:

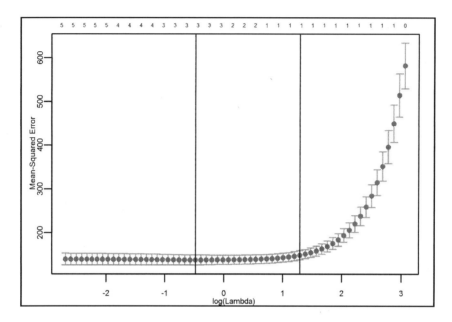

The previous figure includes the cross-validation curve (red dotted line), and upper and lower standard deviation curves along the λ sequence (error bars). As we said in the previous example, in the beginning of the procedure (to the right of the figure), the MSE is very high, and the coefficients are restricted to be too small, and then at some point, it kind of levels off. This seems to indicate that the full model is doing a good job. Lasso not only does shrinkage; it also does variable selection.

There are two vertical lines: the line to the left is at the minimum (`lambda.min`) and is the line which minimizes out-of-sample loss in CV. The other vertical line is within one standard error of the minimum (`lambda.1se`). The `lambda.1se` is the one which is the largest λ value, within one standard error of λ min. The second line is a slightly more restricted model that does almost as well as the minimum, and sometimes, we'll go for that.

At this point, we extract the best lambda value:

```
best.lambda <- CvLassoMod$lambda.min
```

The result is shown in the following:

```
> best.lambda
[1] 0.6202076
```

Once we have the best lambda, we can use the `coef()` function to obtain the coefficients:

```
coef(CvLassoMod, s = "lambda.min")
```

The results are shown in the following:

```
> coef(CvLassoMod, s = "lambda.min")
7 x 1 sparse Matrix of class "dgCMatrix"
                         1
(Intercept) -14.793268375
drivers       0.077943198
front         .
rear          0.005170028
kms           0.000325402
PetrolPrice   .
VanKilled     .
```

We have confirmed that the Lasso method is able to make a selection of variables. Ultimately, we can say that both Lasso and Ridge balance the trade-off bias-variance with the choice of λ. Lasso implicitly assumes that part of the coefficients are zero, or at least not significant. Lasso tends to have a higher performance than Ridge in cases where many predictors are not actually tied to the response variables. In opposite cases, the Ridge tends to have better performance. Both approaches can be compared by cross-validation.

ElasticNet regression

The last type of regularization method that we will analyze is ElasticNet; it is a hybrid of both Lasso and Ridge regression. It is trained with both L1-norm and L2-norm prior as regularizer. A practical advantage of trading off between Lasso and Ridge is that it allows ElasticNet to inherit some of Ridge's stability under rotation. To analyze a practical case of this method, we will use the dataset already used in the Ridge and Lasso regression.

Let's start by loading the `Seatbelts` dataset through the following command:

```
Seatbelts <- data.frame(Seatbelts)
```

As already done before, we will split the dataset into two (before/after the law):

```
BeforeLaw <-subset(Seatbelts,law ==0)
AfterLaw <- subset(Seatbelts,law!=0)
```

To perform ElasticNet regression, we will once again use the `glmnet()` function contained in the `glmnet` package.

First, we load the library through the following command:

```
library(glmnet)
```

To use the `glmnet()` function, we must first set the input matrix and the response variable:

```
x <- model.matrix(DriversKilled~., BeforeLaw)[,-c(1,8)]
y <- BeforeLaw$DriversKilled
```

The `glmnet()` function provides an `alpha` argument that determines what method is used. If `alpha` is between zero and one, extremes excluded, then ElasticNet regression is used:

```
ElasticnetMod <- glmnet(x, y, alpha=0.5, nlambda=100,
                        lambda.min.ratio=0.0001)
```

Let us now see how the coefficient values change according to the lambda value:

```
plot(ElasticnetMod)
```

The following figure shows a coefficient profile plot of the coefficient paths for an `ElasticnetMod` model:

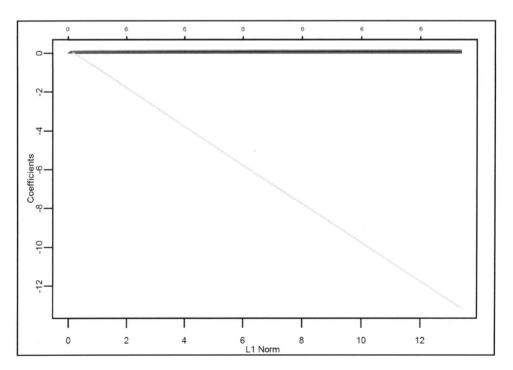

We now perform a k-fold cross-validation for `glmnet` that produces a plot and returns a value for the best lambda value:

```
CvElasticnetMod <- cv.glmnet(x, y, alpha=0.5, nlambda=100,
                             lambda.min.ratio=0.0001)
```

Finally, we plot the cross-validation curve produced by `plot.cv.glmnet()`:

```
plot(CvElasticnetMod)
```

The `plot.cv.glmnet()` function plots the cross-validation curve, and upper and lower standard deviation curves, as a function of the lambda values used, as follows:

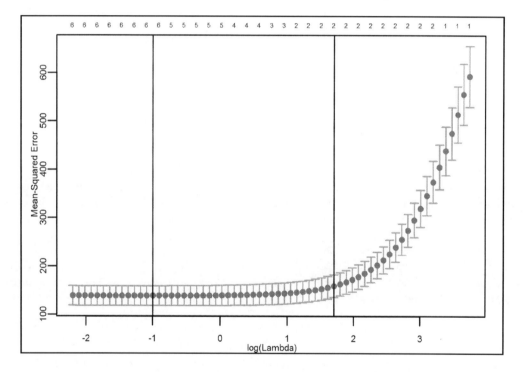

Finally, to summarize, the following are the most important differences between Lasso, Ridge, and ElasticNet: Ridge uses L2-norm term, which limits the size of the coefficient vector. Lasso uses L1-norm, which imposes sparsity among the coefficients, and thus makes the fitted model more interpretable. ElasticNet is introduced as a compromise between these two techniques, and has a penalty which is a mix of L1-norm and L2-norm.

Summary

In this chapter, we learned how to achieve generalization for our models. We explored several techniques for avoiding overfitting and creating models with low bias and variance. In the beginning, differences between overfitting and underfitting were explained.

In general, overfitting occurs when a very complex statistical model suits the observed data because it has too many parameters compared to the number of observations. The risk is that an incorrect model can perfectly fit data just because it is quite complex compared to the amount of data available. Consequently, when the model is used to predict new observations, there is a failure, because it is not able to generalize. On the contrary, underfitting occurs when a regression algorithm cannot capture the underlying trend of the data. Underfitting would occur, for example, when fitting a linear model to nonlinear data. Such a model would have poor predictive performance.

We then discovered the cross-validation procedure through which a dataset is partitioned into a subset of data used to train the algorithm, and the remaining data is used for testing. Subdivision is usually randomly performed to ensure that the two parts have the same distribution. Because cross-validation does not use all of the data to build a model, it is a commonly used method to detect overfitting during training.

Later, we learned how to perform the selection of features. The selection of features is necessary to create a functional model so as to achieve a reduction in cardinality, imposing a limit greater than the number of features that must be considered during its creation. Two techniques were analyzed: stepwise regression and subset selection.

Finally, the regularization methods were explored. These methods involve modifying the performance function, normally selected as the sum of the square of regression errors on the training set. Ridge, Lasso, and ElasticNet regression were performed, with several examples to understand the basis of these concepts.

In the next chapter, the reader will be introduced to the robust regression technique to eliminate the effects of the presence of outliers in our data. The Bayesian regression technique, and how to use information obtained from observing data to update the probability distributions of the model coefficients, will also be explored. Finally, the use of the Poisson regression to treat the count data will be learned.

7
Going Further with Regression Models

In previous chapters, we learned to use different regression models to analyze different types of data. We have therefore fully understood the concept that proposes a regression algorithm for each event, which means that data is not all equal and for each data collection there is a regression algorithm that allows extracting knowledge. Numeric data with many predictors must be treated differently from the data that has only one predictor. Just as, different tools have to be adopted in the presence of categorical data, as well as when we handle data with dichotomous responses. We can safely assert that there is a more suited regression algorithm for each type of data and that a predictive analysis of the data in our possession is crucial to addressing our search for the most suitable algorithm.

Based on what we have said, in this chapter we will continue to deepen regression algorithms by introducing new regression techniques that are particularly suited to the treatment of specific data types. In fact, we start with the problem of the presence of outliers in our data. In Chapter 5, *Data Preparation Using R Tools*, we learned to identify outliers and remove them, thus verifying the performance improvements obtained from the template. Now, we will see that this step can be simply bypassed using a robust regression model. So we will talk about the Bayesian regression technique. The goal of a Bayesian analysis is to update the probability distributions of the coefficients by incorporating information from observed data. Finally, we will analyze the Poisson regression used to model the count of data in contingency tables.

The following topics will be covered:

- Robust linear regression
- Bayesian linear regression
- Poisson regression model

At the end of the chapter, we will be able to build a robust regression model to mitigate the effects of the presence of outliers in our data. We will take a look at the Bayesian regression technique and explore how to use information from observed data to update the probability distributions of the model coefficients. Finally, we learn how to use Poisson regression to treat the count data.

Robust linear regression

So far, we have used the **Ordinary Least Squares (OLS)** estimates for our linear regression models. But these models only become valid when all regression hypotheses are verified. If this is not the case, least squares regression can be problematic. In such cases we can try to locate the problems through residual diagnostics, but this procedure may be slow and requires a great deal of experience. Often, model-fitting problems are due to the presence of extreme values called **outliers**. The following figure shows a distribution with outliers:

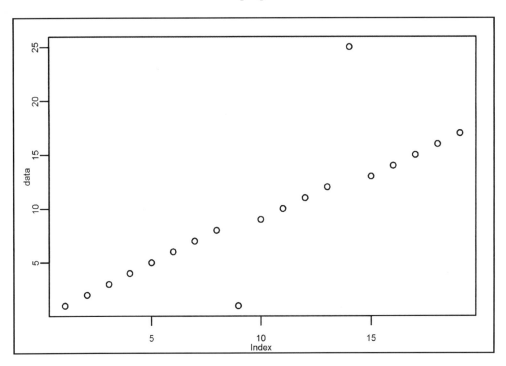

Outliers have a large influence on the fit, because squaring the residuals magnifies the effects of these extreme data points. Outliers tend to change the direction of the regression line by getting much more weight than they are worth. Thus, the estimate of the regression coefficients is clearly distorted. These effects are difficult to identify since their residuals are much smaller than they would be if the distortion wasn't present.

To reduce outlier effects, we can fit our data using robust least squares regression. Robust regression methods provide an alternative to least squares regression; they attempt to dampen the influence of outlying cases in order to provide a better fit to the majority of the data. Robust regression downweighs the influence of outliers, and makes their residuals larger and easier to identify.

The robust regression technique starts by assigning a weight to each data point. Then, a weighing procedure is performed, automatic, and iterative, using a method named **iteratively reweighted least squares** (**IRLS**). First, the weights are initialized, placing them all equally. So, model coefficients are estimated using the OLS algorithm. Iteration is then performed; weights are recalculated so that the points farthest from model predictions in the previous iteration are reduced. The model coefficients are then recalculated using weighing least squares. We will continue this process until the values of the coefficient estimates converge within a specified tolerance.

To perform a robust least squares regression, we will use the `rlm()` function contained in the MASS package. This package includes many useful functions and data examples, including functions for estimating linear models through **generalized least squares** (**GLS**), fitting negative binomial linear models, robust fitting of linear models, and Kruskal's non-metric multidimensional scaling.

The following table lists some of the information on this package:

Package	MASS
Date	February 2, 2017
Version	7.3-47
Title	Support Functions and Datasets for Venables and Ripley's MASS
Author	Brian Ripley, Bill Venables, and many others

Among the many functions contained in the package, we will use the `rlm()` function that fits a linear model with robust regression using an M-estimator. An object of class `rlm` inheriting from `lm` is returned. As always, we start by getting the data to be analyzed.

In Chapter 2, *Basic Concepts – Simple Linear Regression*, we solved a real case: a company at the launch of a new printer model wants to analyze sales at a number of stores to determine the best price. In the dataset named SellingPrintersOutliers.csv, are stored the sales of the product in the last month and the sale prices for these stores. Compared to the dataset used in Chapter 2, *Basic Concepts – Simple Linear Regression*, two outliers were added. We introduced two new stores (Store21 and Store22). These are two special stores. The first, Store21, recorded a large number of sales at an average price. The particular success is due to a contest associated with the sale of printers. The second, Store22, has recorded a low number of sales, again offering an average price. The particular failure is due to the bad character of the seller who mistreats the customers.

To begin, load the dataset into R, to do this, we will use the following code:

```
setwd ("c://R")
Printers=read.csv ("SellingPrintersOutliers.csv", header=TRUE,sep=";")
```

First, setwd(c://R) is used to set the working directory to R contained in the root folder. Then we used the read.csv() function that reads a file in table format and creates a data frame from it, with cases corresponding to rows and variables to columns in the file. To remember what it contains, let's look at the internal structure of the imported data frame:

```
str(Printers)
```

The results are shown in the following:

```
> str(Printers)
'data.frame':   22 obs. of   3 variables:
 $ X          : Factor w/ 22 levels "Store1","Store10",..: 1 12 16
                17 18 19 20 21 22 2 ...
 $ Sold.Items: int   100 150 130 140 110 160 115 135 120 155 ...
 $ Price     : int   60 43 48 45 55 40 53 47 52 42 ...
```

Three variables are stored:

- X: Store
- Sold.Items: Number of printers sold
- Price: Price of the printers

At this point, we will display some data statistics using the `summary()` function. We will then need to compare the two data frames:

```
summary(Printers)
> summary(Printers)
      X          Sold.Items          Price
 Store1 : 1   Min.    : 50.0   Min.    :39.00
 Store10: 1   1st Qu.:115.0    1st Qu.:42.25
 Store11: 1   Median :132.5    Median :47.00
 Store12: 1   Mean    :132.0   Mean    :47.23
 Store13: 1   3rd Qu.:150.0    3rd Qu.:51.75
 Store14: 1   Max.    :210.0   Max.    :60.00
 (Other):16
```

To confirm the two outliers, we draw a plot of the `Sold.Items` against `Price`, as shown in the following figure:

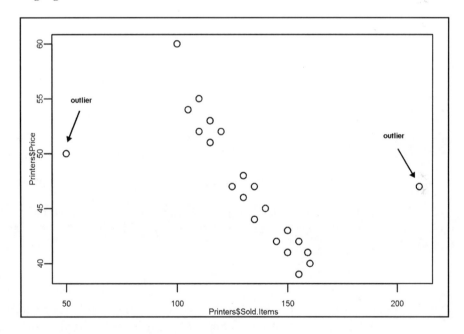

In the previous figure, two outliers are highlighted. Let us now compare the results we get by fitting a linear regression model and a robust linear regression model. Let's begin with the simple linear regression model already used in `Chapter 2`, *Basic Concepts – Simple Linear Regression*, and `Chapter 3`, *More Than Just One Predictor – MLR*:

```
LinMod1 <- lm( Printers$Price ~ Printers$Sold.Items,data=Printers)
```

The resulting model is shown in the following:

```
> LinMod1
Call:
lm(formula = Printers$Price ~ Printers$Sold.Items, data = Printers)
Coefficients:
        (Intercept)    Printers$Sold.Items
             62.538                  -0.116
```

To look at them, let's see a brief summary using the summary() function:

```
summary(LinMod1)
```

The results are shown in the following:

```
> summary(LinMod1)
Call:
lm(formula = Printers$Price ~ Printers$Sold.Items, data = Printers)
Residuals:
    Min    1Q Median    3Q    Max
 -6.738 -3.042 -1.169  3.091  9.061
Coefficients:
                      Estimate Std. Error t value Pr(>|t|)
(Intercept)           62.53762    4.26008  14.680 3.58e-12 ***
Printers$Sold.Items   -0.11599    0.03147  -3.685  0.00147 **
---
Signif. codes:  0 '***' 0.001 '**' 0.01 '*' 0.05 '.' 0.1 ' ' 1
Residual standard error: 4.426 on 20 degrees of freedom
Multiple R-squared:  0.4045,    Adjusted R-squared:  0.3747
F-statistic: 13.58 on 1 and 20 DF,  p-value: 0.001466
```

Now, let's see what happens if we fit a robust linear regression model. As we have anticipated, to do this we will use the rlm() function contained in the MASS package. So, we must first install the package.

Remember, to install a library that is not present in the initial distribution of R, you must use the install.package function. This is the main function to install packages. It takes a vector of names and a destination library, downloads the packages from the repositories, and installs them.

Then, we will load the library through the library command:

```
library(MASS)
```

Now, we can use the `rlm()` function, as follows:

```
LinMod2 <- rlm(Printers$Price~Printers$Sold.Items,data=Printers,
  psi = psi.hampel, init = "lts")
```

Two options are used: Hampel's redescending psi function, and init="lts" to set the coefficients fitted by the FastLTS algorithm as starting points of the iterations. To review all the options available simply type ?rlm. The result model is shown in the following:

```
> LinMod2
Call:
rlm(formula = Printers$Price ~ Printers$Sold.Items, data = Printers,
psi = psi.hampel, init = "lts")
Converged in 3 iterations
Coefficients:
        (Intercept) Printers$Sold.Items
         85.9564656          -0.2939218
Degrees of freedom: 22 total; 20 residual
Scale estimate: 2.01
```

To look at them, let's see a brief summary:

```
summary(LinMod2)
> summary(LinMod2)
Call: rlm(formula = Printers$Price ~ Printers$Sold.Items, data = Printers,
psi = psi.hampel, init = "lts")
Residuals:
    Min      1Q  Median      3Q     Max
-21.260  -1.383   0.223   1.269  22.767
Coefficients:
                    Value   Std. Error t value
(Intercept)        85.9565   1.6512     52.0570
Printers$Sold.Items -0.2939   0.0122    -24.0952
Residual standard error: 2.011 on 20 degrees of freedom
```

A first comparison of the models can be done using `Residual standard error`, which represents the standard deviation of the residuals. It's a measure of how close the fit is to the points. From the results obtained by the `summary()` function, we have the following values:

```
LM1RSE = 4.426 on 20 degrees of freedom
LM2RSE = 2.011 on 20 degrees of freedom
```

This gives us reason to hope. We now extract the coefficients of the two models because we will need to make comparisons:

```
LM1Coef <- coef(LinMod1)
LM2Coef <- coef(LinMod2)
```

To compare the models and to understand the differences better, we can display the original data and the regression line:

```
plot(Printers$Sold.Items,Printers$Price)
abline(coef=LM1Coef)
plot(Printers$Sold.Items,Printers$Price)
abline(coef=LM2Coef)
```

In the code just proposed, we first reported data on the graph so we added the regression lines using the `abline()` function. This function adds one or more straight lines through the current plot. A vector of length two giving the intercept and slope is passed by the `coef` argument. The following figure shows the plots of the two models (**Linear Regression Model** to the left, and **Robust Regression Model** to the right):

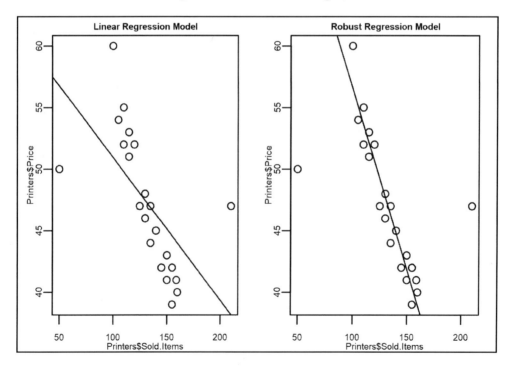

As can be seen, even just two outliers have created a lot of damage. It is clear that the regression line changes considerably: by comparing the two figures the slope is clearly different. But the most important thing is that in the figure to the left (**Linear Regression Model**), the regression line is now unable to fit the data. All this proves that the treatment of outliers, (for example by the **Robust Regression Model**), is crucial in order to obtain a regression model that fits the data very well. The performance of regression analysis methods, in practice, also depends on the quality of the data.

It is important to note that a similar result (on the same dataset) was obtained in Chapter 5, *Data Preparation Using R Tools*, by removing outliers. In this way, we have shown that robust regression is particularly effective in treating outliers. Recall that the robust regression technique gets these results by assigning a weight to each data point. To confirm that, we can plot the weights used in the re-weighted least squares process. This information is stored in the w component:

```
plot(LinMod2$w, ylab="Weight")
```

The following figure shows the weights assigned to the points in the last step of convergence:

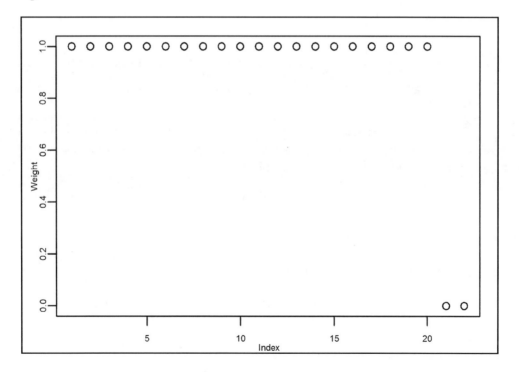

We can note that for almost all points the weight is equal to one while for the two outliers (the last two observations in the dataset), the weight is equal to zero. Then, at the end of the procedure, the model is created giving a weight equal to zero to the two outliers.

Bayesian linear regression

In Chapter 3, *More Than Just One Predictor – MLR*, we have seen that the general **Multiple Linear Regression (MLR)** model for *n* variables is of the form:

$$y = \beta_0 + \beta_1 * x_1 + \beta_2 * x_2 + \ldots + \beta_n * x_n$$

Here, $x_1, x_2, .. x_n$ are the *n* predictors and *y* is the only response variable. The coefficients β measure the change in the *y* value associated with a change of x_i, keeping all the other variables constant.

In order to estimate β, we minimized the following term:

$$RSS = \sum_i [y_i - (\beta_0 + \beta_1 * x_1 + \beta_2 * x_2 + \ldots + \beta_n * x_n)]^2$$

The general linear regression model can be expressed using a condensed formulation:

$$Y = X * \beta$$

Here, $\beta = [\beta_0, \beta_1, \beta_2, \ldots, \beta_n]$. To determine the intercept and the slope through the least squares method, we have to solve the previous equation with respect to β, as follows (we must estimate the coefficients with the normal equation):

$$\beta = (X^T * X)^{-1} * X^T * Y$$

To predict a new value of the response variable, given some new predictors data, we simply multiply the components of the new predictors by the associated β coefficients. So, in estimating a new observation, the β coefficients are treated as fixed values.

In the Bayesian approach, we will see that the interpretation differs substantially, in fact the β coefficients are treated as random variables, rather than fixed, unknown quantities. So, the goal of a Bayesian analysis is to update the probability distributions of the coefficients by incorporating information from observing data.

In Bayesian linear regression, we assign prior probability distributions to the coefficients β_0, $\beta_1, \beta_2, ..., \beta_n$ and use a likelihood function to determine their posterior probability distribution using Bayes' theorem. For a given coefficient β_i, we can write:

$$P(\beta_i | Y) = P(Y | \beta_i) * P(\beta_i)$$

Here, $P(\beta_i)$ is the prior probability of β_i, $P(\beta_i | Y)$ is the posterior probability given the data Y, and $P(Y | \beta_i)$ is the likelihood. Once we have determined the posterior distribution for each β_i, we can set the coefficients for our linear model. It all depends on the loss function we wish to minimize. For a linear loss function we should take the mean, and for a quadratic loss function we should take the median. In order to understand the formula we introduced better, it is necessary to know some basics about probability theory. Those who already have such skills can skip this section, even if a review is always useful.

Basic concepts of probability

Let's spend a few minutes talking about the basic concepts of probability. If you are already familiar with these concepts, you may want to skip this section. Otherwise, it will be interesting to deepen the basic knowledge needed to understand how probabilistic classification algorithms work.

In a bag, there are seven white balls and three black balls. Except for their color, the balls are identical; they are made of the same material, they are the same size, they are perfectly spherical, and so on. I'll put a hand in the bag without looking inside, pulling out a random ball. What is the probability that the pulled out ball is black?

- The balls in all are *7 + 3 = 10*. By pulling out a ball, I have *10* possible cases. I have no reason to think that some balls are more privileged than others, that is, they are more likely to be pulled out. Therefore, the *10* possible cases are equally probable.
- Of these *10* possible cases, there are only *3* cases in which the ball pulled out is black. These are the cases favorable to the expected event.

The `black ball` pulled out event therefore has 3 out of 10 possible occurrences. To define its probability as the ratio between the favorable and the possible cases, and I get:

```
Probability (black ball) = 3/10 = 0.3 = 30%
```

As we have shown in the example, the probability of an event can be expressed:

- As a fraction, for example, 3/10
- As a decimal number, for example, 3/10 = 3:10 = 0.30
- As a percentage, for example, 0.30 = 30%

Resolving this problem gives us an opportunity to give a chance definition of an event.

The probability (a priori) that a given event (*E*) occurs is the ratio between the number (*s*) of favorable cases of the event itself and the total number (*n*) of the possible cases, provided all considered cases are equally probable:

$$P = P(E) = \frac{number\ of\ favourable\ cases}{total\ number\ of\ possible\ cases} = \frac{s}{n}$$

Let's look at two simple examples:

- By throwing a coin, what is the probability that it shows a head? The possible cases are 2, heads and tails {H, T}, the favorable cases are 1{H}. So *P(head) = 1/2* =0.5 = 50 percent.
- By throwing a dice, what is the probability that 5 is out? The possible cases are 6, {1, 2, 3, 4, 5, 6}, and the favorable cases are 1{5}. So *P(5) =1/6 =0.166 =16.6* percent.

To define probability, use the concept of equally likely events. It is therefore necessary to clarify what is meant by equally likely events. To this end, the concept of the principle of insufficient reason (or principle of indifference) can be introduced, which states that:

Given a group of events, if there are no valid reasons to think that some event occurs more or less easily than others, then all group events must be considered equally likely.

To calculate the number of possible and favorable cases, in many cases, combinatorial calculations are required.

Previously, we have defined probability as the ratio between the number of favorable cases and the number of possible cases. But what values can it take? The probability of an event *P(E)* is always a number between *0* and *1*:

$$0 \leq P(E) \leq 1$$

The extreme values are defined as follows:

- An event that has probability *0* is called an **impossible event**. Suppose we have six red balls in a bag, what is the probability of picking a black ball? The possible cases are *6*; the favorable cases are *0* because there are no black balls in the bag. *P(E) = 0/6 = 0.*
- An event that has probability *1* is called a **certain event**. Suppose we have six red balls in a bag, what is the probability of picking a red ball? The possible cases are *6*; the favorable cases are *6* because there are only red balls in the bag. *P(E) = 6/6 =1.*

The classical definition of probability, based on a discrete and finite number of events, is hardly extendable to the case of continuous variables. The ideal condition of perfect uniformity, where all possible outcomes (the space of events) are previously known and all are equally probable, is a weak element of that definition. The latter condition is also imposed before defining the notion of probability, resulting in circularity in the definition.

An important advance compared to the classic concept in which probability is established a priori, before looking at the data, is contained in the frequentist definition of probability; this is instead obtained later, after examining the data. According to this concept, the probability of an event is the limit to which the relative frequency of the event tends when the number of trials tends to infinity. This definition can also be applied without prior knowledge of the space of events and without assuming the condition of equally likely events. However, it is assumed that the experiment is repeatable several times, ideally infinitely, under the same conditions.

We can then say that, in a series of repeated tests a great many times under the same conditions, each of the possible events is manifested with a relative frequency that is close to its probability:

$$relative\ frequency \approx probability$$

In the Bayesian approach, probability is a measure of the degree of credibility of one proposition. This definition applies to any event. Bayesian probability is an inverse probability; we switch from observed frequencies to probability. In the Bayesian approach, the probability of a given event is determined before making the experiment, based on personal considerations. The a priori probability is therefore tied to the degree of credibility of the event, set in a subjective way. With Bayes' theorem, on the basis of the frequencies observed, we can adjust the probability a priori to reach the probability a posteriori. Then, by using this approach, an estimate of the degree of credibility of a given hypothesis before observation of data is used in order to associate a numerical value with the degree of credibility of that hypothesis after data observation.

So far, we've talked about the likelihood of an event, but what happens when the possible events are more than one? Two random events, *A* and *B*, are independent if the probability of the occurrence of event *A* is not dependent on whether event *B* has occurred, and vice versa. For example, if we have two *52* decks of French playing cards. When extracting a card from each deck, the following two events are independent:

- *E1 = The card extracted from the first deck is an ace*
- *E2 = The card extracted from the second deck is a clubs card*

The two events are independent; each can happen with the same probability independently of the other's occurrence.

Conversely, a random event, *A*, is dependent on another event, *B*, if the probability of event *A* depends on whether event *B* has occurred or not. Suppose we have a deck of *52* cards. By extracting two cards in succession without putting the first card back in the deck, the following two events are dependent:

- *E1 = The first extracted card is an ace*
- *E2 = The second extracted card is an ace*

To be precise, the probability of *E2* depends on whether or not *E1* occurs. Indeed:

- The probability of *E1* is *4/52*
- The probability of *E2* if the first card was an ace is *3/51*
- The probability of *E2* if the first card was not an ace is *4/51*

Let us now deal with other cases of mutual interaction between events. Accidental events that cannot occur simultaneously on a given trial are considered mutually exclusive or disjoint. By extracting a card from a deck of 52, the following two events are mutually exclusive:

- *E1 = The ace of hearts comes out*
- *E2 = One face card comes out*

Indeed, the two events just mentioned cannot occur simultaneously, meaning that an ace cannot be a figure. Two events are, however, exhaustive or joint if at least one of them must occur at a given trial. By extracting a card from a deck of 52, the following two events are exhaustive:

- *E1 = One face card comes out*
- *E2 = One number card comes out*

These events are exhaustive because their union includes all possible events. Let us now deal with the case of joint probability, both independent and dependent. Given two events, *A* and *B*, if the two events are independent (I mean the occurrence of one does not affect the probability of the other), the joint probability of the event is equal to the product of the probabilities of *A* and *B*:

$$P(A \cap B) = P(A) \times P(B)$$

Let's take an example. We have two decks of 52 cards. By extracting a card from each deck, let's consider the two independent events:

- *A = The card extracted from the first deck is an ace*
- *B = The card extracted from the second deck is a clubs card*

What is the probability that both of them occur?

- *P(A) = 4/52*
- *P(B) = 13/52*
- *P(A ∩ B) = 4/52 * 13/52 = 52 /(52 * 52) = 1/52*

If the two events are dependent (that is, the occurrence of one affects the probability of the other), then the same rule may apply, provided $P(B|A)$ is the probability of event A given that event B has occurred. This condition introduces conditional probability, which we are going to dive into:

$$P(A \cap B) = P(A) \times P(B|A)$$

A bag contains two white balls and three red balls. Two balls are pulled out from the bag in two successive extractions without reintroducing the first ball pulled out to the bag.

Calculate the probability that the two balls extracted are both white:

- The probability that the first ball is white is 2/5
- The probability that the second ball is white, provided that the first ball is white, is 1/4

The probability of having two white balls is as follows:

$$P(two\ white) = 2/5 * 1/4 = 2/20 = 1/10$$

As promised, it is now time to introduce the concept of conditional probability. The probability that event A occurs, calculated on the condition that event B occurred, is called **conditional probability** and is indicated by the symbol $P(A \mid B)$. It is calculated using the following formula:

$$P(B|A) = \frac{P(A \cap B)}{P(A)}$$

Conditional probability usually applies when A depends on B, that is, events are dependent on each other. In the case where A and B are independent, the formula becomes:

$$P(A|B) = P(A)$$

In fact, now the occurrence of B does not affect the probability $P(A)$.

Let's take an example. What is the probability that by extracting two cards from a deck of 52, the second one is a diamond? Note the information that the first was a diamond too:

```
P(diamonds ∩ diamonds) = 13/52 * 12/51
```

Then, the conditional probability is given by:

```
P(diamonds | diamonds) = (13/52 * 12/51) / 13/52 = 12/51
```

As a further example, you can calculate the probability that you get the number one by throwing a dice, given that the result is an odd number. The conditional probability we want to calculate is that of the event $B\mid A$; that is, getting number one knowing that there will be an odd number, where A is the getting an odd number event and B is the getting the number one event.

The intersection event $A \cap B$ corresponds to the event getting the number one and an odd number (which is equivalent to the getting the number one event, since one is odd). Therefore, the probability of getting an odd number is equal to:

```
P(A)  =  3/6 = 1/2
```

While the probability of getting the number 1 is:

```
P(A∩B)  =  1/6
```

Therefore, it is possible to calculate the conditional probability of event B with respect to event A using the following formula:

$$P(B|A) = \frac{P(A \cap B)}{P(A)} = \frac{\frac{1}{6}}{\frac{1}{2}} = \frac{1}{3} \approx 0.333$$

Let us remember, in this regard, that playing dice is always a loss-making activity, even for a statistician.

Bayes' theorem

In the previous section, we learned to calculate many types of probabilities; it is time to benefit from the acquired skills. We will do this by defining Bayes' theorem as follows.

Let A and B be two dependent events. Previously, we said that the joint probability between the two events is calculated using the following formula:

$$P(A \cap B) = P(A) \times P(B|A)$$

Or, similarly, using the following formula:

$$P(A \cap B) = P(B) \times P(A|B)$$

By analyzing the two proposed formulas, it is clear that they have the first equal member. This implies that even the second members are equal, so we can write:

$$P(A) \times P(B|A) = P(B) \times P(A|B)$$

By solving these equations for conditional probability, we get:

$$P(B|A) = \frac{P(B) \times P(A|B)}{P(A)}$$

Or, in a similar way we can calculate:

$$P(A|B) = \frac{P(A) \times P(B|A)}{P(B)}$$

The proposed formulas represent the mathematical statement of Bayes' theorem. The use of one or the other depends on what we are looking for.

Let's take an example. Suppose you are given two coins. The first coin is fair (heads and tails) and the second coin is biased (heads on both sides). You randomly choose a coin and toss it, getting heads as a result. What is the likelihood of it being the second coin (the wrong coin)?

Let's start by distinguishing the various events that come into play. Let's identify these events:

- A: The first coin was chosen
- B: The second coin was chosen
- C: After the toss comes a head

To avoid making mistakes, let us see what we need to calculate. The question made by the problem is simple. It asks us to calculate the likelihood of choosing the second coin, knowing that after the launch we got heads. In symbols, we have to calculate $P(B|C)$.

According to Bayes' theorem, we can write:

$$P(B|C) = \frac{P(B) \times P(C|B)}{P(C)}$$

Now, compute the three probabilities that appear in the previous equation. Remember that *P(B|C)* is called **posterior probability** and that is what we want to calculate. *P(B)* is called **prior probability**, linked to the second event *(B)*, and is equal to *1/2*, since we have two possible choices (two coins are available):

$$P(B) = \frac{1}{2}$$

P(C|B) is called likelihood and is equal to *1*, as it gives the chances of heads knowing that you have chosen the second coin (which has two heads and so is a certain event). Therefore:

$$P(C|B) = 1$$

Finally, *P(C)* is called **marginal likelihood** and is equal to *3/4*, as the coins have *4* faces (possible cases) of which *3* have heads (favorable cases):

$$P(C) = \frac{3}{4}$$

At this point, we can enter the calculated probabilities in the Bayes' formula to get the result:

$$P(B|C) = \frac{P(B) \times P(C|B)}{P(C)} = \frac{\frac{1}{2} \times 1}{\frac{3}{4}} = \frac{2}{3}$$

Bayesian model using BAS package

To perform Bayesian linear regression, we will use the USCrime dataset contained in the MASS package. This dataset refers to the effect of punishment regimes on crime rates. Criminologists are interested in the effect of punishment regimes on crime rates. This has been studied using aggregate data on 47 states of the USA for 1960 given in this data frame. The variables seem to have been rescaled to convenient numbers.

This data frame contains 47 observations (*47* states of the USA) of the 16 following variables:

- M: Percentage of males aged *14–24*
- So: indicator variable for a Southern state
- Ed: Mean years of schooling
- Po1: Police expenditure in 1960
- Po2: Police expenditure in 1959
- LF: Labor force participation rate
- M.F: Number of males per *1,000* females
- Pop: State population
- NW: Number of nonwhites per *1,000* people
- U1: Unemployment rate of urban males *14–24*
- U2: Unemployment rate of urban males *35–39*
- GDP: Gross domestic product per head
- Ineq: Income inequality
- Prob: Probability of imprisonment
- Time: Average time served in state prisons
- Y: Rate of crimes in a particular category per head of population

To import the data into R, we must first install the MASS package and then load the library:

```
library(MASS)
```

Then we can import the data:

```
UScrimeData<-as.data.frame(UScrime)
```

Let's look at the internal structure of the imported data frame:

```
str(UScrimeData)
```

The results are shown in the following:

```
> str(UScrimeData)
'data.frame':   47 obs. of  16 variables:
 $ M    : int  151 143 142 136 141 121 127 131 157 140 ...
 $ So   : int  1 0 1 0 0 0 1 1 1 0 ...
 $ Ed   : int  91 113 89 121 121 110 111 109 90 118 ...
 $ Po1  : int  58 103 45 149 109 118 82 115 65 71 ...
 $ Po2  : int  56 95 44 141 101 115 79 109 62 68 ...
```

```
$ LF   : int   510 583 533 577 591 547 519 542 553 632 ...
$ M.F  : int   950 1012 969 994 985 964 982 969 955 1029 ...
$ Pop  : int   33 13 18 157 18 25 4 50 39 7 ...
$ NW   : int   301 102 219 80 30 44 139 179 286 15 ...
$ U1   : int   108 96 94 102 91 84 97 79 81 100 ...
$ U2   : int   41 36 33 39 20 29 38 35 28 24 ...
$ GDP  : int   394 557 318 673 578 689 620 472 421 526 ...
$ Ineq : int   261 194 250 167 174 126 168 206 239 174 ...
$ Prob : num   0.0846 0.0296 0.0834 0.0158 0.0414 ...
$ Time : num   26.2 25.3 24.3 29.9 21.3 ...
$ y    : int   791 1635 578 1969 1234 682 963 1555 856 705 ...
```

Now, we will display some data statistics using the `summary()` function:

```
summary(UScrimeData)
```

The results are shown in the following:

```
> summary(UScrimeData)
       M                So               Ed               Po1
 Min.   :119.0    Min.   :0.0000   Min.   : 87.0    Min.   : 45.0
 1st Qu.:130.0    1st Qu.:0.0000   1st Qu.: 97.5    1st Qu.: 62.5
 Median :136.0    Median :0.0000   Median :108.0    Median : 78.0
 Mean   :138.6    Mean   :0.3404   Mean   :105.6    Mean   : 85.0
 3rd Qu.:146.0    3rd Qu.:1.0000   3rd Qu.:114.5    3rd Qu.:104.5
 Max.   :177.0    Max.   :1.0000   Max.   :122.0    Max.   :166.0
      Po2               LF               M.F               Pop
 Min.   : 41.00   Min.   :480.0    Min.   : 934.0   Min.   :  3.00
 1st Qu.: 58.50   1st Qu.:530.5    1st Qu.: 964.5   1st Qu.: 10.00
 Median : 73.00   Median :560.0    Median : 977.0   Median : 25.00
 Mean   : 80.23   Mean   :561.2    Mean   : 983.0   Mean   : 36.62
 3rd Qu.: 97.00   3rd Qu.:593.0    3rd Qu.: 992.0   3rd Qu.: 41.50
 Max.   :157.00   Max.   :641.0    Max.   :1071.0   Max.   :168.00
       NW               U1               U2               GDP
 Min.   :  2.0    Min.   : 70.00   Min.   :20.00    Min.   :288.0
 1st Qu.: 24.0    1st Qu.: 80.50   1st Qu.:27.50    1st Qu.:459.5
 Median : 76.0    Median : 92.00   Median :34.00    Median :537.0
 Mean   :101.1    Mean   : 95.47   Mean   :33.98    Mean   :525.4
 3rd Qu.:132.5    3rd Qu.:104.00   3rd Qu.:38.50    3rd Qu.:591.5
 Max.   :423.0    Max.   :142.00   Max.   :58.00    Max.   :689.0
      Ineq              Prob              Time               y
 Min.   :126.0    Min.   :0.00690   Min.   :12.20    Min.   : 342.0
 1st Qu.:165.5    1st Qu.:0.03270   1st Qu.:21.60    1st Qu.: 658.5
 Median :176.0    Median :0.04210   Median :25.80    Median : 831.0
 Mean   :194.0    Mean   :0.04709   Mean   :26.60    Mean   : 905.1
 3rd Qu.:227.5    3rd Qu.:0.05445   3rd Qu.:30.45    3rd Qu.:1057.5
 Max.   :276.0    Max.   :0.11980   Max.   :44.00    Max.   :1993.0
```

From a first analysis, it is clear that the data has a positive distribution with strong asymmetry. To reduce the effects of data asymmetry in the regression model, we can work on data transformation. For example, we can make a logarithmic transformation of data.

 Remember, logarithmic transformation applies when distribution has positive symmetry, to get a normal distribution. In continuous variables, it is useful to make variances homogeneous when they grow as the average increases.

Any logarithmic transformation has similar effects, though more or less accentuated, since the transformed data differs only for a multiplicative constant. In various situations, logarithmic transformation has multiple effects: it simultaneously serves to stabilize variance, to reduce additive effects to a multiplicative effect, to normalize distribution.

Logarithmic transformation should be used when one desires a more normal distribution from a data distribution characterized by a strong right or positive asymmetry is desired; then we speak of log-normal distribution.

So we make a `log` transformation for all of the variables except column 2, which is the indicator variable of the state being a southern state:

```
UScrimeData[,-2] = log(UScrime[,-2])
```

To compare data distributions before and after logarithmic transformation, we can display data boxplots. The following figure shows the distribution of data before logarithmic transformation (to the left) and after transformation (to the right):

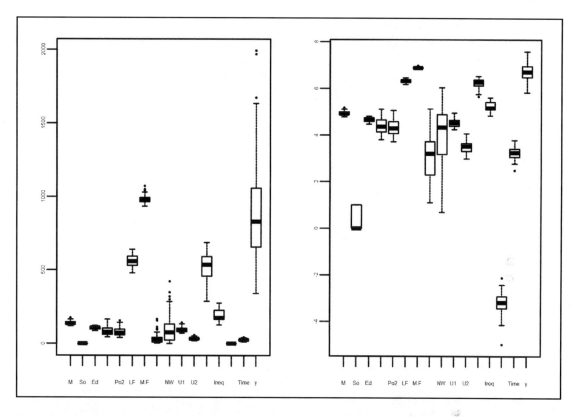

When analyzing the previous figure, it can be noticed that the transformation has considerably reduced the variation range of the values that is passed from *(0;2000)* to *(-4;8)*. In addition, we can observe noticeable reduction effects of the outliers, particularly for the response variable (*y*) (the last to the right of both charts).

To implement Bayesian linear regression in R, we will use the `bas.lm()` function. This function evaluates a set of Bayesian models containing different combinations of features. We can then make predictions using various combinations of the resulting models:

```
USCrimeBas<- bas.lm(y ~ ., data = UScrimeData,prior = 'BIC',
                                modelprior = uniform())
```

We passed a linear model formula for the full model with all predictors using the dot (.) and specify y as the response variable. The function returns inclusion probabilities for each feature, given the data used to fit the models. As prior distribution for regression coefficients, we used the **Bayesian Information Criterion (BIC)**. As a family of prior distribution on the models, we have chosen uniform distribution. The resulting model is shown in the following:

```
> USCrimeBas
Call:
bas.lm(formula = y ~ ., data = UScrimeData, prior = "BIC", modelprior =
uniform())
 Marginal Posterior Inclusion Probabilities:
Intercept          M          So          Ed         Po1         Po2
   1.0000     0.9094      0.2286      0.9920      0.6873      0.4037
       LF        M.F         Pop          NW          U1          U2
   0.1607     0.1677      0.3591      0.7758      0.2263      0.6959
      GDP       Ineq        Prob        Time
   0.3635     0.9992      0.9462      0.4085
```

To display some data statistics, we will use the summary() function:

summary(USCrimeBas)

The results are shown in the following figure:

```
> summary(USCrimeBas)
             P(B != 0 | Y)   model 1      model 2       model 3       model 4       model 5
Intercept      1.0000000     1.00000     1.0000000     1.0000000     1.0000000     1.0000000
M              0.9093806     1.00000     1.0000000     1.0000000     1.0000000     1.0000000
So             0.2286218     0.00000     0.0000000     0.0000000     0.0000000     0.0000000
Ed             0.9919748     1.00000     1.0000000     1.0000000     1.0000000     1.0000000
Po1            0.6872631     1.00000     1.0000000     1.0000000     1.0000000     0.0000000
Po2            0.4037022     0.00000     0.0000000     0.0000000     0.0000000     1.0000000
LF             0.1607246     0.00000     0.0000000     0.0000000     0.0000000     0.0000000
M.F            0.1677401     0.00000     0.0000000     0.0000000     0.0000000     0.0000000
Pop            0.3591253     0.00000     0.0000000     0.0000000     1.0000000     0.0000000
NW             0.7757744     1.00000     1.0000000     1.0000000     1.0000000     1.0000000
U1             0.2263200     0.00000     0.0000000     0.0000000     0.0000000     0.0000000
U2             0.6959277     1.00000     1.0000000     1.0000000     1.0000000     1.0000000
GDP            0.3634938     0.00000     0.0000000     1.0000000     0.0000000     0.0000000
Ineq           0.9992075     1.00000     1.0000000     1.0000000     1.0000000     1.0000000
Prob           0.9462122     1.00000     1.0000000     1.0000000     1.0000000     1.0000000
Time           0.4085486     1.00000     0.0000000     1.0000000     0.0000000     0.0000000
BF                    NA     1.00000     0.7609295     0.5431578     0.5203179     0.4713572
PostProbs             NA     0.03470     0.0264000     0.0189000     0.0181000     0.0164000
R2                    NA     0.84200     0.8265000     0.8506000     0.8375000     0.8229000
dim                   NA     9.00000     8.0000000    10.0000000     9.0000000     8.0000000
logmarg               NA -22.15855   -22.4317627   -22.7689035   -22.8118635   -22.9106871
```

The results show the posterior probability of the top models side-by-side with the zero-one indicators for variable inclusion. The other columns in the summary are the Bayes factor of each model to the highest probability model (hence its Bayes factor is one), the posterior probabilities of the models, the ordinary R-squared of the models, the dimension of the models (number of coefficients including the intercept) and the log marginal likelihood under the selected prior distribution. We can notice that the model with the largest R does not have the largest probability.

Further information can be extracted from the model through a visual analysis. For example, we can use the `image()` function that creates an image of the model space sampled using `bas`. If a subset of the top models are plotted, then probabilities are renormalized over the subset:

```
image(USCrimeBas)
```

The following figure shows the **Log Posterior Odds** for the first *20* models:

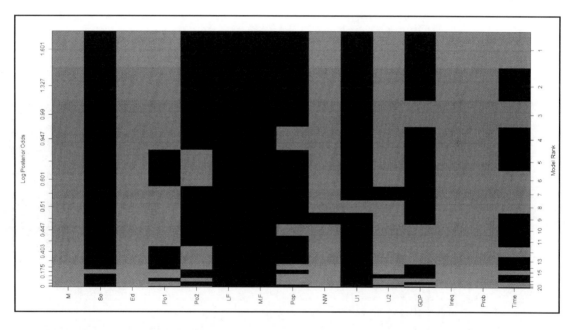

In the previous figure, rows correspond to each of the variables and intercept, with labels for the variables on the *x* axis. The *y* axis corresponds to the possible models. These are sorted by their posterior probability from best on the top to worst on the bottom, with the rank at the right.

Each row represents one of the *20* models. The variables that are excluded in a model are shown in black for each row, while the variables that are included are colored, with the color related to the log posterior probability. The color of each column is proportional to the log of the posterior probabilities (the left *y* axis) of that model. Models that are the same color have similar log posterior probabilities which allows us to view models that are clustered together that have marginal likelihoods where the differences are not significant.

This plot indicates that the police expenditure in the two years, (Po2), do not enter the model together, and is an indication of the high correlation between the two variables. Other variables that do not enter the best model are: So, LF, M.F, PoP, U1, and GDP.

We continue with the visual analysis through some graphical summaries of the output obtained by the plot() function:

```
par(mfrow=c(2,2))
plot(USCrimeBas)
```

The following figure shows **Residuals vs Fitted** values, **Model Probabilities**, **Model Complexity**, and **Inclusion Probabilities**:

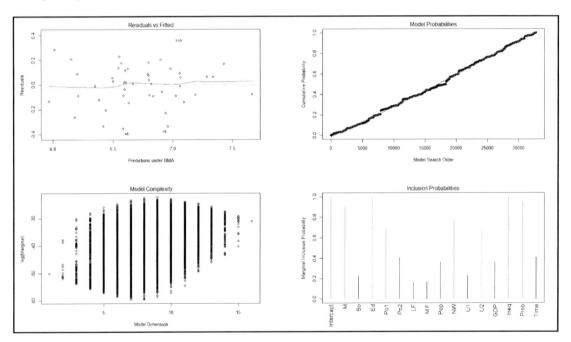

The previous figure shows four plots: the first is a plot of residuals and fitted values under Bayesian model averaging (top left). The residuals appear on the y axis and the fitted values appear on the x axis. There are equally spread residuals around a horizontal line without distinct patterns, that is a good indication you don't have nonlinear relationships.

The second plot displays the cumulative probability of the models in the order that they are sampled (top right). This plot suggests that the cumulative probability is leveled off as each additional model adds only a small increment to the cumulative probability, wherein earlier, there were larger jumps corresponding to sampling high-probability models.

The third plot displays the dimension of each model (the number of regression coefficients inclusive of the intercept) versus the log of the marginal likelihood of the model (bottom left).

The last plot displays the marginal **Posterior Inclusion Probabilities (pip)** for each covariate, with marginal pips greater than *0.5* shown in red (bottom right). The variables with pip is greater than *0.5* correspond to what is known as the median probability model. Variables with high inclusion probabilities are generally important to explain the data or prediction, however marginal inclusion probabilities may be small in case there are predictors that are correlated, similar to how p-values may be large in the presence of multicollinearity.

Count data model

Poisson regression is a form of regression used to model the count of data in contingency tables. For example, counting the number of births or the number of wins in a series of soccer matches. Poisson regression assumes that the response variable Y has a Poisson distribution, and that the logarithm of its expected value can be modelled by a linear combination of unknown parameters. Poisson regression is sometimes also known as a **log-linear model**, especially when it is used to model contingency tables.

Poisson distributions

A distribution tells us how measures of a certain variable are distributed among the various possible values. Each distribution is characterized by an average value and a variance, which adjusts the uncertainty of the measurements obtained. Poisson's distribution, also known as rare event law, is a very useful type of distribution when dealing with extremely rare events, which occur with a well-defined temporal mean. It is an approximation of the binomial distribution, defined for non-negative integer values. Unlike the binomial distribution, it is hypergeometric and unlimited. Examples are:

- The number of phone calls coming to a home in one day
- The number of clients who lodge complaints within a week
- The number of a student's absences in a month
- The number of print errors on a page of a book

Before describing the Poisson formula, it is useful to have the characteristics that a process must satisfy to be considered as a Poisson distribution. Assume that an interval is divided into a very large number of subintervals, so that the probability of an event occurring in each subinterval is very small. The basic hypotheses of the Poisson distribution are:

- The probability of an event occurring is constant for all subintervals
- The event cannot occur more than once in each of the subintervals
- Events occurring at disjointed intervals are independent

Based on these hypotheses, we can write the formula that defines Poisson's probability distribution:

$$P(k) = \frac{\lambda^k}{k!} * e^{-\lambda}$$

Here:

- λ is the rate (per unit of time or space) at which events occur
- k is an integer (0,1,2 … n) indicating for as many values as possible that we want to calculate the probability

The crucial parameter in a Poisson distribution is λ. This is the mean number of events that occurs in a specified interval of time or space. This parameter also represents the variance for a Poisson distribution. The Poisson distribution has the property that its mean and variance are equal. To understand how a Poisson distribution looks, we can create a fictitious one by using the `rpois()` function. In the following the general form of the function is:

```
rpois(n, lambda)
```

The arguments passed are:

- n is the number of random values to return
- lambda is a vector of (nonnegative) means

To generate 60 random numbers from a Poisson distribution with `lambda` = 5 we will write:

```
PD<-rpois(60, lambda = 5)
```

For example, if an emergency service receives 5 calls per minute, this command will simulate 60 minutes, returning the number of calls in each of those 60 minutes. Let's see what we got:

```
> PD
 [1]  3  4  6  6  2  5  7  6  7  8  7  5 14  7  2  5  3
[18]  6  6  3  2  3  2  7  5  7  6  3  1  3  9 10  9  5
[35]  3  8  5  4  2  5  9  7  4  4  9  7  4  4  9  7  4
[52]  6  4  9  4  6 12  5  6  3
```

These are the incoming calls in the last 60 minutes counted in one-minute intervals.

To see the distribution we just created, we must count the frequency of each occurrence. To do this, we will use the `table()` function that uses the cross-classifying factors to build a contingency table of the counts at each combination of factor levels:

```
FPD<-table(PD)
```

Now, we can show on a graph the frequency of occurrence of a specific call count:

```
plot(FPD)
```

The results are shown in the following figure:

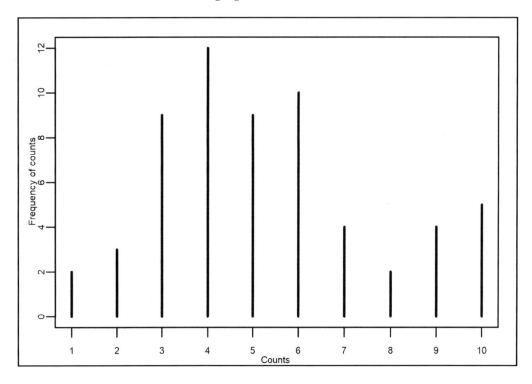

For each group of the data, the frequencies of the occurrences are reported.

Poisson regression model

Suppose that we have a sample of n observations $y_1, y_2, \ldots, y_n$ which can be treated as a Poisson distribution, with:

$$Y_i \sim Poisson(\mu_i)$$

The following variance function:

$$Var(Y_i) = \mu_i$$

Furthermore, suppose that we want to let the mean μ_i (and therefore the variance) depend on a vector of explanatory variables x_i. We can adopt a simple linear model of the form:

$$g(\mu_i) = x_i^T * \beta$$

The linear predictor on the right-hand side of the previous equation can assume any real value, whereas the Poisson mean on the left-hand side, which represents an expected count, has to be non-negative. To solve this problem we can adopt a linear model for the logarithm of the mean instead of the mean itself:

$$log(\mu_i) = x_i^T * \beta$$

Here, the regression coefficient β_j represents the expected change in the log of the mean per unit change in the predictor x_j. That mean increasing x_j by one unit is associated with an increase of β_j in the log of the mean. If we apply the exponential function to both sides of the previous equation we get:

$$\mu_i = exp(x_i^T * \beta)$$

Here $exp\{\beta_j\}$ (exponential of the β_j coefficient) represents a multiplicative effect of the jth predictor on the mean. For every unit increase in X, the predictor variable has a multiplicative effect of $exp(\beta)$ on the mean of Y, that is μ.

Similar to the case of logistical regression, the maximum likelihood estimators for β coefficients are obtained by determining the values that maximize log-likelihood. In general, there are no closed-form solutions, so the model estimates are determined by utilizing iterative algorithms.

Modeling the number of warp breaks per loom

To perform Poisson regression, we will use the `warpbreaks` dataset contained in the `datasets` package. This dataset contains the number of breaks in yarn during weaving. The number of warp breaks per loom is given, where a loom corresponds to a fixed length of yarn. The `warpbreaks` dataset provides the number of warp break imperfections (`breaks` variable) observed in 54 pieces of yarn of equal length. Each piece of yarn is classified according to two categorical variables: `wool`(the type of yarn, with levels A and B) and `tension`(the level of tension applied to that piece—L, M, or H for low, medium, or high). The purpose of the analysis is to determine the effect of `wool` type (A or B) and `tension` (low, medium or high) on the number of warp breaks per loom.

This data frame contains 54 observations on 3 variables, as follows:

- `breaks`: The number of breaks
- `wool`: The type of wool (A or B)
- `tension`: The level of tension (L, M, H)

There are measurements on nine looms for each of the six types of warp (AL, AM, AH, BL, BM, BH).

First, we must import the dataset as a data frame:

```
WPData<-as.data.frame(warpbreaks)
```

Let's look at the internal structure of the imported data frame:

```
str(WPData)
```

The results are shown in the following:

```
> str(WPData)
'data.frame':   54 obs. of  3 variables:
$ breaks : num  26 30 54 25 70 52 51 26 67 18 ...
 $ wool    : Factor w/ 2 levels "A","B": 1 1 1 1 1 1 1 1 1 1 ...
 $ tension: Factor w/ 3 levels "L","M","H": 1 1 1 1 1 1 1 1 1 2 ...
```

One numerical variable and two factor variables are returned. Now, we will display some data statistics using the `summary()` function:

```
summary(WPData)
```

The results are shown in the following:

```
> summary(WPData)
     breaks          wool     tension
 Min.    :10.00    A:27    L:18
 1st Qu.:18.25    B:27    M:18
 Median :26.00            H:18
 Mean    :28.15
 3rd Qu.:34.00
 Max.    :70.00
```

In the following, we will consider breaks as the response variable, which is a count of number of breaks, while the wool type and tension will be taken as predictor variables. To begin, let's look at the distribution of the number of warp breaks:

```
par(mfrow = c(1, 2))
plot(breaks ~ tension, data = WPData, col = "lightgray",
    varwidth = TRUE, subset = wool == "A", main = "Wool
       A",ylim=c(8,72))
plot(breaks ~ tension, data = warpbreaks, col = "lightgray",
    varwidth = TRUE, subset = wool == "B", main = "Wool
       B",ylim=c(8,72))
```

The following figure shows boxplots of **breaks** against **tension** for **Wool A** (to the left) and **Wool B** (to the right):

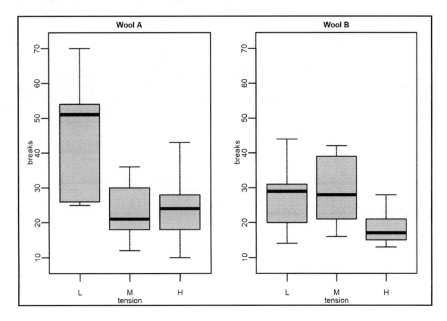

From the comparison between the two boxplots, it is clear that **Wool A** has a greater number of warp breaks at the tension **L** values. Recall that the `warpbreaks` dataset contains observations of the number of **breaks**, (during weaving), under conditions indicated by two grouping factors: **Wool** and **tension**. We said that our purpose is to model the number of **breaks** depending on the type and **tension** of the **Wool**. To do this we can start with a Poisson regression model with interaction between two predictors.

A Poisson regression model can model the relationship between a Poisson distributed response variable and one or more predictors. It is right for modeling the number of events that occur in a given under specific conditions. The predictors can be either numeric or categorical. Interaction terms can also be included in the model.

We can build a Poisson regression model with the `glm()` function. This function is used to fit **Generalized Linear Model (GLM)**, specified by giving a symbolic description of the linear predictor and a description of the error distribution. The Poisson regression is performed by indicating the `family` argument. This argument provides a convenient way to specify the details of the models used by `glm()` function:

```
WPModel1<-glm(breaks~wool+tension, data = WPData, family=poisson)
```

Now, we see the model coefficients:

```
> WPModel1
Call:  glm(formula = breaks ~ wool + tension, family = poisson, data =
WPData)
Coefficients:
(Intercept)        woolB      tensionM      tensionH
     3.6920      -0.2060       -0.3213       -0.5185
Degrees of Freedom: 53 Total (i.e. Null);  50 Residual
Null Deviance:      297.4
Residual Deviance: 210.4 AIC: 493.1
```

We extract the model coefficients that are obtained using the `coef()` function:

```
CoefWP1<-coef(WPModel1)
```

Let's focus on the second coefficient for `woolB`:

```
> CoefWP1[2]
     woolB
-0.2059884
```

How can we interpret this value? In the model, the term `woolA` does not appear, due to the fact that the first level is the reference group by default. So, the coefficient of `woolB` is −0.2059884, so the expected log-count for `woolB` is about 0.2059884 less than those for `woolA` and provides a negative contribution to it (negative sign). Alternatively, we can compute its exponent when speaking about ratios instead of differences:

```
> exp(CoefWP1[2])
     woolB
0.8138425
```

So, the expected number of failures for `woolB` is 0.8138425 times less than for `woolA`. In general, the interpretation goes as: a one-unit increase in predictor multiplies response by *exp(β)*. To look at the model, let's see a brief summary using the `summary()` function:

```
> summary(WPModel1)
Call:
glm(formula = breaks ~ wool + tension, family = poisson, data = WPData)
Deviance Residuals:
    Min       1Q    Median       3Q       Max
 -3.6871  -1.6503   -0.4269   1.1902    4.2616
Coefficients:
              Estimate Std. Error z value Pr(>|z|)
(Intercept)   3.69196    0.04541  81.302  < 2e-16 ***
woolB        -0.20599    0.05157  -3.994 6.49e-05 ***
tensionM     -0.32132    0.06027  -5.332 9.73e-08 ***
tensionH     -0.51849    0.06396  -8.107 5.21e-16 ***
---
Signif. codes:  0 '***' 0.001 '**' 0.01 '*' 0.05 '.' 0.1 ' ' 1
(Dispersion parameter for poisson family taken to be 1)
    Null deviance: 297.37  on 53  degrees of freedom
Residual deviance: 210.39  on 50  degrees of freedom
AIC: 493.06
Number of Fisher Scoring iterations: 4
```

We may notice that all terms inserted in the model are statistically significant, also several statistic values are returned, including the `Null deviance` and `Residual deviance` and `AIC`. `Null deviance` indicates the response predicted by a model with nothing but an intercept. The lower the value, the better the model. `Residual deviance` indicates the response predicted by a model on adding independent variables. The lower the value, the better the model. Deviance is a measure of the goodness of fit of a GLM. Or rather, it's a measure of badness of fit-higher numbers indicate a worse fit.

The analogous metric of adjusted R² in Poisson regression is AIC. AIC is a measure of fit which penalizes models for their number of model coefficients. Therefore, we always prefer models with minimum AIC values.

Finally, the Number of Fisher Scoring iterations is returned. Fisher's scoring algorithm is a derivative of Newton's method for solving maximum likelihood problems numerically. For our model, we see that Fisher's scoring algorithm needed four iterations to perform the fit. This doesn't really tell you a lot that you need to know, other than the fact that the model did indeed converge, and had no trouble doing it.

As we said at the beginning of the section, in a Poisson distribution, the variance and the mean assume the same value. When the observed variance of the response variable is greater than that predicted by the Poisson distribution, overdispersion occurs. Overdispersion is the presence of greater variability in a dataset than would be expected based on a given statistical model. Overdispersion can have a negative impact on the interpretation of results.

A test of the presence of overdispersion can be done by calculating the ratio of the residual deviance to the residual degrees of freedom. If this ratio is much larger than one, overdispersion occurs:

```
> deviance(WPModel1)/df.residual(WPModel1)
[1] 4.207838
```

The result is larger than one. At this point, let's see what happens if we put a term in Poisson's regression model that takes into account the difference between the two categorical predictors:

```
WPModel2<-glm(breaks~wool*tension, data = WPData, family=poisson)
```

Now, we see the model coefficients:

```
> WPModel2
Call:  glm(formula = breaks ~ wool * tension, family = poisson, data =
WPData)
Coefficients:
    (Intercept)              woolB         tensionM          tensionH
         3.7967             -0.4566          -0.6187           -0.5958
woolB:tensionM  woolB:tensionH
         0.6382            0.1884
Degrees of Freedom: 53 Total (i.e. Null);  48 Residual
Null Deviance:      297.4
Residual Deviance: 182.3 AIC: 469
```

As we can see, two coefficients have been added to the previous model that takes into account the interaction between the two predictors. Let's analyze model statistics:

```
summary(WPModel2)
```

The results are shown in the following:

```
> summary(WPModel2)
Call:
glm(formula = breaks ~ wool * tension, family = poisson, data = WPData)
Deviance Residuals:
    Min       1Q   Median       3Q      Max
-3.3383  -1.4844  -0.1291   1.1725   3.5153
Coefficients:
                Estimate Std. Error z value Pr(>|z|)
(Intercept)      3.79674    0.04994  76.030  < 2e-16 ***
woolB           -0.45663    0.08019  -5.694 1.24e-08 ***
tensionM        -0.61868    0.08440  -7.330 2.30e-13 ***
tensionH        -0.59580    0.08378  -7.112 1.15e-12 ***
woolB:tensionM   0.63818    0.12215   5.224 1.75e-07 ***
woolB:tensionH   0.18836    0.12990   1.450    0.147
---
Signif. codes:  0 '***' 0.001 '**' 0.01 '*' 0.05 '.' 0.1 ' ' 1
(Dispersion parameter for poisson family taken to be 1)
    Null deviance: 297.37  on 53  degrees of freedom
Residual deviance: 182.31  on 48  degrees of freedom
AIC: 468.97
Number of Fisher Scoring iterations: 4
```

From the analysis of the results, we can note that the term `woolB:tensionH` is not statistically significant. In order to improve the performance of the model, we could later remove it from the model. But now we focus our attention on the comparison between the two models obtained. We can notice that the last fitted model has better results. I mean `Residual deviance` and `AIC`. These values are lower than those obtained with the previous model.

Again, we will do a test for overdispersion:

```
> deviance(WPModel2)/df.residual(WPModel2)
[1] 3.798024
```

This value also shows an improvement.

Summary

In this chapter, new regression techniques that are particularly suited to the treatment of specific data types are introduced. Starting with the problem of the presence of outliers in our data, we learned to identify outliers and remove them, thus verifying the performance improvements obtained from the template. We have seen that this step can be simply bypassed using a robust regression model.

To reduce outlier effects, we can fit our data using robust least squares regression. Robust regression methods provide an alternative to least squares regression; they attempt to reduce the influence of outlying cases so as to render a better fit to the majority of the data. Robust regression downweighs the influence of outliers, and makes their residuals larger and easier to identify.

Then we explored the Bayesian regression technique. In the Bayesian approach, we see that the interpretation differs substantially, in fact the β coefficients are treated as random variables, rather than fixed, unknown quantities. So, the goal of a Bayesian analysis is to update the probability distributions of the coefficients by incorporating information from observing data.

Finally, we analyzed the Poisson regression used to model the count of data in contingency tables. Poisson regression assumes that the response variable Y has a Poisson distribution, and that the logarithm of its expected value can be modeled by a linear combination of unknown parameters. Poisson regression is sometimes also known as a log-linear model, especially when it is used to model contingency tables.

In the next chapter, the reader will be introduced to several advanced techniques to solve regression problems that cannot be solved with linear models. Some examples will be dealt with to make the use of such algorithms as realistic as possible in real cases. Topics covered will be: nonlinear least squares, **Multivariate Adaptive Regression Splines (MARS)**, **Generalized Additive Model (GAM)**, regression trees, and **Support Vector Regression (SVR)**.

8
Beyond Linearity – When Curving Is Much Better

Some problems cannot be solved with linear models. Often, we must go beyond the simple linearity of models by introducing features that take into account the complexity of the phenomenon. Nonlinear models are more complex (and more prone to overfitting), but sometimes they are the only solution.

In this chapter, we will see an introduction to the most used ones, how to train them, and how to apply them. First, a nonlinear least squares method will be treated, where the parameters of the regression function to be estimated are nonlinear. In this technique, given the nonlinearity of the coefficients, the solution of the problem occurs by means of iterative numerical calculation methods. Then **Multivariate Adaptive Regression Splines** (**MARS**) will be performed. This is a nonparametric regression procedure that makes no assumption about the underlying functional relationship between the response and predictor variables. This relationship is constructed from a set of coefficients and basis functions that are processed, starting from the regression data.

Let's dive into the chapter with a **Generalized Additive Model** (**GAM**). This is a **Generalized Linear Model** (**GLM**) in which the linear predictor is given by a user-specified sum of smooth functions of the covariates, plus a conventional parametric component of the linear predictor. Then, we will introduce the reader to the regression tree. In regression trees, we try to partition the data space into small-enough parts, where we can apply a simple, different model on each part. The non-leaf part of the tree is just the procedure to determine, for each data x, the model we will use to predict it. Finally, we will explore **Support Vector Regression** (**SVR**).

The topics covered are:

- Nonlinear least squares
- MARS
- GAM
- Regression trees
- SVR

At the end of the chapter, you will be able to apply these advanced techniques to solve regression problems that cannot be solved with linear models. Several examples will be dealt with to make use of such algorithms as realistically as possible, in real cases.

Nonlinear least squares

In Chapter 3, *More Than Just One Predictor – MLR*, we have already handled a case in which a linear regression was unable to model the relationship between the response and predictors. In that case, we solved the problem by applying polynomial regression. When the relationships between variables are not linear, three solutions are possible:

- Linearize the relationship by transforming the data
- Fit polynomial or complex spline models
- Fit a nonlinear model

The first two solutions you have already faced in somemanner in the previous chapters. Now we will focus on the third solution. If the parameters of the regression function to be estimated are nonlinear, that is, they appear at a different degree from the first, the **Ordinary Least Squares** (**OLS**) can no longer be applied and other methods need to be applied.

In the multiple nonlinear regression models, the dependent variable is related to two or more independent variables as follows:

$$y = \beta_0 + \beta_1 * x_1 + \beta_2 * x_2 + \ldots + \beta_n * x_n$$

Here, the model is not linear with respect to the unknown coefficients, $\beta_0, \beta_1, \ldots, \beta_n$.

Again, we can use the method of least squares to estimate the values of the unknown parameters. Once again, we must minimize the sum of the squares of the residuals to estimate the vector of coefficients:

$$RSS = \sum_i [y_i - (\beta_0 + \beta_1 * x_1 + \beta_2 * x_2 + \ldots + \beta_n * x_n)]^2$$

Given the nonlinearity of the coefficients, the solution of the problem occurs by means of iterative numerical calculation methods. A general iterative approach follows these steps:

1. Start with an initial estimate for each coefficient (for example random values on the interval *[0,1]*)
2. Produce the fitted curve for the current set of coefficients
3. Adjust the coefficients and determine whether the fit improves
4. Iterate the process by returning to step 2 until the fit reaches the specified convergence criteria

In R, the estimate of the minimum squares in case of nonlinearity in the coefficients can be solved using the `nls()` function (`nls` is the acronym of nonlinear least squares). This function determines the nonlinear (weighted) least square estimates of the parameters of a nonlinear model. The general form of the function is as follows:

```
nls(formula, data, start, control, algorithm, trace, subset,
    weights,na.action, model, lower, upper)
```

The arguments, with a brief explanation, are listed in the following table:

Argument	Explanation
`formula`	A nonlinear model formula, including variables and parameters. Will be coerced to a formula if necessary.
`data`	An optional data frame in which to evaluate the variables in formula and weights. This can also be a list or an environment but not a matrix.
`start`	A named list or named numeric vector of starting estimates. When start is missing, a very cheap guess for start is tried (if algorithm != `"plinear"`).
`control`	An optional list of control settings.

algorithm	A character string specifying the algorithm to use. The default algorithm is a Gauss-Newton. Other possible values are plinear for Golub, Pereyra algorithm for partially linear least square models, and port for the NL2SOL algorithm from the `Port` library (see the references). This can be abbreviated.
trace	A logical value indicating whether a trace of the iteration progress should be printed. Default is FALSE. If TRUE the residual (weighted) sum of squares and the parameter values are printed at the conclusion of each iteration. When the plinear algorithm is used, the conditional estimates of the linear parameters are printed after the nonlinear parameters. When the port algorithm is used, the objective function value printed is half the residual (weighted) sum of squares.
subset	An optional vector specifying a subset of observations to be used in the fitting process.
weights	An optional numeric vector of (fixed) weights. When present, the objective function is weighted least squares.
na.action	A function which indicates what should happen when the data contains NA. The default is set by the `na.action` setting of options, and is `na.fail` if that is unset. The factory-fresh default is `na.omit`. Value `na.exclude` can be useful.
model	A logical value is required. If TRUE, the model frame is returned as part of the object. Default is FALSE.
lower, upper	Vectors of `lower` and `upper` bounds, replicated to be as long as `start`. If unspecified, all parameters are assumed to be unconstrained. Bounds can only be used with the port algorithm. They are ignored, with a warning, if given for other algorithms.

To see how it works, let's look at a simple example. We create an exponential distribution of data in this regard. First we generate the x predictor as 200 integers using the seq() function:

```
x<-seq(0,200,1)
```

The seq() function generates regular sequences. In the previous command, 0 is the starting value of the sequence, 200 is the end value of the sequence, and 1 is the increment of the sequence. Now we need to generate the response variable:

```
y<-((runif(1,8,25)*x)/(runif(1,0,7)+x))+runif(201,0,1)
```

To generate the response, we have used the `runif()` function; it generates random deviates. The general form of the function is as follows:

```
runif(n, min = 0, max = 1)
```

The response variable was generated in accordance with the following formula:

```
y=(a*x/b+x) + noise
```

In this equation the terms are defined as follows:

```
a = runif(1,8,25)
b = runif(1,0,7)
noise = runif(201,0,1)
```

The last term (`runif(201,0,1)`) adds `noise`. Let's look at the data we just created:

```
plot(x,y)
```

The following figure shows the predictor **x** against the response **y**:

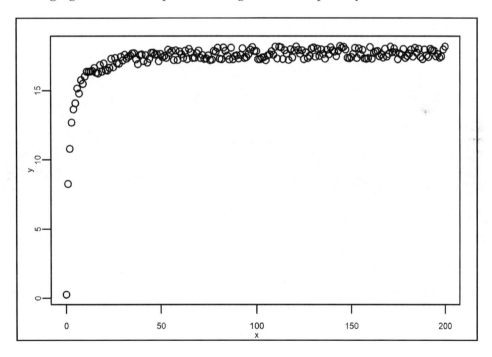

The nonlinear nature of distribution is clearly identifiable. Now, to understand how a linear regression is not suitable for modeling such a distribution, we will first build a linear regression model and then a nonlinear one for comparing. Let's start with the linear model:

```
LModel<-lm(y~x)
```

Now, we will display some data statistics using the summary() function:

```
LMSummary<-summary(LModel)
```

The results are shown as follows:

```
> LMSummary

Call:
lm(formula = y ~ x)

Residuals:
     Min       1Q   Median       3Q      Max
-15.9547  -0.5311   0.4812   0.9926   1.7747

Coefficients:
             Estimate Std. Error t value Pr(>|t|)
(Intercept) 15.965182   0.274745   58.11   <2e-16 ***
x            0.024398   0.002376   10.27   <2e-16 ***
---
Signif. codes:  0 '***' 0.001 '**' 0.01 '*' 0.05 '.' 0.1 ' ' 1

Residual standard error: 1.955 on 199 degrees of freedom
Multiple R-squared:  0.3463,    Adjusted R-squared:  0.343
F-statistic: 105.4 on 1 and 199 DF,  p-value: < 2.2e-16
```

Now let's move to the nonlinear model:

```
NLModel<-nls(y~a*x/(b+x),start=list(a=1,b=0.1))
```

We have passed the formula and the initial values for the parameters. Again, we will display some data statistics using the summary() function:

```
NLMSummary <- summary(NLModel)
```

The results are shown as follows:

```
> NLMSummary

Formula: y ~ a * x/(b + x)

Parameters:
  Estimate Std. Error t value Pr(>|t|)
a 19.86355    0.02954  672.34   <2e-16 ***
b  3.50244    0.06556   53.42   <2e-16 ***
---
Signif. codes:   0 '***' 0.001 '**' 0.01 '*' 0.05 '.' 0.1 ' ' 1

Residual standard error: 0.2964 on 199 degrees of freedom

Number of iterations to convergence: 5
Achieved convergence tolerance: 2.424e-07
```

From the statistics returned, we can extract the Residual standard error for each model to compare them:

```
> LMSummary$sigma
[1] 1.954865
> NLMSummary$sigma
[1] 0.2964455
```

The linear model error is about six times greater than that of the nonlinear one. This shows that the nonlinear model fits better. We look for the same result through a graphic analysis:

```
plot(x,y)
abline(LModel)
lines(x,predict(NLModel),col="red")
```

In the code just proposed, we first reported data on the graph so we added the regression line using the `abline()` function. This function adds one or more straight lines through the current plot. Then, we add the lines using the `lines` function that represent the nonlinear model, as shown in the following figure:

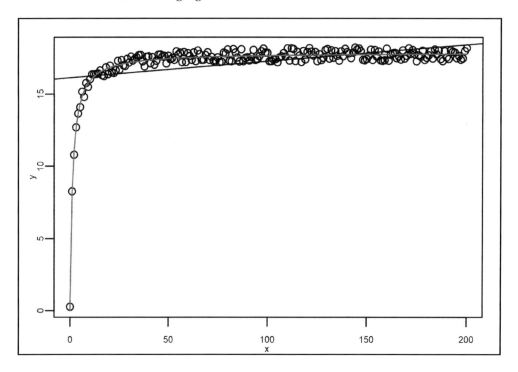

By analyzing the figure, it is possible to confirm that the regression line is unable to predict the starting data. Conversely, the nonlinear model perfectly fits the model.

Multivariate Adaptive Regression Splines

MARS is a form of regression analysis introduced by Jerome H. Friedman (1991), with the main purpose being to predict the values of a response variable from a set of predictor variables.

MARS is a nonparametric regression procedure that makes no assumption about the underlying functional relationship between the response and predictor variables.

This relationship is constructed from a set of coefficients and basis functions that are processed starting from the regression data. The method divides the input space into regions, each with its own regression equation. This makes MARS particularly suitable for problems with a large number of predictors. The following figure shows a distribution with two regression regions:

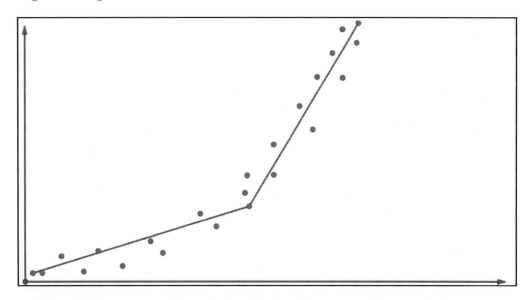

The MARS algorithm operates as a multiple piecewise linear regression, where each breakpoint (estimated from the data) defines the region of application for a very simple linear regression equation.

The general MARS model equation is as follows:

$$y = f(X) = \beta_0 + \sum_{m=1}^{M} \beta_m * h_m(X)$$

Here, y is predicted as a function of the predictor variables X (and their interactions); this function consists of an intercept parameter (β_0) and the weighted by (β_m) sum of one or more basis functions $h_m(X)$.

Each basis function $h_m(X)$ takes one of the following three forms:

- **Constant**: There is just one such term, the intercept.
- **Hinge function**: A hinge function has the form *(t-x)+* and *(x-t)+*, where *t* is a constant. MARS automatically selects variables and values of those variables for knots of the hinge functions.
- **Product of two or more hinge functions**: These basis functions can model interaction between two or more variables.

MARS is particularly popular in the area of data mining because it does not require any particular type of preliminary relationship between predictive variables and response variables. Conversely, models that produce accurate predictions can also be obtained in cases where the relationship between predictors and responses is difficult to derive from parametric models.

 The term MARS is trademarked and licensed to Salford Systems. In order to avoid trademark infringements, many open source implementations of MARS are called **Earth**.

To run a MARS, we can use the `earth` package. This package builds regression models using the techniques in the Friedman papers, *Fast MARS* and *Multivariate Adaptive Regression Splines*. The following table lists some of the information about this package:

Package	`earth`
Date	July 28, 2017
Version	4.5.1
Title	Multivariate Adaptive Regression Splines
Author	Stephen Milborrow. Derived from mda:mars by Trevor Hastie and Rob Tibshirani. Uses Alan Miller's Fortran utilities with Thomas Lumley's leaps wrapper.

To perform a MARS example, as we always do, begin from the data. This time we will use the `trees` dataset contained in the `datasets` package. This data provides measurements of the `Girth` (inches), `Height` (feet) and `Volume` (cubic feet) of timber in *31* felled black cherry trees. Girth is the tree diameter measured at four ft six in above the ground. The goal is the prediction of volume from measurements of girth and height for future trees.

A data frame with 31 observations on 3 variables.

- `Girth`: Tree diameter in inches (numeric)
- `Height`: Height in feet (numeric)
- `Volume`: Volume of timber in cubic feet (numeric)

At first we load the dataset:

```
data(trees)
```

As we have already said, the dataset is contained in the `datasets` package, so to load it we can use the `data()` function. To display a compact summary of the dataset simply type:

```
str(trees)
```

The results are shown as follows:

```
> str(trees)
'data.frame':   31 obs. of  3 variables:
 $ Girth : num  8.3 8.6 8.8 10.5 10.7 10.8 11 11 11.1 11.2 ...
 $ Height: num  70 65 63 72 81 83 66 75 80 75 ...
 $ Volume: num  10.3 10.3 10.2 16.4 18.8 19.7 15.6 18.2 22.6 19.9 ...
```

We have thus confirmed that these are three numeric variables with 31 observations. To extract more information, use the `summary()` function:

```
> summary(trees)
     Girth           Height       Volume
 Min.   : 8.30   Min.   :63   Min.   :10.20
 1st Qu.:11.05   1st Qu.:72   1st Qu.:19.40
 Median :12.90   Median :76   Median :24.20
 Mean   :13.25   Mean   :76   Mean   :30.17
 3rd Qu.:15.25   3rd Qu.:80   3rd Qu.:37.30
 Max.   :20.60   Max.   :87   Max.   :77.00
```

Some statistics are returned with min, max, mean, median, and quartiles for each variable. To understand something more than this distribution, we can perform a preliminary visual analysis. Let's first try to find out whether the variables are related to each other. We can do this using the `pairs()` function to create a matrix of sub axes containing scatter plots of the columns of a matrix:

```
pairs(trees, panel = panel.smooth)
```

The following figure shows a scatter plot matrix of the three variables:

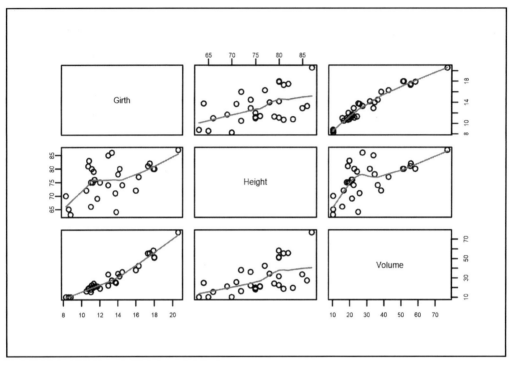

In the previous figure, the plots are scatter plots of the columns of a matrix(the subplot in the ith row and j^{th} column of the matrix is a scatter plot of the ith column against the jth column). As we can see in the figure, scatter plot matrices are a great way to determine roughly whether you have a correlation between multiple variables. This is particularly helpful in locating specific variables that might have mutual correlations, indicating a possible redundancy of data. In the diagonal are the name of the measured variables. The rest of the plots are scatter plots of the matrix columns. Specifically, each plot is present twice; the plots on the ith row are the same as those in the ith column (mirror image).

From a first analysis of the previous figure, you can see several plots showing a nonlinear relationship between the variables. This is the case of the plot showing the relationship between Volume and Girth, as well as between Volume and Height. This trend was confirmed by the smooth curves that are added at each plot. This feature was set by adding the panel argument to the pairs() function:

```
pairs(trees, panel = panel.smooth)
```

The `panel.smooth` value draw a Lowess (locally weighted scatter plot smoothing) curve. A Lowess curve is a smooth curve through a set of data points. In this curve each smoothed value is given by a weighted quadratic least squares regression over the span of values of the *y* axis scatter plot criterion variable. When each smoothed value is given by a weighted linear least squares regression over the span, this is known as a **Lowess curve**. Returns a measure of local regression. From the analysis of the Lowess curves, it is possible to confirm that the distribution is liable to be treated with the MARS technique.

Furthermore, by analyzing the scatter plot matrix we produced, we can notice a greater correlation between the `Volume` variable and the `Girth` variable. At the same time the Lowess curves made it clear that such a relationship is not linear (maybe at times linear). Let's see what happens if we put the `Volume` against `Girth` on a chart by adopting the logarithmic scale for both axes:

```
plot(Volume ~ Girth, data = trees, log = "xy",
            xlab="LogGirth",ylab="LogVolume")
```

The following figure shows **LogVolume** against **LogGirth** by adopting the logarithmic scale for both axes:

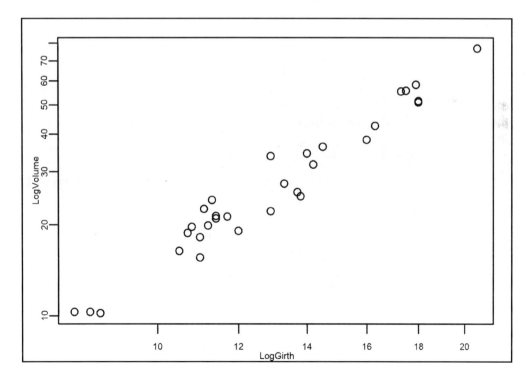

From the analysis of the graph it is easy to identify two zones that show trends that could be fitted by two straight lines, and then at times linear. Where is the variable Height. Let's reintroduce it in the visual analysis we're working on. One way is offered by the coplot() function. This function produces two variants of the conditioning plots. Conditioning scatter plots involves creating a multipanel display, where each panel contains a subset of the data. This subset can be either of the following:

- Those observations that fall in a particular group
- They may represent the values that fall within a particular range of the values of a variable

Each individual panel illustrates the relationship between a pair of variables, over part of the range of the two marginal conditioning variables. The relationship is conditional on one marginal variable lying in one particular interval, and the other lying in a different interval.

In our case, coplot will contain scatter diagrams for the log of Volume as a function of the log of Girth, conditioned by Height (one response variable and one conditioning variable.)

Let's first look at the command to do this:

```
coplot(log(Volume) ~ log(Girth) | Height, data = trees,
                          panel = panel.smooth)
```

First, a formula describing the form of conditioning plot is passed. A formula of the form y ~ x | a indicates that plots of y versus x should be produced conditional on the variable a. Then compare the name of the dataset and the panel.smooth argument. The following figure shows a conditioning plot for log of Volume as a function of the log of Girth, conditioned by Height:

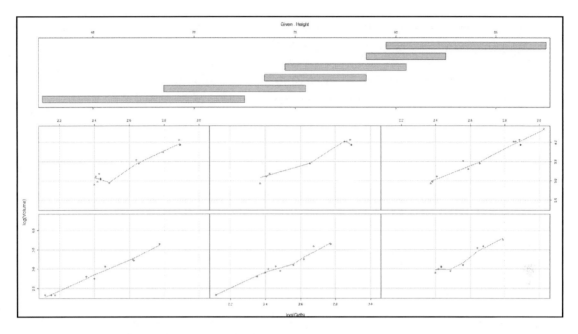

In the top part of the graph are the ranges where the range of existence of the Height variable was subdivided. At the bottom of the graph are the six graphs that contain the log of Volume as a function of the log of Girth for each range of Height. From the analysis of the Lowess curves, it is clear the different trend that LogVolume assumes in each range of the Height variable. The time has come to apply the MARS.

First, we must install the earth package.

 Remember, to install a library that is not present in the initial distribution of R, you must use the install.package function. This is the main function to install packages. It takes a vector of names and a destination library, downloads the packages from the repositories, and installs them.

Then, we will load the library through the `library` command:

```
library(earth)
```

Now we can use the `earth()` function that builds a regression model using the techniques in Friedman's papers *Multivariate Adaptive Regression Splines* and *Fast MARS*:

```
MARSModel <- earth(Volume ~ ., data = trees)
```

Let's see the results:

```
> summary(MARSModel)
Call: earth(formula=Volume~., data=trees)
               coefficients
(Intercept)      29.0599535
h(14.2-Girth)    -3.4198062
h(Girth-14.2)     6.2295143
h(Height-75)      0.5813644
Selected 4 of 5 terms, and 2 of 2 predictors
Termination condition: RSq changed by less than 0.001 at 5 terms
Importance: Girth, Height
Number of terms at each degree of interaction: 1 3 (additive model)
GCV 11.25439    RSS 209.1139    GRSq 0.959692    RSq 0.9742029
```

The following values are returned:

- `coefficients`: The coefficients of the model.
- GCV: The **Generalized Cross Validation (GCV)** is a form of RSS penalized by the effective number of model parameters (and divided by the number of observations).
- RSS: The **residual sum of squares (RSS)** is the sum of the squared values of the residuals. The residuals are the differences between the values predicted by the model and the corresponding response values.
- RSq: RSq (R-squared), also called the coefficient of determination, is a normalized form of RSS, and, depending on the model, varies from zero (a model that always predicts the same value that is the mean observed response value) to one (a model that perfectly predicts the responses in the training data).
- GRSq: GRSq normalizes GCV in the same way that the RSq normalizes RSS.

Now, let's estimate variable importance in the model just created:

```
EvimpMD<-evimp(MARSModel)
```

The following values are returned:

```
> EvimpMD
        nsubsets    gcv      rss
Girth          3  100.0   100.0
Height         1   10.7    11.5
```

In the following list a brief description of the returned values is given:

- `nsubsets`: This is the number of subsets that include the variable
- `gcv`: Variable importance using the GCV criterion
- `rss`: Variable importance using the RSS criterion

A variable's importance is a measure of the effect that observed changes to the variable have on the observed response (or better, the expectation of that effect over the population). It is this measure of importance that `evimp()` function tries to estimate. This function returns a matrix showing the relative importance of the variables in the model. There is a row for each variable. The row name is the variable name, but with unused appended if the variable does not appear in the final model.

We now show the model results in the plot provided by the `earth` package:

```
plot(MARSModel)
```

By default, the `plot()` function shows **Model Selection, Cumulative Distribution** of the residuals, **Residuals vs Fitted** values, and the **Residual QQ** plot. The graphs plotted by `plot()` function are standard tools used in residual analysis and more information can be found in the previous chapter, where we have widely used them.

The following figure shows **Model Selection, Cumulative Distribution** of the residuals, **Residuals vs Fitted** values, and the **Residual QQ** plot:

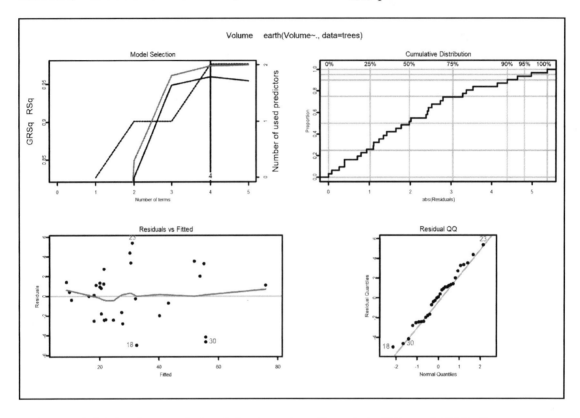

In the **Model Selection** graph (top left of previous figure) the **RSq** and **GRSq** lines run together at first, but diverge as the **Number of terms** increases. This is typical behavior, and what we are seeing is an increased penalty being applied to the **GCV** as the number of model parameters increases. The vertical dotted line is positioned at the selected model (at the maximum **GRSq**) and indicates that the best model has four terms and uses all two predictors (the number of predictors is shown by the black dashed line).

The **Cumulative Distribution** graph (top right of the previous figure) shows the **Cumulative Distribution** of the absolute values of residuals. What we would ideally like to see is a graph that starts at zero and shoots up quickly to one.

The **Residuals vs Fitted** graph (bottom left of the previous figure) shows the residual for each value of the predicted response. By comparing the scales of the axes, you can get an immediate idea of the size of the residuals relative to the predicted values. Ideally the residuals should show constant variance, that is the residuals should remain evenly spread out, or homoscedastic, as the fitted values increase.

The **Residual QQ** plot (bottom right of the previous figure) compares the distribution of the residuals to a normal distribution. If the residuals are distributed normally, they will lie on the line. (Normality of the residuals often isn't too important for earth models, but the graph is useful for discovering outlying residuals and other anomalies.) Following R convention, the abscissa is the normal axis and the ordinate is the residual axis.

To conclude the analysis, we will calculate the accuracy of the model and compare it to that obtained with a linear model. To calculate the accuracy we must first make predictions with the newly built model. To do this, we will use the predict() function, as follows:

```
PredMARSModel <- predict(MARSModel, trees)
```

Now we will calculate the **mean squared error** (**MSE**) that measures the average of the squares of the errors or deviations:

```
mse1 <- mean((trees$Volume - PredMARSModel)^2)
```

The result is shown as follows:

```
> print(mse1)
[1] 6.745608
```

To evaluate the performance of the model, compare it with a linear regression model. To do this, we will do the same thing, that is, we will first build the model, so we will make predictions, and finally calculate MSE:

```
LMModel <- lm(Volume ~ ., data = trees)
```

So we carry out the forecast:

```
PredLMModel <- predict(LMModel, trees)
```

Finally, we calculate MSE:

```
mse2 <- mean((trees$Volume - PredLMModel)^2)
```

The result is shown as follows:

```
> print(mse2)
[1] 13.61037
```

Comparing the two models, the MARS model shows a lower error.

Generalized Additive Model

A GAM is a GLM in which the linear predictor is given by a user-specified sum of smooth functions of the covariates plus a conventional parametric component of the linear predictor. Assume that a sample of n objects has a response variable y and r explanatory variables $x_1, \ldots, x_r$. In these assumptions, the regression equation becomes:

$$F(x) = y = \beta_0 + f_1(x_1) + f_2(x_2) + \ldots + f_r(x_r)$$

Here, the functions $f_1, f_2, \ldots, f_r$ are different nonlinear functions on variables x. Into the GAM, the linear relationship between the response and predictors are replaced by several nonlinear smooth functions to model and capture the nonlinearities in the data.

We can see the GAM as a generalization of a multiple regression model without interactions between predictors. Among the advantages of this approach, in addition to greater flexibility than the linear model, the good algorithmic convergence rate should also be mentioned for problems with many explanatory variables. The biggest drawback lies in the complexity of the parameter estimation method. For this purpose, it is usually used in an iterative backfitting algorithm.

In R, we can fit general additive models by using the `gam()` function implemented in the `mgcv` package. This package contains generalized additive (mixed) models, some of their extensions and other **Generalized Ridge Regression (GRR)** with multiple smoothing parameter estimation by (restricted) marginal likelihood, GCV and similar. It includes a `gam()` function, a wide variety of smoothers, JAGS support and distributions beyond the exponential family. The following table lists some of the information on this package:

Package	`mgcv`
Date	January 09, 2017
Version	1.8-22
Title	Mixed GAM Computation Vehicle with Automatic Smoothness Estimation
Author	Simon Wood

To perform a GAM example, as we always do, begin from the data. This time we will use the `stackloss` dataset contained in the `datasets` package.

It contains data obtained from *21* days of operation of a plant that oxidises ammonia to obtain nitric acid. A data frame with 21 observations on 4 variables, as follows:

- `Air.Flow`: Flow of cooling air
- `Water.Temp`: Cooling water inlet temperature
- `Acid.Conc.`: Concentration of acid [per *1000*, minus *500*]
- `stack.loss`: Stack loss

`Air.Flow` represents the rate of operation of the plant. `Water.Temp` is the temperature of cooling water circulated through coils in the absorption tower. `Acid.Conc.` is the concentration of the acid circulating, *-50*, times *10*: that is, *89* corresponds to *58.9* percent acid. `stack.loss` (the dependent variable) is ten times the percentage of the ingoing ammonia to the plant that escapes from the absorption column unabsorbed; that is, an (inverse) measure of the overall efficiency of the plant.

We want to compare the linear model with an additive model. The analysis begins by uploading the dataset:

```
data(stackloss)
```

As we have already said, the dataset is contained in the `datasets` package, so to load it we can use the `data()` function. To display a compact summary of the dataset, simply type:

```
str(stackloss)
```

The results are shown as follows:

```
> str(stackloss)
'data.frame':   21 obs. of  4 variables:
 $ Air.Flow  : num  80 80 75 62 62 62 62 62 58 58 ...
 $ Water.Temp: num  27 27 25 24 22 23 24 24 23 18 ...
 $ Acid.Conc.: num  89 88 90 87 87 87 93 93 87 80 ...
 $ stack.loss: num  42 37 37 28 18 18 19 20 15 14 ...
```

We have thus confirmed that these are four numeric variables with 21 observations. To extract more information, use the `summary()` function:

```
> summary(stackloss)
     Air.Flow        Water.Temp       Acid.Conc.        stack.loss
 Min.   :50.00    Min.   :17.0    Min.   :72.00    Min.   : 7.00
 1st Qu.:56.00    1st Qu.:18.0    1st Qu.:82.00    1st Qu.:11.00
```

Median	:58.00	Median	:20.0	Median	:87.00	Median	:15.00
Mean	:60.43	Mean	:21.1	Mean	:86.29	Mean	:17.52
3rd Qu.	:62.00	3rd Qu.	:24.0	3rd Qu.	:89.00	3rd Qu.	:19.00
Max.	:80.00	Max.	:27.0	Max.	:93.00	Max.	:42.00

Some statistics are returned with min, max, mean, median, and quartiles for each variable. To understand something more than this distribution, we can perform a preliminary visual analysis. Let's first try to find out whether the variables are related to each other. We can do this using the `pairs()` function to create a matrix of subaxes containing scatter plots of the columns of a matrix:

```
pairs(stackloss, panel = panel.smooth)
```

The following figure shows a scatter plot matrix of the four variables:

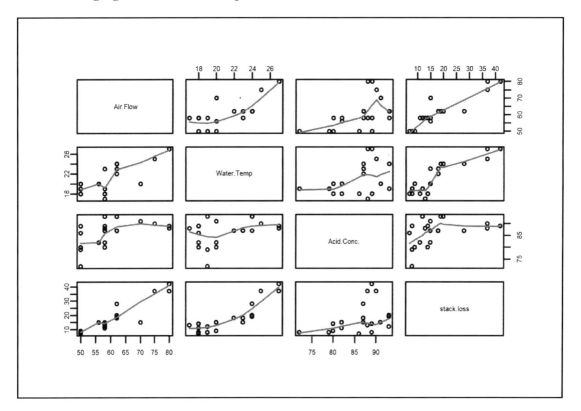

The analysis of the graph confirms the nonlinearity of the relationships between responses and predictors. Now we will see what returns a linear regression model. This analysis will help us later to measure GAM performance:

```
LModel <- lm(stack.loss ~ Air.Flow + Water.Temp + Acid.Conc.,
    data=stackloss)
```

Let's analyze the model statistics:

```
> summary(LModel)

Call:
lm(formula = stack.loss ~ Air.Flow + Water.Temp + Acid.Conc.,
    data = stackloss)

Residuals:
    Min      1Q  Median      3Q     Max
-7.2377 -1.7117 -0.4551  2.3614  5.6978

Coefficients:
            Estimate Std. Error t value Pr(>|t|)
(Intercept) -39.9197    11.8960  -3.356  0.00375 **
Air.Flow      0.7156     0.1349   5.307  5.8e-05 ***
Water.Temp    1.2953     0.3680   3.520  0.00263 **
Acid.Conc.   -0.1521     0.1563  -0.973  0.34405
---
Signif. codes:  0 '***' 0.001 '**' 0.01 '*' 0.05 '.' 0.1 ' ' 1

Residual standard error: 3.243 on 17 degrees of freedom
Multiple R-squared:  0.9136,    Adjusted R-squared:  0.8983
F-statistic:  59.9 on 3 and 17 DF,  p-value: 3.016e-09
```

At first glance the results are not bad at all: the predictors are significant (less than `Acid.Conc.`) and R-squared is high enough. We can better analyze the results by doing a residuals analysis:

```
plot(LModel)
```

The following figure shows a plot of **Residuals vs Fitted** values, a **Scale-Location** plot, a **Normal Q-Q** plot, and a plot of **Residuals vs Leverage**:

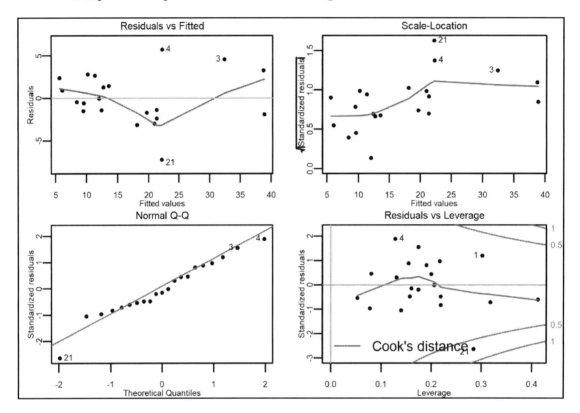

The residuals analysis of the model does not reveal particularly obvious problems. It therefore concludes that the model is well suited to the real situation, with a very high R-squared value.

Let's see what happens now by building GAM. First, we must install the mgcv package.

Remember, to install a library that is not present in the initial distribution of R, you must use the install.package function. This is the main function to install packages. It takes a vector of names and a destination library, downloads the packages from the repositories and installs them.

Then, we will load the library through the library command:

```
library(mgcv)
```

Now we can use the `gam()` function that builds a GAM:

```
GAMModel <- gam(stack.loss ~ s(Air.Flow, k=7) +
                + s(Water.Temp, k=7) + s(Acid.Conc., k=7),
                data=stackloss)
```

In the previous command, the formula is exactly like the formula for a GLM except that smooth terms `s`, can be added to the right-hand side to specify that the linear predictor depends on smooth functions of predictors (or linear functions of these).

In each smooth term, compare the `k` value that is the dimension of the basis used to represent the smooth term. If `k` is not specified then basis specific defaults are used. Note that these defaults are essentially arbitrary, and it is important to check that they are not so small that they cause oversmoothing (too large just slows down computation). The value *k-1* represents the maximum number of actual degrees of freedom attributable to each spline; then it must be checked in output that the specified *k* value is greater than the number of degrees of freedom attributed to the corresponding spline, otherwise the estimates can be quite distorted. In the example for all three splines, a number of nodes equal to seven is set.

The output of the model is examined with the `summary()` function:

```
> summary(GAMModel)
Family: gaussian
Link function: identity
Formula:
stack.loss ~ s(Air.Flow, k = 7) + +s(Water.Temp, k = 7) + s(Acid.Conc.,
    k = 7)

Parametric coefficients:
            Estimate Std. Error t value Pr(>|t|)
(Intercept)   17.524      0.613   28.59 8.66e-15 ***
---
Signif. codes:  0 '***' 0.001 '**' 0.01 '*' 0.05 '.' 0.1 ' ' 1

Approximate significance of smooth terms:
                edf Ref.df     F  p-value
s(Air.Flow)   1.000  1.000 17.500 0.000661 ***
s(Water.Temp) 2.565  3.178  7.044 0.003061 **
s(Acid.Conc.) 1.000  1.000  1.025 0.326916
---
Signif. codes:  0 '***' 0.001 '**' 0.01 '*' 0.05 '.' 0.1 ' ' 1

R-sq.(adj) =  0.924   Deviance explained = 94.1%
GCV = 10.735  Scale est. = 7.8899     n = 21
```

Two significance tables are returned: the first for parametric coefficients (in this case only the intercept), the second for smooth terms. From this second table, it is noted that the effective degrees of freedom (`edf` in the table) of the first and third variables are both one, which is a clear indication that for these terms nothing is gained by introducing smoothing treatment and that well are described by a linear relationship. Let's focus our attention on the second term. We can draw a graph of the smoothness of the smooth function:

```
plot(GAMModel, select=2)
```

The following figure shows the smooth function of the `Water.Temp` variable. Dotted lines identify the confidence interval of the smooth function:

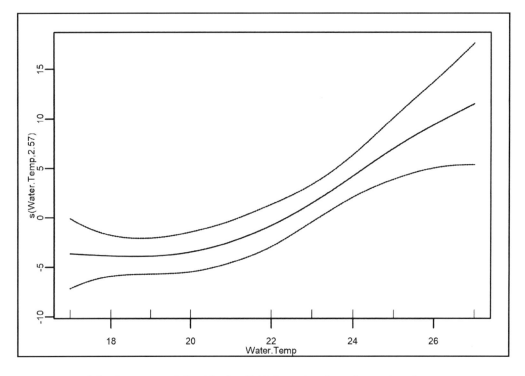

A comparison of the linear model with the GAM can be done by using the `anova()` function. This function computes analysis of variance (or deviance) tables for one or more fitted model objects and returns an object of class `anova`. These objects represent analysis of variance and analysis of deviance tables. When given a single argument, it produces a table which tests whether the model terms are significant. When given a sequence of objects, `anova` tests the models against one another in the order specified:

```
anova(LModel, GAMModel)
```

The results are shown as follows:

```
> anova(LModel,GAMModel)
Analysis of Variance Table

Model 1: stack.loss ~ Air.Flow + Water.Temp + Acid.Conc.
Model 2: stack.loss ~ s(Air.Flow, k = 7) + +s(Water.Temp, k = 7) +
s(Acid.Conc.,
    k = 7)
  Res.Df    RSS    Df Sum of Sq      F  Pr(>F)
1 17.000 178.83
2 15.435 121.78 1.5655    57.053 4.6192 0.03388 *
---
Signif. codes:   0 '***' 0.001 '**' 0.01 '*' 0.05 '.' 0.1 ' ' 1
```

From the analysis of the results it is concluded that the difference between the two models is significant ($P = 0.034$): the additive model best suits the linear model dataset.

Regression trees

Decision trees are used to predict a response or class y from several input variables x_1, x_2,...,x_n. If y is a continuous response, it's called a **regression tree**, if y is categorical, it's called a **classification tree**. That's why these methods are often called **Classification and Regression Tree (CART)**. The algorithm is based on the following procedure: at each node of the tree, we check the value of one the input x_i and depending of the (binary) answer we continue to the left or to the right branch. When we reach a leaf we will find the prediction.

This algorithm starts from grouped data into a single node (root node) and executes a comprehensive recursion of all possible subdivisions at every step. At each step, the best subdivision is chosen, that is, the one that produces as many homogeneous branches as possible.

In the regression trees, we try to partition the data space into small-enough parts where we can apply a simple different model on each part. The non leaf part of the tree is just the procedure to determine for each data x what is the model we will use to predict it.

A regression tree is formed by a series of nodes that split the root branch into two child branches. Such subdivision continues to cascade. Each new branch, then, can go in another node, or remain a leaf with the predicted value.

Starting from the whole dataset (root), the algorithm creates the tree through the following procedure:

1. We identify the best functionality with which to divide the X_1 dataset and the best s_1 division value. The left-hand branch will be the set of observations where X_1 is below s_1 and the one on the right is the set of observations in which X_1 is greater than or equal to s_1.

2. This operation is then executed again (independently) for each branch, recursively, until there is no division possibility.

3. When the divisions are completed, a leaf is created. The leaves indicate the output values.

Suppose we have a variable response to only two continuous predictors (X_1 and X_2) and four division values (s_1, s_2, s_3, s_4). The following figure proposes a way to represent the whole dataset graphically:

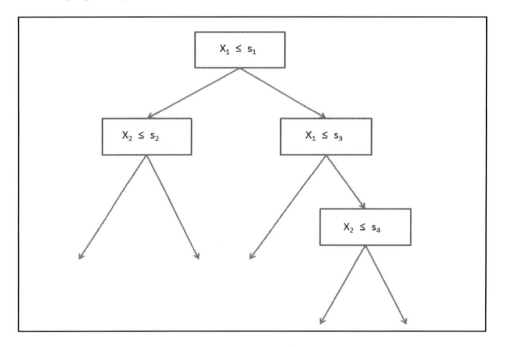

The goal of a regression tree is to encapsulate the whole dataset in the smallest possible tree. For minimizing the tree size, the simplest possible explanation for a set of observations is preferred over other explanations. All this is justified by the fact that small trees are much easier to look at and understand than large trees.

Previously we saw how the regression tree algorithm works. These steps can be summarized in the following processes:

- **Splitting**: The dataset is partitioned into subsets. The split operation is based on a set of rules, for example, sums of squares from the whole dataset. The leaf node contains a small subset of the observations. Splitting continues until a leaf node is constructed.
- **Pruning**: In this process the tree branches are shortened. The tree is reduced by transforming a few nodes of branches into leaf nodes and removing leaf nodes under the original branch. Care must be taken as the lower branches can be strongly influenced by abnormal values. Pruning allows you to find the next largest tree and minimize the problem. A simpler tree often avoids overfitting.
- **Tree selection**: Finally, the smallest tree that matches the data is selected. this process is executed by choosing the tree that produces the lowest cross-validated error.

The process is for finding the smallest tree that fits the data. Usually, this is the tree that yields the lowest cross-validated error.

In R, to fit a regression tree we can use the `tree()` function implemented in the tree package. In this package, a tree is grown by binary recursive partitioning using the response in the specified formula and choosing splits, from the terms of the right-hand side. Numeric variables are divided into $X < a$ and $X > a$. The split which maximizes the reduction in impurity is chosen, the dataset split and the process repeated. Splitting continues until the terminal nodes are too small or too few to be split. In the following table is listed some of the information on this package:

Package	tree
Date	January 21, 2016
Version	1.0-37
Title	Classification and Regression Trees
Author	Brian Ripley

To perform a regression tree example, as we always do, begin from the data. This time we will use the mtcars dataset contained in the datasets package just used in Chapter 6, *Avoid Overfitting Problems – Achieving Generalization*. The mtcars dataset contains gas mileage, horsepower, and other information for *32* vehicles. It is a data frame with *32* observations on the following *11* variables:

- mpg: Miles per gallon
- cyl: Number of cylinders
- disp: Engine displacement (cubic inches)
- hp: Engine horsepower
- drat: Rear axle ratio
- wt: Weight (*1000* lbs)
- qsec: *1/4* mile time
- vs: V/S
- am: Transmission (*0 = automatic, 1 = manual*)
- gear: Number of forward gears
- carb: Number of carburators

The fuel consumption of vehicles has always been studied by the major manufacturers of the entire planet. In an era characterized by oil refueling problems and even greater air pollution problems, fuel consumption by vehicles has become a key factor. In this example, we will build a regression tree with the purpose of predicting the fuel consumption of the vehicles according to certain characteristics.

The analysis begins by uploading the dataset:

```
data(mtcars)
```

As we have already said, the dataset is contained in the datasets package, so to load it we can use the data() function. To display a compact summary of the dataset simply type:

```
str(mtcars)
```

The results are shown as follows:

```
> str(mtcars)
'data.frame':   32 obs. of  11 variables:
 $ mpg : num  21 21 22.8 21.4 18.7 18.1 14.3 24.4 22.8 19.2 ...
 $ cyl : num  6 6 4 6 8 6 8 4 4 6 ...
 $ disp: num  160 160 108 258 360 ...
 $ hp  : num  110 110 93 110 175 105 245 62 95 123 ...
 $ drat: num  3.9 3.9 3.85 3.08 3.15 2.76 3.21 3.69 3.92 3.92 ...
 $ wt  : num  2.62 2.88 2.32 3.21 3.44 ...
 $ qsec: num  16.5 17 18.6 19.4 17 ...
 $ vs  : num  0 0 1 1 0 1 0 1 1 1 ...
 $ am  : num  1 1 1 0 0 0 0 0 0 0 ...
 $ gear: num  4 4 4 3 3 3 3 4 4 4 ...
 $ carb: num  4 4 1 1 2 1 4 2 2 4 ...
```

We have thus confirmed that these are 11 numeric variables with 32 observations. To extract more information, use the summary() function:

```
> summary(mtcars)
      mpg             cyl             disp             hp
 Min.   :10.40   Min.   :4.000   Min.   : 71.1   Min.   : 52.0
 1st Qu.:15.43   1st Qu.:4.000   1st Qu.:120.8   1st Qu.: 96.5
 Median :19.20   Median :6.000   Median :196.3   Median :123.0
 Mean   :20.09   Mean   :6.188   Mean   :230.7   Mean   :146.7
 3rd Qu.:22.80   3rd Qu.:8.000   3rd Qu.:326.0   3rd Qu.:180.0
 Max.   :33.90   Max.   :8.000   Max.   :472.0   Max.   :335.0
      drat             wt             qsec             vs
 Min.   :2.760   Min.   :1.513   Min.   :14.50   Min.   :0.0000
 1st Qu.:3.080   1st Qu.:2.581   1st Qu.:16.89   1st Qu.:0.0000
 Median :3.695   Median :3.325   Median :17.71   Median :0.0000
 Mean   :3.597   Mean   :3.217   Mean   :17.85   Mean   :0.4375
 3rd Qu.:3.920   3rd Qu.:3.610   3rd Qu.:18.90   3rd Qu.:1.0000
 Max.   :4.930   Max.   :5.424   Max.   :22.90   Max.   :1.0000
       am             gear             carb
 Min.   :0.0000   Min.   :3.000   Min.   :1.000
 1st Qu.:0.0000   1st Qu.:3.000   1st Qu.:2.000
 Median :0.0000   Median :4.000   Median :2.000
 Mean   :0.4062   Mean   :3.688   Mean   :2.812
 3rd Qu.:1.0000   3rd Qu.:4.000   3rd Qu.:4.000
 Max.   :1.0000   Max.   :5.000   Max.   :8.000
```

Before starting with data analysis, we conduct an exploratory analysis to understand how the data is distributed and extract preliminary knowledge. Let's first try to find out whether the variables are related to each other. We can do this using the `pairs()` function to create a matrix of sub axes containing scatter plots of the columns of a matrix. To reduce the number of plots in the matrix we limit our analysis to just four predictors: cylinders, displacement, horsepower, and weight. The target is the `mpg` variable that contains measurements of the miles per gallon of 32 sample cars.

```
pairs(mpg~cyl+disp+hp+wt,data=mtcars)
```

To specify the response and predictors, we used the formula argument. Each term gives a separate variable in the `pairs` plot, so terms must be numeric vectors. Response was interpreted as another variable, but not treated specially. The following figure shows a scatter plot matrix:

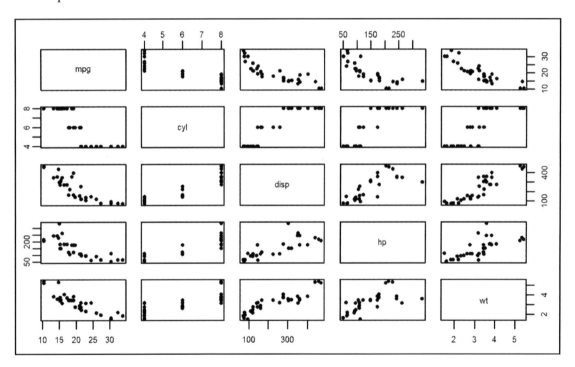

Observing the plots in the first line, it can be noted that fuel consumption increases as the number of cylinders, the engine displacement, the horsepower, and the weight of the vehicle increase.

At this point, we can use the `tree()` function to build the regression tree. First, we must install the `tree` package.

Remember, to install a library that is not present in the initial distribution of R, you must use the `install.package` function. This is the main function to install packages. It takes a vector of names and a destination library, downloads the packages from the repositories, and installs them.

Then, we will load the library through the `library` command:

```
library(tree)
```

Now we can use the `tree()` function that builds a regression tree:

```
RTModel <- tree(mpg~.,data = mtcars)
```

Only two arguments are passed: a formula and the dataset name. The left-hand side of the formula (response) should be either a numerical vector when a regression tree will be fitted. The right-hand side should be a series of numeric variables separated by +; there should be no interaction terms. Both . and – are allowed: regression trees can have offset terms.

Let's see the results:

```
> RTModel
node), split, n, deviance, yval
      * denotes terminal node

  1) root 32 1126.000 20.09
    2) wt < 2.26 6    44.550 30.07 *
    3) wt > 2.26 26  346.600 17.79
      6) cyl < 7 12   42.120 20.92
       12) cyl < 5 5    5.968 22.58 *
       13) cyl > 5 7   12.680 19.74 *
      7) cyl > 7 14   85.200 15.10
       14) hp < 192.5 7   16.590 16.79 *
       15) hp > 192.5 7   28.830 13.41 *
```

These results describe exactly each node in the tree. Information on each node is presented in indented format. It is used to indicate the tree topology: that is, it indicates the parent and child relationships (also referred to as primary and secondary splits). Also, to denote a terminal node an asterisk (*) is used.

In the tree sequence, nodes are labeled with unique numbers. Those numbers are generated by the following formula: the child nodes of a node x are always numbered $2*x$ (left child) and $2*x+1$ (right child). The root node is numbered with one. The following figure explains this rule:

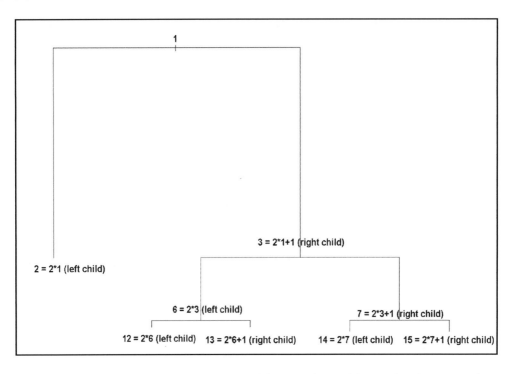

From the analysis of the results we can see a selection of variables, in fact between the 10 available variables only three—wt, cyl, and hp were selected. More information can be obtained from the summary() function:

```
> summary(RTModel)

Regression tree:
tree(formula = mpg ~ ., data = mtcars)
Variables actually used in tree construction:
[1] "wt"  "cyl" "hp"
Number of terminal nodes:  5
Residual mean deviance:  4.023 = 108.6 / 27
Distribution of residuals:
   Min. 1st Qu.  Median    Mean 3rd Qu.    Max.
 -4.067  -1.361   0.220   0.000   1.361   3.833
```

As already mentioned previously, the output of `summary()` indicates that only three of the variables have been used in constructing the tree. In the context of a regression tree, the deviance is simply the sum of squared errors for the tree. Now, we can plot the regression tree:

```
plot(RTModel)
text(RTModel)
```

The first one plots the regression tree, the second one adds the text on the branches to explain the work flow. The resulting plot is shown in the following figure:

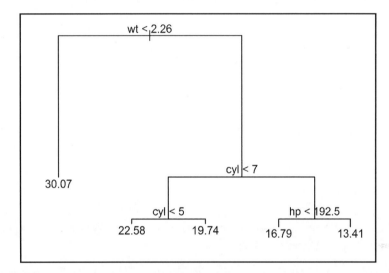

Let's then look at what the regression tree has returned to us. The first thing that seems obvious is a sort of indication of the importance of variables. Already the choice of three predictors for the ten available makes us realize that these three are the ones that most affect the fuel consumption of cars inserted in the dataset. Now we can add that the most important predictor is the weight of the vehicle; in fact a weight less than **2.26** lbs leads us to a terminal knot that gives us a consumption estimate (**30.07** miles/(US) gallon). We can then see that immediately after we find the number of cylinders of the engine, and, finally, the horsepower.

Support Vector Regression

SVR is based on the same principles as the **Support Vector Machine (SVM)**. In fact, SVR is the adapted form of SVM when the dependent variable is numeric rather than categorical. One of the main advantages of using SVR is that it is a nonparametric technique.

To build the model, the SVR technique uses the kernel functions. The commonly used kernel functions are:

- Linear
- Polynomial
- Sigmoid
- Radial base

This technique allows the fitting of a nonlinear model without changing the explanatory variables, helping to interpret the resulting pattern better.

In the SVR, we do not have to worry about the prediction as long as the error (ε) remains above a certain value. This method is called the maximal margin principle. The maximal margin allows SVR to be seen as a convex optimization problem.

Regression can also be penalized using a cost parameter, which becomes useful in avoiding excess adaptation. SVR is a useful technique that provides the user with a great flexibility in distributing the underlying variables, relationship between independent and employee variables, and checking the penalty term.

To perform SVR, we can use the `svm()` function contained in the `e1071` package. This package contains several functions for latent class analysis, short time Fourier transform, fuzzy clustering, SVMs, shortest path computation, bagged clustering, naive Bayes classification, and much more. The following table lists some of the information for this package:

Package	`e1071`
Date	February 02, 2017
Version	1.6-8
Title	Misc Functions of the Department of Statistics, Probability Theory Group (Formerly: E1071), TU Wien
Author	David Meyer, Evgenia Dimitriadou, Kurt Hornik, Andreas Weingessel, Friedrich Leisch, Chih-Chung Chang, Chih-Chen Lin.

To perform a regression tree example, as we always do, begin from the data. This time we will create a series of sample data to understand the functioning of the algorithm better:

```
x <- seq(0, 7, by = 0.01)
y <- sin(x) + rnorm(x, sd = 0.1)
```

In the first line of code, we created the predictor x by using the seq() function. This function generates a regular sequence from zero to seven with an increment of 0.01. In the second line, we created the response y using the sin() function. To make the distribution more real, we added noise with the rnorm() function that generates random deviates with the same length of x and with a standard deviation of 0.1.

Let's start by building a simple linear regression model using the lm() function:

```
LModel<-lm(y~x)
```

Some data statistics of the model are retuned by using the summary() function:

```
> summary(LModel)

Call:
lm(formula = y ~ x)

Residuals:
     Min       1Q   Median       3Q      Max
-1.20079 -0.52952  0.00369  0.47261  1.41470

Coefficients:
            Estimate Std. Error t value Pr(>|t|)
(Intercept)  0.70519    0.04317   16.34   <2e-16 ***
x           -0.18985    0.01068  -17.78   <2e-16 ***
---
Signif. codes:  0 '***' 0.001 '**' 0.01 '*' 0.05 '.' 0.1 ' ' 1

Residual standard error: 0.5721 on 699 degrees of freedom
Multiple R-squared:  0.3114,    Adjusted R-squared:  0.3105
F-statistic: 316.2 on 1 and 699 DF,  p-value: < 2.2e-16
```

To understand how the linear regression model works better, we can plot the distribution and the regression line:

```
plot(x, y)
abline(LModel)
```

The following figure shows the distribution and the regression line:

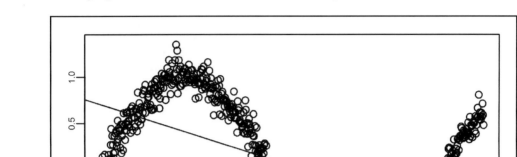

It is easy to perceive that a linear regression model cannot predict this type of distribution.

In order to be able to compare the linear regression with the SVR, that we are going to fit, we can calculate the MSE. The MSE measures the average of the squares of the errors or deviations. To calculate MSE, we first will calculate the predicted value of the model:

```
PredLModel<- predict(LModel)
```

Now, we can calculate the MSE:

```
mse1 <- mean((y - PredLModel)^2)
```

The result is shown as follows:

```
> mse1
[1] 0.3263158
```

This is now the moment to build the SVR model:

```
SVModel <- svm(x, y)
```

The `svm()` function can be used to carry out general regression and classification (of `nu` and `epsilon` type), as well as density estimation. A formula interface is provided to insert more than one predictor. To obtain some statistics of the model, we now use the `summary()` function:

```
> summary(SVModel)

Call:
svm.default(x = x, y = y)


Parameters:
   SVM-Type:  eps-regression
 SVM-Kernel:  radial
       cost:  1
      gamma:  1
    epsilon:  0.1


Number of Support Vectors:  322
```

To compare the SVR model with the linear regression model, we now calculate the MSE. But as we have done before, we must first calculate the predictions of the new model:

```
PredSVModel <- predict(SVModel)
```

Now, we can calculate the MSE:

```
Mse2 <- mean((y - PredSVModel)^2)
```

The result is shown as follows:

```
> mse2
[1] 0.009604251
```

The MSE of the linear model is roughly *34* times greater than that of the SVR model. To get a graphical overview of the goodness of fit of the SVR model, we plot a graph:

```
plot(x, y)
points(x, PredSVModel)
abline(LModel)
```

In the first line of the code just proposed we traced the data distribution. In the second, we have traced the points that represent the predictions of the SVR model. Finally, we have traced the linear regression line, as shown in the following figure:

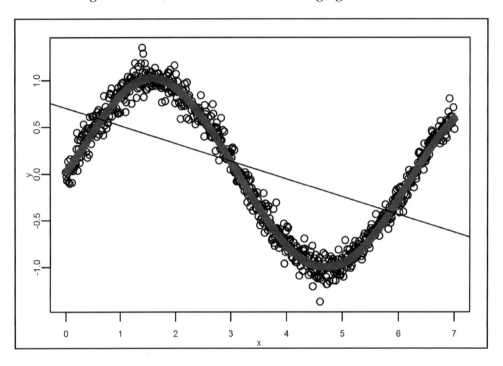

The figure shows the prediction capacity of the SVR model. In addition, the inability of the linear model to represent such distribution is equally clear.

Summary

In this chapter, several advanced techniques to solve regression problems that cannot be solved with linear models were treated. First, a nonlinear least squares method was explored, where the parameters of the regression function to be estimated were nonlinear. In this technique, given the nonlinearity of the coefficients, the solution of the problem occurs by means of iterative numerical calculation methods. Then a MARS was performed. This is a nonparametric regression procedure that makes no assumption about the underlying functional relationship between the response and predictor variables. This relationship is constructed from a set of coefficients and basis functions that are processed, starting from the regression data.

Later, we focused attention on a GAM. This is a GLM in which the linear predictor is given by a user-specified sum of smooth functions of the covariates plus a conventional parametric component of the linear predictor. Then, we introduced the tree regression where we tried to partition the data space into small-enough parts where we could apply a simple different model on each part. The non leaf part of the tree is just the procedure to determine for each data x what is the model we should use to predict it. Finally, we explored the SVR. This technique allows the fitting of a nonlinear model without changing the explanatory variables, helping to interpret the resulting pattern better.

In the next chapter, we will understand the techniques required to perform fitting analysis, pattern recognition, and neural network regression through a series of real cases. We will learn how to prepare data for regression analysis. We will also know how to perform fitting, pattern recognition, and neural network regression analysis in R, and how to perform preprocessing, postprocessing, and visualization to improve training efficiency and assess model performance.

9
Regression Analysis in Practice

In `Chapter 1`, *Getting Started with Regression*, we said that regression models are the most well-understood in numerical simulation. Once we've acquired the necessary experience in regression models, we will be able to understand all other machine learning algorithms. Regression models are easily interpretable as they are based on solid mathematical bases. Perhaps this is the reason behind the extreme ease of understanding of such techniques.

After analyzing in detail the different regression algorithms, it is time to put them into practice. This last chapter is meant to be a short reference, covering some of the major regression algorithms. In this chapter, you will just apply what has been learned. You can explore multiple linear regression, logistic regression, random forest regression, neural networks, and much more as applied to datasets resulting from real cases. The basic concepts we have learned from the previous chapters will now be put into practice. If we need to reinforce these concepts, we can safely retrace our footsteps and review the topics already discussed. We will look at practical examples from raw data to extract as much knowledge as possible.

This chapter starts with solving a real-world regression problem. To perform a regression analysis, a random forest technique will be adopted. Then you'll learn how to use logistic regression to classify a pattern. Finally, we'll perform a neural network regression analysis.

We will cover the following topics:

- Random forest
- Logistic regression
- Neural network regression

At the end of the chapter, we will have understood the techniques required to perform fitting analysis, pattern recognition, and neural network regression through a series of real cases. We will learn how to prepare data for regression analysis. We will also know how to perform fitting, pattern recognition, and neural network regression analysis in R, and how to perform preprocessing, postprocessing, and visualization to improve training efficiency and assess model performance.

Random forest regression with the Boston dataset

In this section, we will run a random forest regression for the Boston dataset; the median values of owner-occupied homes are predicted for the test data. The dataset describes 13 numerical properties of houses in Boston suburbs, and is concerned with modeling the price of houses in those suburbs in thousands of dollars. As such, this is a regression predictive modeling problem. Input attributes include features like crime rate, proportion of non-retail business acres, chemical concentrations, and more.

 To get the data, we draw on the large collection of data available in the UCI Machine Learning Repository at the following link:
http://archive.ics.uci.edu/ml

The following list shows all the variables, followed by a brief description:

- Number of instances: 506
- Number of attributes: 14 continuous attributes (including the class attribute medv), and one binary-valued attribute

Each of the attributes is detailed as follows:

- crim: Per capita crime rate by town
- zn: Proportion of residential land zoned for lots over 25,000 square feet
- indus: Proportion of non-retail business acres per town
- chas: Charles River dummy variable (= 1 if tract bounds river; 0 otherwise)
- nox: Nitric oxides concentration (parts per ten million)
- rm: Average number of rooms per dwelling

- `age`: Proportion of owner-occupied units built prior to 1940
- `dis`: Weighted distances to five Boston employment centers
- `rad`: Index of accessibility to radial highways
- `tax`: Full-value property-tax rate per $10,000
- `ptratio`: Pupil-teacher ratio by town
- `black`: $1000(B_k - 0.63)\text{^2}$ where B_k is the proportion of blacks by town
- `lstat`: Percent of the lower status of the population
- `medv`: Median value of owner-occupied homes in $1000

Of these, `medv` is the response variable, while the other 13 variables are possible predictors. The goal of this analysis is to fit a regression model that best explains the variation in `medv`.

There is a relation between the first 13 columns and the `medv` response variable. We can predict the `medv` value based on the input 13 columns.

As said previously, the objective of this example is to predict the median value of owner-occupied homes value. First, we have to get the data. To do this we can use the `read.table()` function as follows:

```
BHData <- read.table(url("https://archive.ics.uci.edu/ml/machine-learning-databases/housing/housing.data"), sep = "")
```

In this function, instead of the filename, we can also enter a complete URL of a file contained on a website repository. Now, we use the `names()` function to set the names of the dataset according to the list previously viewed:

```
names(BHData) <- c("crim","zn","indus","chas","nox","rm",
        "age","dis","rad","tax","ptratio","black","lstat","medv")
```

The table also includes the names of the variables as they are in the original dataset.

Exploratory analysis

Before starting with data analysis through the multiple linear regression, we conduct an exploratory analysis to understand how the data is distributed and extract preliminary knowledge. Let's start by checking the dataset using the `str()` function. This function provides a compact display of the internal structure of an object. Ideally, only one line for each basic structure is displayed:

```
str(BHData)
```

The results are shown here:

```
> str(BHData)
'data.frame':   506 obs. of  14 variables:
 $ crim    : num  0.00632 0.02731 0.02729 0.03237 0.06905 ...
 $ zn      : num  18 0 0 0 0 0 12.5 12.5 12.5 12.5 ...
 $ indus   : num  2.31 7.07 7.07 2.18 2.18 2.18 7.87 7.87 7.87 7.87
                  ...
 $ chas    : int  0 0 0 0 0 0 0 0 0 0 ...
 $ nox     : num  0.538 0.469 0.469 0.458 0.458 0.458 0.524 0.524
                  0.524 0.524 ...
 $ rm      : num  6.58 6.42 7.18 7 7.15 ...
 $ age     : num  65.2 78.9 61.1 45.8 54.2 58.7 66.6 96.1 100 85.9
                  ...
 $ dis     : num  4.09 4.97 4.97 6.06 6.06 ...
 $ rad     : int  1 2 2 3 3 3 5 5 5 5 ...
 $ tax     : num  296 242 242 222 222 222 311 311 311 311 ...
 $ ptratio : num  15.3 17.8 17.8 18.7 18.7 18.7 15.2 15.2 15.2 15.2
                  ...
 $ black   : num  397 397 393 395 397 ...
 $ lstat   : num  4.98 9.14 4.03 2.94 5.33 ...
 $ medv    : num  24 21.6 34.7 33.4 36.2 28.7 22.9 27.1 16.5 18.9
                  ...
```

So we got the confirmation that it was 506 observations of 14 variables: Twelve numerical and two integer. Now, to obtain a brief summary of the dataset, we can use the summary() function.

Remember, the summary() function is a generic function used to produce result summaries of the results of various model fitting functions. The function invokes particular methods that depend on the class of the first argument.

In this case, the function was applied to a data frame; the results are shown here:

```
> summary(BHData)
      crim                zn              indus
 Min.   : 0.00632   Min.   :  0.00   Min.   : 0.46
 1st Qu.: 0.08204   1st Qu.:  0.00   1st Qu.: 5.19
 Median : 0.25651   Median :  0.00   Median : 9.69
 Mean   : 3.61352   Mean   : 11.36   Mean   :11.14
 3rd Qu.: 3.67708   3rd Qu.: 12.50   3rd Qu.:18.10
 Max.   :88.97620   Max.   :100.00   Max.   :27.74
      chas              nox               rm
 Min.   :0.00000   Min.   :0.3850   Min.   :3.561
 1st Qu.:0.00000   1st Qu.:0.4490   1st Qu.:5.886
```

```
Median  :0.00000    Median  :0.5380    Median  :6.208
Mean    :0.06917    Mean    :0.5547    Mean    :6.285
3rd Qu.:0.00000     3rd Qu.:0.6240     3rd Qu.:6.623
Max.    :1.00000    Max.    :0.8710    Max.    :8.780
      age                 dis                rad
Min.    :  2.90     Min.    : 1.130    Min.    : 1.000
1st Qu.: 45.02      1st Qu.: 2.100     1st Qu.: 4.000
Median : 77.50      Median : 3.207     Median : 5.000
Mean    : 68.57     Mean    : 3.795    Mean    : 9.549
3rd Qu.: 94.08      3rd Qu.: 5.188     3rd Qu.:24.000
Max.    :100.00     Max.    :12.127    Max.    :24.000
      tax               ptratio              black
Min.    :187.0     Min.    :12.60     Min.    :  0.32
1st Qu.:279.0      1st Qu.:17.40      1st Qu.:375.38
Median :330.0      Median :19.05      Median :391.44
Mean    :408.2     Mean    :18.46     Mean    :356.67
3rd Qu.:666.0      3rd Qu.:20.20      3rd Qu.:396.23
Max.    :711.0     Max.    :22.00     Max.    :396.90
     lstat               medv
Min.    : 1.73     Min.    : 5.00
1st Qu.: 6.95      1st Qu.:17.02
Median :11.36      Median :21.20
Mean    :12.65     Mean    :22.53
3rd Qu.:16.95      3rd Qu.:25.00
Max.    :37.97     Max.    :50.00
```

As you can see the variables have different ranges. When the predictors have different ranges, the impact on response variables by the feature having a greater numeric range could be more than the one having a less numeric range, and this could, in turn, impact the prediction accuracy. Our goal is to improve predictive accuracy and not allow a particular feature to impact the prediction due to a large numeric value range. Thus, we may need to scale values under different features such that they fall under a common range. Through this statistical procedure, it is possible to compare identical variables belonging to different distributions and also different variables or variables expressed in different units.

Remember, it is good practice to rescale the data before training a regression algorithm. With rescaling, data units are eliminated, allowing you to easily compare data from different locations.

In this case, we will use the min-max method (usually called **feature scaling**) to get all the scaled data in the range *[0, 1]*. The formula to achieve this is the following:

$$x_{scaled} = \frac{x - x_{min}}{xmax - xmin}$$

Before applying the method chosen for normalization, you must calculate the minimum and maximum values of each database column. To do this, we use the `apply()` function. This function returns a vector or an array or a list of values obtained by applying a function to margins of an array or matrix:

```
max_data <- apply(BHData, 2, max)
```

The first argument of the `apply` function specifies the dataset to apply the function to, in our case, the dataset named `BHData`. The second argument must contain a vector giving the subscripts over which the function will be applied. In our case, one indicates rows and two indicates columns. The third argument must contain the function to be applied, in our case, the `max()` function. What we will do next is calculate the minimums for each column:

```
min_data <- apply(BHData, 2, min)
```

Finally, to normalize the data, we use the `scale()` function, which is a generic function whose default method centers and/or scales the columns of a numeric matrix, as shown in the following code:

```
BHDataScaled <- as.data.frame(scale(BHData,center = min_data,
  scale = max_data - min_data))
```

To confirm the normalization of the data, let's apply the `summary()` function again:

```
> summary(BHDataScaled)
      crim                  zn
 Min.   :0.0000000   Min.   :0.0000
 1st Qu.:0.0008511   1st Qu.:0.0000
 Median :0.0028121   Median :0.0000
 Mean   :0.0405441   Mean   :0.1136
 3rd Qu.:0.0412585   3rd Qu.:0.1250
 Max.   :1.0000000   Max.   :1.0000
      indus               chas                nox
 Min.   :0.0000     Min.   :0.00000    Min.   :0.0000
 1st Qu.:0.1734     1st Qu.:0.00000    1st Qu.:0.1317
 Median :0.3383     Median :0.00000    Median :0.3148
 Mean   :0.3914     Mean   :0.06917    Mean   :0.3492
 3rd Qu.:0.6466     3rd Qu.:0.00000    3rd Qu.:0.4918
 Max.   :1.0000     Max.   :1.00000    Max.   :1.0000
```

```
        rm                    age                   dis
 Min.    :0.0000     Min.    :0.0000     Min.    :0.00000
 1st Qu.:0.4454      1st Qu.:0.4338      1st Qu.:0.08826
 Median :0.5073      Median :0.7683      Median :0.18895
 Mean    :0.5219     Mean    :0.6764     Mean    :0.24238
 3rd Qu.:0.5868      3rd Qu.:0.9390      3rd Qu.:0.36909
 Max.    :1.0000     Max.    :1.0000     Max.    :1.00000
        rad                   tax                 ptratio
 Min.    :0.0000     Min.    :0.0000     Min.    :0.0000
 1st Qu.:0.1304      1st Qu.:0.1756      1st Qu.:0.5106
 Median :0.1739      Median :0.2729      Median :0.6862
 Mean    :0.3717     Mean    :0.4222     Mean    :0.6229
 3rd Qu.:1.0000      3rd Qu.:0.9141      3rd Qu.:0.8085
 Max.    :1.0000     Max.    :1.0000     Max.    :1.0000
       black                 lstat                 medv
 Min.    :0.0000     Min.    :0.0000     Min.    :0.0000
 1st Qu.:0.9457      1st Qu.:0.1440      1st Qu.:0.2672
 Median :0.9862      Median :0.2657      Median :0.3600
 Mean    :0.8986     Mean    :0.3014     Mean    :0.3896
 3rd Qu.:0.9983      3rd Qu.:0.4201      3rd Qu.:0.4444
 Max.    :1.0000     Max.    :1.0000     Max.    :1.0000
```

Now, all variables have values between 0 and 1. Let's go into our exploratory analysis. The first thing we can do is to plot the boxplot of the variables:

```
boxplot(BHDataScaled)
```

In the following figure, the boxplots of all the variables contained in the `BHDataScaled` data frame are shown:

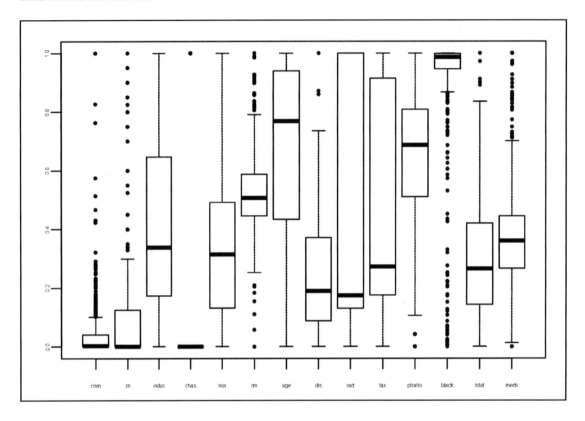

From the analysis of the previous figure, we can note that several variables have outliers, with the `crim` variable being the one that has the largest number.

Outlier values are numerically different from the rest of the collected data. Statistics derived from samples containing outliers can be misleading.

Then we'll see how to handle this problem. Furthermore, from the analysis of the previous figure, we can see that the predictors are many; often this can create problems rather than give us a hand. We can then find which of the available predictors are most correlated with the response variable. A standardized measurement of the relationship between two variables is instead represented by correlation, which can be calculated starting from covariance. In R, correlation coefficients are calculated by the cor() function; it produces a matrix of sample correlation coefficients for a data matrix (where each column represents a separate quantity).

 Remember, the correlation coefficient of two random variables is a measure of their linear dependence.

In the following example, we calculate the correlation coefficients for the BHDataScaled data frame:

```
CorBHData<-cor(BHDataScaled)
```

The following shows the results:

```
> CorBHData
                crim          zn       indus          chas
crim      1.00000000 -0.20046922  0.40658341 -0.055891582
zn       -0.20046922  1.00000000 -0.53382819 -0.042696719
indus     0.40658341 -0.53382819  1.00000000  0.062938027
chas     -0.05589158 -0.04269672  0.06293803  1.000000000
nox       0.42097171 -0.51660371  0.76365145  0.091202807
rm       -0.21924670  0.31199059 -0.39167585  0.091251225
age       0.35273425 -0.56953734  0.64477851  0.086517774
dis      -0.37967009  0.66440822 -0.70802699 -0.099175780
rad       0.62550515 -0.31194783  0.59512927 -0.007368241
tax       0.58276431 -0.31456332  0.72076018 -0.035586518
ptratio   0.28994558 -0.39167855  0.38324756 -0.121515174
black    -0.38506394  0.17552032 -0.35697654  0.048788485
lstat     0.45562148 -0.41299457  0.60379972 -0.053929298
medv     -0.38830461  0.36044534 -0.48372516  0.175260177
                 nox          rm         age          dis
crim      0.42097171 -0.21924670  0.35273425 -0.37967009
zn       -0.51660371  0.31199059 -0.56953734  0.66440822
indus     0.76365145 -0.39167585  0.64477851 -0.70802699
chas      0.09120281  0.09125123  0.08651777 -0.09917578
nox       1.00000000 -0.30218819  0.73147010 -0.76923011
rm       -0.30218819  1.00000000 -0.24026493  0.20524621
age       0.73147010 -0.24026493  1.00000000 -0.74788054
dis      -0.76923011  0.20524621 -0.74788054  1.00000000
```

rad	0.61144056	−0.20984667	0.45602245	−0.49458793
tax	0.66802320	−0.29204783	0.50645559	−0.53443158
ptratio	0.18893268	−0.35550149	0.26151501	−0.23247054
black	−0.38005064	0.12806864	−0.27353398	0.29151167
lstat	0.59087892	−0.61380827	0.60233853	−0.49699583
medv	−0.42732077	0.69535995	−0.37695457	0.24992873

	rad	tax	ptratio	black
crim	0.625505145	0.58276431	0.2899456	−0.38506394
zn	−0.311947826	−0.31456332	−0.3916785	0.17552032
indus	0.595129275	0.72076018	0.3832476	−0.35697654
chas	−0.007368241	−0.03558652	−0.1215152	0.04878848
nox	0.611440563	0.66802320	0.1889327	−0.38005064
rm	−0.209846668	−0.29204783	−0.3555015	0.12806864
age	0.456022452	0.50645559	0.2615150	−0.27353398
dis	−0.494587930	−0.53443158	−0.2324705	0.29151167
rad	1.000000000	0.91022819	0.4647412	−0.44441282
tax	0.910228189	1.00000000	0.4608530	−0.44180801
ptratio	0.464741179	0.46085304	1.0000000	−0.17738330
black	−0.444412816	−0.44180801	−0.1773833	1.00000000
lstat	0.488676335	0.54399341	0.3740443	−0.36608690
medv	−0.381626231	−0.46853593	−0.5077867	0.33346082

	lstat	medv
crim	0.4556215	−0.3883046
zn	−0.4129946	0.3604453
indus	0.6037997	−0.4837252
chas	−0.0539293	0.1752602
nox	0.5908789	−0.4273208
rm	−0.6138083	0.6953599
age	0.6023385	−0.3769546
dis	−0.4969958	0.2499287
rad	0.4886763	−0.3816262
tax	0.5439934	−0.4685359
ptratio	0.3740443	−0.5077867
black	−0.3660869	0.3334608
lstat	1.0000000	−0.7376627
medv	−0.7376627	1.0000000

Due to the large number of variables, the obtained matrix is not easily interpretable. To overcome this inconvenience, we can plot a correlogram. A correlogram is a graph of a correlation matrix. It is very useful to highlight the most correlated variables in a data table. In this plot, correlation coefficients are colored according to the value. A correlation matrix can also be reordered according to the degree of association between variables. We can plot a correlogram in R using the `corrplot` package. The following table lists some of the information on this package:

Package	corrplot
Date	October 17, 2017
Version	0.84
Title	Visualization of a correlation matrix
Authors	Taiyun Wei, Viliam Simko, Michael Levy, Yihui Xie, Yan Jin, Jeff Zemla

A graphical display of a correlation matrix or general matrix is returned. This package, also contains some algorithms to do matrix reordering. In addition, `corrplot` is good at details, including choosing color, text labels, color labels, layout, and so on.

To obtain a correlogram, just use the `corrplot()` function as follows:

```
corrplot(CorBHData, method = "pie",type="lower")
```

Two arguments are used: `method`, and `type`. The first is used to set the visualization method of the correlation matrix. Seven methods are available: `circle` (default), `square`, `ellipse`, `number`, `pie`, `shade` and `color`. The areas of circles or squares show the absolute value of corresponding correlation coefficients. The `type` argument is used to set the type of visualization. The following types are available: `full` (default), `upper` or `lower`, display full matrix, and lower triangular or upper triangular matrix. In our case, we used the `pie` method (classic pie chart) and the `lower` type to display a lower triangular matrix, as shown in the following figure:

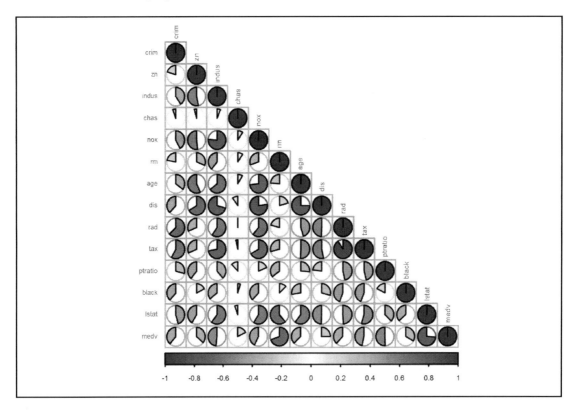

As we are interested in the existing relationship between the response variable (`medv`) and predictors, we will only analyze the last line of the correlation matrix. In it, we can see that the predictors most closely related are: `rm`, `lStat`, `Ptratio`. Indeed, these variables have larger pieces of cake, even if different colors (the different color is due to the positive or negative correlation as shown in the color label at the bottom of the plot).

Multiple linear model fitting

After carefully analyzing the data, it is time to build the multiple linear regression model to obtain a tool capable of predicting the median value of owner-occupied homes of new observations. To fit the multiple linear regression model, we can use the `lm()` function. This function is used to fit linear models. It can be used to carry out regression, single stratum analysis of variance, and analysis of covariance.

To fit a multiple linear regression model for the `medv` response, using all predictors, we can type as follows:

```
LModel1<-lm(medv~.,data=BHDataScaled)
```

The results are shown as follows:

```
> LModel1
Call:
lm(formula = medv ~ ., data = BHDataScaled)
Coefficients:
(Intercept)          crim             zn          indus           chas
   0.480450      -0.213550       0.103157       0.012463       0.059705
        nox            rm            age            dis             rad
  -0.191879       0.441860       0.001494      -0.360592       0.156425
        tax       ptratio          black          lstat
  -0.143629      -0.199018       0.082063      -0.422605
```

Now is the time to clarify the meaning of the values contained in the model. To look at them, let's see a brief summary using the `summary()` function:

```
summary(LModel1)
```

The results are shown as follows:

```
> summary(LModel1)
Call:
lm(formula = medv ~ ., data = BHDataScaled)
Residuals:
      Min        1Q    Median        3Q       Max
 -0.34654  -0.06066  -0.01151   0.03949   0.58221
Coefficients:
              Estimate Std. Error t value Pr(>|t|)
(Intercept)   0.480450   0.052843   9.092  < 2e-16 ***
crim         -0.213550   0.064978  -3.287 0.001087 **
zn            0.103157   0.030505   3.382 0.000778 ***
indus         0.012463   0.037280   0.334 0.738288
chas          0.059705   0.019146   3.118 0.001925 **
nox          -0.191879   0.041253  -4.651 4.25e-06 ***
```

```
rm           0.441860   0.048470    9.116  < 2e-16 ***
age          0.001494   0.028504    0.052 0.958229
dis         -0.360592   0.048742   -7.398 6.01e-13 ***
rad          0.156425   0.033910    4.613 5.07e-06 ***
tax         -0.143629   0.043789   -3.280 0.001112 **
ptratio     -0.199018   0.027328   -7.283 1.31e-12 ***
black        0.082063   0.023671    3.467 0.000573 ***
lstat       -0.422605   0.040843  -10.347  < 2e-16 ***
---
Signif. codes:  0 '***' 0.001 '**' 0.01 '*' 0.05 '.' 0.1 ' ' 1
Residual standard error: 0.1055 on 492 degrees of freedom
Multiple R-squared:  0.7406,    Adjusted R-squared:  0.7338
F-statistic: 108.1 on 13 and 492 DF,  p-value: < 2.2e-16
```

From the results obtained, the model seems to work. In fact, all the predictors used are statistically significant. Also, we have obtained a value of `Multiple R-squared` equal to `0.7406`. In other words, *74.6%* of the variation of `medv` about the average can be explained by the *13* regression variables. This shows that the initial model is appropriate for determining the median value of owner-occupied homes.

To further test the model's capacity in predicting the median value of owner-occupied homes as a function of the thirteen variables assumed, we can display the predicted values against the current ones. To do this, we first perform the prediction on all the observations contained in the starting dataset. We can use the `predict()` function. This is a generic function for predictions from the results of various model fitting functions:

```
Pred1 <- predict(LModel1)
```

Now, we will calculate the **mean squared error (MSE)** that measures the average of the squares of the errors or deviations:

```
mse1 <- mean((BHDataScaled$medv - Pred1)^2)
```

The result is shown as follows:

```
> mse1
[1] 0.01081226
```

Also, we can trace the `Actual` values against the `Predicted` ones:

```
plot(BHDataScaled[,14],Pred1,
     xlab="Actual",ylab="Predicted")
abline(a=0,b=1)
```

In the previous commands, we first plot the actual values against the predicted ones and then we add a line with zero intercept and a *slope=1*, as shown in the following figure:

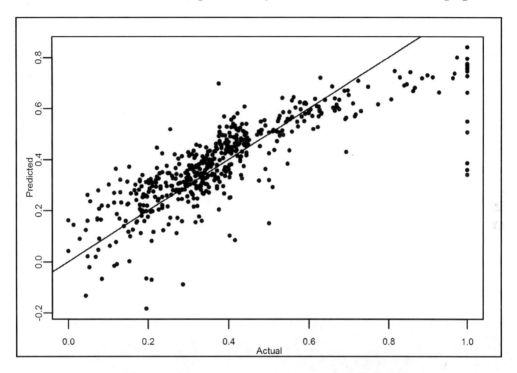

A predicted against actual plot shows the effect of the model and compares it against the null model. For a good fit, the points should be close to the fitted line (the line with the *x=y* equation). Points on the left or right of the plot, furthest from the mean, have the most leverage and effectively try to pull the fitted line toward the point. Points that are vertically distant from the line represent possible outliers. Both types of points can adversely affect the fit. In our case, there are some problems in the right part of the plot.

An important way of checking whether a multiple linear regression has achieved its goal to explain as much variation as possible in a dependent variable while respecting the underlying assumption, is to check the residuals of a regression. In other words, having a detailed look at what is left over after explaining the variation in the dependent variable using independent variables, I mean the unexplained variation.

Ideally all residuals should be small and unstructured; this then would mean that the regression analysis has been successful in explaining the essential part of the variation of the dependent variable. If, however, residuals exhibit a structure or present any special aspect that does not seem random, this challenges the results so far obtained.

To perform a residuals analysis, we can rely on a number of tools in R. Some of these are the diagnostic diagrams that are obtained using the `plot` function on the `lm` class object.

We plot the charts provided by default:

- A plot of residuals against fitted values
- A normal q-q plot
- A scale-location plot of *sqrt(| residuals |)* against fitted values
- A plot of residuals against leverages

Furthermore, we will use the `par()` function to set the graphics window to show four plots at once, in a layout with 2 rows and 2 columns:

```
par(mfrow=c(2,2))
plot(LModel1)
```

The following figure shows four plots: **Residuals vs Fitted** values, **Normal Q-Q**, **Scale-Location**, **Residuals vs Leverage**:

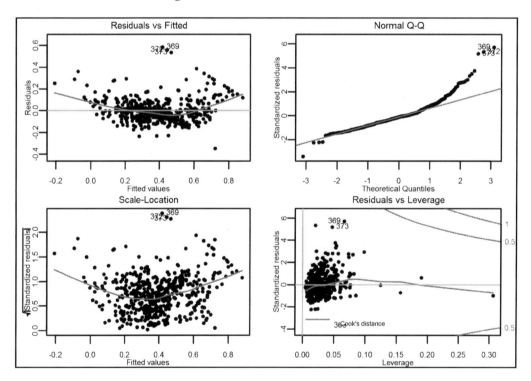

In Chapter 2, *Basic Concepts – Simple Linear Regression*, at the residuals analysis we had repeatedly underlined the need for the residuals to be distributed equally, as a condition necessary for the success of the model. Now we can see that the residuals are equally distributed. In the case of the normal Q-Q plot, the data does not fit very well to the dashed line. All this tells us that the model we have built is able to predict the system with good approximation but at the same time tells us that the model can be further improved.

Earlier, we pointed out that model problems may be due to the presence of outliers. In Chapter 7, *Going Further with Regression Models*, we learned to eliminate these effects with robust regression.

Random forest regression model

The technique of random forests, the extension of the approach to the construction of regression trees, was recently proposed by Leo Breiman. Breiman was a distinguished statistician at the University of California, Berkeley.

The random forests algorithm is based on the construction of many regression trees. Every single case is passed through all the trees in the forest; each of them provides a prediction. The final forecast is then made by averaging the predictions provided by individual regression trees. In accordance with what has been said, the tree response is an estimate of the dependent variable given the predictors.

To perform random forests regression, we will use the randomForest() function contained in the randomForest package. The following table lists some of the information on this package:

Package	randomForest
Date	July 10, 2015
Version	4.6-12
Title	Breiman and Cutler's Random Forests for Classification and Regression
Authors	Fortran original by Leo Breiman and Adele Cutler, R port by Andy Liaw and Matthew Wiener.

So, we must first install the package.

Remember, to install a library that is not present in the initial distribution of R, you must use the `install.package` function. This is the main function to install packages. It takes a vector of names and a destination library, downloads the packages from the repositories, and installs them.

Then, we will load the library through the `library` command:

```
library(randomForest)
```

Now, we can use the `randomForest()` function, as follows:

```
RFModel=randomForest(medv ~ . , data = BHDataScaled)
```

The result model is shown here:

```
> RFModel
Call:
randomForest(formula = medv ~ ., data = BHDataScaled)
                Type of random forest: regression
                      Number of trees: 500
No. of variables tried at each split: 4

          Mean of squared residuals: 0.004825488
                    % Var explained: 88.42
```

From the results obtained, the model seems to work. In fact, we have obtained a value of MSE equal to `0.004825488`, much lower than that obtained in the case of the linear model (*0.01081226*). Furthermore, for this model, *88.42%* of the variation of `medv` about the average can be explained by the 13 regression variables, higher than that obtained in the case of the linear model (*74.6%*). We can also see that `500` regression trees have been implemented. Finally, the number of variables randomly selected at each split is four.

Now is the time to clarify the meaning of the values contained in the model. To look at them, let's see a brief summary using the `summary()` function:

```
summary(RFModel)
```

The results are shown as follows:

```
> summary(RFModel)
          Length Class  Mode
call          3  -none- call
type          1  -none- character
predicted   506  -none- numeric
mse         500  -none- numeric
```

rsq	500	-none-	numeric
oob.times	506	-none-	numeric
importance	13	-none-	numeric
importanceSD	0	-none-	NULL
localImportance	0	-none-	NULL
proximity	0	-none-	NULL
ntree	1	-none-	numeric
mtry	1	-none-	numeric
forest	11	-none-	list
coefs	0	-none-	NULL
y	506	-none-	numeric
test	0	-none-	NULL
inbag	0	-none-	NULL
terms	3	terms	call

In this case, the `summary()` function does not return the usual statistics, but only returns the list of components of the implemented R object. Previously, we had read that 500 regression trees had been implemented for the construction of the model. We can then see the error trend (`mse`) during iteration of the algorithm:

```
plot(RFModel)
```

The following figure shows the **Error** against the number of **trees**:

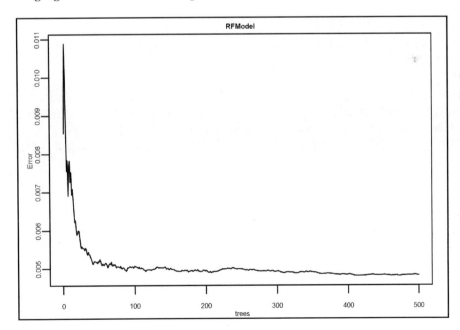

From the analysis of the figure, we can see how the **Error** is dropping as we keep on adding more and more **trees** and average them. Among the components returned by the model, the importance is especially significant. This component extracts a variable importance measure. This means that the random forest model also returns a method for selecting variables. Let's see how to do it:

```
VarImp<-importance(RFModel)
VarImp<-as.matrix(VarImp[order(VarImp[,1], decreasing = TRUE),])
```

In the first line of code, we extracted the evaluation of the importance of the variables as contained in the template. In the second line of code, we ordered it in decreasing order to make reading easier. These are the results:

```
> VarImp
                [,1]
lstat    6.2082684
rm       5.8789901
nox      1.3430405
ptratio 1.3162706
indus    1.2720099
dis      1.2429161
crim     1.2079574
tax      0.7314099
age      0.5599573
black    0.3926114
rad      0.1640457
zn       0.1458600
chas     0.1305161
```

We can now compare these results with those obtained previously with correlation analysis. In both cases, the most important variables are: lstat, rm, ptratio. Another equally effective way of analyzing the importance of variables, is to use the varImpPlot() function that returns a dotchart of variable importance as measured by a random forest:

```
varImpPlot(RFModel)
```

The following figure shows a dotchart of variable importance:

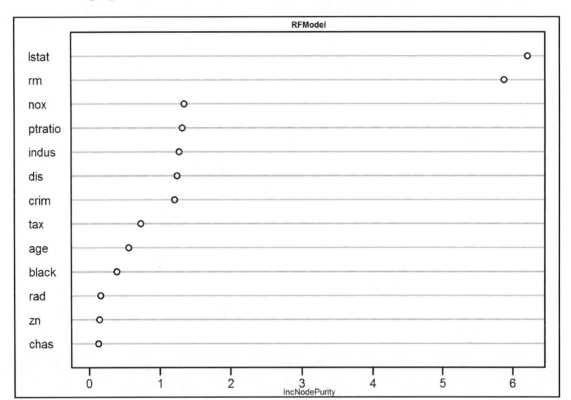

In this way, we can notice that lstat and rm variables take on a greater importance than the others. To further test the model's capacity in predicting the median value of owner-occupied homes as a function of the three variables assumed, we can display the predicted values against the current ones, as already done for the linear model. To do this, we first perform the prediction on all the observations contained in the starting dataset:

```
Pred2 <- predict(RFModel)
```

Now, we can trace the Actual values against the Predicted ones:

```
plot(BHDataScaled[,14],Pred2,
    xlab="Actual",ylab="Predicted")
abline(a=0,b=1)
```

In the previous commands, we first plotted the `Actual` values against the `Predicted` ones and then we added a line with `0` intercept and a slope is `1`, as shown in the following figure:

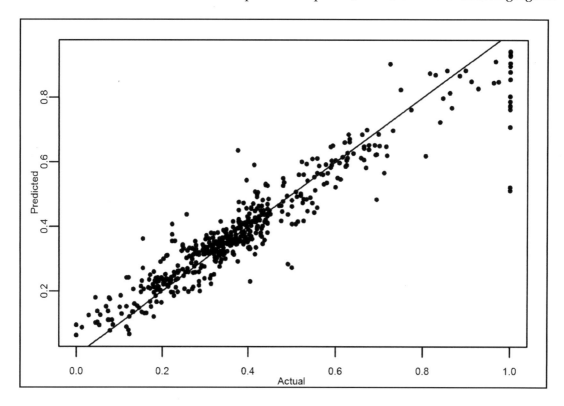

From the analysis of the figure, we have a further insight into how well the random forest model fits. In fact, we can note that the data group around the line is much better than the linear model.

Classifying breast cancer using logistic regression

The breast is made up of a set of glands and adipose tissue, and is placed between the skin and the chest wall. In fact, it is not a single gland, but a set of glandular structures, called **lobules**, joined together to form a lobe. In a breast, there are 15 to 20 lobes. The milk reaches the nipple from the lobules through small tubes called **milk ducts**.

Breast cancer is a potentially serious disease if it is not detected and treated for a long time. It is caused by uncontrolled multiplication of some cells in the mammary gland that are transformed into malignant cells. This means that they have the ability to detach themselves from the tissue that has generated them to invade the surrounding tissues and eventually the other organs of the body. In theory, cancers can be formed from all types of breast tissues, but the most common ones are from glandular cells or from those forming the walls of the ducts.

The objective of this example is to identify each of a number of benign or malignant classes. To do this, we will use the data contained in the dataset named `BreastCancer` (Wisconsin Breast Cancer database). This data has been taken from the UCI Repository of Machine Learning databases as DNA samples arrive periodically as Dr. Wolberg reports his clinical cases. The database therefore reflects this chronological grouping of the data. This grouping information appears immediately, having been removed from the data itself. Each variable, except for the first, was converted into 11 primitive numerical attributes with values ranging from zero through ten.

To get the data, we draw on the large collection of data available in the UCI Machine Learning Repository at the following link:
`http://archive.ics.uci.edu/ml`

The data frames contain `699` observations on `11` variables—one factor, nine integers, and one target class:

- `Id`: Sample code number
- `Cl.thickness`: Clump thickness
- `Cell.size`: Uniformity of cell size
- `Cell.shape`: Uniformity of cell shape
- `Marg.adhesion`: Marginal adhesion
- `Epith.c.size`: Single epithelial cell size
- `Bare.nuclei`: Bare nuclei
- `Bl.cromatin`: Bland chromatin
- `Normal.nucleoli`: Normal nucleoli
- `Mitoses`: Mitoses
- `Class`: Class (two for benign, four for malignant)

As said previously, the objective of this example is to identify each of a number of benign or malignant classes. First we have to get the data. To do this we can use the `read.table()` function as follows:

```
BCData <- read.table(url("https://archive.ics.uci.edu/ml/machine-learning-
databases/breast-cancer-wisconsin/breast-cancer-wisconsin.data"), sep =
",")
```

In this function, instead of the filename, we can also enter a complete URL of a file contained on a website repository. Now, we use the `names()` function to set the names of the dataset according to the list previously viewed:

```
names(BCData)<- c('Id', 'ClumpThickness', 'CellSize','CellShape',
                  'MarginalAdhesion','SECellSize', 'BareNuclei',
                  'BlandChromatin','NormalNucleoli',
                  'Mitoses','Class')
```

The table also includes the names of the variables as they are in the original dataset.

Exploratory analysis

Before starting with data analysis through the logistic regression, we conduct an exploratory analysis to understand how the data is distributed and extract preliminary knowledge. Let's start by checking the dataset using the `str()` function. This function provides a compact display of the internal structure of an object. Ideally, only one line for each basic structure is displayed:

```
str(BCData)
```

The results are shown here:

```
> str(BCData)
'data.frame':  699 obs. of  11 variables:
 $ Id               : int  1000025 1002945 1015425 1016277 1017023 1017122
1018099
                            1018561 1033078 1033078 ...
 $ ClumpThickness   : int  5 5 3 6 4 8 1 2 2 4 ...
 $ CellSize         : int  1 4 1 8 1 10 1 1 1 2 ...
 $ CellShape        : int  1 4 1 8 1 10 1 2 1 1 ...
 $ MarginalAdhesion : int  1 5 1 1 3 8 1 1 1 1 ...
 $ SECellSize       : int  2 7 2 3 2 7 2 2 2 2 ...
 $ BareNuclei       : Factor w/ 11 levels "?","1","10","2",..: 2 3 4 6 2 3
2 2 2 ...
 $ BlandChromatin   : int  3 3 3 3 3 9 3 3 1 2 ...
 $ NormalNucleoli   : int  1 2 1 7 1 7 1 1 1 1 ...
```

```
$ Mitoses          : int  1 1 1 1 1 1 1 5 1 ...
$ Class            : int  2 2 2 2 4 2 2 2 2 ...
```

So we got the confirmation that it was 699 observations of 11 variables: ten integer, and one factor. By analyzing the values of the only non-numeric variable, we notice an anomaly. There is a value equal to ?, indicative of the presence of missing attribute values. We need to remove these values because they may affect our entire analysis. To remove rows with missing values, we can use the following command:

```
BCData<-BCData[!(BCData$BareNuclei=="?"),]
```

The logical operator ! indicates logical negation (NOT). So, with the code we just proposed, we updated the BCData data frame by adding all the rows except those where column BareNuclei contains the ? value. At this point, the BareNuclei variable contains only integer values, so it does not make sense that a factor variable remains. We can convert it to a integer variable using the as.integer() function:

```
BCData$BareNuclei<-as.integer(BCData$BareNuclei)
```

To confirm the success of the operation, we use the str() function again:

```
> str(BCData)
'data.frame':   683 obs. of  11 variables:
 $ Id               : int  1000025 1002945 1015425 1016277 1017023 1017122
1018099
                           1018561 1033078 1033078 ...
 $ ClumpThickness   : int  5 5 3 6 4 8 1 2 2 4 ...
 $ CellSize         : int  1 4 1 8 1 10 1 1 1 2 ...
 $ CellShape        : int  1 4 1 8 1 10 1 2 1 1 ...
 $ MarginalAdhesion: int  1 5 1 1 3 8 1 1 1 1 ...
 $ SECellSize       : int  2 7 2 3 2 7 2 2 2 2 ...
 $ BareNuclei       : int  2 3 4 6 2 3 3 2 2 2 ...
 $ BlandChromatin   : int  3 3 3 3 3 9 3 3 1 2 ...
 $ NormalNucleoli   : int  1 2 1 7 1 7 1 1 1 1 ...
 $ Mitoses          : int  1 1 1 1 1 1 1 5 1 ...
 $ Class            : int  2 2 2 2 4 2 2 2 2 ...
```

As we can see, now all the variables are integer. Now, to obtain a brief summary of the dataset we can use the summary() function.

 Remember, the summary() function is a generic function used to produce result summaries of the results of various model fitting functions. The function invokes particular methods which depend on the class of the first argument.

In this case, the function was applied to a data frame and the results are shown here:

```
> summary(BCData)
      Id              ClumpThickness         CellSize
Min.   :    63375   Min.   : 1.000    Min.   : 1.000
1st Qu.:   877617   1st Qu.: 2.000    1st Qu.: 1.000
Median :  1171795   Median : 4.000    Median : 1.000
Mean   :  1076720   Mean   : 4.442    Mean   : 3.151
3rd Qu.:  1238705   3rd Qu.: 6.000    3rd Qu.: 5.000
Max.   : 13454352   Max.   :10.000    Max.   :10.000
   CellShape        MarginalAdhesion    SECellSize
Min.   : 1.000     Min.   : 1.00     Min.   : 1.000
1st Qu.: 1.000     1st Qu.: 1.00     1st Qu.: 2.000
Median : 1.000     Median : 1.00     Median : 2.000
Mean   : 3.215·    Mean   : 2.83     Mean   : 3.234
3rd Qu.: 5.000     3rd Qu.: 4.00     3rd Qu.: 4.000
Max.   :10.000     Max.   :10.00     Max.   :10.000
   BareNuclei       BlandChromatin     NormalNucleoli
Min.   : 2.000     Min.   : 1.000    Min.   : 1.00
1st Qu.: 2.000     1st Qu.: 2.000    1st Qu.: 1.00
Median : 2.000     Median : 3.000    Median : 1.00
Mean   : 3.217     Mean   : 3.445    Mean   : 2.87
3rd Qu.: 3.000     3rd Qu.: 5.000    3rd Qu.: 4.00
Max.   :11.000     Max.   :10.000    Max.   :10.00
    Mitoses             Class
Min.   : 1.000     Min.    :2.0
1st Qu.: 1.000     1st Qu.:2.0
Median : 1.000     Median :2.0
Mean   : 1.603     Mean    :2.7
3rd Qu.: 1.000     3rd Qu.:4.0
Max.   :10.000     Max.    :4.0
```

The summary() function returns a set of statistics for each variable. To get the number of cancer cases for each classes, we can use the table() function. This function uses the cross-classifying factors to build a contingency table of the counts at each combination of factor levels:

```
table(BCData$Class)
```

Here are the results:

```
> table(BCData$Class)

  2   4
444 239
```

As specified previously, 2 mean benign, 4 mean malignant. So, 444 cases of benign class and 239 cases of malignant class were detected.

Now, let's go into our exploratory analysis. The first thing we can do is to plot the boxplots of the variables. A first idea is already made by looking at the results of the summary() function. Naturally, we will limit ourselves to numeric variables only:

```
boxplot(BCData[,2:10])
```

In the following graph, the boxplots of the numeric variables (from 2° to 10°) contained in the BCData data frame are shown:

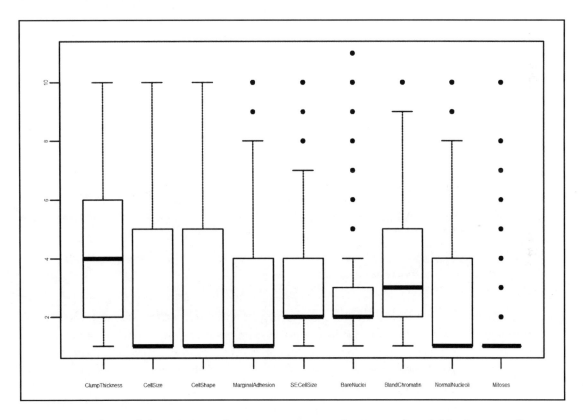

From the analysis of the previous figure, we can note that several variables have outliers, with the variable Mitoses being the one that has the largest number.

Outlier values are numerically different from the rest of the collected data. Statistics derived from samples containing outliers can be misleading.

To better identify the presence of outliers, we can plot histograms of the variables in the database. A histogram is an accurate graphical representation of the distribution of numerical data. It is an estimate of the probability distribution of a continuous variable. To construct a histogram, the first step is to specify the range of values (that is, divide the entire range of values into a series of intervals), and then count how many values fall into each interval. The bins are usually specified as consecutive, non-overlapping intervals of a variable. The bins must be adjacent, and are often of equal size. With a histogram, we can see where the middle is in your data distribution, how close the data lies around this middle, and where possible outliers are to be found.

In the R environment, we can simply make a histogram by using the `hist()` function, which computes a histogram of the given data values. We must put the name of the dataset in between the parentheses of this function. To plot many graphs in the same window, we will use the `par()` function, already used in the previous examples:

```
par(mfrow=c(3, 3))
hist(BCData$ClumpThickness)
hist(BCData$CellSize)
hist(BCData$CellShape)
hist(BCData$MarginalAdhesion)
hist(BCData$SECellSize)
hist(as.numeric(BCData$BareNuclei))
hist(BCData$BlandChromatin)
hist(BCData$NormalNucleoli)
hist(BCData$Mitoses)
```

Since the function `hist()` requires a `vector` as argument, we have transformed the values contained in the `BareNuclei` column into numeric vectors using the `as.numeric()` function. This function creates or coerces objects of the type numeric. The following graphs show the histograms of the numeric variables (from 2° to 10°) contained in the `BCData` data frame:

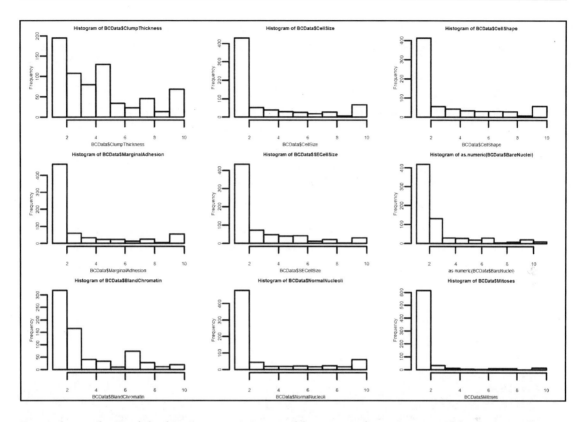

From the analysis of the histograms, it is possible to note that some variables have outliers.

Model fitting

After carefully analyzing the data, it is time to build the logistic regression model to obtain a tool capable of predicting the class of new observations. To fit the logistic regression model, we can use the `glm()` function. This function is used to fit generalized linear models, specified by giving a symbolic description of the linear predictor and a description of the error distribution.

Generalized linear models are extensions of traditional regression models that allow the mean to depend on the explanatory variables through a `link` function, and the response variable to be any member of a set of distributions called the **exponential family** (such as Binomial, Gaussian, Poisson, and others).

The first thing to do is set up the response in a format compatible with the `glm()` function that we will use to fit the model. For the binomial families, the response can be specified in one of three ways:

- As a factor
- As a numerical vector with values between zero and one, interpreted as the proportion of successful cases (with the total number of cases given by the weights)
- As a two-column integer matrix: The first column gives the number of successes and the second, the number of failures

We choose to adopt the second format. Previously, we have seen that the variable class contains two values: 2 mean benign, 4 mean malignant. Then, it's enough to replace 2 with 0 and 4 with 1. In R, to replace values just use the `replace()` function, as follows:

```
BCData$Class<-replace(BCData$Class,BCData$Class==2,0)
BCData$Class<-replace(BCData$Class,BCData$Class==4,1)
```

The following results are obtained:

```
> table(BCData$Class)

  0   1
444 239
```

Now, 0 mean benign, 1 mean malignant. The content of the response is unchanged: 444 cases of benign class and 239 cases of malignant class were detected.

Previously, we have verified that the `Id` variable contains the observation ID. It is clear that this variable can be omitted from the model. On the contrary, at least in the first analysis we will include all the remaining predictors in the model:

```
LoGModel <- glm(Class ~.-Id,
            family=binomial(link='logit'),data=BCData)
```

We now comment on the code used to build the regression model. Logistic regression is called by imposing the family: `family = binomial (logit)`. The `Class ~.-Id` code means that we want to create a model that explains the `Class` variable (benign or malignant breast cancer) depending on all the other variables contained in datasets except `Id`. In practice, `Class` is the dependent variable and all the other variables are the independent variables. Then, we read `data = BCData` to specify the location where the values are contained.

To produce result summaries of the results of the model fitting function, we use the `summary()` function:

```
summary(LogModel)
```

The results are shown here:

```
> summary(LoGModel)

Call:
glm(formula = Class ~ . - Id, family = binomial(link = "logit"),
    data = BCData)

Deviance Residuals:
    Min       1Q   Median       3Q      Max
-3.6922  -0.1128  -0.0588   0.0206   2.6233

Coefficients:
                  Estimate Std. Error z value Pr(>|z|)
(Intercept)      -11.05697    1.24336  -8.893  < 2e-16 ***
ClumpThickness     0.58181    0.12937   4.497 6.88e-06 ***
CellSize          -0.05776    0.20026  -0.288 0.773024
CellShape          0.52133    0.21391   2.437 0.014802 *
MarginalAdhesion   0.38661    0.10949   3.531 0.000414 ***
SECellSize         0.18570    0.14787   1.256 0.209179
BareNuclei         0.21915    0.11224   1.952 0.050887 .
BlandChromatin     0.61953    0.16219   3.820 0.000134 ***
NormalNucleoli     0.14997    0.10936   1.371 0.170251
Mitoses            0.58935    0.35733   1.649 0.099087 .
---
Signif. codes:  0 '***' 0.001 '**' 0.01 '*' 0.05 '.' 0.1 ' ' 1

(Dispersion parameter for binomial family taken to be 1)

    Null deviance: 884.35  on 682  degrees of freedom
Residual deviance: 117.91  on 673  degrees of freedom
AIC: 137.91

Number of Fisher Scoring iterations: 8
```

Let's find out what was being returned to us: the first thing we see is the call, which model we ran, which options we specified, and so on. Next, we see the deviance residuals, which are a measure of model fit. This part of the output shows the distribution of the deviance residuals for individual cases used in the model.

The next part of the summary results shows the coefficients, their standard errors, the z-statistic, and the associated p-values. This is the essential part of the model as it defines the model equation. We can see that not all coefficients are significant (*p-value <0.05*). The logistic regression coefficients give the change in the log odds of the outcome for a one unit increase in the predictor variable. `ClumpThickness`, `CellShape`, `MarginalAdhesion`, `BlandChromatin`, and `Mitoses` are statistically significant.

Following the table of coefficients are fit indices, including the null and deviance residuals and the AIC. `Null deviance` indicates the response predicted by a model with nothing but an intercept. The lower the value, the better the model. `Residual deviance` indicates the response predicted by a model on adding independent variables. The lower the value, the better the model. Deviance is a measure of goodness of fit of a generalized linear model. Or rather, it's a measure of badness of fit—higher numbers indicate worse fit.

The analogous metric of adjusted R-squared in logistic regression is AIC. AIC is the measure of fit which penalizes a model for the number of model coefficients. Therefore, we always prefer a model with a minimum AIC value.

Finally, the `number of Fisher Scoring iterations` is returned. Fisher's scoring algorithm is a derivative of Newton's method for solving maximum likelihood problems numerically. For our model, we see that Fisher's scoring algorithm needed six iterations to perform the fit. This doesn't really tell you a lot that you need to know, other than the fact that the model did indeed converge, and had no trouble doing it.

Now we can run the `anova()` function on the model to analyze the table of deviance:

```
anova(LoGModel, test="Chisq")
```

The results are shown here:

```
> anova(LoGModel, test="Chisq")
Analysis of Deviance Table

Model: binomial, link: logit

Response: Class

Terms added sequentially (first to last)
```

	Df	Deviance	Resid. Df	Resid. Dev	Pr(>Chi)	
NULL			682	884.35		
ClumpThickness	1	425.87	681	458.48	< 2.2e-16	***
CellSize	1	261.91	680	196.58	< 2.2e-16	***
CellShape	1	20.08	679	176.50	7.427e-06	***
MarginalAdhesion	1	21.39	678	155.11	3.750e-06	***

```
SECellSize          1      6.45     677     148.66  0.011112  *
BareNuclei          1      6.98     676     141.68  0.008248  **
BlandChromatin      1     18.42     675     123.26 1.767e-05  ***
NormalNucleoli      1      2.09     674     121.17  0.148710
Mitoses             1      3.26     673     117.91  0.070868  .
---
Signif. codes:   0 '***' 0.001 '**' 0.01 '*' 0.05 '.' 0.1 ' ' 1
```

The difference between the null deviance and the residual deviance shows how our model is doing against the null model (a model with only the intercept). The wider this difference, the better. Analyzing the table, we can see the drop in deviance when adding each variable one at a time. A large p-value here indicates that the model without the variable explains more or less the same amount of variation. Finally, what you would like to see is a significant drop in deviance and the AIC.

At this point, we can use the model to make predictions. To do this, we will use the predict() function. The function predict() is a generic function for predictions from the results of various model fitting functions. This function invokes particular methods which depend on the class of the first argument:

```
LGModelPred <- round(predict(LoGModel, type="response"))
```

In this line of code, we applied the predict() function to the previously built logistic regression model (LoGModel), passing the entire set of data at our disposal. The results were then rounded off using the round() function. Now, we count the cases:

```
> table(LGModelPred)
LGModelPred
  0   1
440 243
```

To analyze the performance of the model in the classification, we can calculate the confusion matrix. In a confusion matrix, our classification results are compared to real data. The strength of a confusion matrix is that it identifies the nature of the classification errors, as well as their quantities. In this matrix, the diagonal cells show the number of cases that were correctly classified, all the others cells show the misclassified cases. The initial way to view the confusion matrix is obtained by the table() function, as follows:

```
table(BCData$Class , LGModelPred)
```

The results are shown here:

```
> table(BCData$Class,LGModelPred)
   LGModelPred
      0   1
  0 432  12
  1   8 231
```

Although in a simple way, the matrix tells us that we only made 20 errors: 8 false negative, and 12 false positive. This simple table is not enough, we want more details. To calculate the confusion matrix we can use the `confusionMatrix()` function contained in the `caret` package. The `caret` package contains functions to streamline the model training process for complex regression and classification problems. The package utilizes a number of R packages but tries not to load them all at package start-up. A description of the `caret` package is contained at the end of `Chapter 1`, *Getting Started with Regression*.

First we will install the package:

```
install.package(caret)
```

Remember, to install a library that is not present in the initial distribution of R, you must use the `install.package` function. This is the main function to install packages. It takes a vector of names and a destination library, downloads the packages from the repositories, and installs them.

Then, we will load the library through the `library` command:

```
library(caret)
```

Now we can apply the `confusionMatrix()` function:

```
confusionMatrix(LGModelPred,BCData$Class)
```

The `confusionMatrix()` function calculates a cross-tabulation of observed and predicted classes with associated statistics, the syntax is similar to the `table()` function, but the positive outcome must be specified. The results are shown here:

```
> confusionMatrix(LGModelPred,BCData$Class,positive="1")
Confusion Matrix and Statistics

          Reference
Prediction   0   1
         0 432   8
         1  12 231
               Accuracy : 0.9707
                 95% CI : (0.9551, 0.982)
```

```
        No Information Rate : 0.6501
        P-Value [Acc > NIR] : <2e-16
                      Kappa : 0.9359
    Mcnemar's Test P-Value : 0.5023
                Sensitivity : 0.9665
                Specificity : 0.9730
             Pos Pred Value : 0.9506
             Neg Pred Value : 0.9818
                 Prevalence : 0.3499
             Detection Rate : 0.3382
      Detection Prevalence : 0.3558
          Balanced Accuracy : 0.9698
           'Positive' Class : 1
```

From the analysis of the confusion matrix, we can see that the logistic regression model has been able to properly classify *663* cases out of *683* available. Classification errors were therefore only *20*. As it is possible to verify, the model has a high `Accuracy` (0.9707), but also the sensitivity and the specificity are greater than *96* percent (0.9665, and 0.9730). Let's say something more about these two results.

The following table shows the confusion matrix for a two-class classifier (caution—in our example the rows and columns are inverted):

Actual values	Predicted positive	Predicted negative
Actual TRUE	*TP*	*FN*
Actual FALSE	*FP*	*TN*

The entries in the confusion matrix have the following meanings:

- *TP* is the number of correct predictions that an instance is positive
- *FN* is the number of incorrect predictions that an instance is negative
- *FP* is the number of incorrect predictions that an instance is positive
- *TN* is the number of correct predictions that an instance is negative

True positive rate (**TPR**) or sensitivity or recall or hit rate is a measure of how many true positives were identified out of all the positives identified:

$$TPR = \frac{TP}{P} = \frac{TP}{TP + FN}$$

Ideally, the model is better if we have this closer to one. To confirm what we got we calculate it:

```
> TPR = 231/(231+8)
> TPR
[1] 0.9665272
```

True negative rate (**TNR**) or specificity is the ratio of true negatives and total number of negatives we have predicted:

$$TNR = \frac{TN}{N} = \frac{TN}{TN + FP}$$

If this ratio is closer to zero, the model is more accurate. We also calculate this:

```
> TNR=432/(432+12)
> TNR
[1] 0.972973
```

In both cases, the results obtained coincide with those returned by the `confusionMatrix()` function.

Another tool to measure the model performance is the **Receiver Operator Characteristic** (**ROC**). ROC determines the accuracy of a classification model at a user-defined threshold value. It determines the model's accuracy using **area under curve** (**AUC**). The AUC, also referred to as the index of acccuracy (A) or concordant index, represents the performance of the ROC curve. The higher the area, the better the model. ROC is plotted between the TPR (y axis) and the FPR (x axis).

The ROC is a curve generated by plotting the TPR against the FPR at various threshold settings while the AUC is the area under the ROC curve. To build a ROC curve, we can use the roc() function contained in the pROC package. The following table lists some of the information on this package:

Package	pROC
Date	June 10, 2017
Version	1.10.0
Title	Display and Analyze ROC Curves
Authors	Xavier Robin, Natacha Turck, Alexandre Hainard, Natalia Tiberti, Frédérique Lisacek, Jean-Charles Sanchez, Markus Müller, Stefan Siegert

The main function of the pROC package is roc(). It builds a ROC curve and returns a roc object, a list of class roc. This object can be printed, plotted, or passed to the functions auc, ci, smooth.roc and coords. Additionally, two roc objects can be compared with roc.test. Let's see how to use it in our case:

```
RocObj<-roc(BCData$Class,LGModelPred)
```

The results are shown here:

```
> RocObj

Call:
roc.default(response = BCData$Class, predictor = LGModelPred)

Data: LGModelPred in 444 controls (BCData$Class 0) < 239 cases
(BCData$Class 1).
Area under the curve: 0.9698
```

Now we can trace the ROC curves from the object of the roc type we just built:

```
plot.roc(RocObj)
```

The results are shown in the following figure:

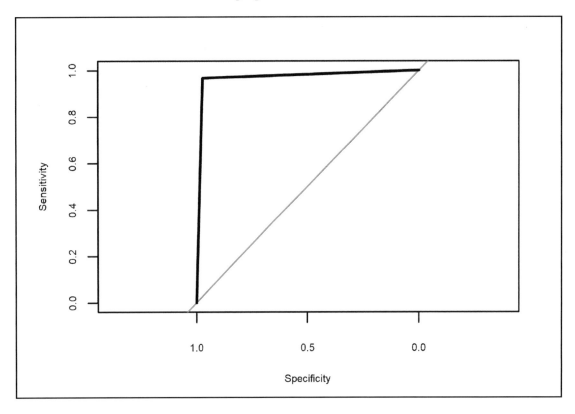

The ROC is a metric used to check the quality of classifiers. For each class of a classifier, ROC applies threshold values across the interval *[0,1]* to outputs. A perfect test would show points in the upper-left corner, with *100%* **Sensitivity** and *100%* **Specificity**. The better the lines approach the upper-left corner, the better is the model performance.

We can add more details such as a measurement of the area under the curve and the values of sensitivity and specificity. We remember that the AUC, also referred to as the index of accuracy (*A*) or concordant index, represents the performance of the ROC curve. While the sensitivity measures the proportion of positive examples that were correctly classified, and specificity measures the proportion of negative examples that were correctly classified. To do this, simply type the following command:

```
plot(RocObj, print.auc=TRUE, auc.polygon=TRUE, grid=c(0.1, 0.2),
            grid.col=c("green", "red"), max.auc.polygon=TRUE,
                auc.polygon.col="blue", print.thres=TRUE)
```

The following figure shows the ROC plot with **AUC**, **Sensitivity** and **Specificity**:

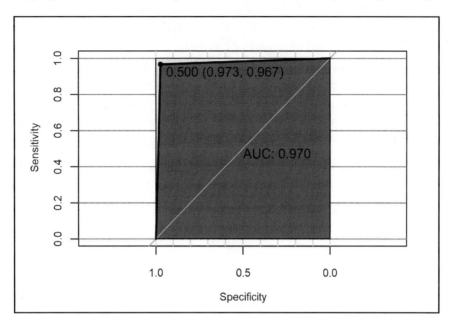

Also in this case, the results obtained coincide with those returned by the `confusionMatrix()` function.

Regression with neural networks

Artificial neural networks (ANN) are mathematical models for the simulation of typical human brain activities such as image perception, pattern recognition, language understanding, sense-motor coordination, and so on. These models are composed of a system of nodes, equivalent to the neurons of a human brain, which are interconnected by weighted links, equivalent to the synapses between neurons. The output of the network is modified iteratively from link weights to convergence. The original data is provided to the input layer and the result of the network is returned from the output level. The input nodes represent the independent or predictor variables that are used to predict the dependent variables, that is, the output neurons. According to these assumptions, it is clear that this tool can also be used to solve linear and nonlinear regression problems.

Neural network regression is the process of training a neural network on a set of inputs in order to produce an associated set of target outputs. Once the neural network fits the data, it forms a generalization of the input-output relationship and can be used to generate outputs for inputs it was not trained on.

The fuel consumption of vehicles has always been studied by the major manufacturers of the entire planet. In an era characterized by oil refueling problems and even greater air pollution problems, fuel consumption by vehicles has become a key factor. In this example, we will build a neural network with the purpose of predicting the fuel consumption of the vehicles according to certain characteristics.

To do this, use the Auto MPG dataset. This data has been taken from the UCI Repository Machine Learning databases.

 To get the data, we draw on the large collection of data available in the UCI Machine Learning Repository at the following link:
http://archive.ics.uci.edu/ml

The `Auto` dataset contains gas mileage, horsepower, and other information for 398 vehicles. It is a data frame with 398 observations on the following nine variables:

- `mpg`: Miles per gallon
- `cylinders`: Number of cylinders between four and eight
- `displacement`: Engine displacement (cubic inches)
- `horsepower`: Engine horsepower
- `weight`: Vehicle weight (lbs)
- `acceleration`: Time to accelerate from *0* to *60* mph (sec)
- `year`: Model year (modulo *100*)
- `origin`: Origin of car (American, European, Japanese)
- `name`: Vehicle name

This dataset was taken from the `StatLib` library which is maintained at Carnegie Mellon University. The dataset was used in the 1983 American Statistical Association Exposition. First, we have to get the data. To do this, we can use the `read.table()` function as follows:

```
AutoData <-
read.table(url("https://archive.ics.uci.edu/ml/machine-learning-
databases/auto-mpg/auto-mpg.data"), sep = "")
```

In this function, instead of the filename, we can also enter a complete URL of a file contained on a website repository. Now, we use the `names()` function to set the names of the dataset according to the list previously viewed:

```
names(AutoData)<-c("mpg","cylinders","displacement",
                   "horsepower","weight","acceleration",
                           "year","origin","name")
```

The table also includes the names of the variables as they are in the original dataset.

Exploratory analysis

Before starting with data analysis through the neural network, we conduct an exploratory analysis to understand how the data is distributed and extract preliminary knowledge. Let's start by checking the dataset using the `str()` function. This function provides a compact display of the internal structure of an object. Ideally, only one line for each basic structure is displayed:

```
str(AutoData)
```

The results are shown here:

```
> str(AutoData)
'data.frame':   398 obs. of  9 variables:
 $ mpg         : num  18 15 18 16 17 15 14 14 14 15 ...
 $ cylinders   : int  8 8 8 8 8 8 8 8 8 8 ...
 $ displacement: num  307 350 318 304 302 429 454 440 455 390 ...
 $ horsepower  : Factor w/ 94 levels "?","100.0","102.0",..: 17 35
                      29 29 24 42 47 46 48 40 ...
 $ weight      : num  3504 3693 3436 3433 3449 ...
 $ acceleration: num  12 11.5 11 12 10.5 10 9 8.5 10 8.5 ...
 $ year        : int  70 70 70 70 70 70 70 70 70 70 ...
 $ origin      : int  1 1 1 1 1 1 1 1 1 1 ...
 $ name        : Factor w/ 305 levels "amc ambassador
                      brougham",..: 50 37 232 15 162 142 55 224 242 2
                      ...
```

So we got the confirmation that it was 398 observations of 9 variables: four numerical, three integer, and two factor. By analyzing the values of the `horsepower` variable, we notice an anomaly. There is a value equal to ?, indicative of the presence of missing attribute values. We need to remove these values because they may affect our entire analysis. To remove rows with missing values, we can use the following command:

```
AutoData<-AutoData[!(AutoData$horsepower=="?"),]
```

The logical operator ! indicates logical negation (NOT). So, with the code we just proposed, we updated the `AutoData` data frame by adding all the rows except those where column horsepower contains the ? value. At this point, horsepower variable contains only integer values, so it does not make sense that a factor variable remains. We can convert it to an integer variable using the `as.integer()` function:

```
AutoData$horsepower<-as.integer(AutoData$horsepower)
```

To confirm the success of the operation, we use the `str()` function again:

```
> str(AutoData)
'data.frame':    392 obs. of   9 variables:
 $ mpg          : num  18 15 18 16 17 15 14 14 14 15 ...
 $ cylinders    : int  8 8 8 8 8 8 8 8 8 8 ...
 $ displacement : num  307 350 318 304 302 429 454 440 455 390 ...
 $ horsepower   : int  17 35 29 29 24 42 47 46 48 40 ...
 $ weight       : num  3504 3693 3436 3433 3449 ...
 $ acceleration : num  12 11.5 11 12 10.5 10 9 8.5 10 8.5 ...
 $ year         : int  70 70 70 70 70 70 70 70 70 70 ...
 $ origin       : int  1 1 1 1 1 1 1 1 1 1 ...
 $ name         : Factor w/ 305 levels "amc ambassador
                  brougham",..: 50 37 232 15 162 142 55 224 242 2
                  ...
```

As you can see, the database consists of 392 rows and 9 columns. The rows represent 392 commercial vehicles from 1970 to 1982. The columns represent the nine features collected for each car, in order: `mpg`, `cylinders`, `displacement`, `horsepower`, `weight`, `acceleration`, `year`, `origin`, and `name`.

Now, we can continue our explorative analysis by tracing a plot of predictors versus target. We recall in this respect that in our analysis, the predictors are the following variables: `cylinders`, `displacement`, `horsepower`, `weight`, `acceleration`, `year`, `origin`, and `name`. The target is the `mpg` variable that contains measurements of the miles per gallon of 392 sample cars.

Suppose we want to examine the `weight` and `mpg` of cars from three different origin, as shown in the next graph, using the following code:

```
plot(AutoData$weight, AutoData$mpg, pch=AutoData$origin)
```

To plot the chart, we used the `plot()` function, specifying what to point on the x axis (`weight`), what to point on the y axis (`mpg`), and finally, which variable to group the data (`origin`), as shown in the following figure:

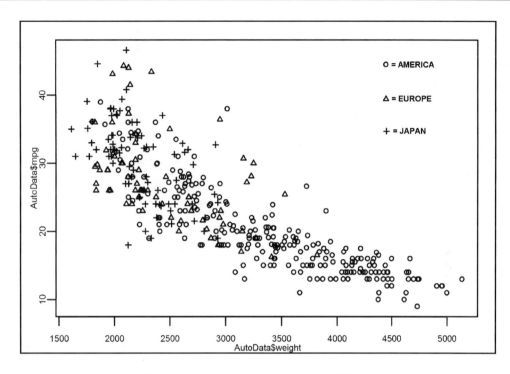

Remember the number in the origin column, corresponds at the following zone: *1= America, 2=Europe, and 3=Japan*). From the analysis of the previous figure, we can find that fuel consumption increases with weight gain. Let's remember that the target measures the miles per gallon, so how many miles are travelled with a gallon of fuel? It follows that the greater the value of miles per gallon, the lower the fuel consumption.

Another consideration that comes from plot analysis is that cars produced in America are heavier. In fact, in the right part of the figure (which corresponds to higher values of weight), there are only cars produced in that area.

Finally, if we focus our analysis on the left of the figure, in the upper part that corresponds to the lowest fuel consumption, we find in most cases Japanese and European cars. In conclusion, we can note that cars that have the lowest fuel consumption are Japanese. Now, let's see the other plots, that is, what we get if we plot the remaining numeric predictors (cylinders, displacement, horsepower, and acceleration) versus target (mpg):

```
par(mfrow=c(2,2))
plot(AutoData$cylinders, AutoData$mpg, pch=AutoData$origin)
plot(AutoData$displacement, AutoData$mpg, pch=AutoData$origin)
plot(AutoData$horsepower, AutoData$mpg, pch=AutoData$origin)
plot(AutoData$acceleration, AutoData$mpg, pch=AutoData$origin)
```

For space reasons, we decided to place the four plots in one. R makes it easy to combine multiple plots into one general figure, using the `par()` function. Using the `par()` function, we can include the option `mfrow=c(nrows, ncols)` to create a matrix of `nrows x ncols` plots that are filled in by row. For example, the option `mfrow=c(3,2)` creates a matrix plot with three rows and two columns. In addition, the option `mfcol=c(nrows, ncols)` fills in the matrix by columns.

The following figure shows four plots arranged in a matrix of two rows and two columns:

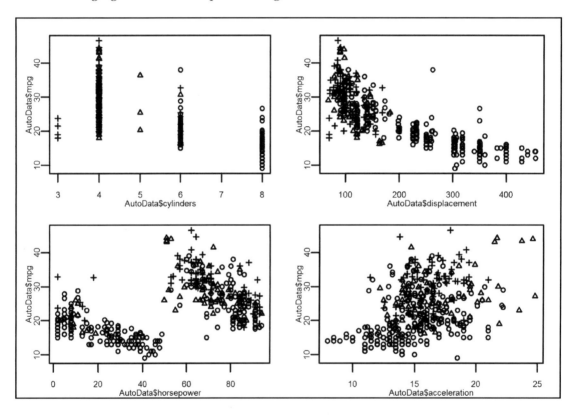

From the analysis of the previous figure, we find confirmation of what has already been mentioned earlier. We can note that cars with higher horsepower have higher fuel consumption. The same thing can be said about the engine displacement; also in this case, vehicles with higher displacement have higher fuel consumption. Again, cars with higher horsepower and displacement values are produced in America.

Conversely, cars with higher acceleration values have lower fuel consumption. This fact is due to the lesser weight that such cars have. Usually, heavy cars are slower in acceleration.

Neural network model

To perform a Neural Network Regression analysis, we will use the `neuralnet` package. The `neuralnet` library is used to train neural networks using backpropagation, **resilient backpropagation (RPROP)** with or without weight backtracking, or the modified **globally convergent version (GRPROP)**. The function allows flexible settings through custom-choice of error and activation function. Furthermore, the calculation of generalized weights is implemented. The following table lists some of the information on this package:

Package	`neuralnet`
Date	August 16, 2016
Version	1.33
Title	Training of Neural Networks
Authors	Stefan Fritsch, Frauke Guenther, Marc Suling, Sebastian M. Mueller

The following lists the most useful functions contained in this package:

- `neuralnet`: Training of neural networks
- `compute`: Computation of a given neural network for given covariate vectors
- `prediction`: Summarizes the output of the neural network, the data and the fitted values of `glm` objects (if available)
- `plot.nn`: Plot method for neural networks

 To learn more about this topic, we recommend reading the book: *Neural Networks with R*, Giuseppe Ciaburro, Balaji Venkateswaran, Packt Publishing.

First, we have to load the libraries needed to run the analysis.

```
library(neuralnet)
```

Remember, to install a library that is not present in the initial distribution of R, you must use the `install.package` function. This is the main function to install packages. It takes a vector of names and a destination library, downloads the packages from the repositories, and installs them. This function should be used only once and not every time you run the code.

Before training a neural network, it's good practice to normalize. With normalization, data units are eliminated, allowing you to easily compare data from different locations.

It is not always necessary to normalize numeric data. However, it has been shown that when numeric values are normalized, neural network formation is often more efficient and leads to better prediction. In fact, if numeric data is not normalized and the sizes of two predictors are very distant, a change in the value of a neural network weight has much more relative influence on higher value.

There are several standardization techniques; in Chapter 5, *Data Preparation Using R Tools,* we introduced several normalization techniques. In this case, we will adopt z scores normalization. This technique consists of subtracting the mean of the column to each value in a column, and then dividing the result for the standard deviation of the column. The formula to achieve this is the following:

$$xscaled = \frac{x - mean}{sd}$$

In summary, the z score (also called **standard score**) represents the number of standard deviations with which the value of an observation point or data is greater than the mean value of what is observed or measured. Values above the mean have positive z scores, while values below the mean have negative z scores. The z score is a quantity without dimension, obtained by subtracting the population mean from a single rough score and then dividing the difference for the standard deviation of the population.

Before applying the method chosen for normalization, you must calculate the mean and standard deviation values of each database column. To do this, we use the `apply()` function. This function returns a vector or an array or a list of values obtained by applying a function to margins of an array or matrix. Let's understand the meaning of the arguments used:

```
mean_data <- apply(AutoData[1:6], 2, mean)
sd_data <- apply(AutoData[1:6], 2, sd)
```

First of all, we will limit the normalization to the first six variables only: The others do not require normalization. The first line allows us to calculate the mean of each variable going to the second line, allowing us to calculate the standard deviation of each variable. Let's see how we used the `apply()` function. The first argument of the `apply()` function specifies the dataset to apply the function to, in our case, the dataset named `data`. In particular, we have only considered the first six numeric variables; the other ones we will use for other purposes. The second argument must contain a vector giving the subscripts which the function will be applied over. In our case, one indicates rows and two indicates columns. The third argument must contain the function to be applied; in our case, the `mean()` function in the first row and the `sd()` function in the second row. The results are shown here:

```
> mean_data
          mpg     cylinders  displacement    horsepower
  23.445918367   5.471938776  194.411989796   52.160714286
       weight   acceleration
2977.584183673   15.541326531


> sd_data
          mpg     cylinders  displacement    horsepower
   7.805007487   1.705783247  104.644003909   29.498054685
       weight  acceleration
 849.402560043    2.758864119
```

To normalize the data, we use the `scale()` function, which is a generic function whose default method centers and/or scales the columns of a numeric matrix:

```
AutoDataScaled <- as.data.frame(scale(AutoData[,1:6],center =
                      mean_data, scale = sd_data))
```

Let's take a look at the data transformed by normalization:

```
head(AutoDataScaled, n=20)
```

The results are as follows:

```
> head(AutoDataScaled, n=20)
              mpg       cylinders     displacement      horsepower
1   -0.69774671923  1.4820530265   1.07591458658  -1.19196722162
2   -1.08211534478  1.4820530265   1.48683158511  -0.58175749110
3   -0.69774671923  1.4820530265   1.18103288853  -0.78516073461
4   -0.95399246960  1.4820530265   1.04724595878  -0.78516073461
5   -0.82586959442  1.4820530265   1.02813354024  -0.95466343753
6   -1.08211534478  1.4820530265   2.24177211729  -0.34445370701
7   -1.21023821996  1.4820530265   2.48067734899  -0.17495100409
8   -1.21023821996  1.4820530265   2.34689041923  -0.20885154467
```

```
 9  -1.21023821996   1.4820530265   2.49023355825  -0.14105046350
10  -1.08211534478   1.4820530265   1.86907995583  -0.41225478818
11  -1.08211534478   1.4820530265   1.80218649096  -0.51395640993
12  -1.21023821996   1.4820530265   1.39126949243  -0.61565803169
13  -1.08211534478   1.4820530265   1.96464204851  -0.78516073461
14  -1.21023821996   1.4820530265   2.49023355825  -0.14105046350
15   0.07099053186  -0.8629107934  -0.77799001142   1.31667278163
16  -0.18525521850   0.3095711165   0.03428777637   1.31667278163
17  -0.69774671923   0.3095711165   0.04384398563   1.38447386280
18  -0.31337809369   0.3095711165   0.05340019490   0.97766737578
19   0.45535915741  -0.8629107934  -0.93088935971   1.07936899754
20   0.32723628223  -0.8629107934  -0.93088935971  -0.07324938233
              weight   acceleration
 1   0.6197483279  -1.2836175968
 2   0.8422576644  -1.4648516041
 3   0.5396920587  -1.6460856115
 4   0.5361601645  -1.2836175968
 5   0.5549969337  -1.8273196188
 6   1.6051468178  -2.0085536261
 7   1.6204516928  -2.3710216408
 8   1.5710051736  -2.5522556481
 9   1.7040398563  -2.0085536261
10   1.0270934624  -2.5522556481
11   0.6892089144  -2.0085536261
12   0.7433646259  -2.7334896555
13   0.9223139336  -2.1897876335
14   0.1276377320  -2.0085536261
15  -0.7129530945  -0.1962135528
16  -0.1702186813  -0.0149795455
17  -0.2396792678  -0.0149795455
18  -0.4598340081   0.1662544618
19  -0.9978592290  -0.3774475602
20  -1.3451621615   1.7973605278
```

Let's now split the data for the training and the test model. Training and testing the model forms the basis for further usage of the model for prediction in predictive analytics. Given a dataset of *100* rows of data, which includes the predictor and response variables, we split the dataset into a convenient ratio (say 70:30) and allocate 70 rows for training and 30 rows for testing. The rows are selected in random to reduce bias. Once the training data is available, the data is fed to the neural network to get the massive universal function in place. The training data determines the weights, biases, and activation functions to be used to get to output from input. Until recently, we could not say that a weight has a positive or a negative influence on the target variable. But now we've been able to shed some light inside the black box. For example, by plotting a trained neural network, we can discover trained synaptic weights and basic information about the training process.

Once sufficient convergence is achieved, the model is stored in memory and the next step is testing the model. We pass the 30 rows of data to check if the actual output matches with the predicted output from the model. The evaluation is used to get various metrics which can validate the model. If the accuracy is too wary, the model has to be re-built with change in the training data and other parameters passed to the neuralnet function.

As anticipated, let's now split the data for the training and the test:

```
index = sample(1:nrow(AutoData),round(0.70*nrow(AutoData)))
train_data <- as.data.frame(AutoDataScaled[index,])
test_data <- as.data.frame(AutoDataScaled[-index,])
```

In the first line of the code just suggested, the dataset is split into 70:30, with the intention of using 70% of the data at our disposal to train the network and the remaining 30% to test the network. In the second and third lines, the data of the data frame named `AutoDataScaled` is subdivided into two new data frames, called `train_data` and `test_data`. Now we have to build the function to be submitted to the network:

```
n = names(AutoDataScaled)
f = as.formula(paste("mpg ~", paste(n[!n %in% "mpg"],
                                     collapse = " + ")))
```

In the first line, we recover all the variable names in the `data_scaled` data frame, using the `names()` function. In the second line, we build a formula that we will use to train the network. What does this formula represent?

The models fitted by the `neuralnet()` function are specified in a compact symbolic form. The ~ operator is basic in the formation of such models. An expression of the form *y ~ model* is interpreted as a specification that the response *y* is modeled by a predictor specified symbolically by model. Such a model consists of a series of terms separated by + operators. The terms themselves consist of variable and factor names separated by : operators. Such a term is interpreted as the interaction of all the variables and factors appearing in the term. Let's look at the formula we set:

```
> f
mpg ~ cylinders + displacement + horsepower + weight +
                                        acceleration
```

Now we can build and train the network. At first, we have to choose the number of neurons, to do this we need to know that:

- A small number of neurons will lead to high error for your system, as the predictive factors might be too complex for a small number of neurons to capture.
- A large number of neurons will overfit your training data and not generalize well. The number of neurons in each hidden layer should be somewhere between the size of the input and the output layer, potentially the mean.
- The number of neurons in each hidden layer shouldn't exceed twice the number of input neurons, as you are probably grossly overfit at this point.

In this case, we have five input variables (`cylinders`, `displacement`, `horsepower`, `weight`, and `acceleration`) and one variable output (`mpg`). We choose to set three neurons in the hidden layer. Do not worry, the best choice is obtained with experience:

```
NNRModel<-neuralnet(f,data=train_data,hidden=3,linear.output=TRUE)
```

The `hidden` argument accepts a vector with the number of neurons for each hidden layer, while the argument `linear.output` is used to specify whether we want to do regression (`linear.output=TRUE`) or classification (`linear.output=FALSE`).

The algorithm used in `neuralnet()`, by default, is based on the resilient backpropagation without weight backtracking and additionally modifies one learning rate, either the learning rate associated with the **smallest absolute gradient (sag)** or the **smallest learning rate (slr)** itself. The `neuralnet()` function returns an object of class `nn`. An object of class `nn` is a list containing, at most, the components shown in the following table:

Components	Description
call	The matched call.
response	Extracted from the `data` argument.
covariate	The variables extracted from the `data` argument.
model.list	A list containing the covariates and the response variables extracted from the `formula` argument.
err.fct	The error function.
act.fct	The activation function.
data	The `data` argument.

net.result	A list containing the overall result of the neural network for every repetition.
weights	A list containing the fitted weights of the neural network for every repetition.
generalized.weights	A list containing the generalized weights of the neural network for every repetition.
result.matrix	A matrix containing the reached threshold, needed steps, error, AIC and BIC (if computed) and weights for every repetition. Each column represents one repetition.
startweights	A list containing the startweights of the neural network for every repetition.

To produce result summaries of the results of the model, we use the summary() function:

```
> summary(NNRModel)
                     Length Class       Mode
call                  5     -none-      call
response            274     -none-      numeric
covariate          1370     -none-      numeric
model.list            2     -none-      list
err.fct               1     -none-      function
act.fct               1     -none-      function
linear.output         1     -none-      logical
data                  6     data.frame  list
net.result            1     -none-      list
weights               1     -none-      list
startweights          1     -none-      list
generalized.weights   1     -none-      list
result.matrix        25     -none-      numeric
```

Three features are displayed for each component of the neural network model:

- Length: This is component length, that is how many elements of this type are contained in it
- Class: This contains specific indication on the component class
- Mode: This is the type of component (numeric, list, function, logical, and so on)

To plot the graphical representation of the model with the weights on each connection, we can use the `plot()` function. The `plot()` function is a generic function for the representation of objects in R; generic function means that it is suitable for different types of objects, from variables to tables to complex function outputs, producing different results.

Applied to a nominal variable, it will produce a bar graph. Applied to a cardinal variable, it will produce a scatter plot. Applied to the same variable, but tabulated, that is, to its frequency distribution, it will produce a histogram. Finally, applied to two variables, a nominal and a cardinal, it will produce a boxplot:

```
plot(NNRModel)
```

The neural network plot is shown in the following figure:

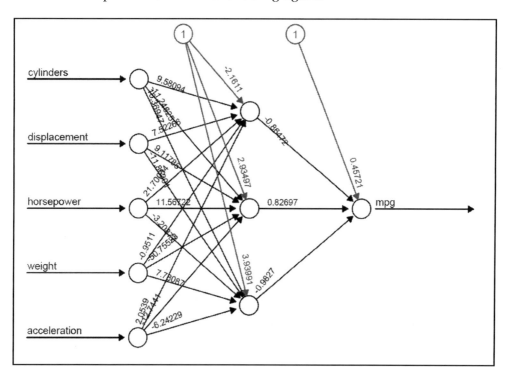

In the previous figure, the black lines (these lines start from input nodes) show the connections between each layer and the weights on each connection, while the blue lines (these lines start from bias nodes which are distinguished by number one) show the bias term added in each step. The bias can be thought of as the intercept of a linear model.

Though over time, we have understood a lot about the mechanics that are the basis of the neural networks, in many respects, the model we have built and trained remains a black box. The fitting, weights, and model are not clear enough. We can be satisfied that the training algorithm is convergent and then the model is ready to be used.

We can print on video, the weights and biases:

```
> NNRModel$result.matrix
                                          1
error                        26.424835868163
reached.threshold             0.008474056829
steps                      4002.000000000000
Intercept.to.1layhid1        -2.161104082217
cylinders.to.1layhid1         9.580940970808
displacement.to.1layhid1      7.522657555673
horsepower.to.1layhid1       21.700335681606
weight.to.1layhid1           -0.951102324090
acceleration.to.1layhid1      2.053898171391
Intercept.to.1layhid2         2.934972348178
cylinders.to.1layhid2       -11.246250332359
displacement.to.1layhid2      9.117852748780
horsepower.to.1layhid2       11.567216632838
weight.to.1layhid2          -50.755230886812
acceleration.to.1layhid2    -12.744100558643
Intercept.to.1layhid3         3.939907601551
cylinders.to.1layhid3        10.369471194932
displacement.to.1layhid3    -11.853014211539
horsepower.to.1layhid3       -3.208773904311
weight.to.1layhid3            7.780873230268
acceleration.to.1layhid3     -6.242289197064
Intercept.to.mpg              0.457209941798
1layhid.1.to.mpg             -0.864715366867
1layhid.2.to.mpg              0.826968142618
1layhid.3.to.mpg             -0.982700104708
```

As can be seen, these are the same values that we can read in the network plot. For example, `cylinders.to.1layhid1` is `9.580940970808` is the weight for the connection between the input cylinders and the first node of the hidden layer.

Now, we can use the network to make predictions. For this, we had set aside 30% of the data in the `test_data` data frame. It is time to use it:

```
PredNetTest <- compute(NNRModel,test_data[,2:6])
```

In our case, we applied the function to the `test_data` dataset, using only the columns from 2 to 6, representing the input variables of the network. To evaluate the network performance, we can use the MSE as a measure of how far away our predictions are from the real data:

```
MSE.net <- sum((test_data$mpg - PredNetTest $net.result)^2)/nrow(test_data)
```

Here `test_data$mpg` is the actual data and `PredNetTest$net.result` is the predicted data for the target of the analysis. Here is the result:

```
> MSE.net
[1] 0.264248305
```

It looks like a good result, but what do we compare it with? To get an idea of the accuracy of the network prediction, we can build a linear regression model. So, we build a linear regression model using the `lm()` function. This function is used to fit linear models. It can be used to perform regression, single stratum analysis of variance, and analysis of covariance:

```
LModel <- lm(mpg~., data=train_data)
```

The results are shown as follows:

```
> LModel

Call:
lm(formula = mpg ~ ., data = train_data)

Coefficients:
 (Intercept)       cylinders  displacement      horsepower
 0.010700025   -0.101019978  -0.021560871     0.003760324
      weight    acceleration
-0.683865020     0.082811946
```

To produce a summary of the results of the model fitting obtained, we have used the `summary()` function, which returns the following results::

```
summary(LModel)
```

The results are shown as follows:

```
> summary(LModel)

Call:
lm(formula = mpg ~ ., data = train_data)

Residuals:
      Min          1Q      Median          3Q         Max
-1.22975887 -0.36312202 -0.04769433  0.30793937  2.07580191

Coefficients:
                Estimate   Std. Error   t value           Pr(>|t|)
(Intercept)    0.010700025  0.033431009  0.32006          0.749170
cylinders     -0.101019978  0.115758663 -0.87268          0.383620
displacement  -0.021560871  0.142820872 -0.15096          0.880117
horsepower     0.003760324  0.039964723  0.09409          0.925107
weight        -0.683865020  0.099575435 -6.86781 0.000000000045379 ***
acceleration   0.082811946  0.041956379  1.97376          0.049436 *
---
Signif. codes:  0 '***' 0.001 '**' 0.01 '*' 0.05 '.' 0.1 ' ' 1

Residual standard error: 0.5521387 on 268 degrees of freedom
Multiple R-squared:  0.6995484, Adjusted R-squared:  0.693943
F-statistic: 124.7981 on 5 and 268 DF,  p-value: < 0.00000000000000022204
```

We have obtained a value of `Multiple R-squared` equal to 0.6995484. In other words, 69.9% of the variation of `mpg`, about the average, can be explained by the five regression variables. Also, only two predictors are statistically significant.

Now we make the prediction with the linear regression model using the data contained in the `test_data` data frame:

```
PredLModel <- predict(LModel,test_data)
```

Finally, we calculate the MSE for the regression model:

```
MSE.lm <- sum((PredLModel - test_data$mpg)^2)/nrow(test_data)
```

Here is the result:

```
> MSE.lm
[1] 0.296002603
```

From the comparison between the two models (neural network model versus linear regression model), the neural network wins (0.26 versus 0.29). We now perform a visual comparison by drawing on a graph the actual value versus the predicted value, first for the neural network and then for the linear regression model:

```
par(mfrow=c(1,2))
plot(test_data$mpg,predict_net_test$net.result,col='black',main='Real vs
predicted for neural network',pch=18,cex=4)
abline(0,1,lwd=5)
plot(test_data$mpg,predict_lm,col='black',main='Real vs predicted for
linear regression',pch=18,cex=4)
abline(0,1,lwd=5)
```

The comparison between the performance of the neural network model (to the left) and the linear regression model (to the right) on the test set is plotted in the following figure:

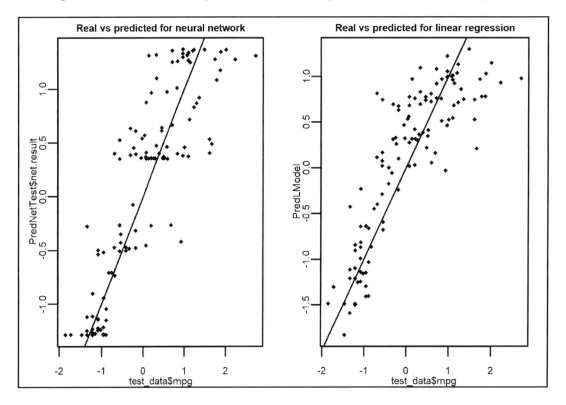

As we can see, the predictions by the neural network are more concentrated around the line than those by the linear regression model, even if you do not note a big difference.

Summary

In this final chapter, we have explored multiple linear regression, logistic regression, random forest regression, and neural network techniques applied to datasets resulting from real cases. We started from a random forest regression for the Boston dataset to predict the median value of owner-occupied homes for the test data. The random forests algorithm is based on the construction of many regression trees. Every single case is passed through all the trees in the forest; each of them provides a prediction. The final forecast is then made by averaging the predictions provided by individual regression trees. In accordance with what has been said, the tree response is an estimate of the dependent variable given the predictors.

Then, we have used a logistic regression technique to classify breast cancer. Logistic regression is a special case of a generalized linear model having as a `link` function the `logit` function. This is a regression model applied in cases where the dependent variable y is of the dichotomous type referable to the values zero and one, as are all the variables that can only assume two values. Through this technique, it's possible to extend the regression analysis to classify patterns.

Finally, we have used a neural network to perform a regression analysis. ANN are mathematical models for the simulation of typical human brain activities, such as image perception, pattern recognition, and so on. Generally, these techniques are used in classifying and clustering problems. In this example, we have learned how to use the neural network to solve a regression problem.

Other Books You May Enjoy

If you enjoyed this book, you may be interested in these other books by Packt:

Machine Learning Algorithms

Giuseppe Bonaccorso

ISBN: 978-1-78588-962-2

- Acquaint yourself with important elements of Machine Learning
- Understand the feature selection and feature engineering process
- Assess performance and error trade-offs for Linear Regression
- Build a data model and understand how it works by using different types of algorithm
- Learn to tune the parameters of Support Vector machines
- Implement clusters to a dataset
- Explore the concept of Natural Processing Language and Recommendation Systems
- Create a ML architecture from scratch

Statistics for Machine Learning
Pratap Dangeti

ISBN: 978-1-78829-575-8

- Understand the Statistical and Machine Learning fundamentals necessary to build models
- Understand the major differences and parallels between the statistical way and the Machine Learning way to solve problems
- Learn how to prepare data and feed models by using the appropriate Machine Learning algorithms from the more-than-adequate R and Python packages
- Analyze the results and tune the model appropriately to your own predictive goals
- Understand the concepts of required statistics for Machine Learning
- Introduce yourself to necessary fundamentals required for building supervised & unsupervised deep learning models
- Learn reinforcement learning and its application in the field of artificial intelligence domain

Leave a review - let other readers know what you think

Please share your thoughts on this book with others by leaving a review on the site that you bought it from. If you purchased the book from Amazon, please leave us an honest review on this book's Amazon page. This is vital so that other potential readers can see and use your unbiased opinion to make purchasing decisions, we can understand what our customers think about our products, and our authors can see your feedback on the title that they have worked with Packt to create. It will only take a few minutes of your time, but is valuable to other potential customers, our authors, and Packt. Thank you!

Index

A

accuracy 143
action of regressing 8
Akaike Information Criterion (AIC) 130
apodixis 8
area under curve (AUC) 380
artificial neural networks (ANN) 383

B

BAS package
  used, for creating Bayesian linear regression
   283, 291
batch GD 107
Bayes' theorem 281, 283
Bayesian Information Criterion (BIC) 288
Bayesian linear regression
  about 274, 275
  Bayes' theorem 281, 283
  creating, with BAS package 283, 291
  probability, basic concepts 275, 278, 281
binning
  using, for discretization 188, 190
BLR package
  about 41
  BLR 41
  sets 41
Boston dataset
  random forest regression 346
Box-Cox power transformation 37
breast cancer
  classifying, with logistic regression 366

C

car package
  ANOVA 36

cookd 36
durbin.watson 36
levene.test 36
linear.hypothesis 36
ncv.test 36
outlier.test 36
caret package 38
caret package, functions
  defaultSummary 38
  knnreg 38
  plotObsVsPred 38
  predict.knnreg 38
  train 38
  trainControl 38
  varImp 38
categorical data
  multiple logistic regression 143, 147, 152, 153,
   155
categorical variables
  about 96
  dichotomous variables 96
  nominal variables 96
  ordinal variables 96
certain event 277
classification 121
Classification and Regression Tree (CART) 329
classification tree 329
Comprehensive R Archive Network (CRAN)
  URL 27
conditional probability 280
Cook's distance 78
correlation
  about 44, 46, 47, 48, 49, 50
  versus regression 18, 21
count data model
  about 291
  Poisson distributions 292, 294

Poisson regression model 294, 295
warp breaks per loom, modeling 296, 298, 300, 301
covariance 44, 46, 47, 48, 49, 50
cross-validation
k-fold 214
Leave-one-out cross-validation (LOOCV) 214
used, for overfitting detection 213, 218, 221, 224, 226
Cumulative Distribution 319, 320
customer satisfaction analysis
with multiple logistic regression 136, 139, 143

D

data scaling 181
data wrangling
about 164
data, viewing 164, 166, 167
datatype, modifying 167, 169
empty cells, removing 169
incorrect value, replacing 170
missing values 170, 173
NaN values 173
decision trees 329
deduction 15
Department of Transportation (DOT) 65
dependent 18
diagnostic plots 72, 74, 75, 76, 77, 78
dimensionality reduction
about 195
principal component analysis 195, 198, 201, 203, 205, 206
discretization
about 187
by binning 188, 190
by histogram analysis 191, 194
dummy coding 24

E

Earth 312
ElasticNet regression 261, 263
explanatory variables 7
exponential family 127

F

feature scaling
about 181, 350
min-max normalization 182, 185
z score standardization 185, 187
feature selection
about 228
regression subset selection 237, 240, 243, 244
stepwise regression 229, 232, 235, 237
Federal Highway Administration (FHWA) 65
File Transfer Protocol (FTP) 28
Fitted values 74, 76
Free Software Foundation's (FSF) 24
Froude number 231

G

Galton universal regression law 12
General Public License (GPL) 24
Generalized Additive Model (GAM) 303, 322, 325, 327, 329
Generalized Cross Validation (GCV) 318
generalized least squares (GLS) 37, 267
Generalized Linear Model (GLM)
about 35, 121, 127, 250, 298, 303
simple logistic regression 127, 132, 134
Generalized Ridge Regression (GRR) 322
glmnet package, function
deviance.glmnet 39
glmnet 39
glmnet.control 39
plot.glmnet 39
predict.glmnet 39
print.glmnet 39
globally convergent version (GRPROP) 389
Gradient Descent (GD) 103, 104, 105, 106, 107

H

histogram analysis
using, for discretization 191, 194

I

impossible event 277
independent 18

indicator variables 24
induction 15
inference 15
Integrated Development Environment (IDE) 31
interquartile range (IQR) 174
iteratively reweighted least squares (IRLS) 267

K

K-Nearest Neighbor (KNN) regression 38

L

Lars package
  about 41
  lars 42
  plot.lars 42
  predict.lars 42
  summary.lars 42
lasso regression 254, 257, 261
least absolute deviations 255
least absolute errors 255
least squares 255
least squares regression 55, 56, 57, 58, 59, 60,
    61, 62, 63
Leverage 77
linear regression model
  about 103, 104, 105, 272, 273
  creating 64, 65, 66, 67, 68
  diagnostic plots 72, 74, 75, 76, 77, 78
  model results, exploring 69, 70, 71, 72
  statistical significance test 69
  with SGD 108
linear regression
  with SGD 109, 110, 111, 112
linear relationships
  searching 51, 52, 53, 54
lobules 366
Log Posterior Odds 289
log-Iteration 111
log-linear model 291
log-odds 126
logistic regression
  about 122
  exploratory analysis 368, 373
  logit model 124, 126

model, fitting 373, 379, 383
  used, for classifying breast cancer 366
logit 126
Lowess curve 315

M

marginal likelihood 283
MARS model equation 311
Mean Square Error (MSE) 111, 220, 321, 358
milk ducts 366
min-max normalization 182, 185
model results
  exploring 69, 70, 71, 72
Model Selection 319
model
  building 97, 98, 99, 100, 101, 102, 103
multicollinearity 246
multinomial logistic regression 156, 160, 162
multiple linear model
  fitting 357, 359
Multiple Linear Regression (MLR) model
  about 274
  building 90, 92, 93, 94, 95
  categorical variables 96
  concepts 84, 85, 86, 87, 88, 89
  model, building 97, 98, 99, 100, 101, 102, 103
  with categorical predictor 96
multiple logistic regression
  about 135
  customer satisfaction analysis 136, 139
  with categorical data 143, 147, 152, 153, 155
  with customer satisfaction analysis 143
Multivariate Adaptive Regression Splines (MARS)
    303, 310, 312, 313, 315, 317, 320, 322
multivariate models 23
multivariate multiple regression 23

N

National Weather Service (NWS) 183
neural networks
  about 389, 393, 397, 400
  exploratory analysis 385, 389
  using, for regression 383
nonlinear least squares 304, 305, 308, 309, 310

nonlinear least squares, arguments
  about 305
  algorithm 306
  control 305
  data 305
  formula 305
  lower bounds 306
  model 306
  na.action 306
  start 305
  subset 306
  trace 306
  upper bounds 306
  weights 306
Normal Q-Q plot 95
Not a Number (NaN) 166
null hypothesis 69

O

Ordinary Least Squares (OLS) 44, 252, 266, 304
outliers
  about 266
  searching, in data 174, 178, 179, 180
overfitting
  about 210, 213
  detection, with cross-validation 213, 218, 221, 224, 226

P

partial 135
penalized quasi-likelihood (PQL) 37
perfect linear association
  modeling 78, 79, 80, 81
Poisson distributions 292, 294
Poisson regression model 294, 295
polynomial regression 112, 113, 115, 117, 119
Posterior Inclusion Probabilities (pip) 291
posterior probability 283
precision 143
Principal Component Analysis (PCA) 195, 198, 201, 203, 205, 206
principal components 195
prior probability 283
probability

basic concepts 275, 278

R

R environment 24, 27
R packages
  BLR package 41
  car package 35
  caret package 38
  glmnet package 39
  Lars package 41
  R stats package 34
  sgd package 40
  using, for regression 34
R
  installing 27, 29
  installing, on Linux 30
  installing, on macOS 30
  installing, on Windows 30
  precompiled binary distribution, using 29
  source code, installation 31
random forest regression
  about 361, 364, 366
  exploratory analysis 347, 353, 356
  multiple linear model, fitting 357, 359
  with Boston dataset 346
Receiver Operator Characteristic (ROC) 380
regression subset selection 237, 240, 243, 244
regression towards mediocrity 11
regression tree
  about 329, 332, 335, 337
  pruning 331
  splitting 331
  tree selection 331
regression
  about 14
  applications 12, 14
  origin 8, 12
  R packages, using 34
  types 21, 23, 24
  versus correlation 18, 21
  with neural networks 383
regularization
  about 245
  ElasticNet regression 261, 263
  lasso regression 254, 257, 261

ridge regression 245, 247, 249, 252, 254
resampling
  bootstrap resampling 215
Residual QQ 321
Residual Sum of Squares (RSS) 245, 318
Residuals 74
Residuals vs Fitted values 319
resilient backpropagation (RPROP) 389
response variable 7
ridge regression 245, 247, 249, 252, 254
Road Casualties Great Britain (RCGB) 247
Road Traffic Accidents (RTA) 247
robust linear regression 266, 267, 269, 271, 274
Robust Regression Model 272, 273
RStudio
  about 31, 33
  URL 31

S

sensitivity 382
sgd package 107
sgd package, functions
  plot.sgd 40
  predict.sgd 40
  print.sgd 40
  sgd 40
simple logistic regression 127, 132, 134
smallest absolute gradient (sag) 394
smallest learning rate (slr) 394
specificity 142, 382
standard score 185, 390

Standardized residuals 75, 76, 77
statistical significance test 69
stepwise regression
  about 229, 232, 235, 237
  backward method 229
  forward method 229
  stepwise method 229
stochastic 107
Stochastic Gradient Descent (SGD) 40, 83, 107, 121
Support Vector Machine (SVM) 338, 339, 341, 342
Support Vector Regression (SVR) 303

T

Theoretical Quantiles 75
TIOBE
  URL 26
True Negative Rate (TNR) 142, 380
true positive rate (TPR) 380

U

UCI Machine Learning Repository
  URL 384

V

variables
  relationships 44, 46, 47, 48, 49, 50

Z

z score standardization 185, 187, 390

Made in the USA
San Bernardino, CA
10 December 2018